SECULAR RITUAL

SECULAR RITUAL

edited by

SALLY F. MOORE
BARBARA G. MYERHOFF

1977

VAN GORCUM, ASSEN/AMSTERDAM, THE NETHERLANDS

© 1977 VAN GORCUM & COMP. B.V. – Postbox 43, Assen, The Netherlands

ISBN 90 232 1457 9

Printed in the Netherlands by Van Gorcum, Assen

To Lita Osmundsen
Director of Research of the Wenner-Gren Foundation
With gratitude for all that she has done for Anthropology

TABLE OF CONTENTS

ACKNOWLEDGEMENTS

The conference at which these papers were originally presented was held from August 24 to September 1, 1974 at Burg Wartenstein, Austria, and was sponsored by the Wenner-Gren Foundation for Anthropological Research. The meeting, entitled, "Secular Rituals Considered: Prolegomena toward a Theory of Ritual, Ceremony and Formality", was organized by Max Gluckman, Victor Turner and Sally F. Moore. Its purpose was to explore the nature of non-religious ritual, ceremony, and formality in social life. The conference week was one of those happy occasions which can only be described as a feast of ideas. Participants were all put in a convivial mood by the excellent management of the Wenner-Gren staff headed by Karl Frey, to whom we wish to express heartfelt thanks. The intellectual excitement and warmth of the interchange was greatly enhanced by the participation of several persons whose conference presentations are not included in this volume, but whose presence and stimulating contributions we wish to acknowledge with gratitude. They are: Erving Goffman of the University of Pennsylvania, Philadelphia, Pennsylvania; Chie Nakane of the Institute of Oriental Culture, University of Tokyo, Tokyo, Japan; James Peacock of the University of North Carolina, Chapel Hill, North Carolina; M.N. Srinivas of the Institute for Social and Economic Change, Bangalore, India; and M.J. Aronoff of Tel Aviv University, Ramat Aviv, Israel. To Dr. Aronoff special thanks are due for introducing the editors to the publishers of this volume. We also wish to thank Julia Kessler, who was rapporteur of the conference, and to acknowledge the friendly help we had from Elizabeth Colson who gave us all of her excellent notes on the discussions. The editors also wish to acknowledge a personal debt to the National Science Foundation which funded some of the research on which Myerhoff's and Moore's papers were based and which also afforded typing and other assistance (GI - 34953 X).

It also should be noted that the editors' interest in the subject matter was originally sparked at a seminar on Secular Ritual held at the University of Southern California, 1972-73. We thank the University for providing an atmosphere in which such exploration could flourish.

Acknowledgements

The meeting turned out to be the last occasion on which many of Max Gluckman's friends were to see him. He died the following spring in Israel. His sense that he might be saying "goodbye" was expressed with great dignity to the conference and to individuals. His heightened awareness of the value of collegiality and his urgent sense of commitment to the profession permeated the meeting and gave it an unusual intensity. It is with sorrow that we note that his paper in this book was his last.

The editors.

PART 1

THEORETICAL AND DEFINITIONAL STUDIES

CHAPTER 1
INTRODUCTION:
SECULAR RITUAL: FORMS AND MEANINGS

Sally F. Moore and Barbara G. Myerhoff

Since social life has some order, yet moves continuously – on the grand scale through historical time – on the micro-scale through each hour, its movement requires a great deal of subtle meshing between the regular and the improvised, the rigid and the flexible, the repetitive and the varying. Social life proceeds somewhere between the imaginary extremes of absolute order, and absolute chaotic conflict and anarchic improvisation. Neither the one nor the other ever takes over completely. There is endless tension between the two, and also remarkable synchrony. This idea is implicit in Victor Turner's phrase, "structure and anti-structure." He sees the two as existing in a perpetual dialectical relationship over time (1969:112,203). With such a view of culture and social life in mind, collective ritual can be seen as an especially dramatic attempt to bring some particular part of life firmly and definitely into orderly control. It belongs to the structuring side of the cultural/historical process.

In anthropology the study of ceremony and ritual has been confined largely to consideration of religious and magical procedures. With Tylor, Durkheim, Weber and Frazer in the background, the association between those formalities we call "ritual" and their religious or magical purposes has been so strong that analysis of the two has almost invariably proceeded together. No doubt that is partly because anthropologists have so often dealt with societies in which everything has a religious significance, in which all of daily life is imbued with the sacred, in which the unseen spirit world is present all the time and intervenes in the visible world. But if religion is defined in the Tylorian manner as having to do with spirits, then surely the sacred is a wider category than the religious. An essential quality of the sacred is its unquestionability. Unquestionable tenets exist in secular political ideologies which are as sacred in that sense as the tenets of any religion. Secular ceremonies can present unquestionable doctrines and can dramatize social/moral imperatives without invoking the spirits at all. If the realm of the religious and the realm of the sacred are not treated as co-terminous, then it is possible to analyze the ways in which ceremony and ritual are used in the secular affairs of modern life

3

to lend authority and legitimacy to the positions of particular persons, organizations, occasions, moral values, view of the world, and the like. In these matters, ritual and ceremony are employed to structure and present particular interpretations of social reality in a way that endows them with legitimacy. Ritual not only belongs to the more structured side of social behavior, it also can be construed as an attempt to structure the way people *think* about social life.

This book is assembled to address the question of what happens to theories of ritual if analogous formal procedures are inspected in secular contexts. What new material becomes visible if the supernatural element is stripped away and this-worldly ceremonies and their outcomes are considered? What are the implications of *new* ceremonies if past theory has been built on the ethnography of traditional rites? The first consequence, as the reader will see, is that the category analysed is very broadly and loosely defined by certain kinds of ritual-like formalities, rather than being defined by the double criteria of religious or magical purpose as well as form. Secular ritual so construed is a vast subject that could encompass everything from individual ritualized behavior and its psychological significance (vide Freud) to collective ceremony. This book confines itself to collective ceremonial forms in order to keep the social context at the center of attention, and uses the term ritual in its non-technical meaning in order to make the religious analogy visible throughout.

The chapters of this volume consider out of what stuff secular rituals are constructed, what such rituals say, or show, or mean, or do, and what their outcome is, or is supposed to be. Each chapter analyses a particular collective ceremonial occasion. While that is the unit analysed, such a complex entity cannot be understood without extensive allusions to the social and cultural background that lies behind it. The specific ethnographic details of the ceremony itself are drawn from observed behavior. But the meaning of that behavior is inferred from a wide range of materials. In every case, there is little doubt about what the ethnographer saw, or thought he or she saw, but there may be disagreement about what it meant. An interpretation of one ritual may illumine the understanding of another by bringing attention to a previously unobserved dimension. The contributors to this book offer an assortment of approaches for comparison, reflection and for what they may stimulate in further work.

Secular ceremonies are common in industrial societies and are found in all contexts (See, for example, Bocock 1974 on England). Meetings, court trials, installations, graduations, and other formal assemblies of many kinds are part of the ordinary fabric of collective social life. What do any of these occasions have in common other than their stylized and conventionalized forms? Why do they have formality in common? In what processes of social life is form emphasized and why? These are some of the theoretical questions that are raised here. And by extension, any general answer to them, or part of one, is likely to apply to religious rituals as well as secular ones.

To social anthropologist and layman alike, a collective ceremony is a dramatic occasion, a complex type of symbolic behavior that usually has a statable purpose, but one that invariably alludes to more than it says, and has many meanings at once. With Durkheim's paradigm deeply learned, social anthropologists frequently have looked at particular rituals as they reflect social relationships. This approach explicates ritual in terms of the manner in which a particular rite states, reiterates or reinforces traditional social ties, or expresses social conflicts, or delineates social roles (See Gluckman, 1958, 1962, 1963, 1965; Kuper, 1944, 1972; Nadel, 1954; Rappaport, 1968; Turner, 1957, 1964, 1968a, 1968b). But an emphasis on the social meanings of ritual in anthropology has not excluded consideration of the way in which ritual not only propagates cultural ideas, but shapes those ideas (Geertz, 1966; 36, 41; Turner, 1966, 1969). One of the least disputable contentions of this book is that a balance should be sought between these two ways of looking at the problem of meaning. Neither should be neglected. Ritual may do much more than mirror existing social arrangements and existing modes of thought. It can act to reorganize them or even help to create them. This is particularly striking in the secular ceremonies of our own day, which often are put together and performed precisely for that purpose. It may well apply equally to traditional religious ritual. This book is concerned with the *creation*, the *performance*, and the *outcome* of secular ceremonies, and with their myriad meanings.

When Durkheim analysed the ritual forms of the Australian aborigines as he understood them, he was by implication asking the sociocentric question, "How does religion perpetuate this kind of society?" He made the argument that the rites and collective representations of the aborigines symbolized the social cohesion of their assembled groups and simultaneously acted as the vehicle for bringing about that very social solidarity. There is a circularity in the argument. It rests on certain important but unstated premises, principally on assumptions about the analytic and temporal priority of *existing* social relationships and cultural forms which must be perpetuated over time. It pictures ritual as endlessly repetitive, as being performed again and again, year after year, cyclically celebrating and renewing a going social group through the restatement of its fixed cultural forms (Durkheim, 1912, 1961 ed.; 388, 391-432). Because Durkheim was thinking in terms of an established totemic cult, an existing society and an already formed culture, he was occupied with its maintenance, the periodic creation and recreation of its "faith" (Ibid,: 464). He did not address himself at all fully to the creation of new rituals, yet many of his arguments could have applied equally well not to the continuation of an old cult but to the creation of a new one.

Since, for Durkheim, the referent of religious ritual was "society," he attributed to religious ritual social-symbolic qualities which are found in many other settings. As Goody remarked when speaking of Red Army parades and July 4th celebrations,

> "Not infrequently he [Durkheim] allocates to religion the functions and properties which might more properly be assigned to a phenomenon of greater generality, mass ceremonial." (1962: 146)

Durkheim did not explore at any length what ceremony might be or create in secular contexts nor in heterogeneous and changing socities full of skeptics. He obviously considered the possibility, though, when he mentioned patriotic enthusiasms of the French Revolution as quasi-religious (1912, 1961 ed.: 244-45). But his sharp dichotomy between mechanical and organic solidarity, and his association of the elementary forms of religion with the first prevented him from extending and complicating his analysis of ritual. In *The Division of Labor*, he differentiated between an all-embracing primitive religion participated in by all members of a society, coextensive in meaning with social life, and a religion in a complex society, where it is a specialized institution, distinct from politics, economics and the like, and occupies only one compartment of social life. He says of the evolution of societies that as they become more developed, "there is a decreasing number of collective beliefs and sentiments which are both collective enough and strong enough to take on a religious character" (1893, 1964 ed: 169-70). What, then, are we to make of secular ceremonies and rituals? Are they indicators of islands of collective "beliefs and sentiments" in seas of heterogeneity? Clearly, in a complex specialized and differentiated society rites, often have this character and are used to show a limited commonality, or even to create it.

The combination of strangers in common action certainly is one of the hallmarks of modern life. Ceremonies that make visible a collective connection with some common symbol or activity can minimize for a ceremonial moment their disconnections and conflicts in a crowd, even while depicting them. Along these lines, Da Matta (this volume) has described two Brazilian national celebrations which involve "all classes, categories and social groups which make up Brazilian society." He stresses the "combinatorial" syntheses of symbols and persons which these celebrations embody.

Underlying Durkheim's idea about religion, there were assumptions about its efficacy, a certainty that through ritual the Australian tribesmen were all readily made enthusiastic believers and moral conformers to a common code. While *The Elementary Forms* concedes that the aborigines needed their faith renewed and livened up from time to time, there is no extended discussion of the possibility that ritual might fail in this. His book accepts at face value the success of the very messages that many rituals are designed to propagate: the myth of cultural unity and social continuity, the myth of unchanging common tradition, the myth of shared belief.

Leaving aside for the moment the question of actual success, and taking as true the proposition that ritual can and often does carry a message about social/cultural perpetuation, what is it about collective ritual that so often gives it this tradition-celebrating role? Why is it a suitable vehicle for this task? It is our contention that certain formal properties of that category of events ordinarily called collective ritual (or ceremony) all lend themselves singularly well to making ritual a "traditionalizing instrument" (a phrase borrowed from Apter who used it in a different but related context, 1963: 69). As the papers in this book indicate, collective ceremony can traditionalize new material as well as perpetuate old traditions. Some of its formal properties mimic its message in this regard. These are:

1 *Repetition*: either of occasion, content or form, or any combination of these.

2 *Acting*: a basic quality of ritual being that is not an essentially spontaneous activity, but rather most, if not all of it is self-consciously "acted" like a part in a play. Further, this usually involves doing something, not only saying or thinking something.

3 *"Special" behavior or stylization*: actions or symbols used are extra-ordinary themselves, or ordinary ones are used in an unusual way, a way that calls attention to them and sets them apart from other, mundane uses.

4 *Order*: collective ritual are by definition an organized event, both of persons and cultural elements, having a beginning and an end, thus bound to have some order. It may contain within it moments of, or elements of chaos and spontaneity, but these are in prescribed times and places. Order is the dominant mode and is often quite exaggeratedly precise. Its order is often the very thing which sets it apart.

5 *Evocative presentational style; staging*: collective rituals are intended to produce at least an attentive state of mind, and often an even greater commitment of some kind; ceremony commonly does so through manipulations of symbols and sensory stimuli.

Victor Turner's paper (this volume) emphasizes the ways in which
ritual may be a framework that engenders creativity in individuals
both through mandatory improvisation (liminal periods, trance,
visions) and through highly structured, rule-bounded activities,
both of which produce a concentration so extreme that there is a
loss of self-consciousness, and a feeling of "flow."

6 *The "collective dimension"*: by definition collective ritual has a
social meaning. Its very occurrence contains a social message
(Rappaport, 1971).

In the repetition and order, ritual imitates the rhythmic imperatives of the
biological and physical universe, thus suggesting a link with the perpetual
processes of the cosmos. It thereby implies permanence and legitimacy
of what are actually evanescent cultural constructs. In the acting, stylization and presentational staging, ritual is attention-commanding and de-
flects questioning at the time. All these formal properties make it an ideal
vehicle for the conveying of messages in an authenticating and arresting
manner.

Clearly, each of these formal characteristics of collective ceremony is
found in other categories of behavior. In fact, all of them in combination
are founds in such activities as drama and games. The formal properties
of ceremony are thus not sufficient to distinguish it from other cultural
phenomena, and it overlaps them in this regard. It is in the area of meaning and effect that the distinction may be more clearly drawn and this is
the subject of the Gluckmans' contribution, "On Drama, and Games and
Athletic Contests" (this volume).

Myerhoff proposes conceptualizing collective ceremony in its formal aspect as a container, a vessel which holds something. It gives form to that
which it contains. Ritual is in part a form, and a form which gives certain
meanings to its contents. The work of ritual, then, is partly attributable to
its morphological characteristics. Its medium is part of its message. It can
contain almost anything, for any aspect of social life, any aspect of behavior or ideology, may lend itself to ritualization (Nadel, 1954: 99).
And once used in collective ceremony, whether performed for the first
time or the thousandth, the circumstance of having been put in the ritual
form and mode, has a tradition-like effect. Even if it is performed once,
for the first and only time, its stylistic rigidities, and its internal repetitions of form or content make it tradition-like. Myerhoff's chapter (this
volume) describes such a once-and-only event, a graduation ceremony in
an urban social center for the aged. The graduation combines many elements from the several cultural backgrounds of the members to make a
unique composite. Such a ceremony may fail to convince outsiders but it

is intended for insiders. Though performed only once it is supposed to carry the same unreflective conviction as any traditional repetitive ritual, to symbolize for the participants all that they share in common, and to insist to them that it all fits together by putting it together as one performance. Incongruity is disallowed. In this way an entirely new ceremony, though performed only once, not only represents, but interprets the assorted experiences of its audience, and makes them tradition-like. This ceremony represented not a society but an amalgam of the collective past of one little group of people, and was an effort to have that past make sense in the situation of their peculiar collective present.

In so far as Durkheim set ritual within religion, and religion wholly within an organized community, he linked ritual with community, and that insight illuminates many secular ceremonies (Durkheim, 1912 [1961 ed.]: 62). Yet as Leach pointed out, in some rituals the solidarity of the participating group may be only momentary (1954:281). Secular ceremony certainly often takes place outside of community in the sense of "corporate group" and outside of community in the sense of "common culture." There are secular ceremonies invented and produced for persons who have come together just for one particular occasion. The participants even may be of different cultures. For example, Gluckman described a dedication ceremony that took place in Zululand (1958). In it African notables and white officials gathered together to celebrate the opening of a bridge Gluckman persuasively analysed the ceremony as "representing" two segments of a single social "structure." But it is clear that the personal ties between the two sides were fragile and tenuous. The ceremony itself may have been an attempt to mask that, and to exaggerate the collective effort, the common cooperation and the collective benefit, the way in which strangers may contribute to the same enterprise. It provided a formal theatrical medium in which the people could be together without interacting very much, but in which their symbols could be juxtaposed in time and space to give apparent unity.

When a building was dedicated on a University campus the ceremony assembled for a "once and only once" occasion certain wealthy donors, administrative officers of the College, and a handful of professors and students who would ultimately use the building. A more motley crew is hard to imagine. Such a ceremony was not celebrating the existence of a corporate *group* of any sort, but rather marked the temporary conjuction of some persons and groups at one of the many network-crossroads of modern life. It was performed once, never to be repeated as such.[1] Such "junction" ceremonies are not uncommon in modern life, and the part of the Durkheimian paradigm that equates ritual with group perpetuation does not help in their analysis.

These dedicatory ceremonies were staged with certain intentions. They certainly had some effects. Each ceremony reorganized and rearranged certain information and called attention to the status of certain persons. It made public declarations of thanks and amity. It declared the moral value of what had been built and the use to which it would be put. It did something, just as clearly as a marriage ceremony marries people, or a curing ritual may heal. It ended the making of a building and began the period of its use. The ceremony was a process in which certain changes were made and marked as surely as in any *rite de passage*. Borrowing from Victor Turner, then, one may think of the ritual process as potentially an active thing, not invariably as a restatement of a static or even cyclic state of affairs, but equally capable of making and marking a shift in a situation (1969). Moore has argued along these lines that legal hearings may be interpreted as rituals of situational transformation (1975a). That a traditionalizing medium should be used to accomplish this, that the ceremonial form should make and mark change as often as it celebrates repetitions and continuities is one of the many paradoxes that the form encompasses. Colson's chapter (this volume) about a birthday party in a Senior Citizens' Center is a remarkably good example of this. There the birthday party form is used in a totally new setting with many modifications to introduce strangers to each other, and to give them a collective experience to share. Held once a month to honor those whose birthdays fall in that month, it serves to construct something new out of old cultural materials, and to define a group through a new common "tradition."

The Dimensions of Explanation Offered by Ritual and of Ritual: Doctrinal and Operational Efficacy

Religions give explanations of the cosmos, of "where it all began" and "where it is all going" and "what it means." Such explanations are part of the presumed background of religious ritual. They are part of a logical system in which the ritual itself makes sense. Since secular ceremonies are also events in larger cultural nexes of ideas and practices, it is reasonable to ask whether there is any comparability between the cultural-idealogical referents of secular ceremony and the kind of creed that lies behind a religious ritual. If a religious ritual is simultaneously a *declaration about* religion and a *demonstration of* its operation, what does a secular ceremony declare and what does it demonstrate?

The answer is that a secular ceremony may, but need not be "attached" to a worked-out, elaborate ideology. A Red Army parade is attached in this way, but there are many secular ceremonies that are not. Indeed, there may be more rather than less elaboration of ritual in secular circumstance, precisely because more presentation and persuasion, more communication of information, is needed when ideology is scanty or fragmentary, and context not reliable as when background and presumptions of shared belief and comprehension are limited.

The matter of presumed "background meaning" moves one into slippery territory because it addresses questions about the connectedness of parts of culture. The interrelation between religious ritual and religion is explicit, worked out, stated, and conscious. The connection between many secular ceremonies and the larger sets of customs and attitudes which comprise the context in which they make sense need not be explicit. They are sometimes a matter of common understandings that are not specifically declared, as, for example, a middle class American child's birthday with its conventional giving of gifts and cake with candles. It would be hard to identify any specific ideological, creedal referent for such a ceremony. On other occasions, such as the celebrations of national holidays, public figures may take the opportunity to make quite explicit the official "symbolic" meaning of the occasion, by referring to political creeds, national history, past political glories and future goals of the state. Secular ceremony seems connected with specialized parts of the social/cultural background, rather than with the all-embracing ultimate universals to which religious rituals are attached. But how does one determine the limits of reference?

On the most general level all parts of a culture are vaguely associated through mere contemporaneity, so any part can, by a series of chains, be shown to touch, though often at some considerable remove, many others. A sentence implies a language, a single economic transaction (a written contract, a deferred cash payment with interest) may in its form imply a complex legal and economic background. When can such referential scope be inferred from a secular ceremony? What techniques can be used to ascertain the limits of semantic content? This level of specific but implied meanings presents difficult exegetical and analytical problems. This problem is exemplified in Manning's description (this volume) of the elaborate displays which are mounted in two Caribbean societies; their drama and elaboration and implied meanings account for their effectiveness more than overt ideology.

However, despite the difficulties, some tentative generalizations can be made. In particular, the referential scope of secular ceremonies can be compared with that of religious rituals with respect to their explanatory content. It is almost a matter of definition that when a secular ceremony is not attached to an elaborately worked out ideology, its implied explanatory range is bound to be more limited than that of religious ritual. Religions have something to say about life and death, the beginning and end of time, and the source of all things. Ceremonies, religious or secular, may be occupied with relatively shallow periods of time, and with the experience of special and particular segments of the population and with their immediate concerns. They may be quite situationally specific in their explicit emphasis. When religious rituals are situationally specific (the funeral of a particular person, the marriage of two individuals) by implication they link these specific occasions to all deaths and all marriages and the nature of life, and eventually to the religious doctrine itself. When secular rituals are situationally specific, they also may link the immediate with a larger reality, but they do not, even in a vague way, invariably attach to a total explanation.

Religious rituals, too, are postulated to have consequences beyond their social effects. Built around cosmic explanations, these rituals are often supernaturally dangerous to some degree, as social ceremonies are not. Middleton (this volume) draws attention to the taboos which surround religious rituals and which serve to make them a distinctive social category. Tampering with supernatural powers, powers beyond human control and understanding, he reminds us, often requires protection against breaches which may inadvertently create cosmic disruptions which surpass the social relations and definitions attendant on their performance.

What Moore calls the *doctrinal efficacy* of religous ritual is provided by the explanations a religion itself gives of how and why ritual works. The explanation is within the religious system and is part of its internal logic. The religion postulates by what causal means a ritual, if properly performed, should bring about the desired results. A religious ritual refers to the unseen cosmic order, works through it and operates on it directly through the performance. The gods, the ancestors or the spirits are moved. At one and the same time a religious ritual *affects* the spirit-world and *demonstrates* the postulated validity of the explanations the religion offers of causal processes. The religion may refer to and act upon the social order as well, either explicitly or by implication. In any case, causal explanation internal to the religious doctrine postulates that the ritual shall be efficacious. Do secular rituals also have doctrinal explanations of their efficacy?

Doctrinal efficacy must be distinguished from social/psychological effectiveness, here called *operational efficacy*. Doctrinal efficacy is a matter of postulation. As the intrinsic explanation, it need merely be affirmed. It lacks the dimension of outcome or consequence which is attributed to operational efficacy. Results, successes, failures, are part of the operational effects of a ritual. These are the empirical questions in analysis. For example, healing ceremonies may or may not make a patient feel better. Political ceremonies may or may not succeed in rearranging images, may succeed or fail in attaching positive or negative balances to certain ideas or persons. Rites may vary greatly in successfully convincing their participants and communicating their messages. Such questions about communicative, social/psychological effects are operational.

Though the outcome of a ritual is an empirical question, it is one that is often hard to answer. A field worker is confronted with difficult technical problems if he/she wants to ascertain the specific effects on all the individuals present at a collective ceremony. Numbers are an obstacle. Further, much information may be inaccessible for many reasons: psychological, cultural and technical. In the absence of an ideal universe of complete, precise information the field worker must rely on what people tell him/her, piecing data together, drawing on empathy and intuition – not a very scientific procedure, but the best available for the moment. However refined our field techniques may eventually become, analyses of ritual can never be exhaustive and definitive because participants themselves cannot explain some of the effects of ritual upon them. Exegetical analysis does not help in determining the unconscious consequences of ritual, consequences that may or may not occur at all, may occur in every shade of intensity from an image in the mind, to a slight murmur of the heart, to a profound ecstasis. They may occur in only one or a few participants, may be simulated for myriad reasons, particularly by those specialists responsible for staging and conducting of the ritual.

One of the most subtle and analytically elusive of psychological consequences in ritual is that state of mind which Langer (1942) called "transformation." A transformation occurs when symbol and object seem to fuse and are experienced as a perfectly undifferentiated whole. Such apparent fusion may be the ultimate goal of some religious rituals but is never the exclusive criterion for success, because it is ultimately unpredictable. Emotion and imagination operate more like fountains than machines (James [1937]), and as such, transformation is invited but not commanded by ritual performances. Boas (1911), Freud (1918), and Langer (1942) have dwelt upon the compelling quality of ritual which has the capacity to transform experience as word-bound thought usually cannot. "Transformations" of this kind occur when ritual symbols fire the imagination, and insight, belief and emotion are called into play, "altering our conceptions ... at a stroke" (Langer 1942: 20). Then, participants are able to conceive the invisible referents of symbols used in rituals. Sometimes, especially in religious rites, they have the sense of envisaging the essential pattern of human life, its relation to the natural and cosmic orders, and achieve thereby an immediate triumphant sense of knowledge and belief. When its symbols rarely or never fire, rituals may become cold, empty forms. They may still be sufficiently viable to provide a sense of continuity and predictability, albeit without great vitality, as for example, in etiquette, where mere conformity is required. Thus even without being capable of arousing emotional-perceptual transformations, ritual performance may have significant effects, and may succeed on the operational level.

Some immediate part of what is deposited in the mind or is stimulated by collective ritual may be discovered from behavior and statement. It remains much more difficult to assess the long-term consequences, the effect of a ritual event in a long flow of events, the cumulative place of ritual communication in the context of other communications.[2] The fact is that an empirical assessment of the *total* consequences for individuals and groups of a ritual performance may be impossible. That means that not only is doctrinal efficacy a matter of faith, but frequently the anthropologically or politically presumed social and psychological "effects" of ritual necessarily are something more inferred than proved. For example, in Vogt and Abel's chapter (this volume) we see an analysis that supplies a functional rationale for a no-choice, one-candidate "election" in Mexico. Staged trials and planned "demonstrations" are a familiar part of the recent history of many nations. Thus there are traditions and ideologies as well as conventions of sociological interpretation which postulate that declared political objectives will be enhanced by a particular ceremonial display, or ritual performance.

All of these are ideologically, though perhaps not sociologically, different in kind from religious rituals. They offer internal explanations of their own efficacy which are distinct in obvious ways from those of religious rituals. The latter are other-worldly in rationale, the former exclusively this-worldly. The religious ritual moves the other world to affect this one. The secular ceremony moves this world and this world only. Hence two quite different explanations of causality underlie the two performances. Yet this very difference brings out an important similarity between religious and secular rituals. They both "show" the unseen. Religious ritual "shows" the existence of the other world through the display of attempts to move it. Analogously, a secular ceremony "shows" by acting in terms of them the existence of social relationships (the Government, the Party, etc.) or ideas or values which are inherently invisible most of the time. It objectifies them and reifies them (Berger and Luckmann [1966]). It displays symbols of their existence and by implicit reference postulates and enacts their "reality." Moore's chapter (this volume) shows how newly independent Tanzania tries to give its national government and socialist ideology palpable immediacy through the medium of

14

regular local political meetings. In such a setting questions of doctrinal and operational efficacy are urgent political issues.

Certainly one common objective of religious and secular ritual is to influence this world. Both are supposed to have consequences, actual social or communicative psychological effects on living persons. And among those effects both may reiterate implied postulates about causality and "reality." A religious ritual always has an explicit doctrinal dimension that explains, however mysteriously or vaguely, the basis of its efficacy. A secular ceremony is less likely to have as well-developed a rationale of how it works. A doctrinal dimension enhances the efficacy of a ceremony by establishing congruent working connections between the particular performance and a larger system of postulated beliefs and ideas. As Rappaport has said, it implies that any lack of credence in the immediate ceremonial performance suggests a skepticism about a much wider and more-difficult-to-challenge range of associations (Rappaport 1971).

Assessing the outcome of a ritual, the work it has done, involves questions of meanings as well as of efficacy. Certainly the reception of a message cannot be considered unless the message is identified. If specific action is supposed to follow and does, one may be sure the message was received. But if the nature of the ceremony is such that no action is expected, how is the impact to be judged? In looking at the particular cases described in the chapters in this volume, it is evident that the messages carried by rituals are extremely complex with implicit and unconscious elements not easily interpreted, and consequences difficult to measure.

Perhaps because of exaggerations of the emotional side, it is often said that rituals are expressive acts par excellence. Frequently a radical separation is made between these and instrumental behaviors (Beattie 1966). But instrumental actions are too often accompanied by and advanced by ritual to justify taking refuge in this dichotomy. Instrumental actions may be performed in a ritualized manner. An army may move in a marching formation. A meeting may be highly formal. Ritualization may have both purposive and communicative properties though it is not exhausted by these descriptions. This being so, the problem of assessing the effects of particular collective rituals becomes all the more complex.

Dimensions of Ritual Outcomes

Five ways of looking at the outcome of secular ritual were distinguished at the symposium. The subject could assuredly be sorted out in other categories, but these seemed clarifying in our discussion, hence we repeat them here:

1. *Explicit purpose*: Rituals and ceremonies often are mounted with a declared and explicit purpose. This is the manifest meaning, the simplest to understand, and often likely to be the most superficial. A meeting is held to attend to specific business, a parade to celebrate a holiday, a graduation to mark the end of a course of study. Some explanation of why the ceremony is construed as appropriate to its purpose is at least implicit in its performance, if not expressed in some formal doctrine or ideology.

2. *Explicit symbols and messages*: Another part of the work done by ritual is to present symbols and messages and allusions. A ceremony activates or presents selected ideas necessarily related to larger cultural frameworks of thought and explanation. Thus some of the work of ritual is to make momentarily visible an idealogy, or part of one, a basic model or a "root metaphor" (Turner 1974). It may also make available many symbolic elements which are fragmentary, separate and evidently unsystematized.

3. *Implicit statements*: At a subtler level, the ceremony may iterate all manner of less conscious social and psychological materials. It may express deep contradictions in the social or cultural system − all kinds of troubles, uncertainties, conflicts and paradoxes. Or, just the opposite, it may be designed to mask these, to deny and disguise them and gloss the difficulties they present. It may be an act of affirmation, a declaration of structural strength, a presentation of apparent certainties, continuity, and the like. A ceremony may formulate, pattern or transform such materials; it may reiterate or present afresh ideas about social relationships, cultural or specific models, connecting them with universal personal experiences, linking or dividing, aggrandizing or diminishing, blurring or clarifying.

4. *Social relationships affected*: At any or all of these levels of communication there may be effects on the participants which directly involve their social roles, identities, sense of collective contact, attitudes toward other persons, and the like. It can be analytically useful to divide the social effects from the messages conveyed, and from the inventory of paradigms and symbols displayed since these are not always congruent. Indeed, one social message may be given and quite a different one acted upon.

5. *Culture versus chaos*: Last, at its most general level, all collective ceremony can be interpreted as a cultural statement about cultural order as against a cultural void. As Kenneth Burke has remarked, cultures are built on the edge of the abyss. Ceremony is a declaration against indeterminacy (See Moore 1975b). Through form and formality it celebrates man-made meaning, the culturally determinate, the regulated, the named, and the explained. It banishes from consideration the basic questions

raised by the made-upness of culture, its malleability and alterability. Every ceremony is par excellence a dramatic statement against indeterminacy in some field of human affairs. Through order, formality, and repetition it seeks to state that the cosmos and social world, or some particular small part of them are orderly and explicable and for the moment fixed. A ceremony can allude to such propositions and demonstrate them at the same time. In other words, a dialectical relationship exists between the formed and the indeterminate. Ritual is a declaration of form *against* indeterminacy, therefore indeterminacy is always present in the background of any analysis of ritual. Indeed there is no doubt that any analysis of social life must take account of the dynamic relation between the formed and the indeterminate (Ibid).

Order: Connection and Predictability

Order, as used here, calls attention to two features in particular: connections and predictability. Connections are established or asserted and some systematic relationships are suggested, whenever items are ordered. By definition, the connection provides an explanation, implies meaning and comprehensibility. Rituals always provide meaning, of varied scope and kind in this way.

These relationships or connections are given repetitively in ritual. Certainly one of the purposes accomplished by such repetitiveness is the message of predictability. The repetitive insists and may even persuade that its messages are durably true, now and in the future. It gives information that affairs and states, attitudes and understandings are stable; we may count on them, make plans in terms of them. As such, rituals are promises about continuity. The studies of the social rituals we call etiquette, the greetings and departures, gestures/manners, and "social forms," are germane here. The well-known work of Goffman (1967) on the rules of social conduct emphasize the necessity for predictability among social interactants, concerning their conceptions of themselves, one another, the social order, indeed, the nature of the cosmos. Social reality and social relationships are endlessly stated and restated in allegedly empty ritual behaviors, which when viewed analytically are found to convey a wealth of social agreements essential for ongoing interactions.

Ritual must be orderly because it frequently interrupts or manages or accompanies various forms of disorder, ranging from the ordinary rough and tumble confusion of everyday life, through the disorder of choice, and the multiplicity of inconsistencies in ideologies and in social arrangements. It veils the ultimate disorder, the non-order, which is the unconceptualized, unformed chaos underlying culture. The degree and kind of disorder taken up by ritual varies. Sometimes it is merely annoying, other times truly terrifying and in between it concerns matters which trouble us deeply.

And underlying all rituals is an ultimate danger, lurking beneath the smallest and largest of them, the more banal and the most ambitious – the possibility that we will encounter ourselves making up our conceptions of the world, society, our very selves. We may slip in that fatal perspective of recognizing culture as our construct, arbitrary, conventional, invented by mortals. Ceremonies are paradoxical in this way. Being the most obviously contrived forms of social contact, they epitomize the made-up quality of culture and almost invite notice as such. Yet their very form and purpose is to discourage untrammeled inquiry into such questions. Ceremonies convey most of their messages as postulates.

Ritual discourages inquiry not only because it presents its material authoritatively, as axiomatic. It is itself a message stated in a form to render it unverifiable, separate from standards of truth and falsity. (It may be good or bad, effective or ineffective, but it cannot be tried by the usual empirical standards of verifications). So often, as Langer (1942) has pointed out, symbols used in ritual are presentational rather than discursive. Their substance is conveyed dramatically, appealing to the senses, which, once engaged, offer their own unarguable definitions of reality and conviction. This presentational form is not fortuitous. For rituals frequently portray unknown and unknowable conditions – ideals or imaginings – and make them tangible and present, despite the fact that they are ineffable and invisible. Thus it is, as Geertz points out, "In a ritual, the world as lived and the world as imagined, fused under the agency of a single set of symbolic forms turn out to be the same world..." (Geertz 1966: 28). That is, of course, the essence of obsessive compulsive rituals since the very thing which they explicitly banish is by implication their central concern (Freud 1907). Thus compulsive washing legitimates a covert preoccupation with dirt through its exaggerated concentration on cleanliness. Similarly the preoccupation of ritual with order and organization is an explicit turning away from an acknowledgement of the possibility of non-culture or open choice, or even of chaos and disorder (Moore 1975b). Any such "indeterminacy" is excluded by ritual order often because its very *form*, let alone its message, inherently closes choice.

Ritual, then, closes possibilities, but this is not to say that it may not provide for elements of indeterminacy within its overall format. Myerhoff observed (1976 and this volume) that in extended rituals there is a tendency for fixed segments to alternate with open or variable segments. Often the former are associated with sacred externally-originating elements, the latter with secular, regional, or highly particular elements. Such juxtapositions are attempts to suggest that the optional, particular segments are as axiomatic as the fixed pieces which usually precede, follow and regularly punctuate the improvised, or localized sections. And reciprocally, the axiomatic matters are enlivened and made relevant by their association with specific, immediate affairs.

Does this mean that ritual segments are merely vehicles for calling attention to the contents in between "frames," to use Goffman's term (1974). Can one say that what "really happens" is in the open rather than the fixed sections? In our discussions Chie Nakane provided an illuminating example which warned us away from such assumptions. In Japanese wrestling matches, she pointed out, the wrestlers' body contact may last mere moments. The body contact is framed by elaborate rituals, conveying a wealth of information. A Westerner might regard the body contact and the outcome as the content and the real meaning of the event, but the Japanese audience responds to the totality, frame *and* combat, as a communication. Terence Turner's discussion (this volume) reiterates this point, reminding us that at our peril we ignore the form of ritual since that is always an essential carrier of its unique message. Ritual may "bracket" open segments, but the brackets must always be included as an aspect of the communication (See Goffman 1974).

Sacred and Secular

Mary Douglas has made the argument that there are secular societies, primitive as well as complex (1970). She offers the Ituri Pygmies and the Basseri as examples of peoples with very little ritual, hence in her terms "secular." Her contention is that secular societies are organized around ego-centered networks (grid), rather than bounded groups. Conversely, she argues that ritual elaboration occurs in societies with well developed group structures. One part of the argument seems founded on Durkheimian notions about the functions of collective religious ritual for group life. That discussion is unexceptionable. To the extent that collective rituals celebrate group life, it follows that they are bound to be correlated with its presence. It is the other side of the argument that is more difficult to accept, the argument that secularism occurs in societies predominantly organized around ego-centered networks of social relations, and that there is a causal connection between the two.

While one can only agree that the ethnographic evidence does not show much ritual elaboration for the Pygmies and the Basseri, it does not necessarily follow that these are secular societies in any ordinary meaning of the term. There seems no absence of mystical ideas and conceptions of supernatural powers among either people. There is no evidence of the kind of disbelief and anti-religiosity, or of that specialized, explicit non-religiosity which appear in many modern industrial societies (see Needham, 1972, on the modern advent of disbelief *and* belief). There are even some rituals. There is simply a non-elaboration of collective ritual. The sacred and unquestionable for the Pygmies and the Basseri certainly cannot pertain to the boundaries of groups they do not have, but is attached to other relationships and ideas.

Obviously, Douglas has quite different problems in mind from those addressed here when she uses the term "secular." Her argument is an intricate one, with chains of reasoning having many links. It cannot be properly detailed here. But the brief outlines of her discussion indicated above point up a number of theoretical and methodological matters. They suffice to show how much hangs on what one understands by religious/secular, sacred/mundane, ritual/non-ritual, and on one's associated presumptions of causality.

The general absence of consensus about these matters complicates all discussion. The issue is not one of defining words for the sake of it. That is, after all, a game all sides can play endlessly. The issue is much more serious. It is a question of which kinds of social phenomena should be distinguished, and which lumped together for the purpose of advancing the understanding of ceremony, ritual and formality in social life. That is a theoretical question, not a semantic one. It follows that since terms must be used to discuss anything, the terms used will reflect theoretical positions and analytic categories. Douglas addresses the secular/religious issues in terms of whole societies and whether they are "more" or "less" secular. She sees secularism as a kind of cosmology, setting great weight on certain pervasive ideas of order, and certain basic metaphors, such as that of the body, with its boundaries. In this volume, our concern is first with particular ceremonies or rituals, not with whole societies. The approach is from the micro-ethnographic end of the problem. The unit of analysis is *a* ceremony, not a society. The entire context is necessarily used as a resource for the interpretation of the ceremony. But the quality of a whole society as more or less given to ritualization is not addressed here.

What the organizers of the symposium sought to do was to focus on the meaning of ceremony and formality in any modern context excepting the exclusively religious. As the discussions developed it seemed clarifying to distinguish the religious from the sacred. If sacred is understood in the sense of "unquestionable" and traditionalizing, then something may be sacred, yet not religious. A four-fold set of categories, religious/non-religious, sacred/non-sacred provides a framework for considering non-religious sanctity, and for noting that religious symbols are sometimes exhibited on inherently non-religious occasions. Examples of this last would be a prayer said at the opening of a session of Congress, or an oath taken on the Bible in a courtroom. These terms also make it easier to discuss the fact that religious institutions such as churches have non-religious non-sacred aspects, such as their finances. Of course there are also sacred, non-religious objects and ideas: the flag, patriotism, loyalty to family and country, and the like. The codes of acceptable social behavior also may be unchallengeable, their unquestionable aspects only becoming obvious in the breach. These objects, symbols and behaviors and ideas may be charged with more or less emotion and may be variously defined as important or trivial, but they all have in common a certain degree of unquestionability. The four-fold categories we propose are capable of generating more combinations than Durkheim's sacred/profane, and are susceptible of less confusion (we refer especially to the problem of the mundane, discussed later in this section). As many of the ceremonies which take place in modern situations use a variety of symbols, having both religious and non-religious referents, their dissection is facilitated by such a framework.

The looseness of the concept of ritual, as Goody (this volume) points out, is a serious obstacle to investigation of the subject. There are problems everywhere one turns and these were reiterated and explored but not resolved in the Burg Wartenstein Conference on which this volume is based. In dealing with religious rituals, the disunity is not as troublesome since such ritual is conventionally understood, as Victor Turner puts it, to refer to "formal behavior for occasions not given over to technological routine, having reference to beliefs in mystical being or powers" (cited in Goody, this volume). Gluckman (1962) has advocated limiting the term "ritual" to practices involving mystical forces or "supra-sensible qualities." But much ceremony in modern industrial societies does not refer to mystical powers. Gluckman's solution is to speak of "ceremonious" rather than ritual behaviors in discussing secular contexts. A number of the symposium participants adopt the same terminological distinction as Gluckman and abjure the term "secular ritual" entirely.

It is clear that the articles in this volume do not reflect consensus on these matters and their usage remains inconsistent. Most often the terms, *ritual* and *ceremony*, were used interchangeably despite the general awareness of the confusion surrounding them. Goody (this volume) argues that even accepting the distinction between ritual and ceremony leaves many problems, since ceremony is a category so broad and general as to be very hard to cope with. If secular ceremonies are merely "formal behaviors in the non-technological realm" how is one to distinguish ceremony from all formal actions?

There was general agreement at the conference that if social behaviors were put on a continuum, with the extreme of prescribed formality at one end and the most open, optative, spontaneous behavior at the other, that almost any complex social occasion involved both, in various permutations and combinations. Which of such performances constitute rituals and which merely have formal or ritualized elements? Locating the precise point where ceremony begins on such a continuum, if indeed it were possible to do so at all, does not have any heuristic importance for the present discussion. What is of much greater interest is to consider the meaning of formal elements wherever they occur. In this matter Rappaport's discussion of sanctity and religious ritual is very useful (1971). "Sanctity," he says, "is the quality of unquestionable truthfulness imputed by the faithful to unverifiable propositions" (Ibid: 69). Leaving out the matter of belief, which we have already identified as an empirical question about the operational efficacy of ritual, we argue that formality as such often conveys an element of presented certainty. It is our conviction that one level of meaning of many formal actions is to present or refer to the culturally postulated and the socially unquestionable. It is an attempt to reify the man-made (see Berger and Luckmann 1966). That which is postulated and unquestionable may but need not be religious. It may but need not have to do with mystical forces and the spirit world. Unquestionability may instead be vested in a system of authority or a political ideology or other matters. If ritual is considered a set of formal acts which deal with or refer to postulated matters about society or ideology (or matters those mounting the ritual *want* to be unquestioned) then the notion of a secular ritual is not a contradiction in terms. Using the terms ceremony and ritual interchangeably emphasizes a common formalism, rather than emphasizing doctrinal difference.

Conventionally "secular" exists only as a counterpart of "religious." They can be defined only by implying each other. In using these as discontinuous and exclusive categories, one seems to walk arm in arm with Durkheim in a two-part universe in which all things are either sacred or profane. All things religious are sacred. All things non-religious are profane (1912, 1961 ed.: 52). For Durkheim the sacred included both God and the Devil. The demonic manifestation of the sacred is made very clear in Kapferer's discussion of Sinhalese exorcism ritual (this volume) and indeed in magical cures one frequently encounters the manipulation of evil forces in the context of sacred rituals. Durkheim appreciated the inextricable association of God and the Devil. For Durkheim the secular or profane was simply the mundane (Ibid.: 345, 468). The sacred had to be kept separate from the mundane, the ordinary life, the not "special" nor set-apart. "In general, all acts characteristic of the ordinary life are forbidden while those of the religious life are taking place. The act of eating is of itself profane: for it takes place every day . . . and is a part of our ordinary existence" (Ibid: 345).

Durkheim's radical distinction between sacred and mundane creates difficulties conceptually and proves to be at variance with much ethnographic evidence. It is clear that in some societies, the mundane itself is contained by the sacred. All of life may be sacralized in this way so that every breath drawn, every social amenity or implement used is a manifestation of the cosmic order, and an expression of cosmic will. The sacred/mundane distinction is a culture-bound dichotomy rather than a universal one. Hunt (this volume) touches the question when she asks whether there can ever be a totally non-sacralized society. One can imagine a non-religious society, but it is difficult to imagine a society that holds nothing sacred, that treats everything as open to question, and sets nothing apart.

Durkheim himself had a very broad conception of the sacred. Any object might become invested with sacredness in his terms, since sacredness is not inherent, but is a quality given to things (Ibid: 261). An object or symbol is sacred not because of what it is, but because of the way it is treated. Vogt remarked at the symposium that in such a classification, Lenin's tomb might be counted sacred, as might the idea of Communism itself. That is indeed what Durkheim meant, and he used the French Revolution as a secular example (Ibid.: 245).

Inevitably, discussion of the putative sanctity of Lenin's tomb leads to consideration of the coercive uses of ritual and the relationship between sanctity and authority. In discussion Colson pointed out the great rigidity evident in political rituals in oppressive circumstances, or recently established, still precarious conquests. In these conspicuously secular settings, strict obedience to form is demanded, and this is in sharp contrast to the operation of accepted sacred rituals, whose authority issues from their profound embeddedness through many spheres of society and culture. This point was made vivid by Srinivas' description to the symposium of a crowded, noisy Hindu wedding where sanctity issued from the embededness of sacred symbols. The sacrality of the event was demonstrated, not undermined, by the informality and ease which characterized the participants' behavior. The mundane and the ceremonial dimensions were inseparable, blended and utterly appropriate. So too, Myerhoff observed, the Huichol Indians of Mexico in the presence of their deities, during their most sacred ritual moments are often jolly and casual, even boisterous and ribald. The authority accruing to sacred symbols which are completely embedded in a culture does not need external expression, and decorous attitudes need not be required. Colson and Vogt's descriptions of sanctity externally enforced by secular authorities resulting in extremely formal, rigid respectful demeanor provided sharply contrasting illuminating examples.

Although ceremony seems to be an ideal medium in which to make statements about matters that are postulated, or unquestionable, it seems sensible to view unquestionability as a matter of degree rather than kind. A political ritual, a formal greeting, a graduation, may differ in terms of the extent of questioning permissible, the extent of belief and commitment expected. But the form itself gives its messages some degree of what Rappaport calls "certification" (Ibid., 1971).

Since ritual is a good form for conveying a message as if it were unquestionable, it often is used to communicate those very things which are most in doubt. Thus where there is conflict, or danger, or political opposition, where there is made-upness and cultural invention, ritual may carry the opposite message in form as well as in content. Action itself may be soothing, and Malinowski (1948) stressed this in his interpretation of ritual. It may be the expression of potence and optimism, especially in situations of technological inadequacy, danger and anxiety. Ceremony can make it appear that there is no conflict, only harmony, no disorder, only order, that if danger threatens, safe solutions are at hand, that political unity is immediate and real because it is celebrated, and so on. Ritual can assert that what is culturally created and man-made is as undoubtable as physical reality. Whether a ceremony succeeds in its purpose is another question, a question about operational efficacy. But the connection between ritual and the unquestionable is often at the core of its doctrinal efficacy as much in social and political settings as in religious ones.

To explore these questions, to ask about a particular ceremonial performance to what postulated and presumed truths it refers, what social relationships it involves, what doctrines it presents, what symbols it uses, raises tantalizing theoretical and methodological questions. The reward, as the articles in this volume amply demonstrate, is a glimpse into the way people in society represent their situation to themselves.

NOTES

[1] Description of this event was offered at a seminar on Secular Ritual by two students, Richard Morantz and Gregory Dimmitt, University of Southern California, 1973.

[2] There is an analogy in the difficulty of ascertaining the effects of television watching or the impact of other mass-communication media.

CHAPTER II
AGAINST "RITUAL": LOOSELY STRUCTURED THOUGHTS ON A LOOSELY DEFINED TOPIC

Jack Goody

I begin by saying that what I am offering is an abuse of the written mode, but since conferences now turn upon the circulation of documents, so that the phrase "presenting one's thoughts" has to be interpreted as "reading a paper," the oral mode is relegated to the off-hand comment on the formal script. What I have to say needs to be spoken rather than written, at least read living rather than circulated dead.

A whole set of terms used in the anthropological discussion of the area generally referred to as "religion" are virtually useless for analytic purposes and have done little but confuse the attempt to understand human behavior. I do not refer only to the kind of discussion that has centered around totemism, mana, sorcery and the like, but to other, more general, terms like magic, myth and above all ritual.

In the first place, the terms are vagueness itself; witness the time and effort that go into the definitional problem, which gives rise to whole books whose main problematic turns out to rest on nominalistic criteria, Steiner on taboo, Lévi-Strauss on totemism.

In the second place, these terms often accept, implicitly or explicitly, a dichotomous view of the world which may be based upon a directional distinction of the kind crudely illustrated in the recent comment of that boisterous psychoanalyst, Thomas S. Szasz: "if you can talk to God, you are praying; if God talks to you, you have schizophrenia." More usually, the basis is a "religious-secular" distinction, of the kind: pray to God, talk to father. Or, more seriously, of the kind: they have myths (the men of old), we have *storia*. The categories are based upon a we/they distinction, which operates in a temporal context (traditional/modern), or in a geographical frame (we the people/they the savages), or by reference to a particular set of assumptions, for example, world religions (like Christianity) as against other local beliefs, like magi(c) or withcraft, and so forth until we reach the ultimate dichotomy on which so much thinking in this field is based; we = science/logic, they = religion/magic, or we = rationality, they = irrationality (or non-rationality).

I do not overlook the fact that some of these categories are emic, actor-based ones that are plainly visible at the observer level. In LoDagaa,

special verbs exist for speaking (praying) to supernatural agencies, for offering (sacrificing) them material objects, and so forth. On the other
hand some have no recognizable base in the societies in which I have
worked, and these would include magic, myth, symbol, ritual and religion
(not to speak of the sacred and the profane).

When we look around the field of the analysis of ritual, we find widespread confusion. Let us take the definition of the field offered in a recent book entitled *Ritual in Industrial Society*. Pointing out that some
writers have restricted the word ritual to "religious" acts, the author himself uses the term to cover "both religious ritual and other types of ritual,
which might be called 'ceremonies' by others" (Bocock 1974: 15). The
illustrations to the book indicate the range of social action reviewed in
this short monograph, ranging from coronations, to funerals, Christmas,
dances, football, theatre, gymnastics, brass-bands, pop festivals, to student
demonstrations. Include elections, schools, work groups and the rituals of
family living, and you have covered much of social life in Britain today.
Indeed much the same catholicity is shown in the outline to this conference where we range from parties and music to holidays and negotiations.

If one adopts the view that *ritual* forms an aspect of all social action,
then such an oecumenical definition is perhaps understandable. But what
does one do with the definition when you've got it? If, on the other hand,
you are looking for *rituals* as a category of action requiring some special
kind of interpretation, then such universalism is of little help. The only
thread that one can see through this diversity (whether of aspects of
behaviour of of behaviours) is the observer's categorisation of the means-
ends relationships, indicated by the title to the first chapter of the book
named above, "Man shall not live by bread alone." What isn't bread (i.e.,
the non-rational area of life) needs some other justification, i.e., an "explanation" in terms of symbolic value (dominant, core or key), hidden
code or social solidarity. But the eating of bread can be just as symbolic,
solidary, meaningful, etc. as any other act, indeed more so just because of
its close entailment in the "rational" sphere, where means-ends relationships approach more closely to the model of the economist, the political
scientist, the taxi-driver or the engineer, i.e. the logico-empirical.

It seems doubtful if the thinking (or rather, the assumptions, since the
"thought" is usually implicit) behind this categorisation can be of much
use in the analysis of human behavior. Confined to the religious sphere it
has some minimal utility. But used in the wide manner of ethologists (the
rituals of copulation), archaeologists (with their ritual objects), the sociologists (discovering rituals of family living) and the anthropologist (rituals, more rituals, yet more rituals), there is little to be gained either from
the term itself or from further subdivision.

I have taken Bocock's work as an example of the disutility of the concept of ritual. I am not meaning to single out his work; it happens to deal with "Ritual in Industrial Society", and is subtitled, "A sociological analysis of ritualism in modern England." It is therefore concerned with "secular" as well as religious rituals, the dichotomy that appears in the preamble to the conference as well as in the conference papers themselves. One of his findings is that "rituals are of far greater importance in an industrial society such as modern Britain than is often realised." But if we include in our definition of ritual "hand-shaking, teeth cleaning, taking medicines, car riding, eating, entertaining guests, drinking tea, or coffee, beer, sherry, whisky, etc., taking a dog for a walk, watching television, going to the cinema, listening to records, visiting relatives, routines at work, singing at work, children's street games, hunting and so on,' then one can, at the author rightly perceives "go on adding activities *ad infinitum*" (1974: 15). And what's the point? We then have a category that includes almost all action that is standardised in some way or other, and we then have to begin all over again breaking it down into some more meaningful categories. However, given the initial vagueness, perhaps it is better to build up from nothing rather than break down from everything.

In his valuable collection of essays, *The Forest of Symbols*, Victor Turner defines ritual as "formal behaviour for occasions not given over to technological routine, having reference to beliefs in mystical beings or powers. The symbol is the smallest unit of ritual . . ." (1967: 19). This is not a definition I would wish to dispute in any way. For secular rituals then we simply omit the last phrase of the first sentence, "having reference to mystical beings." We are left with formal behaviour in the non-technological realm. But while this is (for me) acceptable, it is also of very limited significance, largely because the category is so engulfing it seems likely to block research, but also because of the gap between the observer's and actor's categories at this point. "Technological" is the differentiating factor, hence relating the action to what is empirically determined, what is intrinsic to the means-end relationship here the standpoints are likely to be very different.

S.J. Tambiah has tried to get round this difficulty in his recent discussion of the "form and meaning of magical acts" (1973). He argues that: "while both 'magic' and 'science' are characterised by analogical thought and action, they comprise differentiated varieties whose validity it would be inappropriate to measure and verify by the same standards. Magical acts, usually compounded of verbal utterance and object manipulation, constitute "performative" acts by which a property is imperatively transferred to a recepient object or person on a analogical basis. *"Magical acts are ritual acts,* and ritual acts are in turn performative acts whose position and creative meaning is missed . . . if . . . subjected to . . . empirical verification associated with scientific activity" (1973: 199).¹ I find the argument leads us back to where we started from, for my experience has been that the actors in "rituals of affliction" do indeed expect to have their afflictions relieved. And again, I find the planting of grain as "symbolic", often as "formal", certainly as "repetitive" as any other kind of action.

In the volume mentioned above Turner divides Ndembu rituals into two main types, life-crisis rituals and rituals of affliction. With regard to the first he writes that "there are a number of ceremonies or rituals designed to mark the transition from one phase of life or social status to another" (1967: 7). This Van Gennepian position has been maintained by many, including myself. But its significance is again very limited. Translate "rituals" into the neutral "ceremonies" or the even more neutral "public acts" or social interacts, and the statement becomes almost a tautology. The announcement of birth, the celebration of marriage, the burial of the dead, what special theory or approach could deal with these, *grosso mode*? Yet the use of the term "ritual" suggests there is some key we can discover that will unlock this universe of social action, some common code that will reveal all to the enquiring mind.

That there are elements (possibly "structural elements") of meaning (we can dispense with symbol as we can dispense with ritual) that are often common to these ceremonies located in the life cycle, there is no doubt. But here is plenty of doubt about the utility of locating such action in a field defined according to "technological" criteria, whether or not we add the criteria of religious or the mystical. Indeed seen from this angle, there can be little point in asking what light the study of religious ritual can shed on secular rituals, since neither the dichotomy of religious/ secular nor that of ritual or non-ritual carry much analytic weight. What would a life crisis look like without "ritual"? What would a funeral look like without a reference to continuity after death; even if such continuity does not always involve spiritual beings, the pressure to accept a functional equivalent to a religious "ritual" is strong. Of course if one defines ritual as a formalistic type of behaviour, leaving out any connotation of "religion", then it would be absurd (read "lacking in any theoretical base") to suppose that "ritual" was any less common in Western societies than in any other. "Routinisation", regularisation, repetition, lie at the basis of social life itself.

Let us turn specifically to secular "rituals". In my view, any analytic system that cannot (or does not) discriminate between performances of Rattigan's French without Tears (I take what's playing at the local Theatre as I write), the State Opening of Parliament and the Mass is wasting our time by trivialising the study of social behaviour. One is well aware, since Chambers, that our main source of modern English drama were the Mystery plays of Medieval England, that there was a move from Church to Procession to Theatre. There may be something to be said about the general or specific characteristics of "formal" actions, or the meaning of words and gestures, or even of their (mass) behaviour of people in crowds. But to approach this enquiry in terms of the meaning, role, classification of ritual seems (to me) like blindfolding oneself before looking for the way out of a maze.

If one accepts the trend of this argument then questions like "What does ritual do?" and "What is the meaning of ritual?" or attempts to subdivide ritual into subcategories (even "rites of passage") can lead nowhere. In the first instance the same questions can be posed of any aspect of human behaviour: in the second, the subcategories would apply to all action, and would anyhow be of little value unless directed towards the understanding of variations within or between human groups – yet the use of such an all-embracing "concept" inhibits the study both of variation and of association. There is nothing to demonstrate either way, nothing to prove or disprove, support or contradict; all is equally acceptable.

The middle: function: the fit and the unfit; formality and informality

A widespread view of ritual in the earlier part of this century saw ritual as the verbal counterpart of myth e.g., Jane Harrison. The idea continued to be vigorously applied by the myth and ritual "school" e.g., S.H. Hooke and was in some way implicit in Malinowski's view of myth as a "charter" for other forms of social behaviour. This view was quite consistent with all forms of functional approach. In 1954, Leach put the view in a very explicit way, seeing myth and ritual as two sides of the same coin.

The "structural" study of myth did away with all that. Not "at a stroke," since Griaule's discussion of Dogon myth had already insisted upon the philosophical elements in *le mythe* and ritual was left to follow its own course. But the functional study of ritual has recently taken a new direction in the works influenced by the study of cultural ecology.

In his interesting analysis of Maring ritual, Rappaport claims that the regulatory function of ritual "helps to maintain an undegraded environment, limits the fighting to frequencies that do not endanger the existence of the regional population, adjusts man-land ratios, facilitates trade, distributes local surpluses of pig in the form of pork throughout the regional population, and assures people of high quality protein when they need it" (1968: 224). Well may the reader see this as an essentially functionalist contribution. Not that there is anything wrong in patterns. That's what we're looking for at one level or another. But the limitation here is the broadness of the category of ritual and the impossibility of falsification.[2]

If we assume any kind of functional or structural relationship of "ritual", than its formal and repetitive nature must tend to inhibit change in other parts of the social system, whether these relationships lie on the same or a different level of the system.[3] It is not surprising, therefore, to find that ritual is so commonly seen as system-maintaining, group-maintaining, as eufunctional. But formality, repetitiveness also means culture lag and loss of meaning. In asking "how should this be done" of a Coronation in Britain, a sixty year Sigi ceremony amoung the Dogon or installation of a Tallensi chief, one is attempting to reproduce the acts of the previous occasion as accurately as one can. In so far as the attempt is successful, the new performance will repeat the physical and verbal acts associated with the earlier ceremony. Meanwhile the social situation may have changed, and (even in the most "static" of societies) the meaning will certainly have done.

The meaning changes in two ways. Firstly, by the process of forgetting or elaboration. Many societies in West Africa use the "code" 3 = man, 4 = woman. Of two adjacent groups (A and B), one leaves the association at that point, whereas another "explains" 3 = penis plus testicles of man, 4 = four lips of a woman.

Presuming a common base, this difference represents a process whereby one group has forgotten the wider associations or the other has elaborated a less complex original. The same processes clearly occur in the same society over time; consequently the same acts would have a different meaning at T_1 and T_2. Secondly, any society, no matter how simple, experiences the continuous creation of meaning in another range. A particular event, a new song, a topical phrase, will have its effect upon the network of meaning and thus change the system in one direction or another. The advent of an elephant into the village, a sudden display of its destructive power, may alter the meaning of elephant as totem, as symbol, as metaphor, as element in a ceremony. In Africa the ebullient creation of new meaning (V.C. 10 = gin, hijack = elope, etc.) is a recurrent feature of the use of language, even when that language is a secondary one.

One may argue that diversity of meaning, as with three and four constitutes a set of variations (transformation) on a common theme, reflecting, expressing, deriving from one common structure. Perhaps. The argument is difficult to falsify. Nevertheless, at the actor level of meaning, the fit between actor and interaction must vary with the presence or absence of an explicit sexual reference.

Exact recollection (to return to the Coronation), formalisation, repetition, may only lead to solidarity (many public displays have this effect); it also leads to a loss of meaning. Take the election of a Master of a Cambridge College. The election in the chapel involved a declaration before God of one's belief that X was the right man. Nowadays the verbal vote seems an infringement of personal liberties (enshrined in the voting reforms of the 19th century). Yet ceremony preserves the emptied if not empty form, now shorn of meaning because that is how things are done. The formal repetitive character of "ritual" leads to continuity, yes, but the perjorative implications of formal, ritual, convention, etiquette, are in fact embedded in their very substance, intrinsic to their nature.

What I am saving here has certain implications which, while corresponding to experience of our own society, are often brushed aside in considering other cultures. Namely, that the central meaning for the spectators lies at a fairly simple level; they too need an explanation of the meaning of the sceptre and the orb, let alone the fine rainments preserved in the crypt. The nuances of wedding tent require exegesis even for the main participants, let alone the watchers of the screen.

This situation is of course affected by the way in which "occasions" are communicated (the nature of the media), but the relative superficiality of such communication is not to be entirely derived either from the mass audience or the rapidity of change. It is intrinsic to the nature of ritual and it gives rise to different interpretations by the actors (exegesis) as well as by the observers (sociology). Both can vary greatly, but whereas the first set of variants constitute a set of interesting sociological facts about the society, the latter testify to the often circular, speculative, untestable and even simple minded character of much that passes for explanation.

Perhaps I could illustrate the point of interpretation from two recent articles on two adjacent (and very much interesting) peoples in Ghana. In an account of spirit mediums among the Ga, Marian Kilson notes that these roles are mainly filled by women who are not only illiterate but are also either childless or "women who disclose deep ambivalance about the maternal role itself" (1972: 174). Redress is obtained by becoming married to the (male) god (monogamously) and producing acolytes as "children" (174, 176). Meanwhile of Ashanti initiates into "traditional" medical practice (i.e. what Fortes and others have called "medicine shrines"), P.A. Twumasi notes that the final rite of the long training includes the phrase uttered by the new male priest (or practitioner): "God so and so accept this sheep and eat; today you have completed marriage with me . . ." (52). In the first instance, the role of women as mediums is explained by their compensating status as wives of male gods; in the second, it appears that the concept of marriage can easily be stripped of its sexual connotations.

An example of variation in ritual occurs in the Gonja marriage ceremonies described by Esther Goody (1973: 94). Here many of the elements are widely distributed not only in Gonja but among other groups influenced by Islam; different groups, even different families, make use of different elements in this pool and appear to make additions of their own much in the manner of family celebrations at Christmas. But the number of elements included in all marriage formalities in the society is small indeed and subject to differential interpretation. One common element in Muslim marriages throughout the area is the unravelling of string wrapped around some kola nuts. Even here the interpretation may vary, some seeing the halves of the nut as representing the spouses and the whole nut their union, an association which others do not make.

Given this situation, and setting aside for one moment our qualms about the category, there is some reason for doubting Monica Wilson's statement, quoted approvingly by Victor Turner and offered in similar form by many anthropologists (particularly those believing in or looking for "a key to culture"),[5] to the effect that "Rituals reveal values at their deepest level . . . men express in ritual what moves them most, and since the form of expression is conventionalized and obligatory, it is the values of the group that are revealed. I see in the study of rituals the key to an understanding of the essential constitution of human societies" (1954: 241, quoted by Turner 1969: 6). I suggest it is misleading to assert that "rituals" provide a key to deep values more than any other type of human behaviour. Indeed, I would be tempted to argue that they conceivably provide less of a clue, for the reasons I have stated, their formality, the element of culture lag, the component of public demonstration, their role as masks of the "true" self. Communication that takes place in a "conventional" ritual is often much less "meaningful" than currently supposed. However this may be in non-literate societies, I do not believe it possible to maintain that the public rituals of our secular society really provide "decisive keys to the understanding of how people think and feel about (economic, political and social) relationships, and about the natural and social environments in which they operate" (Turner 1968: 6). There has certainly been a change of considerable magnitude, but it is perhaps not only in "secular" societies that rituals may be formal and repetitive, representative of the old rather than the new, occasions where action is automatic rather than thought out, hence possibly less central to human life than the afflictions or crises that have provided the occasion.

This (potential) separation of ritual from "values", "self", "core", "meaning", is a constant theme in European history. In the Greek city state, for example, compliance in ritual was demanded, not acceptance of belief. Other differentiated societies demanded participation in ritual as a mark of obeisance, knowing full well that the maranos of Spain and Arab lands, did not believe. The English Test Acts bear witness to the same divide. The acknowledgement of ritual does not necessarily affect deeper values, for participation may be a function of political power. So too perhaps with rituals of rebellion, where the tension inherent in the situation of dominance is given explicit recognition. Indeed it is often the rejection of ritual that is seen as revealing the truth; hence its rejection by Protestant and Evangelical sects, as a prelude to creating their own particular formalitties.

The end

Since I am against "ritual", I don't have to offer a way forward, only a way out. But nagging problems remain, especially if one has invested a lot of time working in myth, ritual and the vague and unsatisfactory fields mentioned at the beginning.

If we reject the use of the term "ritual", except for expressive purposes (or as a vague pointer, a highly generalized orientation) what can we do instead? As an opening gambit, we can attempt to translate the term ritual each time it is used. This I believe would separate two trends: firstly, acts which are repetitive, formal or both repetitive and formal; all formal acts are repetitive, repetition tends to formalize behaviour, though not all repetition involves "formality" in the more extreme sense of the word. There are two meanings of the word "formal" which are of special relevance to this discussion. One meaning has to do with regularity, pattern, convention; it is just what most social scientists are looking for. The other, related usage is perjorative; "excessively regular or symmetrical, stiff", even "perfunctory, having the form without the spirit." Of course, all "normative" behaviour is in some degree repetitive (hence, "formal" in the weaker sense); that is what we generally mean by social behaviour. The notions of custom, habits, etiquette, norms, expectations, structure, continuity, solidarity, all these privileged concepts of the sociologist involve this notion. We hardly need the concept "ritual" to deal with table manners, or courting behaviour, or personal idiosyncrasies; indeed to bring them together under one such heading in no way increases our understanding.

Secondly, we can take a tip from the title of M. Varignan's treatise of

1725, *Ecclaircissemens sur l'analyse des infiniment petits*. This adverse
direction leads us towards the study of what Goffman has called "the sociology of occasions," the close systematic study of "small behaviours"
that begins with a description of the "natural units of intreaction," from
the smallest facial expression to the week-long conference. Goffman enti-
tles his book *Interaction Ritual* and speaks of "the ritual roles of the self"
(in contrast to the sacred self), of "player in a ritual game," of "riutal
codes" (1972: 31-34) and "ritual care" (1972: 36). Since one of the
values of Goffman's work is to subject all "encounters" to similar forms of
analysis, it is not clear what is gained by this particular phraseology, except perhaps a certain detachment from such behaviour (as well as its
detachment from the self "qua object of ultimate worth" rather than "qua
actor") which enables the analysis to develop. Other "rituals" consist of
large-scale ceremonies but the building blocks often consists of such
small behaviours, the formal units of performance, the idioms and metaphors of action. Here the structure of ceremony, the order in which such
behaviours are put together, requires particular attention.

The other point suggested by the reference to Varignan is the possibility of quantification, though this is a difficult area and one could suggest
only crude techniques.

Thirdly, there is the area of meaning and exegesis, which has a very
long way to go. We all accept types of explanation and evidence for other
cultures that we would not accept for our own.

Finally, the function of "ritual" can be better elucidated under changing rather than static conditions, here again the field presents us with special difficulties which cannot be solved by slight of hand or mind.

I conclude with an example taken from what might be expected to be a
fraternal subject among the sciences of man, but is more often looked
upon as the enemy who are not even affines. Writing recently of some aspects of psychological research, Mittler comments, "One of the reasons
why the nature-nurture controversy proved relatively unproductive in the
1930's was that the questions and the terminology were too global. We
are now beginning to see that terms such as "heredity", "environment",
"intelligence", "personality" are themselves of limited value in research,
even though they provide convenient abbreviations with a common core
of meaning for general discussion. Psychologists are becoming increasingly dissatisfied with global constructs such as "intelligence", "language", "perception", "memory" and "learning": recent theoretical and
psychometric efforts have concentrated on attempts to isolate, identify
and measure specific cognitive processes. General intelligence has never
been satisfactorily defined . . . intelligence is now seen as consisting of a
number of hierarchically organised skills and processes . . ." (1971: 149).

Is it possible to carry out the same kind of paradigm shift in anthropology? Or would the whole edifice fall to the ground?

NOTES

[1] Though not all ritual is magical, of course (p. 228).

[2] I don't ignore the criticisms of Popper, but they touch upon more detailed aspects of these views.

[3] "In attempting to discover how it is that these conventions are maintained in force as guides to action, one finds evidence to suggest a functional relationship between the structure of the self and the structure of spoken interaction" (Goffman 1972: 36).

[4] I am indebted to Robert Launay for this observation on Dyala marriage in the Savannah area of West Africa.

[5] See J. Goody. Turning the tables: literacy and classification. ASA (volume in press).

CHAPTER III
VARIATIONS ON A THEME OF LIMINALITY

Victor Turner

Liminality is a concept, borrowed from the Belgian folklorist Arnold Van Gennep, which like a pebble, I tossed speculatively into the pool of my anthropological data about a dozen years ago, to try to make more sense than I had previously been able to do of ritual processes I had observed in Central Africa. Since then it has been spreading rings in my work and thought over wider ranges of data drawn not only from preindustrial societies, but also from complex, large-scale civilizations. My theoretical focus has correlatively shifted from societies in which rituals involve practically everyone, to societies in which, as Durkheim puts it, "the domain of religion", if not perhaps of ritual, has "contracted", become a matter of individual choice rather than universal corporate ascription, and where, with religious pluralism, there is sometimes a veritable supermarket of religious wares. In these societies, symbols once central to the mobilization of ritual action, have tended to migrate directly or in disguise, through the cultural division of labor, into other domains, esthetics, politics, law, popular culture, and the like.

We will briefly examine liminality, what Van Gennep meant by it, and how I have elaborated his formulation. Van Gennep examined rites of passage in many cultures, and found them to have basically a tripartite processual structure, even when they had many isolable episodes. He defined *rites de passage* as "rites which accompany every change of place, state, social position, and age." I will use "state" as a metonym for the other terms; it refers to any type of stable or recurrent condition that is culturally recognized. These rites of transition, says Van Gennep, are marked by three phases: separation; margin (or *limen*); and re-aggregation. The first and last speak for themselves; they detach ritual subjects from their old places in society and return them, inwardly transformed and outwardly changed, to new places. A more interesting problem is provided by the middle, (marginal) or liminal phase. It is interesting in itself, but more so perhaps on account of its implications for a general theory of sociocultural processes. The term "marginal" has been preempted by various sociologists (for example, Stonequist, Thomas, Znanieki, and Riesman) for their own purposes – so we are left with "liminal".

A *limen* is a threshold, but at least in the case of protracted initiation rites or major seasonal festivals, it is a very long threshold, a corridor almost, or a tunnel which may, indeed, become a pilgrim's road or passing from dynamics to statics, may cease to be a mere transition and become a set way of life, a state, that of the anchorite, or monk. Let us refer to the state and process of mid-transition as "liminality" and consider a few of its very odd properties. Those undergoing it – call them "liminaries" – are betwixt-and-between established states of politico-jural structure. They evade ordinary cognitive classification, too, for they are neither-this-nor-that, here-nor-there, one-thing-not-the-other. Out of their mundane structural context, they are in a sense "dead" to the world, and liminality has many symbols of death – novices may be classed with spirits or ancestors or painted black; in Central Africa the place of circumcision in the boys' initiation rites is called "the place of dying." They are also "polluting", as Mary Douglas might say, because they transgress classificatory boundaries. Sometimes they are identified with feces; usually they are allowed to revert to nature by letting their hair and nails grow and their bodies get covered with dust. Their structural "invisibility" may be marked not only by their seclusion "from men's eyes" but also by the loss of their preliminal names, by the removal of clothes, insignia and other indicators of preliminal status; they may be required to speak in whispers, if at all. They may have to learn a special liminal vocabulary; normal word-order may be reversed or even randomly scrambled. As against these emblems of death or limbo, other symbols and symbolic actions portray gestation, parturition, lactation, weaning. The novices at times may be treated as embryos in a womb, as infants being born, as sucklings, and as weanlings. Usually, there are words and phrases which indicate that they are "being grown" into a new postliminal state of being. But the most characteristic midliminal symbolism is that of paradox, or being *both* this *and* that. Novices are portrayed and act as androgynous, or as both living *and* dead, at once ghosts and babes, both cultural and natural creatures, human *and* animal. They may be said to be in a process of being ground down into a sort of homogeneous social matter, in which possibilities of differentiation may be still glimpsed, then later positively refashioned into specific shapes compatible with their new postliminal duties and rights as incumbents of a new status and state. The grinding down process is accomplished by ordeals; circumcision, subincision, clitoridectomy, hazing, endurance of heat and cold, impossible physical tests in which failure is greeted by ridicule, unanswerable riddles which make even clever candidates look stupid, followed by physical punishment, and the like. But reducing down overlaps with reconstruction. The rebuilding process is by instruction, partly in practical skills, partly in

37

tribal esoterica, and proceeds both by verbal and nonverbal symbolic means. Sacred objects may be shown, myths recited in conjunction with them, answers may be given to riddles earlier left unexplained. Very often, masked figures invade the liminal scene – usually framed in a sacred enclosure, cave, *temenos*, or other sequestered site – these masked figures being themselves liminal in their bizarre combinations of human, animal, vegetable and mineral characteristics. Such maskers and monsters are often composites of factors drawn from the culture of mundane, quotidian experience, but split off from their normal, expectable contexts and recombined in grotesque, weird, even anatomically impossible configurations, which have as at least one of their functions, that of provoking the novices or initiands, the "liminaries", into thinking hard about the elements and basic building blocks of symbolic complexes they had hitherto taken for granted as "natural" units. Actuality, in the liminal state, gives way to possibility, and aberrant possibilities reveal once more to liminaries the value of what has hitherto been regarded as the somewhat tedious daily round. A manheaded lion, leaping in firelight from the bush, may make one think about the abstract nature both of human heads and of feral bodies, or of the relationship between culture which can *manufacture* monsters, and nature which generates lions, or of the symbolism of social control – a chief has lion-like powers; each culture will stress its own salient dichotomies and draw its own lessons. And this is one of the simpler monsters; the Chinese dragon, a complex monster indeed, has been claimed by Elliot Smith to be a cultural construct in its entirety; every part of its body has cosmological significance; the colors and shapes of its eyes, limbs, wings, tail, its scales, its claws, its postures – all derive from the principles and symbolic lexicon of a cosmological system. Thus masks and monsters may be as much pedagogical devices as instruments of coercion through terror and awe; like other liminal things they are probably both.

This is, of course, a synoptic account. Not all preindustrial societies have protracted *rites de passage*; some stress particular themes and symbolic processes, and play down others. Here I wish to show that where transition in space-time is ritualized, *how* it is ritualized, the nature and properties of the ritual symbols and of their interrelations, give us clues not only to the cherished values of the society that performs the rituals, but also to the nature of human sociality itself transcending particular cultural forms.

This is not the place to discuss in any detail the distinction between sequestered and public liminality – which roughly corresponds to the difference between initiation rites and major seasonal feasts. In the former, the liminaries are humbled and levelled to make them fit for a higher status

or state; in the latter, the liminaries are everybody in the community, and
no one is elevated in status at the end of the rites. But by way of compensation such major rites as sowing and harvest festivals, first-fruits festivals, change of season rites or rites celebrating important points on the
sun's ecliptic from northern to southern solstice very frequently involve
symbolic status-reversal or the creation of mock-hierarchies for the
mundanely poor and humble.

Humbling and submission to ordeal, whether inflicted by self or others,
goes with preparation for elitehood – whether in this world or the next;
while having an extremely good time, and play-acting at having superior
status, goes with a basic persisting secular egalitarianism among those
who become liminaries for the occasion.[1]

Here, another question must be raised: whatever happened to liminality in *post*tribal societies? The answer will involve me in a brief discussion
of a set of concepts which may help towards an explanation. These are:
work, leisure, play, flow, and communitas. I am not, in this essay, going
to use liminality in a metaphorical sense. I am going to look at cultural
phenomena, which may either be shown to have descended from earlier
forms of ritual liminality, or are, in some sense, their functional equiva-
lents.

Work

In tribal and archaic societies what people do in ritual is often described
by terms which we might translate as "work". Raymond Firth speaks of
the "work" of the Gods in Tikopia as a native description of the annual
ritual cycle of these Polynesians. Bantu-speaking peoples in Africa use
the same term for a ritual specialist's activity as for what a hunter, a cul-
tivator, a headman, or today a manual laborer does. Our own term "liturgy" is from the Greek *leos* or *laos*, "the people" and *ergon* "work" (cog-
nate as our linguists here well know with Old English *weorc,* and German
werk, and ultimately derived from the Indo-European base *werg-o* "to
do, act"). I could cite many other examples, but the point I wish to make
is that the ritual round in tribal societies is embedded in the total round
of activities, and is part of the work of the people which is *also* the work
of the gods. We are dealing with a universe of work, in which the whole
community participates, as of obligation not optation. Furthermore,
though there are special rites for special categories of persons, and for
particular points in the culturally defined life-cycle of each person, soon-
er or later no one is exempt from ritual duty, just as no one is exempt
from economic, legal or political obligations. Communal participation,
obligation, the passage of the whole society through crises, communal or

individual, directly or by proxy, these are the hallmarks of the "work of the gods" and sacred human work. Without sacred work profane human work would be, for the community, impossible to conceive.

But, on the other hand, the ritual "work" to which I am referring is not quite what we, from our stance on the hither side of the Industrial Revolution and perhaps the Protestant Ethic, might regard as "work". For it includes what we might think of as *"play"*, or, more solemnly put since Huizinga, the "ludic". In many tribal rites, there is built into the liturgical structure, a good deal of what we and they would think of as amusement, recreation, fun, and joking; furthermore, there is often the actual "playing" of games, ceremonial lacrosse among North American Indians, for example, the exhausting combined race and ball-game of the Tarahumara of Mexico, or the "push-of-war" contests found among the West-Central Bantu of Africa. Among the maskers are *clowns*; among the myths, *Trickster* stories. Liminality is particularly conducive to play. Play is not to be restricted to games and jokes; it extends to the introduction of new forms of symbolic action, such as word-games or masks. In short, parts of liminality may be given over to experimental behavior. I mean here by "experiment", any action or process undertaken to discover something not yet known, *not* scientific experimentation nor what is based on experience rather than theory or authority. In liminality, new ways of acting, new combinations of symbols, are tried out, to be discarded or accepted. Ritual, and particularly liminality, should not be regarded as monolithic. A tribal ritual of any length and complexity is in fact an orchestration of many genres, styles, moods, atmospheres, tempi, and so on, ranging from prescribed formal, stereotyped action to a free "play" of inventiveness, and including symbols in all the sensory codes mentioned by Lévi-Strauss – visual, auditory, olfactory, gustatory, tactile, kinesthetic, and so on. It has free and formulaic verbal behavior – bodily acts of many kinds. The essence of ritual is its multidimensionality, of its symbols their multivocality. Merely to equate such ritual with the obsessional "rituals" of Western neurotics, as Freud did, is to rob it of its creative potentials, and of its nuanced interplay of thought and mood. Ritual's multiplicity of elements allows for great flexibility and gives it an immense capacity to portray, interpret, and master radical novelty. This same complex flexibility makes it adaptable to change. I am here referring to tribal ritual, where ritual is the nerve-center of cultural sensitivity.

But whatever happened to liminality, and to the richness, flexibility, and symbolic wealth of tribal ritual? As an adherent to one of the religions of the Book, I regret the deliminalization of Christian liturgy – except on rare occasions such as Christmas or Easter, where some liminal sonorities of song and language are allowed to linger. With the deliminalization seems to have gone the powerful play component. Other religions of the Book, too, have regularly stressed the solemn at the expense of the festive. Fairs, fiestas, carnivals exist, of course, but not liturgically. Other major historical religions have fared less badly. Thus, in Vedic India, according to Alain Danielou, the "gods" (the *sura* and *deva*, who are the objects of serious sacrificial ritual, which is the "work" of the householder *ashram* – *grihasta* – stage of life), the gods *play*. The rise, duration, and destruction of the world is their *game*. Creation is not only the "work of the gods", but also the "play of the gods". And human ritual is both earnest and playful. Modern *Bhakti* movements still have this spontaneous, "performative," ludic quality – where Eros sports with Thanatos, and not as a grisly Danse Macabre, but to symbolize a complete human reality.

Leisure

We have spoken of "work" and "play," now let us consider "work" and "leisure." Of recent years much has been written of this pair of concepts. Joffre Demazedier has recently argued strongly for the view that true leisure only exists when it complements or rewards work. Thus he refused to classify the idle state of Greek philosophers and sixteenth century gentry as 'leisure," since this cannot be defined *in relation to* work, but rather *replaces work altogether*, work being done by slaves, peasants, or servants. For Dumazedier, then, "leisure" presupposes "work." It is a non-work, even an anti-work phase in the life of a person who also works. Leisure, he holds, arises under two conditions: (1) the first is that society ceases to govern its activities by means of common ritual obligations; some activities, including those of work and leisure, become, at least in theory, *subject to individual choice*. (2) Secondly, the work by which a person earns his or her living is "set apart from his other activities; its limits are no longer natural but arbitrary" – indeed, it is organized in so definite a fashion that it can easily be separated, both in theory and practice, from his free time. Now it is in industrial and industrializing societies that we mostly find these conditions. Here work is organized by industry, by clocking in and out, by office hours, and so on, so as to be separated from "free time," which includes, of course, in addition to leisure, attendance to such personal needs as eating, sleeping, and caring for one's health and appearance, as well as familial, social, civic, political, and religious obligations. In tribal society all these would have been parts of the work-play sacred-profane continuum and would have been done with substantially the same group of people, not as in industrialized society with different bunches for each segmental activity spun off
 Leisure, again, tends to be mainly an urban phenomenon – we see by the division of labor.

41

early forms of it perhaps in the fourteenth century Italian city state. When the concept of leisure begins to penetrate rural societies, this is because agricultural work is tending towards an industrial, "rationalized" mode of organization, and because rural life is being penetrated by urban, industrial values. Dumazedier follows Isaiah Berlin in arguing that leisure has aspects both of "freedom *from*" and "freedom *to*." Leisure is *freedom from* a whole array of institutional obligations prescribed by the basic forms of technological and bureaucratic organization in the work domain. It is also *freedom from* the forced, chronologically regulated rhythms of factory and office, and a chance to recuperate and enjoy natural, biological rhythms again, on the beaches and mountains, and in the parks and game reserves provided as liminoid retreats. More positively, it is *freedom to* enter, even for some to help generate, the symbolic worlds of entertainment, sports, games, diversions of all kinds. It is *freedom to* transcend social structural normative limitations, freedom, indeed, to *play* – with ideas, with fantasies, with words (in literature, some of the "players" have been Rabelais, Joyce, and Samuel Beckett), with paint (think of the Pointillistes, Surrealists, Action Painters, and so forth), and with social relationships (new forms of community, mating, sensitivity training, and so on). And now we are getting closer to our lost liminality, for in this modern "leisure," far more even than in tribal and agrarian rituals, the experimental and the ludic are stressed. There are many more options in complex, industrial societies: games of skill, strength, and chance may serve (to use Clifford Geertz's terms) both as models *of* past work experience and models *for* future work behavior. Football, chess, and mountaineering are undoubtedly exacting and governed by rules and routines at least as stringent as those of the work situation, but, being optional, they remain part of the individual's freedom of his growing self-mastery, even self-transcendence, as we shall see when I discuss the notion of "flow." They are imbued more thoroughly with pleasure than are those many types of industrial work in which men are alienated from the fruits and results of their labor. Leisure is thus potentially capable of releasing creative powers, individual and communal, either to criticize or prop up dominant social structural values.

This is not the place to discuss the effects of the Protestant Ethic and bureaucratization on even the entertainment genres of industrial leisure, making for professionalization of the arts and sports, and giving rise to the notion that art itself is a quasi-religious vocation, with its own asceticism and total dedication – exemplified by Blake, Kierkegaard, Baudelaire, Proust, Rilke, Cezanne, Gauguin, Mahler, Sibelius, and so on. Here I wish to draw attention to some similarities between the *leisure* genres of art and entertainment in complex industrial societies and the *rituals and myths* of archaic, tribal, and early agrarian cultures. It is, I suppose, possible to conceive of leisure as a betwixt-and-between, neither-this-nor-that domain between two lodgements in the work domain, or between, on the one hand, occupational, and, on the other, familial and civic activities. Leisure is derived from the old French *leisir*, itself derived from Latin *licere*, "to be *permitted*." Interestingly enough, the Latin comes ultimately, according to Skeat, from the Indo-European base *leik*, "to offer for sale bargain," referring to the "liminal" sphere of the market, with its implications of choice, variation, contract – a sphere that has connections, in archaic and tribal religions with such Trickster deities as the Yoruba and Fon Elegba and Eshu, and the Greek Hermes. Exchange and marketing are more "liminal" than production – as the focused fantasies of modern commercial advertising still attest.

We have now seen how tribesmen *play* with the factors of liminality, with masks and monsters, symbolic inversions, parodies of profane reality, and so forth. So also do the genres of industrial leisure: theater, ballet, film, the novel, poetry, classical music, rock music, art, pop art, and so on, pulling the elements of culture apart, putting them together again if often random, grotesque, improbable, surprising, shocking, sometimes deliberately experimental combinations. But there are certain important differences between the tribal genres, relatively few in number, of liminality, and the prolixity of genres found in modern industrial leisure. I have called the latter "liminoid" by analogy with *ovoid*, "egg-*like*" and *asteroid*, "star-*like*." I wish to convey by it something that is akin to the ritually liminal, or like it, but not identical with it. The "liminoid" represents, in a sense, the dismembering, the *sparagmos* of the liminal; for various things that "hang together" in liminal situations split off to pursue separate destinies as specialized arts and sports and so on, as liminoid genres.

Furthermore, the liminoid is very often secularized. Many of the symbolic and ludic capacities of tribal religion have, with the advancing division of labor, with massive increase in the scale and complexity of political and economic units, migrated into nonreligious genres. Sometimes they have taken their sacred tone with them, and one speaks of "high priests" and "priestesses" of this or that art form or of criticism. Certainly, symbol and ritual have gotten into drama and poetry, while on the one hand, literary critics speak of the nineteenth century *Bildungsroman*, the story of "our hero's" progress from poverty to glory, innocence to experience, as a *"rite de passage"* or „an initation," with a linear irreversible monological diachronic progression; while Julia Kristeva on the other hand, writes of the "carnivalization" of the novel – the kind of synchronic, dialogic, nonlinear, reversible, multigenred work such as Rabelais, Cervantes, Lawrence, Sterne, Joyce, Virginia Woolf and others have produced – which may have its ultimate roots in seasonal rituals of reversal and celebration of fructifying chaos, rather than rituals of status elevation. One striking piece of "secularization" seems to have occurred after the massive burning of images of the Virgin Mary by Thomas Cromwell in Chelsea in 1500's. Devotion came by the end of the century to be addressed to a secular Virgin Queen, Gloriana or Oriana, Elizabeth the First, to whom the liminoid humanists, the secular poets and dramatists, dedicated their rich symbolic offerings. Other arts have developed quasi-liturgical properties, or alternatively, have laid claim to the prophet's mantle. Music, for example, has often been called "the religion of the intellectuals" while poetry as Blake and Rimbaud saw it was the language of the prophet and *voyant*.

Continuing to contrast "liminal" and "liminoid" we may say that *liminal phenomena* tend to be collective, concerned with calendrical, meteorological, biological, or social-structural cycles and rhythms, or with crises in social processes whether these result from internal adjustments, external adaptations, or unexpected disasters (earthquakes, invasions, plagues, and the like). Thus they appear at what may perhaps be called "natural breaks" in the flow of natural or sociocultural processes. *Liminoid phenomena*, on the other hand, may be collective (carnivals, spectacles, major sports events, folk drama, national theater, and so on), and when they are so, are often directly derived from tribal liminal antecedents, but are more characteristically produced and consumed by known named individuals, though they may of course, have collective or "mass" effects. They are not cyclical, but continuously generated, though in times and places sequestered from work settings in the "leisure" sphere.

Liminal phenomena are centrally integrated into the total social process, forming with all its other aspects a complete whole, and in its specific essence representing the "negativity" and "subjunctivity" of that total process, rather than its "positivity" and "indicativeness"; its possibility rather than its actuality, its "may be" and "might have been" rather than its "is," "was," and "will be," or even a *via negativa* entered by everyone, not just by mystics. On the other hand, *liminoid phenomena* develop most characteristically *outside* the central economic and political processes, along their *margins*, on their *interfaces*, in their "tacit dimensions" (though, later, liminoid ideas and images may seep from these peripheries and cornices into the center). They are also, in contrast to liminal phenomena, plural, fragmentary and experimental – by "fragmentary" I mean the total inventory of liminoid thoughts, words, and deeds. Individual liminoid productions may, of course, be highly coherent because they have passed, as Ben Johnson said, through "the second fire on the Muses anvil," craftsmanship.

Liminoid phenomena, being produced by specific named individuals or particular groups, "schools," "coteries," tend to be more idiosyncratic and quirky than *liminal* phenomena, which one generalized and normative. They compete with one another in the cultural market, and appeal to specific tastes – while *liminal* phenomena tend to have a common intelectual and emotional meaning for all the members of the widest effective community. *Liminal* phenomena, may, on occasion, portray the inversion or reversal of secular, mundane reality and social structure. But *liminoid* phenomena are not merely reversive, they are often subversive, representing radical critiques of the central structures and proposing utopian alternative models.

Another whole set of topics can be spun off this set of distinctions, for example, the ways in which both liminal and liminoid phenomena constitute metalanguages, (including nonverbal ones) devised for the purpose of talking *about* the various languages of everyday, and in which mundane axioms become problematic, up for speculative grabs, so to speak, where the cherished symbols of the forum, agora, and stoa are reflected upon, rotated, and given new and unexpected valences. I see the germ of such metalanguages and reflexivity in certain of the phenomena of tribal liminality – where we observe parodies of the sacred, and even playful mockery of the gods, let alone of chiefs, priests, and patriarchs.

Again, I can hardly do more than touch here upon the obvious fact, that even in so-called tribal societies, there is an easily recognized *"liminoid zone"* of culture. All anthropologists have encountered this: the great woodcarvers and painters who produce for delight as well as for ritual occasions, the singers of tales and composers of folklore, the manifold children's games, some of which ironically comment on the practices and beliefs of their elders, the satirists who employ keen malicious wit to put down prigs and bosses and one another for the delectation of their mass audiences. On the other hand, there is a well-marked *"liminal zone"* in our own culture: in the liturgies and services of surviving religions, in the initiation rites of clubs, fraternities, Masonic orders, Elks, Lions, Knights of Columbus, secret societies, political and criminal, in the *rites de passage* of Academia (anthropologists will recall Meyer Fortes' analysis of the Anglican rites by which the atheist Sir Edmund Leach was inducted into the office of Provost of King's), or of even more celebrated Academies – some will have read Claude Lévi-Strauss' address after he had been formally and ceremonially admitted as Fortieth "Immortal" into the Académie Française, where he compared the rites, point by point, with those through which he had been given honorary tribal membership in a group of North-West Coast Indians – thereby calling attention to certain universal, symbolic structures in liminal ritual. Furthermore, there can be "reliminalization" of the liminoid. I think this is what may have happened to pilgrimages in the later Middle Ages. Formerly, like all liminoid phenomena, an effect of multiple individual choices and-arising spontaneously as a counterthrust to the corruption of ordinary life in manor and village and town, pilgrimage became built into the structure of Christian culture as a "penitential system," as a rite of passage for readmitting criminous and reprobate individuals into the *Unam Ecclesiam* and, indeed, into civil society. Again, when a group of liminoid artists constitutes itself as a coterie, it tends to generate its own admission rites, providing a liminal portal to its liminoid precinct, a portal, to throw in a liminal monster or two, guarded by three-headed dogs and flaming-sworded angels. Nevertheless, despite the coexistence of liminal and liminoid phenomena in all societies, it remains true that in complex societies today's liminoid is yesterday's liminal.

Here I will add a few comments on some social and psychological aspects of liminal and liminoid processes. I have often spoken of "communitas," or social antistructure, meaning by it a relation quality of full, unmediated communication, even communion, between definite and determinate identities, which arises spontaneously in all kinds of groups, situations, and circumstances. I distinguish between three types of communitas: (1) the *spontaneous*, "existential" type I have just mentioned, the wind which bloweth where it listeth, and which defies deliberate cognitive and volitional construction; (2) *normative* communitas, the attempt to capture and preserve spontaneous communitas in a system of ethical precepts and legal rules, something akin to Weber's "routinization of charisma" – though here the charisma is "pentecostal," something that-descends on a group and is evanescent, rather than a constant personal attribute; and (3) *ideological communitas*, the formulation of remembered attributes of the communitas experience in the form of a utopian blueprint for the reform of society – "ideological communitas" seems already to fall into the class of liminoid phenomena. At the opposite pole to spontaneous, existential communitas is "social structura," in the sense of American and British structural-functionalist sociologists and anthropologists. Robert Merton puts it as well as any, when he defines structure, not as Lévi-Strauss would, as a system of unconscious categories, but as "the patterned arrangements of role-sets, status-sets, and status-sequences," on the whole consciously recognized and regularly operative in a given society. When we participate in social structure thus regarded, we gain through being presented with an orderly social world, with a recognized system of social control, with prescribed ways of acting towards people by virtue of our incumbency of status-roles. But we lose immediacy, we are constrained by laws and conventions, and we are usually limited in the degree to which we can "play" with ideas or innovate behavior. Recognition should be given, if this view of the social is a valid one, to *both* key modalities of human relatedness, structure and communitas, if the social process and personal life are to develop fruitfully and usefully. Hypertrophy or atrophy of either may well produce social conflicts and psychological problems. Repressed communitas may be as warping as sexual repression.

Now one of the social aspects of "liminality" is probably to produce optimal conditions in small-scale preindustrial societies for the emergence of communitas among liminalities, particularly among those jointly undergoing initiation. The levelling and stripping processes I mentioned earlier – the reduction of initiands to a sort of common human *prima materia*, may have the effect of strengthening the bonds of communitas even as it dissolves antecedent social structural ties. Initiands frequently lose their very names, their previous kinship ties are situationally annulled, similarly their former residential and political connections. But they are often allowed, even encouraged, to form small groups of friends in the seclusion camp – and such ties of friensdhip often endure, whether institutionalized or not, throughout life. Friends of this type, among Ndembu, may even act as mediators if there is a blood-feud between their respective lineages. Liminally-originated friendship exists in our own society, of course. Members of the same class at Sandhurst or West Point, regardless of national, state or class origin, continue to meet ceremonially, whenever possible, throughout life. The same is true of gatherings of alumni on American campuses in the summer, a liminoid time of leisure.

So I am speculating that certain kinds of liminality may be conducive to the emergence of communitas. Again, there is a difference between the tribal-liminal and the industrial-liminoid. In the former, the whole group is engaged in this process, directly or through its representatives. In our society, it seems that the small groups which nourish communitas, do so by withdrawing voluntarily from the mainstream not only of economic but also of domestic familial life. The social category becomes the basis of recruitment. People who are similar in one important characteristic – sex, age, ethnicity, religion or some aspect of a religion, or in the possession of a common physical or mental condition, often pathological, standing in a local community, trade, profession, and so forth, withdraw symbolically, even actually, from the total system, from which they may in various degrees feel themselves "alienated," te seek the glow of communitas among those with whom they share some cultural or biological feature they take to be their most signal mark of identity. Through the route of "social category" they escape the alienating structure of a "social system" into "communitas," or social antistructure.

This may well be "normative communitas" only, but there is no doubt, if one listens to enthusiastic members of street gangs, the Lion's Club, branches of the women's movement, Catholics for Peace, the New Minyan movement, Rock Climbers' clubs, poetry reading and writing groups that subjectively these people have a sense of being at times what Buber would call, "an essential We," or what David Schneider would call "symbolically sharing common substance." Furthermore, in the retreats these groups make for themselves, they generate sensorily perceptible rituals and symbols which frame and consolidate their identity as a communitas. The paradox of such groups is that while existential communitas is in feeling-tone a striving towards the universal, to an open society and an open morality, the normative communitas they achieve often separates them as so many symbolically framed "in-groups" even more completely from the environing society. The social-engineering trick, I suppose, is to keep the pipeline open between the society in general and each of its communitas groups, so that the former is seen as an amplification of the latter, and the latter is seen as an "organ" of the former. There are, however dangers of "totalism," in all this which are highly undesirable, the danger of the "corporate state", for example.

Finally. I want to focus on a concept, "flow," which has recently been the subject of some fascinating research by a Chicago colleague of mine, a social psychologist, Mihali Csikszentmihalyi. The precise nature of the connection between "flow" and "communitas" is in question: as we shall see, Csikszentmihalyi stresses the competitive, "agonistic" frames of "flow," while I see communitas as often arising out of the cessation of agonistic processes. In an article in a recent number of the *Journal of Humanistic Psychology*, "Flowing: A General Model of Intrinsically Rewarding Experiences," Csikszentmihalyi speaks of "flow" as the "holistic sensation present when we act with total involvement," and is "a state in which action follows action according to an internal logic which seems to need no conscious intervention on our part." Csikszentmihalyi's earlier work was in the study of play and sport, and he collected many responses from mountaineers, rock-climbers, footballers, hockey-players, chess-players, long distance swimmers, basketball players, and made his preliminary generalizations about the state of low on the basis of these. Now he is extending "flow" beyond sport to the "creative experience" in art and literature, and to religious experiences. Tentatively, he has located six elements or qualities or distinctive features of the "flow experience." These are:

(1) *The experience of merging action and awareness:* there is no dualism

in flow; while an actor may be aware of what he is doing, he cannot be aware that he is aware – if he should do so there is a rhythmic behavioral or cognitive break – self-consciousness makes him stumble. Pleasure gives way to problem, to worry, to anxiety. The player loses the point, the rock-climber slips, the swordsman gets pinked. A personal cavil here: is it not precisely through the effort to resolve such problems of reflexivity that knowledge advances?

(2) In Csikszentmihalyi's view, this merging of action and awareness is made possible by a *centering of attention on a limited stimulus field*. Consciousness must be narrowed, intensified, beamed in on a limited focus of attention. Past and future must be given up – only *now* matters. How is this to be done? Here conditions that normally prevail must be "simplified" by some definition of situational relevance. Bracketing and framing are employed. Sometimes this is by physiological means – drugs (including alcohol) which do not so much "expand consciousness" as limit and intensify awareness. I can see some help from this for the study of liminal and liminoid rituals, where social structure is simplified – elders and juniors, initiators and initiands – and action may be retualized. But Csikszentmihalyi looks for his first model in Western games and sports. There intensification is brought about by, on the one hand, formal rules, and, on the other, by motivational means, for example, competitiveness. A game's rules dismiss as irrelevant most of the "noise" which makes up uncontrolled, daily social reality, the multiform stimuli that impinge on our consciousness and sensorium. When we play football or chess we have to abide by a limited set of norms. Then we are motivated to do well by the game's intrinsic structure, often to do better than others who subscribe to the same set of rules. Our minds and wills are thus focused sharply in certain known directions. *Rewards* for good knowledge and invincible will, when harnessed to tactical skill, complete, for Csikszentmihalyi, the focusing. But he is much more interested in the flow induced by these means than in the rules, motivations, or rewards. He believes that this is what makes the participants accept the rules, too, for the sake of a flow experience. The participants should also have "inner resources," the "will to participate" (like other liminoid attributes this goes back to valuntariness, one *chooses* to play), the capacity to shift emphases among the structural components of a game or to innovate by using the rules to generate unprecedented performances – the sort of thing a great coach can do, as well as the players in team games.

(3) *Loss of ego* is another "flow" attribute. The "self" which is normally the "broker" between one person's actions and another's, simply becomes irrelevant, when flow begins. Translating it into my terms, the "self" Csikzentmihalyi is talking about, is the broker that functions in the field

of "social structural" relationships. The non-self or non-mind of flow awareness is highly characteristic of existential communitas, as well as of what Suzuki would call "Zen-awareness." For Csikszentmihalvi's games view of flow, the actor is immersed in flow – he accepts the rules which are binding on the other actors – no "self," in the ordinary sense, is needed to bargain about what should or should not be done. Reality, says Csikszentmihalyi, tends to be thus "simplified to the point that is understandable, definable, and manageable." He then insists that this also applies to "religious ritual and artistic performance" as well as to "games." Consensus about framing is a necessary if not sufficient condition for flowing.

(4) An actor in flow, says Csikszentmihalyi, finds himself *"in control of his actions and of the environment."* He may not know this at the instant of flow, but reflecting on it he may realize that his *skills were matched to the demands made on them by ritual, art, or sport.* This helps him to build up "a *positive self-concept."* For, outside flow, such a subjective sense of control is difficult to achieve, due to the multiplicity of stimuli and cultural tasks – especially, I would hold, in industrial societies with their complex social and technical division of labor. Perhaps, there is a similar motivation behind the withdrawal of persons into initially categorical groups based on selected characteristics, I mentioned earlier, and participation in sport – each helps people to build up a positive self-concept, in the face of the many-selved "Protean man" of social structure, by means of the no-self flow experience. Anyway, it is certain, Csikszentmihalyi argues, that with control, in, say, the ritualized limits of a game or the form of a poem, a person may cope, worry goes, and fear. Even, as in rock climbing or Formula One driving, when the dangers are real, the moment flow is elicited and the activity is entered, the flow delights eliminate the consciousness of danger and problem.

(5) *A fifth feature of flow is that it contains coherent, non-contradictory demands for action,* and provides clear, unambiguous feedback to a person's actions. This is entailed, Csikszentmihalyi says, by the limiting of awareness to a restricted field of possibilities. Culture reduces the flow possibility to defined channels – chess, polo, gambling, the stock market, liturgical action, miniature painting, yoga exercises, and the like. You can confidently "throw yourself" into the cultural design of the game or art, and know whether you have done well or not when you have completed the round of culturally prefigured acts – in the extreme case, as in completing the race at Le Mans, if you survive you have performed adequately – in other cases, the public, the crowd, the audience, or the professional critics have an important say, but if you are a real "pro," the final judge is yourself, looking back on your work or performance with estab-

lished criteria in mind. Csikszentmihalyi shows himself here as being in the classical not the romantic tradition, in his stress on self-imposed limitations or accepting the rules of the game. For him, "flooding" is not "flow." Flow is channeled and terminable by fiat. For the true romantic, the formal rules that center attention are only the beginning, discarded when Fancy starts to fly. Shelley, for example, in his "Lament for Adonais," after Keat's death, uses a conventional poetic form to get started. but finds himself – fairly quickly – "driven darkly and fearfully afar" to where "the soul of Adonais, like a star, beacons from the abode where the Eternals are." The same distinction would probably hold between priestly and shamanic ritual.

(6) Finally, *flow is autotelic*, in the sense, that it seems to need no goals or rewards outside itself. Cultural forms such as sports and arts, according to this view, are set up for the sake of the flow they may induce, not for the particular rewards they may appear to offer, the prizes, trophies or fame.

Relating "flow" to "communitas." I would have to say that while I go along with Ccikszenlmihalvy's notion that flow involves a merging of action and awareness, an ego-less state that is its own reward, and that communitas, too, has these attributes, as he writes in a recent monograph, I do not agree with him that flow requires "formal rules" and circumscription in space and time as preconditions. Communitas *is* a sort of shared flow – but it can and does occur both in structured and unstructured situation. On the other hand, any games, sports, artistic performances, musical compositions, poems, and attempts at meditation, are totally without flow, frustrating in the extreme to those who have recourse to them primarily for the "flow" experience. In protracted games, too, the moments of genuine flow are few and far between, even in some regarded as "classical" and "memorable." What the framing of sociocultural processes may do, however, is to call attention to the presence of flow, even perhaps to amplify it. But such framing is not necessary for flow-production. Flow clearly has strong physiological, including sexual overtones: flow of milk, flow of semen, flow of blood, flow of urine; there are also metaphorical uses, such as flow of thought, flow of ideas, flow of work, flow of production. Flow clearly crosses the work/leisure divide I spoke of earlier. But the work domain itself is heterogeneous and complex and has its liminal aspects. All these usages imply some kind of psychosomatic basis and they imply too an endogenous process that has a definite beginning and end. This processual form is not imposed from without by rules: as William Blake said of fire: "Fire finds its own form." So flow finds its own form. Nevertheless, since we are animals with culture, flow elicitation may well be a function of certain key symbols. Again, it is a matter of particular cultural symbols in concrete situations not of abstract systems of symbols. Group experience may lead to the selection of certain symbols as the best flow-elicitors. My guess is that these would be liminal or liminoid symbols or symbolic actions, precisely those which are associated with social anti-structure, and which are initially associated with ritual process. These tend to be levelling, frame-breaking, hierarchy-toppling sorts of symbols. They may be in the ludic form of verbal and practical jokes, *jeux de mots*, witty paradoxes, and so forth, or in the serious form of reference in terms of the shared experience of the group to what equalizes us all, the biological facts of "birth, copulation, and death," and "the troubles of our proud and angry dust" which teach us that we *are* dust, to compound T.S. Eliot, A.E. Houseman, and the Ash Wednesday liturgy. If we focus, for example, on the liminoid genres of literature, on scenes and moments famous for the quality of their communitas and flow, such as Achilles's encounter with Priam in the *Iliad*, the episode of Raskolnikov's and Sonya's long, painful discovery of one another in *Crime and Punishment*, so well discussed by Paul Friedrich, the communitas of the liminary outcasts, Lear, Tom O'Bedlam, Kent, and the Fool, in the scene on the heath in King Lear, in the serious vein; and the women's *communitas* in Aristophanes' *Lysistrata*, and many episodes in *Tom Jones, Don Quixote*, and other "carnivalized novels", in the ludic, my hunch is that there will be key symbols which "open" up relationships to communitas. And that in life, too, key symbols, will emerge to presage experiences of communitas.

Let me conclude by saying that in all societies "flow" symbols are most likely to be found in association with beginnings and transitions, genesis and exodus. In tribal society they are linked with the liminality of rites of passage and seasonal feasts; in complex large-scale societies, primarily with the liminoid genres of leisure. And "flow" symbols, often but not always, go with the capacity to "play", just as in sexuality and lactation, foreplay elicits physiological flow. The study of such transitional processional, liminal, and transformative phenomena will surely help us to "loosen up" structural anthropology, and possible to "disalienate" the work process.

CHAPTER IV
TRANSFORMATION, HIERARCHY AND TRANSCENDENCE:
A REFORMULATION OF VAN GENNEP'S
MODEL OF THE STRUCTURE OF RITES DE PASSAGE

Terence S. Turner

I. VAN GENNEP'S MODEL OF THE STRUCTURE OF RITES DE PASSAGE[1]

Van Gennep's formula for the structure of what he called rites of passage has become an anthropological commonplace, perhaps even a cliché (1909). The features which he was the first to identify as comprising the universal pattern of such rituals are so well known as hardly to need recapitulation here.[2] The essential idea is that rituals that mark transitions between temporal periods, spatial zones, or social states or relations of various kinds take the form of a sequence of three distinct types of rites, corresponding to and expressing the three phases of the process of transition itself: rites of separation, rites of the *limen* or *marge,* to use Van Gennep's terms, or of transition, to use the equivalent adopted by his English translators; and rites of aggregation (incorporation or reincorporation). Of the general points adduced by Van Gennep in elaborating his basic scheme, I will mention only one. Van Gennep noted that the rites of the medial, liminal or transitional phase tended to display characteristics different from those of the initial and final phases of the ritual, which often amounted to inversions of the properties of profane social organization or secular space-time bracketing the rite as a whole. This inverted quality of the liminal phase was summed up by Van Gennep in his notion of the "pivoting of the sacred," whereby those actually going through the rites of the limen, who are thereby set apart from the rest of (profane) society, view the latter as if *it* were "sacred" and therefore prohibited or dangerous to them.

The validity of Van Gennep's formulation as a descriptive framework for the structure of *rites de passage* has been confirmed by subsequent research,[3] but the pattern which he identified has never been successfully accounted for in theoretical terms. Van Gennep himself made almost no attempt to do so, beyond the general affirmation that the phase-structure of the ritual reflects that of the social transitions it mediates (he stressed, for example, that different phases of the ritual might be stressed depending upon the type of social transition involved, e.g. rites of separa-

53

tion would be relatively stressed in funerals). The questions of why there should exist an iconic relationship between the structure of rituals and that of the social transitions they mediate, of why the three phases of separation, transition, and incorporation should be the particular features selected as the focus of this iconic relationship, and why the liminal rites should exhibit their peculiar characteristics were scarcely entertained, either by Van Gennep or, with one or two exceptions, by any subsequent investigator.

Victor Turner's work on the ritual process, focusing in particular upon rites of the liminal period and allied phenomena, constitutes the major exception to this generalization (V. Turner 1962, 1964a, 1969). The model I propose in this paper draws upon Turner's work in certain respects, while differing from it in others.

Turner's central contribution to the theoretical understanding of the liminal phase in particular, and the structure of *rites de passage* in general, seems to me to lie precisely in his emphasis upon the relatively unstructured, undefined, potential (rather than completed or realized) qualities which he has correctly identified as the distinctive features of liminal phenomena. The principle notion underlying Turner's model of liminal rites is that they assert the polymorphous potential of social actors as a ground for the transformation and recombination of statuses and roles at the level of normative, profane secular social structure. As Turner points out, this assertion tends to be associated with powers, qualities, and patterns of relationship of a different order than those associated with profane social structure (1964a, 1969). In Turner's formulation, the liminal phase, as the pivotal point of the transformation from phase to phase or state to state of the profane social order, appears as, at one and the same time, the conditional negation of both states or phases of secular social identity, the common ground of both, and the power to transform the one into the other.

Implicit in these general notions is an insight of fundamental importance into the structure and function of such rites. This is the notion that the phenomena of the liminal phase constitute, in structural terms, a different (and higher) level of the same system of relations as that represented by the secular order of social relations. The existence of such a hierarchical relationship between the liminal phase of a *rite de passage* and the social relations with which it deals, considered together with the transformational character of this relationship and the regulatory functions it performs within its social setting, strongly suggests that what is at work is an underlying structure of "cybernetic" type.

II. A MODEL OF THE GENERAL STRUCTURAL FEATURES OF SOCIAL TRANSITIONS OF THE TYPE RITUALIZED IN RITES DE PASSAGE

Without further ado, then, let me present what seem to me to be the general features of this structure. These features, and their bearing upon the features of ritual structure under discussion, can be most easily grasped in relation to a concrete example. Let us take, then, as an example the minimal system made up of the two status/role categories, "boy" and "man," and the transition of a male individual from the one status to the other. As categories, "boy" and "man" form a simple binary matrix of roles. This matrix of role relations may be thought of as a classification constructed of combinations of features of role-relationship. These features, defined as discrete dimensions of binary contrast, would minimally include those of sex (by which both man and boy are defined as sharing a common identity in contrast to the corresponding female categories, woman and girl) and generation (in terms of which man and boy are contrasted as the opposing feature-values of adult and child, respectively). In all societies, the gross role-categories defined by these features are associated for practical and for many normative social purposes with a whole set of other, more specific role-contrasts (e.g., father/son, husband/brother, sexually active/sexually inactive, jurally responsible/jurally irresponsible), each of which is defined by its own set of constituent features. These roles and their features would form part of the total matrix or classification of role relations involved in the boy/man contrast.

Such a matrix appears, at any given moment of social time, as a static structure, the contrasting role categories of which stand in fixed, mutually exclusive relationships to each other. An actor's transition from the status ("role category") of "boy" to that of "man", on the other hand, constitutes a relationship between the two categories (boy/man) that differs fundamentally in its structural properties from the status, classificatory definition of the relationship between them at any given moment of social time. Instead of a clear-cut, static definition of the relationship between opposing values of features within a matrix considered as a single state or invariant pattern of the relationships involved, it takes the form of a transformational operation. Such an operation can be thought of as consisting of the concrete social process through which the transformation in question is realized in actual social life, together with the formal principle that regulates the transition from one role-category (or set of role-categories) to another.

It is the specific formal nature of this transition, and not merely its gross character as a change or transition *per se*, that defines it as a "transformation" in the precise sense of the word. The formal character of the operation involved in such a transition can be illustrated by referring to the example of the boy-man transition. A "boy" (who is also defined in associated roles, in a given society, as a son, a brother, a pre-sexual or sexually inactive male, as a jurally irresponsible minor) makes the transition, upon reaching the socially prescribed age, to the contrasting status or role category of "man" (involving, in the society in question, the assumption of the complementary opposite roles to those just listed, e.g., father, husband, etc.). What has happened is that two contrastive sets of role categories, which in any given state of the matrix or role-classification stand in a mutually exclusive relationship as far as the ability of the same actor to occupy both sets is concerned, have been treated as non-exclusive in a sense permitting a single actor to pass from one set of roles to the other. This is accomplished, in formal terms, by relating the two sets of roles, not as it were within the same state of the matrix of role relations, but as components of two different states of the same matrix related by a transformation.[4] The actor has in effect shifted from one set of role categories, in which he played certain roles towards other actors occupying the complementary set of role categories, to become himself an occupant of the complementary set of role categories, playing the same roles towards others as were played to him by others when he occupied the first set of roles. The actor has, from his point of view, inverted the pattern of role relations defined by the matrix. Such an inversion is a form of transformation.

Such an inversion may or may not be a total transformation of the actor's whole field of relationships. While becoming transformed from "boy" to "man" and commencing to play the various adult male roles entailed by the latter status towards other actors, he may retain (in a suitably attenuated form) the boyish roles of son and brother towards those to whom he originally related in those roles. The point is that his new set of relationships is a transformation of the old; the integration of the two sets within the same actor's overall field of relations therefore implies a higher level of structure than the level represented by either set of relations considered separately. This higher level is comprised of two states of the basic matrix connected by a transformation. To sum up: any actor's total field of relationships of which that field consists, should be conceived as consisting, in formal terms, of three basic components: the classificatory matrix in terms of which the relationships in question are defined in relation to one another; the transformational operations by which the different states of the matrix called for by the society are generated; and finally the socially prescribed pattern of coordination of the various transformational operations in question.

Transformational operations can be said to be *more powerful* than the simpler classificatory operations (e.g., binary opposition) that comprise the structure of the matrix of role relations because they are capable of linking pairs or series of mutually contradictory states of such matrices as permutations of one another. Their greater power is, to put it differently, expressed in their ability to transform relationships and categories that are mutually exclusive at the lower levels of structure constituted by individual states of the matrix of relations (or, in simpler terms, any classification of relations considered as a fixed, static structure) into non-exclusive categories that may coexist or pass into one another within the same field of relations. It is only by calling upon the power of transformational operations in this sense, or (which comes to the same thing) by ascending to the higher level of structure they constitute, that it becomes possible to reclassify an actor or entity initially classed within one of a pair of mutually contrasting categories (e.g., "boy") within the opposite category (i.e., "man"). Coordinated sets of transformations of this type form the structure of processes of social transition such as those associated with *rites de passage*.

This discussion of the simple example of the transition from the social category of "boy" to that of "man" has been intended to illustrate the general properties of a very large class of social and cultural structures, which includes not only social structures *per se* but also the rituals that mediate them. The generic features of this class of structures, as they are relevant to social and ritual processes alike, may be defined, drawing upon the preceding discussion, by the following four-point model.

1. The system of social relations within which the ritual process takes place is organized on a hierarchy of levels. A "level" is defined as a type of relationship between classes generated by a specific type of operation (e.g. classificatory operations such as binary opposition, transformational operations such as inversion, or, at a still higher level, the coordinating operations that comprise the culturally prescribed pattern of correlation among transformations).
2. The lower levels of the system consist of specific states (individual permutations) of the matrices of relations defined by the structural features of the system, stratified according to their differing degrees of generality or inclusiveness. The upper levels of the system consist of transformations (or, at the highest levels, coordinated sets of transformations) of the specific configurations of features and relations comprising the lower levels of the system.
3. The upper levels of the system thus comprise the generative principles and, in the sense in which this term was used in the above example, the "common ground" of the discrete categories and relations comprising the lower levels. The upper levels are, on the other hand, defined only in relation to the lower levels, as the transformations that mediate be-

tween their elements. A relationship of feed-back or reciprocal interdependence of an asymmetrical and dynamic type thus exists between the upper and lower levels.

4. The lower levels of the system essentially consist of statis matrices or sets of relations, categories and groups. The upper levels, consisting of the operations that generate and mediate between these groups, cannot be defined as the additive sum of the lower level categories or groups, or even as merely more general, abstract or inclusive forms of these entities, because they constitute operations of a different structural order (transformations and principles of coordination between transformations). The higher levels of the system, in other words, cannot be formulated or described, and therefore cannot be easily controlled, in the terms appropriate to the lower levels. It follows that

a. when higher-level transformations must be controlled, and therefore in some way formulated or described, from the standpoint of the lower levels, the description will tend to be couched in terms of paradox, or the negation or inversion of lower-level criteria such as normative definitions of categories, relations between statuses and groups, etc.[5]

b. The upper levels will, in general terms, be seen from the standpoint of the lower levels as standing to them in a relation of becoming to being, generalized potential to specific realization, dynamic to static, and transcendent to immanent.

c. The upper level will also tend to be seen, from the standpoint of the lower level, as both the indispensable, generative ground of the system, a source of powers of a higher order, and at the same time as a domain of relatively uncontrollable and therefore dangerous powers. The essential form of this danger is the implied negation, through mediation or transcendence, or the boundaries of specific categories, relations or groups, and the fixed relations among such entities that comprise the lower level of the structural order.

III. APPLICATION OF THE MODEL TO THE STRUCTURE OF RITUAL

A. *Social dynamics and ritual structure: some general points*

The first point to emphasize about the model outlined in the last section is that it is not specifically a model of ritual structure, but rather of the structure of the social context of ritual. It is, in other words, an attempt to identify, in the most general possible terms, the structural form of what Van Gennep called the social *tendances sous-jacentes* and *nécessités sociales,* the "transitions" and "movements" that, as he correctly perceived, comprise the true "constants of social life" and form the reference of *rites de passage*.

The model, at the same time, generates the main features of the structure of *rites de passage*. That it does so exemplifies the main point of this paper: that formalized ceremonial or ritual behaviors are essentially to be understood as hypostatizations or models of common features of the structure and dynamics of social processes. These features, as defined by the model, are not in themselves of an essentially "sacred", "ritual", or "ceremonial" character, and are in many cases dealt with without the aid of "sacred" ceremonial forms.

From the standpoint of this thesis, the first requirement for an adequate theory of ritual and ceremonial behavior is that it should specify what general features of the structure of social relations become the objects of such behavior. The second requirement is that it be capable of giving an account of the dynamic relationship between ritual and its social context (i.e., the "effectiveness" of ritual from the point of view of its participants). Finally, as the third and clinching requirement, it should be capable of accounting for the main features of the structure of ritual and ceremonial behavior as the products of the dynamic relationship between ritual and its social context.

The question of the functional or dynamic relationship between ceremonial and ordinary, nonritualized social action and the question of the nature of the structure of ceremonial or ritual itself must, then, be seen as aspects of the same question, not distinct and mutually independent questions as they have almost invariably been treated by anthropologists. This is the major difference between the approach formulated in this paper and functionalist formulations like that of Gluckman to ritual phenomena of this and other kinds (cf. Gluckman 1962). It would perhaps be as well to clarify the essence of this difference before moving on to take up the substantive questions raised in the preceding paragraph.

The best place to begin is by stressing the considerable area of agreement between the two positions. Like Van Gennep and Gluckman, I start from the assumption that the key to the understanding of ritual, both as a form of social action and as a symbolic structure, is an understanding of the social *tendances sous-jacentes* and *nécessités sociales* that comprise the sociological context of the ritual act, Like Van Gennep but unlike Gluckman, I proceed from the further assumption that the symbolic form and content of the ritual act is itself the most direct expression of, and thus the most reliable guide to, the features of the sociological context that bear most directly upon the problem. In other words, I follow Van Gennep's insight that ritual is primarily to be understood as a direct or iconic embodiment of social "transitions" and "movements", and that this iconic quality is in some way the basis of its dynamic or functional effectiveness. This position may be contrasted with the functionalist position of Gluckman that the relation between ritual and its social context, and thus the nature of ritual itself, is to be understood primarily in terms of the dynamic effects of ritual upon its social setting, considered apart from the formal properties of the medium through which those effects are exercized: i.e., the structure of the ritual itself.

B. *Dynamics: the functions and effectiveness of ritual*

The four-point model presented above represents an attempt to outline, in general terms, the features of social and cultural structures that enter into the definition of the ritual situation (including, under the latter term, both the social context of ritual and ceremonial behavior, and the ritual performance itself). It represents, in short, an effort to fulfill the first of the three requirements for a general model of ceremonial and ritual action laid down in the last section. I now attempt to deal with the second of the requirements: that is, to give a general account of the dynamics of the ritual situation, that is, the functional relation between ritual and its social context, together with the sources and mechanisms of the effectiveness of ritual in fulfilling these functions.

1. *The ritual situation.* Ritual and ceremonial behaviors develop in response to situations in which some transition, ambiguity, conflict, or uncontrollable element threatens a given structure of relations either explicitly or, simply by remaining beyond control, implicitly.

Such a situation of ambiguity, disorder, or lack of control (e.g., the arrival of a boy at the age of transition to manhood) may appear as a "horizontal" conflict among incompatible categories of the same level of structure (e.g., "boy" and "man"). It may, alternatively, be perceived as a "vertical" disturbance in the hierarchical relationship between a given state of matrix that includes those relational categories in question (i.e., the state in which the actor plays the roles of "boy", jural dependent, sexually inactive male, etc.) and the higher-level transformational principles that comprise its transcendental "ground". A situation of this type, of course, involves both dimensions or axes in equal measure and its ritual treatment normally pays some attention to both. Ritual, as a symbolic mechanism of regulation or control, typically has recourse to the transformational operations forming the "vertical" dimension of the system in attempting to reorder the relations and categories comprising its horizontal dimension, while at the same time manipulating the "horizontal" dimension of relations among categories of the same level to influence, summon, or banish the transformational powers inherent in the "vertical" dimension. These two dimensions of the problem of structure, ambiguity, disorder and control are, as the model outlined above makes clear, simply complementary aspects of the same structure.

2. *General dynamic properties of ritual and ceremonial behavior.* Ritual and ceremonial behavior constitutes, above all, a controllable, unambiguous, orderly pattern of action (as far as its own rules are concerned: some of its symbols, acts or aspects may, of course, seem highly ambiguous and disorderly from the standpoint of ordinary, normative social behavior). This controllability is essential to ritual's primary functions as an effective mechanism for manipulating or reordering the uncontrollable, ambiguous, or otherwise dangerous aspects of the situation in relation to which it is defined, and, by the same token, reorienting the actors involved to the reordered situation in controlled, stereotyped or unambiguous ways.

There are thus two aspects of the effectiveness or dynamic function of ritual. The effectiveness of rituals and ceremonies as means of controlling or ordering otherwise uncontrollable or ambiguous and disorderly situations is grounded in their capacity to model both the objective and subjective aspects of such situations, and to transform the relationship between these two aspects in a determinate way. The coding of ceremonial behavior in concrete symbolic terms that can appeal directly to the actors' subjective experience has the effect of including the subjective orientations of actors among the relations that are affected, and thus to an extent controlled, by ritual acts. Ceremonial behavior, in this sense, comprises a mechanism for manipulating or reordering the subjective orientations of actors to a situation (that is, the meaning and form of the actors, experience of both the situation and of themselves as participants by manipulating the objective structure of the situation.

At a more fundamental level, however, the basis of the effectiveness of both the objective and subjective aspects of ritual or ceremonial action is its ability to model the hierarchical relationship between a conflicted or ambiguous set of relations and some higher-level principle that serves, at least for ritual purposes, as its transcendental common ground. This hierarchical framework of relations, as I have argued above, is identical with the structure of the social order itself, considered as a self-regulating and self-regenerating system. Ritual, as a symbolic model of social order that also attempts to be an effective means of regulating that order, is grounded upon the same fundamental structural and dynamic principles as society itself.

Ritual may be defined as formulaic patterns of symbolic action for ordering or controlling relatively disorderly or uncontrollable situations by controlling the hierarchical relationship between the levels of the structure within which the relations in question are defined. My argument is that rituals are able to serve as mechanisms for exercising such control because they directly model, in their own structures, the hierarchical mechanism of control that forms an intrinsic part of the structure of the situations in question. The structure of ritual action, in other worlds, directly embodies its own principle of effectiveness.

3. *The effectiveness of ritual as a medium for controlling the objective situation.* The "modelling" relationship of ritual to the hierarchical relationship between the generative principles comprising the higher level of a given structure of relations and the lower level of disordered or conflicted relations that becomes the focus of the ritual consists in a iconic correspondence between the structure of the ritual or ceremony and the hierarchical structure of the relations in question. This iconic relationship is normally expressed on three levels, and invariably on at least one.

The first of these is that the relation between the ritual or ceremonial act as a whole and the social relations to which it refers parallels the hierarchical and objectively "effective" relationship between the higher-level transformational operations that regulate the social relations in question and the lower-level relations themselves. The second is that the internal structure of the ritual or ceremony (that is, its symbolic elements and the transformations in the relations among them effected in the course of its performance), may directly model the ambiguous or conflicted set of relations that comprise its social context, together with their relation to the higher-level structural principles which order or transform them. Thirdly and finally, the internal structure of the individual symbolic elements of ritual and ceremony may reflect aspects of the pattern of lower-level relations comprising the situational context of the ritual or of its hierarchical structure. To sum up: the effectiveness of ritual and ceremony as means of bringing about the reordering, or preventing the disordering, of a set of relations is a function of the ritual's or ceremony's character as an iconic model of that set of relations and its relation to the higher-level, transformational operations that control or have power over it.

The iconic relationship works in two directions. In one direction, the ritual's character is an iconic model of the structure of social relations as the basis of its acceptance as an embodiment of the same higher-level transcendent principles or transformational operations that order (or disrupt, as the case may be) the social relations in question. The performance of the ritual, given this direct, "embodied", connection between it and the set of transformational operations in question, therefore becomes in itself an iconic model of the act of controlling or affecting the social relations concerned. The same attribution of objective effectiveness to the iconic connection, in other words, now applies in the opposite direction, i.e., as the attribution of objective effectiveness to the ritual performance. The effectiveness of the ritual as a mechanism for affecting objective reality may be said to consist in the interaction of these two directions of the iconic relationship.

4. *The effectiveness of ritual as a medium for regulating the subjective experience of actors.* The iconic relationship of the ritual to the objective situation it models also has a subjective dimension. The concrete iconic imagery and formal structural parallelism through which the ritual reflects the content and structure of social relations also reflects the cognitive and affective forms in which these relations appear to social actors (i.e., participants in the relations in question). Ritual, in short, typically collapses sociocentric (i.e., relatively "objective") and egocentric (i.e., "subjective") levels of iconic representation within the same condensed symbolic vehicle. It thus provides a means of imbuing the objective, sociocentric order with the subjective meanings it encodes, and of manipulating both dimensions of meaning as a function of one another. This aspect of the effectiveness of ritual has been well characterized by Munn in her observation that ritual

> . . . achieves its instrumental aims through its capacity to reorganize the actor's experience of the situation . . . symbolic forms provide external templates for inner experience, and operations within the external, symbolic sphere are aimed (implicitly or explicitly) at adjusting internal orientations . . .

> Finally, at a still more fundamental level, ritual symbols may be said to regulate and affirm a coherent symmetrical relationship between individual subjectivity and the objective societal order (1973: 605-606).

5. *Summary.* The dynamic mechanisms or aspects of ritual acts, I have suggested in the preceding sections, can be reduced, at the most general level, to two: firstly, the manipulation of the relationship among a set of objects through the manipulation (explicit or implicit) of the hierarchical relationship between those elements and superordinate structural principles comprising higher levels of the structures of relations in which they take part; and secondly, the manipulation of the structure of the subject's orientations to the situation in which he or she participates as actor.

These two functions, I have argued, are interconnected and rely upon a common instrumentality: iconic symbolism, which comprises the basic medium of ceremonial and ritual action. "Iconicity" in the ritual context is, I have suggested, a more complex affair than is often recognized. It is a quality not only of the individual symbolic elements of rites and ceremonies, but of their overall structures and the modality of their relationship to their social contexts as well. At all three of these levels, the iconic character of ceremonial and ritual behavior has two primary references or coordinates, constituting the structural manifestations of the two primary dynamic aspects cited above. These coordinates are, firstly, the dynamic relationship between the hierarchically related levels of the structure of the set of relations modeled by the rite or ceremony, and secondly, the correspondence between the objective and subjective aspects of the structure of relations in question. Any instance of ritual behavior, I would maintain, more or less implicitly embodies or reflects these two aspects of the social relations it mediates, both in its symbolism and in the form of its relationship to the social relations in question.

C. *Structure: Formal aspects of the routinization of transcendence.*

The forms of ceremonial behavior vary with the nature of the stituation and the purpose of the ceremonial acts involved. I shall attempts no typology of the forms of ritual action here, but will rather suggest an alternative approach to the problem of the generic structural features of ritual acts. This approach is based on the notion that certain broad structural features are exhibited by all types of ceremonial behavior, and that these arise directly from the two main dynamic aspects of ritual action defined in the preceding sections. The specification of these general features of ritual structure, proceeding from the analysis of the dynamics of ritual action and the structural properties of the social situations in which it arises presented in earlier sections, represents the fulfillment of the last of the three requirements of the general model outlined at the beginning of this part of the paper.

One structural feature of a general kind has already been implied in the foregoing discussion of the iconic properties of ritual structure (as well as of the individual symbolic elements of which it is comprised). This is that the structure of the ritual act (defining "structure" in the broadest sense to include the relationship between the ritual and the profane, unritualized aspects of the social relations to which it refers) symbolically collapses or condenses two iconic aspects of the structure of relations which it mediates. These two aspects are, firstly, some aspect of the objective structure of the relations in question (e.g., to return to the above cited example, the contrasting male generational categories of boy and man and the transformation that connects them), and secondly, the structure of the culturally defined subjective orientations in terms of which social actors relate to this objective situation. This feature of ritual structure proceeds from the second of the two basic dynamic aspects of ritual discussed above.

A concern with the separation or establishment of boundaries between categories and with the mediation of these boundaries comprise the second and third general features of the structure of ritual with which I shall deal here. Both of these two related features arise directly from the first of the two general dynamic functions defined above: the mediation of the relationship between categories comprising a given level of the structure of a situation through the manipulation of the superordinate transformational principles, defined at a higher structural level, that comprise what I have called the "transcendental ground" of that situation.

This hierarchical relationship, as I have defined it (pp. 3-9), entails both dynamic interdependence and structural distinctness. The various contrasting categories of lower-level relations are both *generated* as specific permutations by the higher-level operations and *endangered*, in their capacity as mutually contrasting and exclusive categories standing in a fixed relationship to one another, by the transformational power of the higher-level principles. This power, by definition, represents the capacity not only to generate but to transform, negate or transcend and thus to disrupt any particular state or pattern of relations at the lower level.

Any system or subsystem of social relations (or, for that matter, of relations between social and natural or cosmic entities) depends for the regulation and regeneration of its structure upon some degree of contact with such higher-level transformational principles. Any such system is, by the same token, threatened by them, since they have the power to disrupt it but remain (if they represent the highest levels of structure of the system as a whole) to a degree beyond its power to formulate or control. The need for both contact (or mediation) and separation (or insulation) are thus inherent and correlated aspects of the hierarchical relationship between any system of relations and the higher-level principles comprising its transcendental ground. The model of ritual structure outlined in this paper is based on the idea that ritual behavior constitutes a means of dealing with this ambivalent and ambiguous relationship between the levels of a structure.

The concern with boundaries and the separation of opposing or mutually exclusive categories of relations, which forms the second of the three generic structural features of ritual mentioned above, derives directly from this dynamic functional role within the context of the hierarchical structural framework that has been described. The point of the present discussion is that this concern is not merely a preoccupation with the maintenance of order *per se,* conceived as a static array of relations and categories comprising a given level of classification or social organization, but a concern with regulating the relationship between such an order of categories or relations and the higher-level, generative mechanisms upon which it depends for its maintenance, periodic transformation and regeneration. It is this dynamic, hierarchical relationship that is called in question by disorder, conflict, or ambiguity at a given level of classification or relationships.

Such disorder implies that the generative principles upon which the order as a whole depends may break down or become disrupted, with consequences that might reach far beyond the focus of conflict or disorder in question. Hierarchical structure is a two-way affair: it implies not only the "top-down" generative relationship between higher and lower levels, but the reciprocal "bottom-up" relationship by which the higher-level principles are defined in relation to the lower-level order of relations. The maintenance of the proper order of distinctions among the categories of the lower level of a structure thus represents a dynamically effective if indirect means of controlling the more powerful, higher-level principles upon which the system as a whole depends, and which by their nature remain beyond the direct control of the lower level.

The same point can be formulated the other way around, as it implicitly is in many ritual observances. The avoidance of the juxtaposition of contradictory attributes, categories or relations, as in taboo and much purification ritual, serves to insulate a given set of relations from direct contact with the more powerful (higher-level) principles required to subsume such normally incompatible features as aspects of a common reality. Unregulated contact between a system of relations and such powerful principles, comprising the "transcendental ground" not only of itself but of other, normally incompatible states or relations, would produce not order but chaos.

The same considerations lead to the separation (conceptual, if not always behavioral and concrete) between ritual behavior and the profane order of relations and behavior which it serves to facilitate and protect. As the medium through which contact between levels is made, ritual embodies the very phenomenon from which it serves to insulate the profane social and conceptual order: the direct and potentially disruptive contact between structural levels of discrepant power and generality. This applies even if the "contact" made by a particular instance of ritual or ceremony takes the negative form of insulation, or the prevention of direct contact between levels: the insulation itself must still come into contact with both of the levels or categories involved.

The third general structural feature mentioned above is the preoccupation with the mediation or establishment of regulated contact between levels (or between incompatible or contradictory categories of the same level of structure, which indirectly calls in question higher levels of structure) for the purpose of generating power to effect transformations or to regenerate some aspect of the structure of the system of relations in question. This is obviously the complement of the second feature (the concern with separation) that has just been discussed. Just as the avoidance of the juxtaposition of contradictory attributes or categories serves to avoid disruptive contact between higher-level transformational principles and lower-level sets of relations, so the deliberate juxtaposition of such attributes within a controlled setting may serve as a means of gaining access to powers of a transcendent order, and thus the capacity to transform or regenerate the set of relations in question.

As a final point, it should be emphasized that "transcendence" and the qualities associated with it, including generative power, disruptive potential, and the other attributes listed under point four of the general model set forth earlier are relative, not absolute qualities. They inhere in the principles or relations of a given level only from the vantage point of a lower level of the system.

With this last point about the relativity of transcendental properties, we rejoin Van Gennep and his notion of the relativity, or as he called it the "pivoting" of the sacred. Having returned by a different route to my starting point, I shall attempt to show that the model I have developed can provide answers to the questions raised in connection with Van Gennep's model.

The questions that I suggested earlier that Van Gennep and his model had raised but did not answer were, first, why should there be an iconic relationship between the structure of rituals and that of the social transitions they mediate; second, why should the three-phase pattern of separation, *limen,* and aggregation be considered the appropriate "iconic" pattern; and third, why should the rites of the liminal phase have such peculiar and distinctive properties, in contrast to those of the two terminal phases of the ritual and to normative social structure.

Since I have already dealt with the general issue of the iconic relationship between the structure of rituals and the social situations to which they apply, I shall pass directly to the question of the nature and iconic reference of the three-phase structure. Here the model that has been proposed renders a simple and clear-cut answer. The structure of the rites does indeed, as Van Gennep intuited, reflect the structure of the social transitions they mediate, but this structure has a vertical or hierarchical dimension which he did not recognize. It is, in short, not merely a sequence of consecutive phases, representing relations of the same level, but involves a hierarchical relationship between adjacent (higher and lower) levels. Rather than a simple triadic sequence, in short, the elementary structure of *rites de passage* identified by Van Gennep is really composed of a pair of cross-cutting binary contrasts. These can be conceived as intersecting vertical and horizontal axes. The horizontal axis consists of the contrast between the two categories (e.g., "boy" and "man") between which the passage takes place. The vertical axis comprises the relationship between this pair of categories and the higher-level transformational principles that regulate the passage between them. The point is that the structure of *rites de passage* models both of these axes simultaneously, in a way that defines each as a function of the other. The rites of separation and aggregation, in other words, mark the vertical (inter-level) separation between the level at which the initial and final social states or status-identities of the transition are defined and the higher level comprised by the principle of transformation between them, as well as the horizontal (intra-level) separation from the first of the two statuses and aggregation with the second.

The liminal phase of the ritual, as this implies, is the direct expression of the higher level of transcendent, transformational principles which form the ground and mechanism of the social transition in question. It is this hierarchical relation between the liminal phase and the profane social states or categories that form the terminal points of the ritual process which in turn accounts for the peculiar properties of the rites associated with this phase. The inverted, paradoxical, "anti-structural" qualities of these rites are of precisely the sort which characterize the relationship of a higher to a lower level (from the point of view of the latter) within the terms of the model outlined above (point four, pages 3-9).[6] Even Van Gennep's notion of the "pivoting of the sacred" as a characteristic of the liminal phase is accounted for by the relativistic aspect of the hierarchical relationship between the levels of the model, as observed at the beginning of this discussion.

As a final point, I would stress that, in accounting for the essential common features of the form and content of *rites de passage* on purely structural grounds, the model I have outlined leaves room for the full range of observed variability in the content of such rites. Specifically, the model presupposes that the transformational principles which comprise the principal content of the liminal rites are defined in each case with reference to the specific states or statuses that form the terminal points of the ritual. The contents of the liminal stage are thus defined by the model as situationally and culturally dependent variables. The common features of the expression of the variable content of liminal rites are accounted for on the basis of the *relative* transcendental (hierarchical) relationship of the principles expressed by such rites in any given instance to the lower-level relations or states comprising the terminal points.

I am greatly indebted to Prof. John Middleton of the School of Oriental and African Studies, London, Prof. Nancy Munn of the University of Massachusetts, and Jane Fajans of Standford University for their critical comments and suggestions on earlier drafts of this paper.

NOTES

[1] The term "transcendence" and its derivatives (e.g., transcendent) is used here and in the remainder of this paper to denote structural principles or relations of a level lying above or outside the level of structure taken as the point of reference (usually the normative or secular order of social relations considered at a given point in time, or within a given stage of development). "Transcendence" is, in these terms, an intrinsic feature of the relations between the levels of hierarchically organized structures, and carries no necessary connotations of "sacredness."

[2] Van Gennep's model of rites of passage was, of course, heavily indebted to the earlier work of Mauss and Hubert on sacrifice, and in a more fundamental sense to Robertson Smith's notions of ritual as a movement between separated sacred and profane zones (Mauss and Hubert 1898; Robertson Smith 1880, 1889).

[3] By this I do not mean that the comparative study of rituals has shown that Van Gennep's model, in its simple form as a series of three consecutive phases, is universally found as the structure of *rites de passage*. It is more common to find more complex patterns, in which rites that Van Gennep would categorize under different headings (e.g. "separation", "margin", etc.) are combined in the same phase of ritual activity, while rites of the same Van Gennepian category (e.g., "marginal" or "liminal") recur in several distinct phases of the ceremony. In many cases, one or more of Van Gennep's three categories of rites seems to be entirely missing, or at least cannot be identified as such, and the ritual as a whole may seem to consist of only a single "phase". It remains true, however, that Van Gennep's set of three categories has been found to provide the best general descriptive classification for a very broad class of ritual acts, and that the logical relationship among the three categories of his model often holds for the structural or meaningful relations among rites or parts of rites in complex ceremonies that do not occur in the temporal sequence he indicated. In this paper I attempt to develop a more powerful model of the structure of relations to which Van Gennep's model refers in a more arbitrarily schematic way and at a more descriptive level, which can apply more directly to the broad spectrum of ritual behavior that has resisted classification according to Van Gennep's relatively rigid and simplistic schema.

[4] A "state" or single (and therefore "static") "moment" or a matrix or classification of relations is defined, for purposes of this discussion, as an instance of the pattern of relations defined by the matrix in which an actor occupies a single cluster of associated role identities,, e.g., boy, son, brother, jurally irresponsible minor, pre-sexual male, etc.

[5] There is an analogy here to the principle embodied in Godel's famous proof that any relatively complex system of logical propositions is necessarily incapable of serving as the basis for deducing all of the axioms necessary to demonstrate its own

69

logical consistency. It may be suggested that, in an analogous manner, social and cultural systems will have difficulty in formulating the basic (highest-level) principles responsible for their own coherence and integration in terms of the principles and criteria applicable within the system (i.e., the principles of what I have termed the lower levels of the structure).

[6] I use V. Turner's term "anti-structure" in quotation marks because the basic interpretation of liminal rites put forward in this paper is that they are an integral part of *processes of structuring,* and as such are no less "structural" than the lower-level classificatory structures of relations they mediate. The notion of "anti-structure" conceived as a level of being alien to "structure" and set over against it as it were in binary opposition, has no foundation in the model presented here, and appears to stem rather from an equation of the notion of "structure" with what I have called the *lower levels* of structure, i.e., static classificatory matrices of relations. (V. Turner, 1969:passim)

PART 2

TRADITIONAL SETTINGS

CHAPTER V
RITUAL AND AMBIGUITY IN LUGBARA SOCIETY

J. Middleton

I

This paper is concerned with what have been called "non-religious rituals" and "secular ceremonial". Since these are only part of a single spectrum of forms of formalized behavior, I shall discuss them in this wider context. I see no point here in presenting an introductory discussion of past usages of these similar terms, since it has been done excellently some years ago by Goody (1961). I shall place this discussion in a particular ethnographic context, that of the Lugbara of Uganda; but I have space to mention only a few of the many rites and ceremonies performed by this people.

When we speak of religious, ritual, ceremonial, and so on, this is usually to distinguish and define various types of social behavior. In my view this approach is too rigid a one and distorts what actually takes place. It would be more accurate to consider religious and non-religious, or ritual, or ceremonial, rather aspects of behavior. It would seem impossible to find any organized, conventional or expected behavior in any society that does not contain some element of more than one of these aspects. Even the most technical behavior contains some touch of the ritual; and even the most religious act some aspect of the technical. This is a commonplace but we do not always remember it. So if we see these as aspects of behavior rather than as types of behavior we can expect to make greater sense of the social reality before us. Besides seeing them as aspects of behavior we should also regard these various "types" of behavior as representing positions on a continuum. We may see an item of behavior as being more or less ritual, or more or less ceremonial, instead of being qualitatively distinct. Some behavior is both ritual and ceremonial, some is ritual but with virtually no ceremonial; some is ceremonial but with virtually no ritual. Clearly, I am here using "ritual" as being essentially "religious" or at least as including a religious element.

The behavior among the Lugbara that I wish to consider is performed and/or controlled by persons whose roles are recognized and whose statuses are named and defined: rainmakers, prophets, chiefs, kinsmen, and so on. All their activities are formalized, in the sense of being conventional, normal, ceremonial, regular, or observant of form (all from the Oxford English Dictionary). The terms "rite" and "ritual" refer to something very similar. The main distinction between rite and ceremony would seem to be that a rite is a performance that is not only ordered or formal but which also makes for or brings order in experience, and so in social organization. Again according to the Oxford English Dictionary, there is nothing inherently religious about a rite, although a religious connotation has entered ordinary usage. Also we may generally accept that those who carry out a rite believe that it is effective by its performance. A ceremony, on the other hand, is rather a formal pattern of behavior that in itself does not "work" in the sense of making for order in experience, although it may express the desirability or assumed existence of order, and its performance may be effective in inculcating values in the minds of those taking part. Here we come to Gluckman's definition of the process of ritualization, which he sees as being central to ritual (Gluckman 1962: 24).

On a rather different level it has usually been accepted that a crucial distinction between a religious and a non-religious act, whether referred to as a rite or a ceremonial, is that the former involves occult or mystical powers, which are thought by the participants to make it effective, whereas the latter does not. To define behavior by reference to the occult is clearly difficult, since the definition of what is occult is bound to be ethnocentric and thus unsuitable for or difficult in comparative analysis. The oft-quoted definition from Evans-Pritchard's book on the Azande, for example, refers to "supra-sensible qualities which ... are not derived from observation or cannot be logically inferred from it, and which (the phenomena) do not possess" (Evans-Pritchard 1937: 12). This definition is difficult to use, because the area of experience to be referred to will vary from one society to another. This variation is in itself, of course, significant, but it is then the variation that we need to analyse comparatively rather than the qualities themselves. But the main difficulty is who is to make the logical inference to which Evans-Pritchard refers, or who is to state that the phenomena do not possess these qualities.

In brief, the central problem is in the relationship between those forms of behavior that may be called "formal" or "ritual" or "ceremonial" on the one hand, and on the other a belief in the participation or intervention of spiritual forces or powers, since the existence of these powers cannot be accepted as an objective fact but is part of the belief system of any given people. We should perhaps try to get round this particular difficulty by taking as our criterion not the believed participation of a spiritual power but rather the particular item of behavior that is resorted to on formal, ritual, or ceremonial occasions to deal with or control the believed power: this behavior can be observed in a sense that is not true of the belief that is behind it. Power, in the sense of power without authority, is in all societies regarded as being dangerous to those who come into contact with it and who must therefore be protected from it. We come here to the notion of taboo, which would seem to offer a more workable criterion for the definition of the religious aspect of behavior. The observance of taboos marks off this aspect of behavior from other aspects and situations, although of course the symbolic details of the taboos will vary from one society to another. In brief, let us take the observance of a taboo as being critical rather than the belief in an exterior power against which the taboo is directed: the taboo can be analysed comparatively whereas to do so with the content of a religious belief is more difficult and leads to confusion. In this paper I start from this notion in order to work out in a meaningful manner the significance of the distinction between religious and non-religious (or more religious and less religious) behavior. It provides a useful starting point to my central approach, which is to analyze ritual and ceremonial behavior in its relationship to the inhibition and resolution of social ambiguity and conflict.

Their main argument is a simple one and has three main parts. The first is that the event or period of formal behavior is marked off or bracketed by acts that bound it and so define and mark it. These marking items are given many forms: the observance of taboos; the use of particular forms of speech, gesture, attire, or ornament; the entry into particular spaces or areas; the exclusion of particular categories of people. The second is that these marking items are not equal in emphasis or degree of prescription; they may be invariable and stressed, slight and almost voluntary; but they always occur. The third point is the question of the factors that determine this variation. In Lugbara thought the main one would seem essentially to be the danger and strength of what external divine or spiritual powers are thought to participate in the main formal event. I think it credible and useful to regard this as a function of the kind and degree of conflict that the behavior is intended to resolve, and I therefore base my ethnographic materials on the types of conflict found in Lugbara and the means used to resolve them.

II

It is useful at this point to present certain features of Lugbara society (see Middleton 1965). The Lugbara are small-scale peasant farmers, lacking a king or traditional chiefs although today they have administrative chiefs and headmen. The largest traditional political unit, the jural community, is the sub-tribe, formed around a sub-clan, the local core of a dispersed clan. A sub-tribe has an average population of about four thousand persons. Each sub-tribe is segmented into from three to six levels of territorial rial section, the sections being formed around the lineages that are the segments of a sub-clan. The smallest section is the family cluster based upon a minimal lineage of some three to seven generations. The head of this small lineage, the elder, is also thereby the head of the family cluster. A feature of the Lugbara system is the low level of effective lineage authority, the elder being the only holder of authority in the lineage system (see Middleton 1958).

Something should be said about Lugbara cosmological notions of the nature and relationship of men, spirits, and divinity. Divinity, a power outside the total understanding or control by men, omnipotent and everlasting, is experienced at three levels. These are the universe (*Adroa*, the Creator, the Divine Spirit, in the sky); the surface of the earth (*Adro*, the immanent aspect of divinity, in the bushland); and the individual psyche (*adro*, the source of idiosyncratic and anti-social behavior). Spirit is different from and opposed to the soul (the responsible element of a living man) and the ancestor or ghost (into which the soul is transformed at death). Throughout all Lugbara thought, whether overtly "religious" or not (a distinction that we may make but which is not made by the Lugbara themselves), runs the basic differentiation between the two spheres of the "home" (*aku*) and the "outside" (*amve*). The former pertains to the social, moral, predictable, controllable, to authority, to men, the lineage dead; the latter pertains to the asocial, amoral, unpredictable, uncontrollable, to power without authority, to women, and the world of spirits. For Lugbara, the "home" and the "outside" together form a conceptualization of the totality of human experience (see Middleton 1968). All societies have some such mode of conceptualizing experience (and may have others also) but the detailed criteria vary and the boundary between them varies from one society to another on the continuum from the social to the asocial, from the human to the divine or spiritual, whatever terms we care to use.

III

In this paper I essentially discuss means by which the members of this particular society cope with conflicts, contradictions, and ambiguities within their social structure and social experience, and with the inevitability of change and development within a system which is seen by its members as ideally unchanging. Despite this ideal, the Lugbara realize that they do have to accept change and underlying structural conflict that are brought about by ecological, demographic, and technological factors, and also by external causes such as Arab slavery, colonial rule, and Independence. These conflicts cannot easily be resolved by deliberate action by the Lugbara themselves, or at least they do not appear to have been so resolved in the past. Other, more everyday, conflicts are less radical and these the Lugbara know that they can deal with more easily by conventional and expected means, principally by ritual and ceremonial activities.

The terms conflict, dispute and others refer to different levels and aspects of relationship and situation. We may clearly recognize and distinguish three as being distinct aspects of social relations. First there are underlying structural conflicts which are essentially insoluble. Following Gluckman (1965:109) I shall refer to these as contradictions rather than as conflicts. These contradictions express the stresses that have arisen (in living memory, and we may assume there were earlier ones also throughout history) from changes in ecology and demography due to sudden and serious animal and human epidemics that largely changed the patterns of wealth, settlement, and political relations between territorial groups; and by changes in the patterns of money and labor that have brought changes in the "traditional" relations between men and women and between old and young. Secondly we may distinguish recurrent struggles associated with the continual maturation of individuals and the cyclical development of groups. And thirdly we distinguish disputes between individuals and groups over land and other resources, when they are not closely related and do not share close common ancestors.

We may, perhaps properly, argue that disputes are usually expressions of struggles, and that struggles are in their turn usually expressions of contradictions. But this is rather too rigid a view and it would be more accurate to say that they are aspects of all conflict rather than different types of conflict. In addition the factor of social distance between the parties concerned in any level of conflict is highly significant, so that we may regard these three kinds or levels of conflict as being on a single continuum.

Among the Lugbara the various contradictions, struggles and disputes are related to different levels of social grouping and networks of social relations, each of which is in a state of continual development, whether cyclical or not. Contradictions are found at the level of the jural community, the sub-tribe; essentially, these contradictions are insoluble, being an inherent quality of social structure at that level. Struggles are at the level of the lineage, especially of lower-level lineages. Disputes are found anywhere in the system, but here the crucial point is that the close lineage ties that characterize intra-lineage struggles are lacking, so that these disputes are either between individuals whose kin ties are temporarily irrelevant, or between lineages and neighborhoods more distantly related to each other than are the members of the minor or minimal lineage. I cannot discuss at any length either the different developmental cycles of different groups and fields or relationships, or the highly significant variations in these cycles found from one part of Lugbara to another (see Middleton 1974). What I can do, however, is to discuss these levels of conflict from another viewpoint. I have so far mentioned them from that of an external observer and wish now to present them rather from that of the people themselves, one which is somewhat different although no more nor less justified.

The Lugbara see "conflict" as having two aspects. One is that of cosmological and categorical confusion and ambiguity; the other is that of actual physical dispute. The network of social relations – between kin, neighbors, affines, and others – within any one social grouping is regarded as having a proper form: relationships of "respect" and authority should be ordered, recognized, accepted, and maintained in behavior. When they are not so ordered and maintained, then ambiguity, uncertainty, and confusion appear. These are regarded as the manifestations of disorder from the sphere of the "outside" impinging upon and entering that of the "home". The group – in the persons of its senior authority-holders – then performs rites and ceremonies that are believed to remove disorder and to reinstall relations of order and certainty.

There are two points to be made in this regard. The first is that the sanctions for the maintenance of order are ultimately controlled by certain forces – Divinity, the dead, or the living, according to the identity of the group concerned. The second is that of the precise meaning for the Lugbara of "certainty", "ambiguity" and similar notions. It is convenient to discuss the second first, even though briefly. This point is essentially that of free will and choice in interpersonal behavior. I have described elsewhere Lugbara notions of soul and spirit (Middleton 1960). The soul is associated with responsibility and adherence to accepted norms; the spirit is associated with irresponsibility, the individualistic, the idiosyncratic, with evil and the anti-social. The soul is part of the sphere of the "home", the spirit is linked with that of the "outside", as it were, an extension of extra-social divine power into the person within the "home". When there is order, the soul is uppermost; when there is disorder it is the spirit that takes control. This rather simplistic view of the situation is not a distortion. Another way of expressing this is to say that when there is order, there is no individual choice to be made, but that disorder is caused by the exercise of individual choice, particularly when irrational or irresponsible. I realize that these latter terms need lengthy analysis for which there is no space here, but I think that the general sense of the argument is clear enough. It leads to the fact that choice is a highly significant factor in the performance of rite and ceremony and that it is closely associated with the proper relationship between individuals and the remainder of their moral universe.

I now return briefly to the first of the two points mentioned above, that of the ultimate sanctions behind ordered behavior – that is, behind the acceptance of the proper norms and the abandonment of the exercise of too great a degree of individual choice and self-definition. If for the moment we accept, for ease of discussion, the three levels of conflict that I have mentioned earlier – even though the boundaries between them cannot be made too rigid – we see that these ultimate sanctions rest in different areas in each case, and that each is associated with different categories whose confusion, disturbance, and uncertainty are seen by Lugbara as associated with different levels of conflict.

IV

Among the Lugbara there are many holders of statuses and offices whose behavior is formalized and defined in space and in time by certain rules and taboos. Some of these appear as mainly secular or non-religious persons: the chief, the headman, the market organizer, the shopkeeper, the kinsman, the neighbor, the friend. As against these, using our own ethnocentric viewpoint, are personages whose behavior is more "religious", defined as being behavior directed to and/or controlled by presumed beings, forces or powers that are either non-human (spirits) or transformed humans (ancestors). These include elders when sacrificing, rainmakers, diviners, prophets and evangelists. This distinction is of course a situational one rather than one of basic social status.

I now wish to present examples of some rites and ceremonies performed by Lugbara in order to resolve and also, hopefully, to inhibit open conflict of the three main categories I have mentioned – and I stress that these are areas of a continuum rather than distinct types of conflict. The first example has to do with conflict within the lineage, the type referred to above as struggle over the changing relationships between persons and between groups as part of their maturation and development.

The most noticeable and important ritual performances in Lugbara are the sacrifices made to the dead – to ghosts and ancestors. They are made mostly by the members of the family cluster, the basic domestic, land-owning and land-using unit. The minimal lineage, on which it is based undergoes a cycle of development and segmentation that lasts on the average about twenty-five years. At the beginning of the cycle there is more or less congruence between the accepted genealogy of the group and its internal authority and status structure. The elder is accepted as effective head, and the senior men of constituent segments recognize both his overriding authority based on his being the representative of the dead members of the lineage, and their own respective relations of seniority and juniority as regards one another. As they and their dependent family members grow older, marry, die, move in and out of the cluster, and as they and their dependents' requirements in land, livestock, and wives change, so do tensions and struggles for authority, and uncertainties and ambiguities in the accepted genealogical reckoning, develop and increase.

Sacrifices are made as part of the process of settling internal struggles over the allocation and exercise of authority, to "purify the home", and to re-establish a properly recognized pattern of authority, sanctioned by genealogical statement, within the local group. The process begins with the sickness of a member of the lineage, who is shown by oracular consultation to have offended a senior lineage member. Sickness has been sent by the dead, usually after having being invoked by the senior member concerned, to "show" the offender his "sin". A beast is dedicated for sacrifice, which is performed when the offender has recovered. At the sacrifice living and dead share the oblation; the offender is purified; and the dispute is brought into open discussion in which participants must speak the truth, settled, and resolved. Either the past authority network or a revised one is affirmed and expressed at the sharing of the oblation. The central part of this process, the sacrifice itself, is marked by various defining signs: the presence of the sun or lack of rain and dark clouds; the formal exclusion of non-lineage kin and neighbors, including wives of lineage members in the area of the actual sacrifice; the use of sacred leaves at the ritual addresses; speaking with solemn and measured voice and making slow and deliberate gestures and movements. The central act of sacrifice, the placing of meat and blood in the shrines, is marked by the sacrificing elder taking on symbolic attributes of "inversion", mainly by his observing sexual taboos and using the left hand when at the shrines. The elder is at that time at least partially "outside", in contact not only with the dead, who are in the "home" as they are buried under the compound floor, but also with Divinity who is outside it altogether. (See Middleton 1960 for a fuller account of these matters).

There are several kinds of ancestral sacrifice but all share this basic form and follow the same pattern: the events leading up to the first ritual address which marks the formation of the congregation; the sacrifice proper at the shrines; then, following the second ritual address, the anointment and commensal sharing of sacrificial meat among lineage representatives. Any breach of the customary and proper is thought to be followed by the approval of Divinity, expressed in rain or dark clouds: the rite is then ineffective and regarded as void and must be performed again.

This behavior, associated with the "home", is obviously ritual behavior, with an essentially religious element. It reaffirms and reinforces an existing field of social relations; it takes place within a ritually defined place and time that represent the perpetual identity of the lineage; it expresses an unchanging pattern of lineage relations that transcends the patterns of relations of local neighborhood and interpersonal kinship that are in actuality continually changing. It makes for order within temporary disorder, the basic function of all ritual activity.

V

There are also occasions of formalized behavior which should not be regarded as religious ritual but perhaps (using Gluckman's terminology) as ceremonious ritual, although some of them are as far as their function is concerned very close to the ancestral ritual I have just described. They comprise forms of intergroup hostility and fighting. I shall discuss only one here: others (e.g., death dances) show the same basic features and more ethnographic detail cannot be given here. These occasions are all those of the resolution of disputes, in the sense used above, between groups not closely related in lineage terms.

The main form of ceremonious intergroup hostility is the feud. This no longer occurs but since older men have experienced it in the past (up to about 1930) they can still discuss it in detail; also they still try to set it in motion, to be stopped by the chiefs before it grows too serious. The feud is a jural mechanism, an expression in action of the segmentary lineage system. It is also a ceremonial performance, which is, of course, a central factor in its efficacy as a jural mechanism. (I have discussed some aspects of feud and warfare in Middleton 1958).

The participants are men who are related by clanship but not by close lineage ties, and the form of a particular outbreak of feud is known and accepted (I here use the ethnographic present tense). The feud is typically part of a dispute over the allocation or use of productive resources, which has been the subject of tension, open quarrelling, and some serious insult or injury which has led to demands for compensation or vengence. Threats and warning of feud should be given by the injured group. It must be carried out in sunny weather and not in heavy rain or in darkness. The men of the group advance, uttering their *cere*, long falsetto whoops, the words and tone patterns each of which is "owned" by an individual man; to call a *cere* shows the caller's formal status and identity in a situation where these should be unequivocally stated. They carry weapons, and fight along the intergroup boundary, each group standing apart making runs towards the other but not getting closer than the distance needed accurately to throw a spear or shoot an arrow. Great care is taken not to shoot at uterine kin on the other side, warnings being shouted to them to stand out of the way before a man shoots. Feud takes place only in the dry season, when there is no work to be done in the fields, there are no crops in the fields and so visibility is easy, when there is still plenty of food and beer, and when the passing of time is regarded as coming almost to a standstill (I return to this point below). At nighttime the warriors may wish to court the girls of the other side and they may then freely visit them. Women are not attacked and may pass openly from one side to another.

There are thus known rules which are strictly followed. Breach of them leads to purification after the feud, to continued fighting, to later suspicions of sorcery (those injured continue to fight by mystical means), or to curses by the sub-clan rainmaker. An important factor is that of the outcome in deaths and wounding, that is to say, of choice within the content of the performance. In most feuds for which I have information, there are either no deaths or only one death, that of the original offender or his brother (men try to shoot their arrows at these men). But "accidental" deaths do occur, in which case the killer becomes a recognized homicide and requires purification after the feud is ended unless he is actually killed in retribution first. Until purification the killer is "outside", analogous to the hunter of animals in the bushland. Wounding occurs frequently and is usually accepted as a fit conclusion to the original dispute. Once it is agreed by the use of intermediaries (usually women) that the feud has achieved its main purpose, it is formally brought to an end by the sub-clan rainmaker who threatens to curse the participants with sterility if they continue to cross a boundary which he marks out between them. The rainmaker chooses his time so as to cause no loss of face or prestige on either side; and after the feud is over, although there is no formal feasting to mark the resumption of clanship, there may be somewhat formal drinking between the two sides and displays of friendship and esteem made on the next occasion when they meet as participants in a lineage sacrifice.

These performances of feud (and of warfare, which has some similarities for which there is no space here) clearly resemble games, although they are perhaps more clearly defined as to content and have a slight degree of mystical control. The resemblance to Classical games and the "games" of the American Indians is close. For the Lugbara they may be regarded as containing much of the ceremonious and little of the religious aspect of ritual.

Today feud no longer takes place, its jural function as a means of settling what I have referred to as "disputes" being taken by chiefs' courts. Much of the content persists although the form is different. The form of court procedure is accepted in custom, and behavior is highly formalized, including both periods of apparent argument and shouting (equivalent to the actual fighting in the feud), followed by periods of calm and dignified behavior by both chief and accused. As in the feud, the main aim is to bring about reconciliation between the parties and it is regarded as unseemly for anyone to win a case against another with too great a degree of success; after a decision both parties are expected to drink together at a beerhouse to show that ties have been restored. (For further information on courts and moots, see Middleton 1956).

As far as the Lugbara are concerned there is a significant distinction between the ritualization in the process of ancestral sacrifice and the statements about interlineage relations made in the feud and today in court actions. It is not merely that the former reaffirms and redefines a set of kinship relations. To say that is not perhaps to say very much. The former redefines genealogical statements about authority: it is for this reason that the intergenerational relationship between living and dead members of the lineage is restated. The dead exercise authority over the living, and the senior living exercise authority over their own juniors precisely because they are regarded as representatives of the dead. In the interlineage relations that are reaffirmed by feud, authority is irrelevant. The elder of the minimal lineage is genealogically the most senior man with lineage authority; the genealogical heads of minor and major lineages may act as representatives of those lineages at the rites performed by collateral lineages but they exercise no formal authority over anyone other than the members of their own minimal lineages. The point is that for Lugbara the process of ritualization has not as aim to redefine and reaffirm networks of social relations as such, but more precisely to redefine specific relations of authority. Those social relationships that lack the content of authority are certainly redefined and reaffirmed, but by ceremonious performances that lack ritualization. With this difference goes another that is significant as far as the degree of religiosity is concerned. The sacrificial rite is defined by the observance of taboos by the main performer. There are no taboos observed in the feud or in court cases, although there is great formality. In place of an external power, from which participants are protected in sacrifices by the taboos observed by the elder, the power in the feud situation is that of the protagonists themselves. Only if they step outside this situation, by breaking the rules by killing outside the expected program of the feud, do they become liable to the effect of mystical powers and need later to be purified.

VI

I come now to performances by two kinds of functionaries who are themselves clearly regarded as sacred: prophets and rainmakers (for longer accounts, see Middleton 1963, 1971, 1973, 1974). They are significant in those situations in which what I have referred to above as "contradictions" become manifest.

The Lugbara prophets of whom we know anything first appeared at the turn of the century and were believed to have the power to remove the recently arrived Europeans and certain epidemic sicknesses, all destructive to traditional Lugbara society. The greatest prophet was Rembe, a Kakwa, who lived in Lugbara for some months in 1916-1917. His power was said to come directly from Divinity in the form of sacred water, drawn from a pool and dispensed to his followers. It gave them everlasting life and immunity to bullets. He introduced new forms of divination by which he revealed the "words" of Divinity to his followers. They were organized on an egalitarian basis, the principles of cult organization being radically opposed to those of traditional society based on descent, sex, and age: all these principles were ignored according to the Divine instructions received by the prophet. The central part of his activities was the holding of meetings at which people attended, drank the sacred water, danced irrespective of lineage affiliation, sex or age, and had sexual intercourse irrespective of clan or lineage affiliation. These performances were marked off from ordinary social activities not only by disobeying traditional principles of organization, but by being held in the bushland away from the settlements, at nighttime, under the influence of drugs and by being led by a prophet who was given "inverted" attributes of many kinds. The performances symbolized the destruction of the contemporary political situation and the introduction of a "perfect" form of society as it had been at the beginning of the world. By acting as though that society had come into being again it was in a sense brought into existence, even though only for short periods of time during the night and in the bushland and so away from ordinary everyday life of lineage settlements.

The role of rainmaker is different from that of prophets and in certain ways more germane to this paper, so I discuss it at greater length. The rainmaker is the genealogically senior man of his sub-clan and is given attributes that symbolically mark him off from other men. He is regarded as in a way socially dead after his succession, as can be seen from his burial which is totally different and in detail contrary to those of ordinary people. He manipulates rainstones (which have features that symbolize their being of both sky and earth and which represent "all the words of men, those of yesterday, of today, and of tomorrow"), inside his rain-grove ("the vagina of the world"), a place kept secret to everyone except rainmakers. The more important attributes for our concern here are first, that he is the repository and the custodian of divine knowledge about the nature of "society" at the beginning of the world as told in myth, before present day society was formed. This knowledge is secret and he does not tell it to ordinary men (as does a prophet, who does not however under-stand the meaning of what he says and must therefore give it out in "tongues", as it is too dangerous to put into words). Secondly, his knowl-edge and his words are regarded as being totally true; ordinary men may think that they can speak the truth, at ancestral rites, but in fact their truth is only partial and incomplete. A rainmaker knows the absolute truth, "the words of Divinity", but he cannot tell it to ordinary people since it is so dangerous, its utterance being able to destroy and re-create all categories of experience. Thirdly, he stands outside the ordinary passing of time and he can both know of things in the past and in the fu-ture, and also control the passing of time. Fourthly, he is associated with rain, that links sky and earth and represents fertility of land, livestock, and women; he can prevent death at feud and by acting as sanctuary for a homicide, he is himself above death.

His activities to do with rain are clearly central to his role. I have men-tioned that the rainmaker "makes rain" in his raingrove; also he is said to have done so in the past by the killing of a captive alien. The latter was rare and a last and rather desperate resort, done at the end of a dry sea-son that continued overlong. But the manipulation of rainstones with the raingrove is of a very different character, in two ways. One is that it is to-tally secret, as he does it alone out of the sight of ordinary people. It is said that he goes there to perform his "work" (*azi*). Azi means "work" and also "labor"; but it has in this context also the connotation of "duty" or proper activity according to basic human and social condition.

The other difference is the occasion for this "work". The rainmaker enters his grove at fairly regular intervals throughout the year. But there are two periods when people can expect him to do so more often and for greater lengths of time than usual. These are towards the end of the dry season, when anxiety is general about the advent of the main rains, the sign for planting crops; and towards the end of the growing season when people are waiting for crops to ripen for harvesting. Both depend on the weather being as expected and anxiety rises especially if the coming of the proper weather is late when measured against the rise and fall in the sky of certain constellations of stars and the rise and fall of the moon.

If there is a discrepancy it is a sign that "time" has become confused or "wrong".

The rainmaker does not really "make rain" except on very rare occasions. Rather he knows the true significance of rain, the link between heaven and earth. He controls time, change, fertility, and death; and he does these things mainly by stating formally when planting and harvesting should be done, the two most crucial points in the agricultural calendar. He exercises little actual technical control or leadership, since each family can best judge exactly when to plant or harvest. The only thing that they cannot themselves ensure is peace; planting and harvesting are the only occasions when open force cannot be permitted, and only the rainmaker can ensure this.

But there is more to it than that. The periods before planting and harvesting are both in a sense without time. These are the periods when shortages of land, of grazing, of food or water, all become the objects of disputes. There is then little farming work to be done, there is much mortality of both humans and livestock and it is the time when feuding takes place. Being without certainty of time they are occasions for weakening of ordered social relations and activities. Their termination is open to uncertainty. Signs are there: the climate, the position of stars, the state of the crops and of the ground; but these do not occur in perfect unison and the "work" of the rainmaker, who through his knowledge of the real truth can understand the relationship between these signs, is to decide what is the "true" time of their conjuction.

The rainmaker thus becomes a focus of conflict within the jural community, conflict which has been called contradiction. We must ask how this actually works – how does he purify his community of sin and trouble. Purification of the jural community caught up in dispute and unhealth is mainly done by his being blamed for them, since it is he who controls "time" and "knows the secret words of truth". Contradictions are focused on him precisely because they express ambiguities of purpose, uncertainties, events and relations that are out of precision. His knowledge can destroy, create, and repair disorder or change, and he knows the ideal or true form and structure of society. Ordinary people can never know these things.

By using his secret and true divine knowledge he ensures the proper relationship between the rain, the moon, the stars, and men's behavior on earth. By doing this he controls the overt expression of conflict and tensions between groups on the land. And by inhibiting and controlling tensions he creates the "proper" or "true" relationship between the spheres of the "home" and the "outside". In many respects he is like a king: his role or his "work" is merely to be a rainmaker, to exist. He performs rituals continually in his raingrove, but in a sense his entire life is a single performance, marked off not only by temporary signs and taboos such as entering the grove, but also by his being symbolically dead and of almost a different nature from that of ordinary people.

VII

Let me return to the questions of what are the Lugbara doing, and what they think that they are doing, when they perform these various rites and ceremonies, organized by various symbolic attributes that define their relationship to divine power, and which lie along the continuum of religious to non-religious ritual and which have differing kinds and degrees of marking or bracketing from everyday activities. They are trying to resolve various levels of contradictions, struggles, and disputes, some of which are soluble by these means, at least temporarily, some of which are not. But the people themselves do not see the performances in these terms. They are of course perfectly well aware that disputes can be settled by taking an opponent to court or by wounding him with a spear. Yet they are also aware that to do so is still a kind of a game, a formal ceremonial, and has other significance as well.

They regard what we may refer to as various levels and aspects of conflict in terms of areas of categorical ambiguity. I have mentioned the basic cosmological distinction between the spheres of the "home" and of the "outside". The Lugbara hold two views of the ideally socially ambiguous: one is that of a social field in which the network of authority which is stated and validated by genealogy, is completely accepted; the other is that of the mythical world, in time before the formation of society by the Heroes, in space in the "outside", and in detail unknown to ordinary men today. The first, Lugbara recognize explicitly, never lasts for very long even, indeed, if it ever actually occurs at all in everyday experience. The second is hoped for at times of structural crisis and Lugbara attempt to realize it through the activities of prophets. It is obvious that these ideal views are contradictory, but this is so only at first glance. They refer to different situations, to different levels of social organization. The first is the ideal organization of the jural community and its segments in the everyday world of the "home". The second is the ideal structure of the ideally unchanging world under the authority of Divinity, as it was once and one day will be again when men have re-acquired the secret knowledge that they lost when Divinity, who once lived with them, separated them from the sky and left them to their own devices on earth.

The Lugbara, like anyone else, wish to live in a condition of certainty and unambiguity of social categories. Yet they find that in actuality they cannot do so. They have two main recourses open to them – more accurately, their responsive behavior has two levels or aspects, distinguished largely by the identities of the leaders of the ritual performances.

The first is action taken to remove the ambiguity in relations of lineage and neighbourhood, the former being those of authority and the latter lacking authority. This is the area of the everyday, in which categories are always somewhat unclear. But social life can continue despite these petty uncertainties that are due essentially to the vagaries of minor individual wishes, ambitions, and envies. In time these uncertainties increase due to the normal maturation of ordinary people. They lead to conflicts at two levels: struggles within the lineage over the exercise of authority, and disputes between lineages over the enjoyment of resources. The first is settled by the performance of ancestral rites, the latter by the performance of feud and the operation of courts. The latter are the more easily settled, in the sense that they in fact can be settled, and their religious content and degree of bracketing and the importance in them of taboos are all slight. The former are deeper seated, due less to individual choice and idiosyncracy and more to the necessary cycles of development of local groups, and can therefore never easily be settled for very long: their religious content, degree of bracketing and importance in them of taboos are all much greater.

The second level of recourse is more complex. It is attempted only when the underlying structural contradictions and tensions become so serious that the basic principles of organization become disturbed throughout the country, not merely at the local level. The general positions of old and young, men and women, wealthy and poor, powerful and weak, all become confused due to large-scale ecological and other factors that are both beyond the control and also the understanding of men. Therefore they are seen as emanating from the "outside", the sphere of Divine power. Since Divinity is invisible and not comprehensible, the external power is regarded as a spiritual power associated with a particular historical force – Europeans (Rembe's cult) and in other cults that I have mentioned here that have occurred at various times, Azande (Mmua) and Baganda (Balokole) – which happen to be in evidence at the time but whose identity is in a sense fortuitous. Men try to remove this total ambiguity and confusion by attempts to return to the only form of society that is known to them from their experience, that of the egalitarian "society" of the beginning of the world as recalled in myth. At that time Lugbara say that men lived together with Divinity in a state of changelessness in social relations; so they try to restore that ideal community by appealing to Divinity, by calling him into the sphere of the "home" from the "outside" in order to make the ambiguous and polluted sphere of the "home" vanish altogether. Men cannot actually call in Divinity since they cannot speak to him, so they call in prophets as his representative. Prophets try to re-establish the egalitarian community but fail, Lugbara say, because they are merely mouthpieces of Divine secrets which they themselves do not actually understand, even though they utter them in "tongues". But the rainmakers do understand them and so take over the prophetic movements when these falter and also take on themselves the seasonal settlement of conflicts that erupt at "timeless" periods of agricultural stagnation and neighborhood tension. Because both prophets and rainmakers are of the "outside", they are given powerful bracketing attributes that symbolize their external and liminal status. Between them they know how to re-order social and cosmic categories: they have the dangerous secret truth to destroy and to re-shuffle categories, in order to achieve the ideal society by re-creating order anew from the disorder they have found in society at a time of great crisis and turbulence. But because their experience of the world is limited historically and because these ideas are not clearly articulated, the re-ordering of categories has very much the same pattern as before, one which people have in fact been brought up to regard as normal and one which in any event they cannot change.

VIII

I should like to have made some comparisons between the Lugbara and other societies in respect of the points made above, but there is not the space to do so here. The Lugbara have no striking rites of initiation, and the only important rite marking change of status is at death, when mortuary rites may continue for up to a year after the burial. Their rites and ceremonies are performed almost entirely at periods of contradiction, struggle and dispute within and between lineages and neighborhoods, with the exception of performances by rainmakers at certain points in the agricultural year. But these are also dependent largely on the eruption of intergroup tension and are called for by the people who do not themselves take part in or even witness the performances, the degree of bracketing to set them apart from the everyday being so extreme.

The significance of this is of course that at base the distributions along a continuum of the kinds of conflict I have mentioned, and of the degree of religious content of the performances made to resolve the conflicts, vary from one society to another. The Lugbara have a particular distribution that is unique to them. I use the word "distribution" advisedly, as it would seem that the nature of contradictions, struggles, and disputes is more or less invariable. The factors that are relevant here, basically those of ecology, demography, and history, are outside the immediate concern of this seminar, although essential to any comparative analysis of the ways in which societies actually work. And I stress again the concept of distribution in the religiosity or otherwise of the performances: to state that there is some simple division between religious rituals and non-religious rituals is to misunderstand the nature of social process entirely. We are dealing always with a continuum, a single complex, with aspects of behavior rather than with discrete bits of social activity. In one sense our problem is to be able to make comparisons from one social system to another, to show how the points on the continuum – which itself would seem to be common to all societies – vary, and what are the factors that are relevant to that variation. The problems faced by different societies are basically the same – how to ensure perpetuity and certainty of role-networks, to accommodate insoluble conflicts and inevitable changes in organization and in structure. I have tried to separate out some of the key notions: conflict, authority, ambiguity, truth, defining by bracketing and others, none of them very unusual. It is the ways in which they are grouped, differentiated, and used that merit our discussion, and which I have tried to analyse with regard to one particular society.

I am grateful to the members of the Wenner-Gren Foundation seminar for comments on my original paper, and also to Professor T. O. Beidelman for reading and commenting on the revised paper.

CHAPTER VI
FIRST CLASS TO MARADANA:
SECULAR DRAMA IN SINHALESE HEALING RITES

Bruce Kapferer

Sinhalese healing rituals in southern and western Sri Lanka combine and oppose, in performance, religious and secular elements.[1] My general aim in this paper is to show that there are discernible shifts in the organizational medium through which symbolic object and action are presented and within which particular definitions of meaning are sustained or transformed as the exorcisms proceed from the more clearly religious sequences, or episodes of marked supernatural reference, to those dominantly secular in content.

The category of rituals with which I concern myself here is designed to cure illness caused by the attention of a malign demon (*yakka*). There are many rituals used by Sinhalese to exorcise malign demons and spirits but my description is confined to one small group of rituals or *yak tovil* which typically are performed over a period of a least twelve hours (or thirty Sinhalese hours) from sunset to sunrise, and which perhaps are the most elaborately produced of all Sinhalese exorcisms. These rituals, of which there are a number of available descriptions in varying detail,[2] as well as having extended magical and occult sequences, which refer almost exclusively to the non-human world of deities, demons and ghosts, also later include elaborate dramatic episodes involving mime, masked actors, and often extremely comic dialogue; indeed they have been referred to as folk dramas (Sarachandra 1966).

There is no doubt that these dramatic sequences are viewed as highly popular entertainment by members of the Sinhalese peasantry and urban working class among whom they are the most frequently performed. The actors in these episodes model their characters not only on the figures which populate the supernatural world as depicted in myth and legend but also upon popular movie stars and characters (often infamous) encountered in everyday life. The scenes they portray refer to daily domestic and economic troubles. They provide a commentary upon local and national political events, factional clashes, difficulties with governments bureaucracies and so on. The dramatic sequences are cast in the idiom of the everyday whereas the other ritual episodes are not. The dramatic dialogue is in the corase and often bawdy language of the market-place, of the peasant or working class Sinhalese community. Fun and enjoyment derives from the lampooning of elements encountered as part of normal, everyday Sinhalese social experience. It is, in fact, the prospect of a down-to earth secular enjoyment that swells the ranks of spectators to as many as five hundred – particularly when a well-known and skillful exorcist group is performing.

Of course the dramatic scenes are part of a single religious ritual context. The episodes flow directly out of the more esoteric ritual sequences which precede them. The fun produced by them, and indeed the evident attempts by the exorcists-actors to evoke laughter, not just from an audience but also from a patient and concerned kinsfolk, is consistent with the curative aims and developmental logic of ritual exorcisms (Kapferer 1976). They have vital transformational significance, as I show later in the analysis. Through them the progress of the patient from a state of defined sickness to one of defined health is effected and receives public expression. Moreover, they enable a reality, constructed in the course of ritual performance, to be destroyed and re-assembled in accordance with a conception of reality consistent with that of those who must participate in a "normal" everyday secular world.

Exorcists stress that the dramatic episodes illustrate and represent in a form easily understood by non-exorcist participants and audience the meaning and purpose of the previous magical exorcist acts and incantations. They are equated by some exorcists with the dramatic representations (*alawaka damanaya*), performed in some temples in the south of the island, of Buddhist preaching (*bana*), which usually involves the recounting of an event in the life of Gautama Buddha or an event in one of his previous lives. The presence of dramatic acting episodes, often of a markedly secular nature, performed within a religious or ceremonial context is a relatively widespread phenomenon. It is an element of Indian religious ritual (Gargi 1966) and has been well documented as an aspect of medieval church worship (e.g., Young 1933; Collins 1972). In many medieval church dramas, as with Sinhalese exorcism ritual, there was not only an element of buffoonery and comedy but also the dramas were often performed "on the periphery of the main liturgical structure" (Young 1933: 399). Comic and tragic drama was also a feature of ancient Greek religious ritual. Their appearance specifically as adjuncts to rituals of healing in the cult of Asclepius is particularly noteworthy (Edelstein 1945).

But these aspects of comparison aside, the point which I stress is that even though the dramatic episodes occur in the religious context of a Sinhalese exorcism they are of an indubitably secular tone. It is this together with their highly exotic, enjoyable and spectacular qualities which renders them amenable to being performed outside the context of exorcism. They are important elements in government-sponsored cultural competitions and are performed independently before tourists and before visiting Sinhalese official dignitaries.

What is of central interest for the subsequent analysis is that these later dramatic episodes of an exorcism both in the organization of action and in the symbolic medium in which they are set differ substantially from the earlier ritual sequences. Because of this they permit, in the Sinhalese cultural context, some distinction to be made, I argue, between ritual activity where the reference is dominantly supernatural and mystical in nature and ritual activity where the reference is dominantly to the everyday and mundane. While the dramatic episodes I describe occur within an undeniably ritual framework, at least as anthropologists conventionally use the term "ritual", a consideration of them might have wider methodological value.

The anthropological study of religious ritual has yielded both insight and to some extent an analytic frame for the study of secular behaviour, particularly where this behaviour is highly symbolic, stereotyped, stylized and repetitive. While the results of such an approach might be enlightening, the unqualified labelling of behaviour as ritual, irrespective of its secular or religious aspect, could lead to the overlooking of significant differences in the organization of symbolic object and action in secular contexts as distinct from religious contexts. There is a real danger, inherent in the use of common analytical frameworks together with unqualified labels, of treating qualitatively different phenomena as if they were the same. A variety of symbolic and organizational devices commonly found in the religious ritual contexts studied by anthropologists will of course be evident in those occasions termed secular ritual. But a concentration on these to an exclusion of the other properties of these "ritual" performances might deny certain aspects of their form, and the way elements of their content are organized into it, essential to an understanding of their meaning and the way they interrelate and organize those who participate in, and witness, them.

Because the dramatic sequences with which I am chiefly concerned here appear in the context of exorcisms designed to heal a sick patient, I will start with a short account of Sinhalese ideas about illness and cure. This will be connected with a description of major aspects of the supernatural world as it relates to the performance of an exorcism, to be followed by a description of the main ritual sequences, in particular the main dramatic episodes and their role in the overall ritual process.

Exorcism and some Sinhalese ideas on the cause of illness and the order of the supernatural world

Sinhalese Buddhists recognize that diseases can be caused by supernatural or natural agents (Obeyesekere 1969: 1974). Sanskritic *Ayurveda* provides both a method of treatment and a theory of causation for disease caused by natural agents. However, local practitioners (*vederala*) of ayurvedic medicine will often use *mantra* and other magical spells in order to increase the potency of their herbal decoctions. Ayurvedic diagnosis and treatment is based upon a theory of humoural disorder of which there are three: wind (*vata*), bile (*pitta*) inclusive of blood, and phlegm (*sema*). They are collectively known as the three troubles or *tri* or *tun dosa* (*op. cit.* 1975). When there is an excess in the body of any one of these the humoural balance is thrown into disequilibrium and sickness follows. Although ayurvedic specialists are operating, in the Sinhalese view, in a different system from exorcists[3] (*adura*) who are well versed in the "science" of manipulating demons and other malign beings (*yaksha bhuta vidyava*) there is considerable overlap in the basic principles which organize their spheres of expertise.[4]

Thus the major demons which cause illness do so by fixing a patient (*aturaya*) in their gaze (*yaksha disti*). This results in a humoural imbalance which brings on sickness. Indeed the major demons, or specific forms (*avatara*) of them, are linked with particular humours and through this to specific physiological symptoms indicative of certain types of illness or disease. The humours are associated with specific colours and these same colours are also symbolic of specific demons.[5] Thus black is associated with the humour of wind and both are linked with *Mahasona* (great cemetery demon) whose gaze can induce fits of vomiting, stomach disorders, etc., connected with humoural imbalance caused by an excess of wind. The colour red is indicative of the humour of bile and blood and also *Riri Yakka* (blood demon) whose gaze is predominantly linked with illness caused by an imbalance in this humour. Likewise, white represents phlegm and *Sanni Yakka* and is also symbolic of nasal and chest complaints related both to the phlegm humour and to *Sanni Yakka*. Thus black, red and white colour symbolism is a recurrent motif throughout the performance of exorcisms and is expressed together with its attendant meaning in the dress of the exorcists, actors and dancers and in clay images (*bali*) and pictorial representations of demons at the ritual performance.

Demons most often afflict people when they are alone (*tanikama*). As Obeyesekere states, "Aloneness is not simply physical aloneness but psychological aloneness as well. It refers to a state when one's psychological defenses are weak. Generally physical aloneness is a precondition, sets the state for, psychological aloneness, which produces the demonic attack. Illness produced by demonic attack when a person is "alone"[6] is called *tanikam dosa*. Its importance in Sinhalese views regarding the etiology of demonic illness is so great that this term is often used as a synonym for the wider class of misforutnes caused by demons" (op. cit. 176-177). Patients who are under the gaze of a demon are typically left alone by all except close kin. Most of the patients I visited who were suffering from severe illness or misfortune at the result of demonic attacks restricted their social interaction.

Exorcism deals with the causes of physiological and mental ailment in as much as these are seen to relate to the real and imagined attention of malevolent demons and spirits to a patient. It is important to emphasize here that exorcists see their curative task as being twofold: the severing, cutting (*kapanava*), of a demon's malign hold over a patient, and the removal of any idea a patient might have that he is still subject to the will of a demon. A characteristic of most patients I have interviewed is that they present an over-determined understanding of their condition. Thus patients interpret all past as well as present unusual experience and misfortune as being the result of demonic attacks. They see every aspect of their behaviour as being subject to demonic control.

Exorcists are concerned to act upon and change what they and others consider to be a patient's conception of a supernatural reality and the way a patient understands himself to relate to this reality. There are many excellent descriptions of the supernatural order as Sinhalese Buddhists view it (see especially Ames 1964, 1966; Gombrich 1971; Obeyesekere 1963, 1966; Yalman 1962, 1973), but generally those who are not afflicted by demons typically regard the supernatural world as being ordered into a hierarchy with the Buddha at the head. Below the Buddha are the deities and especially the four main Sinhalese deities, Saman, Nata, Vishnu and Kataragama, and below deities are the demons followed by ancestor spirits (*pretaya*) and various other maleficent spirits. The particularly capricious and malicious demons were, according to myth, banished by Buddha from the world of man and placed under the control of King Vesamuni.[7] The ordering of the supernaturel world is reflected in the nature of the ritual offerings and the named category within which they come and this in turn organizes, as Ames (1966) has argued, supernatural beings along a "sacred"/"profane" dimension. Thus deities receive "pure" offerings (*adukku),* which denote their sacred position in the supernatural hierarchy, such as various coloured flowers, fruits, areca-nut flowers, camphor, coins, etc. Demons are given "impure" offerings (*dola),*[8] indicative of their profane status, such as fried vegetables, burnt, fried or roasted meats sweetmeats made from oil and country rice, and sometimes marihuana, opium and various types of fecal matter (Obeyesekere 1964; Yalman 1973). Flowers are also given to demons, as well as deities, but the lower position of demons is indicated by the blooms being torn into small pieces.[9]

The relation of human beings to supernaturals in the view of healthy Sinhalese is one of veneration for the Buddha and subordination to the deities and of superiority, albeit uncertain, to demons and ghosts. Demons are powerful and terrifying but display behaviour which is antithetical to Buddhist virtue and is beneath contempt. A patient's understanding that he is subject to the will of malicious demons essentially elevates these beings in the hierarchy of supernaturals to a position almost equivalent to that of deities. Specific demons are in the normal Sinhalese conception subject to the will of certain deities but when they cause affliction to human beings they have broken free from this restraint. Demons no longer occupy a fixed and clearly defined position in a supernatural hierarchy. In addition, human beings by seeing themselves as subordinates to demonic malevolence have conceptually inverted what should otherwise be their normal relationship with demons.

A major objective of exorcists, therefore, in the performance of an exorcisms is to readjust the patient's conception of reality in conformity with the way the non-afflicted see it. This is critical, for exorcists consider that if a patient continues to view himself as subject to the control and whims of demons then the illness will continue or else recur. If the patient's mind remains fixed on the idea that malign demonic forces condition his reality, then his body humours will persist in a state of disequilibrium and the illness will continue. It is partly for this reason that exorcists regard the elaborate exorcism rituals which contain dramatic episodes to be more effective as treatment (because they actively seek to alter the mental orientation of a patient) than other shorter exorcisms which do not have extended dramatic sequences. These shorter exorcism rituals, often attempted as treatment before a more expensive and elaborate exorcism is performed, are more designed to sever what is considered to be the real connection between a malevolent agent and a patient rather than being directed as readjusting the patient's conception of the reality which surrounds him.[10]

The four most elaborate and most frequently performed ritual exorcisms enacted in Galle Town and its environs on the south coast of Sri Lanka are, in order of frequency, the *Mahasohon Samayam* (great cemetery demon exorcism), the *Sanni Yakuma* (disease demon exorcism), the *Rata Yakuma*[11] (foreign country demon exorcism) and the Sunniyam (sorcery demon exorcism). The early ritual episodes in the first three exorcisms are basically similar but differ considerably in their episodic content and organization from the Sunniyam. For this reason I confine the following description to the first three ritual exorcisms.

Diagram 1. The setting of an exorcism

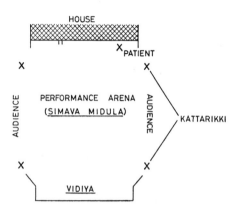

The group of exorcists which has been hired by a patient's household to perform an exorcism normally arrives in the early afternoon and begins immediately to make the various structures and props essential to the performance. The objects and structures to be used in the ritual are made from materials provided by the patient's close kinsfolk. The main performance arena (*simava midula*) for the enactment of the exorcism is clearly marked out by the positioning of the various offering tables and erection of ritual structures such as the *vidiya* or place from which the dancers and actors make their entry at various stages in the exorcism (see Diagram 1.). The space behind the *vidiya* is used by exorcists as a resting and changing place. The audience is usually seated along the perimeter of the performance arena, either side of the *vidiya* and between this structure and the patient's house. Men normally sit outside on chairs and benches, whereas women stand on the house verandah near the patient or else inside the house.

Diagram 2. presents a schematic outline of the three exorcism rituals upon which I have based this description. The rituals proceed through basically three successive stages, which, in the way the ritual performance interrelates the patient, the patient's kin and other members of the audience, undergo significant transformations in organization. The rituals gradually develop whereby a patient who, in the early ritual sequences is separated from an everyday reality, is eventually re-introduced into it.

97

Diagram 2. The placement of major ritual episodes in exorcisms.

ARTICIPANTS	I	II	III
AUDIENCE	AUDIENCE NON-ATTENTIVE	AUDIENCE ATTENTIVE BUT NOT PARTICIPANT	AUDIENCE JOKES WITH ACTORS
PATIENT'S KIN	CLOSE RELATIVES ASSIST PATIENT IN MAKING OFFERINGS	CLOSE RELATIVES ATTEND PATIENT	CLOSE RELATIVES STOP ATTENDING PATIENT - JOIN AUDIENCE
PATIENT	ABSTRACTED UNCONSCIOUS	PATIENT ENTERS TRANCE	PATIENT CONSCIOUS & MAKES OWN OFFERINGS
TIME	6pm	→ 10.30-11pm → 12.30-1 am	→ 6am
ORDERING OF RITUAL EPISODES IN EXORCISM	OFFERINGS TO DEMONS — NAMASKARAYA — OFFERINGS TO MAIN DEMONS — AVA MANGALE (death time) — SEATING OF PATIENT	B R E A K — MAJOR DANCE EPISODES	B R E A K — DRAMATIC SEQUENCES — MAHASONA — MANGARA PELA PĀLIYA — RATA YAKUMA — NANU MURA PĀLIYA (toilet of the princesses) — SANNIYA YAKUMA — ATA PALIYA — DEATH OF MAHASONA (Mahasona played by masked actor) — KAPU UPATA (making of the cloth) — NALAWILLI PĀLIYA (washing the baby) — DAHATA-SANNIYA — SHORT CONCLUDING OFFERINGS
PRESENCE OF MUSIC & DANCE	DRUMMING SINGING SIMPLE DANCE STEPS USE OF ESOTERIC RITUAL LANGUAGE	ELABORATE DRUMMING & DANCING	MUSIC & DANCING CEASE, USE OF EVERYDAY VERNACULAR

Coincident with this, the patient undergoes important behavioural trans-formations indicative of a progress from a state of illness to health. There is a correspondence here with Van Gennep's classic observation of the three stages of rites of transition into separation, margin (or *limen*) and aggregation (see also V. Turner 1967: 94). The early ritual sequences are complex and this partly derives from the fact that although an exorcism ritual is held under the primacy of one particular demon, a number of de-mons and spirits are invoked and propitiated.

The analysis in this paper concentrates on the later dramatic episodes and it is for this reason (and restrictions placed on length) that I give a very much shortened account of the preceding sequences. My analysis of the dramatic sequences rests on the contrast between the symbolic mode in which the dramatic-acting phases of the ritual are couched as distinct from the symbolic mode of the previous ritual events. It is crucial, there-fore, that the reader grasp an understanding of the form and manner of presentation of the earlier sequences.

The first phase: The summoning of the demons

The first phase of the ritual typically begins at 6:00 p.m. and expresses and marks the patient's separation from the everyday secular world. A rapid beating of a drum signals the beginning. The patient is ritually seat-ed on a mat, often very comfortably reclining on pillows, and is sur-rounded by a variety of objects, some of which have the property of ab-sorbing elements of the illness, others giving protection against a possible fatal attack by demons. Praises (*namaskaraya*) are uttered for the Bud-dha and the main deities. This is said by some exorcists to calm the pa-tient before a terrifying reality dominated by malevolent demons is ritu-ally constructed around the patient. Offering baskets (*tattuva*)[12] to the main demons to be propitiated are proferred one at a time, and eventually removed to stands (*kattarikki*) at the border of the performance arena. Mantra and songs (*kavi*) are chanted by an exorcist and chorused by oth-ers seated on mats behind him. They tell of the myths of origin of the various demons.

Once this phase is completed, the *ava mangale* (death time) ritual act begins. This is for *Riri Yakka* (blood demon) or various forms (*avatara*) of him. The exorcist stretches out on a mat in front of the patient. A number of further offerings are made. This episode itself takes the form of an elaborate subterfuge or trick (though performed in a serious vein), whereby the exorcist presents himself as a corpse in an effort to lure the demon's attention away from the patient. This rite and the first phase of the ritual process concludes when the exorcist is rolled in the mat and carried to the side of the performance arena by the close male relative of the patient. The crying and howling in mock mourning of these relatives as they perform this act is the first point in the ritual where signs of the comic and ludicrous enter, all the preceding ritual acts being conducted in complete seriousness.

The ritual and magical acts conducted in the early phases of the exorcism develop and represent a reality consistent with the one understood to have caused the patient's illness. Symbolic action proceeds in accordance with rules which accept as valid the premises upon which the patient construes the reality in which he has been caught up and within which he is subject to the capricious will of demonic forces. The ritual conjuring of this reality establishes the necessary conditions for the exorcist to apply successfully his occult skill and knowledge in severing the relationship between the patient and demons. Through these early ritual episodes the exorcist can step into the world of the patient and by dint of magical art and clever subterfuge domesticate, control and tame the afflicting devils.

In the early phases, ritual action and the medium within which this action is carried involves a suspension of the realities and rules which relate to and organize behaviour in the everyday world. This suspension of mundane realities and an entry into a malign supernatural world is effected and realized by inversions expressed in ritual action. In his magical utterances the exorcist addresses demons as *devatava* (godlings), elevating them to the position of deities in the supernatural order. Human beings give demons offerings (*dola*) with a respect and deference normally accorded to deities, and this symbolizes a momentary subordination of human beings to the will of demons.

But, additional to such common ritual devices as inversion, the ritual medium through which a diabolical reality is presented is highly important. The ritual medium ensures not just the construction of a supernatural reality and the suspension of other everyday realities but also the sustaining of a particular supernatural reality in the wider context of alternative everyday understandings. The language of the mantra and much of the song in the early ritual sequences is in an esoteric ritual language or in a form which cannot be easily understood by a patient, kin and other members of the audience.[13] The intoning of the main exorcist as he signs verses in communion with the supernatural and the chorusing of these verses in response by the other exorcists gathered around reduces the ease with which an audience can follow what is said. In any case the ritual language in these episodes is magical, the power of which is greater the less it can be comprehended and interpreted by a lay audience. The song style, the ritual gesture and simple dance steps of the exorcist, the monotonous drum rhythm, the other smells and sounds produced in the course of ritual action, all serve to establish a reality apart.

The organization of ritual action is such that it erects a frame or relatively impermeable membrane (Bateson 1955: 44; Goffman 1961: 20; Handelman and Kapferer 1972; Kapferer 1976) around the activity clearly defining who can legitimately participate in the proceedings and who cannot. The ritual action is tightly focused on the patient and certain close kin seated nearby. More distant kin, neighbours, friends and other members of the audience are excluded as ritual participants. The exorcists restrict their operations to a small part of the performance arena, their eyes and body movements (the audience in the early stages of the exorcism is presented with the backs of the exorcists and is rarely faced by them) being directed at the patient. The frame around the ritual action is of a kind that elements of the outside everyday world which might occasionally enter, pass through it unnoticed. Members of an audience will often walk into the house, edging past the exorcist and stepping over the patient, in search of refreshments or to talk with a friend. They do so with no disruption to the proceedings and are ignored by active ritual participants. The way ritual activity is organized narrows the range of meaningful reference of symbolic object and action. All symbolic objects and acts relate to and refer back to a supernatural reality. Symbol is piled upon symbol with no extension in the range of meaningful reference, as they are received and understood by ritual participants.

An exorcism ritual and the reality it constructs is subject to the threat of subversion and destruction. It is performed in the secular context of a Sinhalese household, enacted by specialists who outside the application of their occult art otherwise live secular lives and participate in normal everyday activities, and is played before a non-afflicted audience which recognises that the exorcism is portraying a reality, important elements of which involve an inversion of a supernatural order as the healthy should conceive it. The intertwining of sound, verse, symbol and movement into a restricted code (Bernstein 1972) seals off the early parts of the ritual performance and the reality created by it from the potentially subversive nature of the wider secular context in which the ritual is set. That the organization of ritual action and the medium of ritual presentation guards against subversion is important if certain important ritual aims are to be achieved. Any subversion of a demonic reality early in the ritual would, for example, inhibit the attraction of demons to the ritual site and would interfere with the exorcist's ability to ply his esoteric knowledge and skill in driving demons away from and severing their malign connection with the patient.

The second phase: The dance of the demons

Upon the completion of the early offering sequences, extended and elaborate dance and drumming episodes being normally lasting through to midnight and, dependent on the type of ritual exorcism performed, often through to 2:00 a.m. Three or more dancers participate accompanied by the magnificent and varied rhythmic beat of a number of drums. The dancers in colourful attire perform dance steps which increase in complexity and swiftness of execution as the night wears on. Different named dance and drumming episodes are organized in sequence. The dances contain curative elements, possessing the power to draw out aspects of the sickness. At the same time they are a medium for the presentation of key symbolic objects used to assist the patient towards a cure, and attract and control demons. Thus in the *Rata Yakuma* there is the brazier-resin dance (*anguru-dummala pade*) and the arrow dance (*igaha pade*), while in the *Mahasona,* the arrival of the main demon to be propitiated is represented and mythical figures related to the exorcisms and around whom they are structured, as in the *Rata Yakuma* and *Sanni Yakuma,* are portrayed and honoured in dance. The extended dance episodes of the *Rata Yakuma* depict the arrival of the Seven Princesses (*Ridi Bisava*) at their bed chambers. In some performances of the *Sanni Yakuma* I have witnessed there is a dance of the Lichavis of the city of Visala. Myth relates (Obeyesekere 1969: 213) that these people suffered from disease wrought by *Kola Sanniya,* the major demon of the Sanni Yakuma. In addition to this the dance episodes are understood by exorcists to provide general entertainment for demons and malign spirits in order to please and influence them to loose their hold upon a patient and also to provide entertainment for an audience.

The combined effect of swirling dance, the throbbing rhythm of drums, the juggling of lighted torches and other acrobatic feats communicate to participants and audience that the ritual is rapidly approaching a zenith. If a patient becomes possessed by the afflicting demon, which does not always occur, he dances across the performance arena to the structure (vidiya) from which the dancers emerge. The exorcists bring the patient back under the control of human beings and sever the relationship between patient and demon. The major dance sequences are concluded by the dancers approaching individual members of the audience and the patient's household, and, in return for monetary payment, executing short dance steps (*adawe*).

These main dance episodes develop and proceed within the terms of reference of the reality created during the earlier offering sequences. The dancing elaborates on the earlier themes and plunges the patient into the full depth of the reality he has constructed around himself. He is induced, according to exorcists, to explore the full range of the reality which has consumed him and is brought to the threshold of another – the world of the non-afflicted. This is expressed in the changes, incumbent on the performance of the dance episodes, in the way participants and audience are organized around the ritual action. The earlier offering sequences established a ritual frame around the activity of the patient and close attendant kin, so separating them from the other members of the audience that the realities they represented were largely irrelevant to the ritual proceedings. Whether the audience is attentive or not to the ritual activity is unimportant. But in the extended and elaborate dance sequences which make use of the entire space set aside for the ritual performance, the attentiveness of the audience is actively sought. The audience, though still maintained in the initially passive role of onlookers, is invited to take part in the ritual. Members of the audience are brought to the margin of the ritually constructed world of the patient who is in turn brought to the margin of the everyday mundane realities of an audience. The greater involvement of the audience in the ritual action, through the recognition of their physical presence and the addressing of ritual action to them as well as to the patient and the patient's close concerned kin, established a potential basis for the eventual subversion of a reality which has been further elaborated on in the dance episodes. Nevertheless, it is the world of the patient, through the organization and restricted meaning reference of symbolic object and action, which continues to dominate and subdue the other realities surrounding it. The full potential of those elements now organized into the ritual activity to subvert the reality erected by the ritual is only realized in the major dramatic acting episodes which follow.

Before I describe and illustrate certain aspects of the dramatic performances which follow on from the main dance interludes it is important to note the changes produced in the behaviour of the patient as he proceeds towards a cure and the stage the exorcists have reached in the application of their curative skills. The patient, in the early offering sequences particularly, appears relatively abstracted, dazed and, according to my observations and questioning of patients, is unaware of the human beings acting out the reality around him. Conversations with patients after an exorcism suggest that they believe and understand themselves to be immersed in a world peopled by demonic forms. This achieves a full demonstration during the dance sequences, particularly if the patient becomes possessed. With the ending of the sequences, however, there is a marked change in the behaviour of the patient who appears more conscious and alert to the surrounding activity. I suggest that the heightened emotional state ritually induced, especially in the exciting dance sequences, psychologically as well as physically, brings the patient to the margin of a reality as actors, and the non-afflicted audience, perceive it.

What is of note here is that as the patient becomes more aware of the world of human beings which surrounds him so he is better prepared and more amenable to the activity of others directed at the readjustment of his conception of reality. Exorcists maintain that by the time the major dramatic acting episodes of an exorcism begin they have exhausted much of their esoteric knowledge and skill in so far as it is designed to cut the relationship between patient and demons. Although from time to time in the later ritual sequences offerings and magical incantations will be performed, exorcists argue that the mystical relationship between patient and demons has been magically severed. What remains, according to exorcists, is for the patient to be brought to a realization that malign spirits no longer control his action and furthermore to impress upon him a view of a supernatural reality and its relationship to everyday mundane events and experiences which conforms with the way healthy others see it. Then the possibility of continued malevolent attention by demons causing illness (brought about by sustained humoural imbalance related to the patient's persistent obsession with a world subject to demonic control) is at last averted.

At this point I stress that exorcisms, of the type I describe here, develop upon and progressively express a basic contradiction. The presence of a patient suffering from demonic illness contradicts a reality conceived by healthy, non-demonically affected, Sinhalese. An exorcism is organized to resolve this contradiction. But throughout most of the early phases this contradiction is not realized in the developing ritual context. Rather one side of the contradiction, the reality of the patient, is constructed and elaborated. However, in the spectacular dance phases, aspects of the contradiction, between the reality of the patient and the reality of the audience, begin to emerge. Thus at one point a dancer approaches the patient with his face partly covered by the wing of a cock. The patient usually recoils in apparent fright, an action which is interpreted by exorcists and audience alike that the patient sees the dancer as a manifestation of a demon and not for what he really is, a human being. There are many acts like this especially during the dance episodes and later. They constitute both a confirmation of the reality of the patient depicted in the ritual and a further surfacing, and emerging realization, in the context of the ritual performance of the contradiction between audience and patient views of reality; a contradiction which only began to become apparent at the concluding stage of the *ava mangale* episode. The dance episodes are of key transitional significance in the ritual process and establish the conditions for the transformation of the ritual structure, the reality upon which it had hitherto been premised and the resolution of the contradiction between patient and audience perspectives. I have explored this significance of the dance episodes in greater detail in another paper (Kapferer 1976) concerned with a single exorcism performance.[14] Suffice it to stress here that one of the conditions for ritual transformation established in the dance sequences is the extension of a limited license to the unafflicted members of an audience to participate in the ritual activity. This license is further extended in the major dramatic episodes. It is during these dramatic sequences that a realization of the contradictory realities of audience and patient is fully expressed, the ritual transformed and a resolution effected.

The third phase: A Comedy of Errors

The time at which dramatic episodes are performed in ritual exorcisms varies considerably. They can begin as early as 12:30 or as late as 3:00 in the morning. Specific dramatic acts should always be performed with certain types of ritual exorcism but this does not prevent them from being added to other rituals of a different type. The usual style of dramatic presentation is for an actor to open a dramatic sequence by first respectfully greeting the senior member of the household and then the patient. The sequence is closed, and also often acts within a linked series, by the actor taking a symbolic object, used as a prop in the sequence, or else an offering basket and passing it three times (signifying the *tun dosa* – three humours) over the patient. This functions partly also to re-focus attention upon the patient, a focus which is often lost in the preceding periods of comic action and dialogue when the actors direct most of their performance to the audience.

Where dialogue is part of the dramatic action it usually involves one of the drummers, who plays the part of the straight man, engaging an actor in comic interchange. In masked interludes, when the actor takes the role of a demon, the structure of the dialogue is such that the drummer tries to ensnare and overcome the "demon" by skillful wit and repartee. The content of the dialogue, especially in exorcist groups who regularly work together, varies only slightly from one performance to another but occasionally includes new material.

Set forth below are some short examples of the dialogue typically found in specific dramatic sequences of three of the most frequently performed ritual exorcisms. As the reader will observe, the comedy is often raw and bawdy, but obvious too will be the way in which the actors elaborate on the meaning of ritual symbol and concept linking them to the everyday secular world.

105

Bruce Kapferer

(i) *Rata Yakuma*

The short section of dialogue reproduced here is from "the weaving of the cloth" sequence which depicts one scene in the myth of the Seven Princesses The Seven Princesses were over-zealous in assisting the Black Prince (*Kalu Kumaraya*) in persecuting women and girls and were imprisoned by King Vesamuni. However, they secured their freedom by weaving a white cloth for Dipankara Buddha. But this freedom was only allowed on condition that they did not kill but only made women barren, a blight which they would withdraw upon being given offerings (see Wirz 1954: 65-66). The sequence follows immediately upon a dramatic miming interlude which presents the toilette of the Seven Princesses (*nanu mura paliya.*) The "weaving of the cloth" scene begins with a mat being spread out on the ground before the patient. An actor representing the Seven Princesses sits at one end, and a member of the exorcist group, representing Dipankara Buddha, at the other. This man remains silent throughout the interlude and becomes the main butt of jokes developed out of the interchange between the actor and one of the drummers.

Ridi Bisava:	*Gurunanse*[15] (teacher) – who is this man?
Drummer:	He is your husband.
Ridi Bisava:	My man? My husband?
Drummer:	Yes, your own husband.
Ridi Bisava:	Seven Deaths! My husband is a very youthful man. Why, he can only be 3,500 years old. Not very old, eh? (audience laughs) He will rot if not used.

(A cotton spindle is placed on the mat so that the actor and his partner can wind the cotton which has been grown.)

	Do you know that this spindle comes from Koratuwa? (This is a quick allusion to one of the tough areas in the centre of Galle Town.)
Drummer:	Not Koratuwa – Moratuwa (a town on the southern outskirts of Colombo, renowned for its furniture-making and the making of various kinds of craft machinery).
Ridi Bisava:	Now we must weave the cotton. Seven Deaths! What a bunch (*valukurak,* means alternative "bunch" or "stick" and has in colloquial usage clear sexual reference) my man has here (the audience laughed uproariously). I hope I get him in the next life.

(A cloth is eventually woven and is held up for all to see. It has

106

an enormous hole in it, which evokes gales of laughter from the audience.)

(ii) *Mahasohon Samayam*

The following dialogue is part of the *Mangara pela paliya*[16] (presentation for God Mangara).[17] It is performed immediately after the major dance episodes and immediately before the masked appearance of an actor in the guise of *Mahasona* in which the actor dramatically enacts the death of this demon before the patient (see Kapferer 1976). *Mangara* is the deity to whom Mahasona is directly subservient and the episode represents in mock form a religious procession (*perahara*) in Mangara's honour. Twelve acts are performed in sequence and various objects having symbolic reference and meaning are introduced. These objects represent in turn a sacred canopy, an umbrella, a flag, the sun and moon symbol, horns, drums, a stick game, the tying of a wild elephant, the tying of a wild buffalo and so on. As each object is introduced and act performed the drummer asks the actor what he is doing and what the object he is using represents.

Drummer:	An umbrella and a flag should now be presented.
Actor:	What's an umbrella?
Drummer:	An umbrella protects you from the sun and rain.
Actor:	It can't do two things at once. What's it look like?
Drummer:	Like a bat.
Actor:	A bat umbrella? Where can I find one?
Drummer:	The schoolmistress has one. You know, the one that breaks into two or three bits and is carried under the arm.
Actor:	Are you going to break up the schoolmistress?
Drummer:	If you did that her teacher husband would break your neck. I am talking about modern umbrellas not those ancient ones. You know, the ones that fold into four or five pieces. All the young people have them now.
Actor:	Really! When I talk of an umbrella I mean the umbrella which is held over the sacred tooth relic in the procession at the Dalada Maligawa (Temple of the Tooth in Kandy).
Drummer:	You are right. This is the power of the umbrella you must bring.

The actor twirls the umbrella until it breaks.

(iii) Sanni Yakuma[18]

The main dramatic episodes of this ritual are the *Ata paliya* (eight presentations) and the *Dahata sanniya* (eighteen disease spreading demons).[19] There is no break between them and the two sequences are often known jointly as the *Dahata paliya*. Their performance follows on a half-hour break in the ritual proceedings and usually starts at approximately 3:00 a.m. The beginning of these sequences, which involve one or more actors wearing a variety of masks signifying different demons and apparitions, is signalled by a roaring of the actor within the *vidiya* and his violent shaking of it. As the masked actor emerges he spins a structure (*Kapala Kuduva*)[20] which has been set on a rice poinder in front of the *vidiya*. The performance of this dramatic sequence, which can last for over three hours, is not limited to the *Sanni Yakuma*. It is commonly performed with the other major exorcisms, usually towards the end, such as the *Rata Yakuma, Mahasohon Samayam* and the *Sunniyam*. I include excerpts from two recorded sequences. The first is taken from the *Ata paliya* and concerns *Kalas paliya* (pot-bearing apparition). The second involves one of the most feared *sanni* demons, *Maru Sanniya* (death demon) who normally appears towards the end of the *Dahata sanniya* episodes.

Drummer:	My sweetheart, my darling, my little lollipop – what should I call you?
Member of audience:	
	Karunawattie (a name meaning "kind-hearted girl").
Drummer:	Not Karunawattie – she should be called Bakalawattie (bow-legged woman). Seven Deaths! She is already making a pass at someone. (The masked actor has seated himself on the lap of a member of the audience.)
Kalas paliya:	Annee, annee . . . (to the drummer). You are ugly.
Drummer:	Look at that! She is wriggling so much that her backside looks heavier than her top.
Kalas paliya:	Annee – you are ruining my reputation.
Drummer:	Really – we can all see that she's been ruined by the shape of her arse. Come here my little one.
Kalas paliya:	Leave me alone!
Drummer:	Why did you come disguised as a woman, a whore?
Kalas paliya:	I have come to meet my lover in Galle. He promised me some Gunasiri toffee (a popular sweet).

> I have come dressed as a woman because I am the goddess of the earth (*Polowa mahi Kantawa, Bumi Devi),* who once defended Buddha against *Maraya.*

Shortly after this announcement the sequence ends. Much later Maru Sanniya enters.

Drummer:	Where are you off to?
Maru Sanniya:	I am off to Maradana (a suburb of Colombo) by a first class express bus.
Drummer:	You must do a lot of travelling. Why, what was it I saw you doing only yesterday? You pissed near the sacred *Bodhi* tree, then shitted on the temple grounds after which you stole a monk's robes. What else have you done? Why, you also stole a ration book and visited the barber shop to have your head shaved.
Maru Sanniya:	You *peretaya* (ghost)!!! (These are conceptualized by Sinhalese as greedy, pot-bellied, long-haired, ill-kept, filthy beings; very similar to the way demons are portrayed in the ritual drama. The term *peretaya* is often used colloquially as a term of abuse.)
Drummer:	Aah – you are only a mad demon – beneath contempt.

More mutually insulting exchanges follow which progressively become more and more obscene to the obvious delight of the audience. This is ended when Maru Sanniya suddenly pointed to the patient.

Maru Sanniya:	Gurunanse, the patient is showing some signs of amusement. (The patient at this time was recoiling in apparent fright.) Look here (Maru Sanniya addressed the patient), look at my face, show a bit of movement. If you don't speak I will beat you on the head.
Drummer:	Stop that.
Maru Sanniya:	Look! The patient is beginning to giggle. Now she is starting to behave more like a young woman. (The patient was holding her hands over her face but occasionally opening her fingers to steal a peek at the demon.) Look here--you must look at my face. Simply move those hands away. If you don't look at or talk with me . . . I will beat you on the head.

Drummer:	Stop that.
Maru Sanniya:	Come on woman . . . Smile.
Drummer:	(to the patient) Open your eyes. (to the audience) He (Maru Sannuya) wants the patient to say out aloud what has caused her illness. He would go if she showed signs of amusement or laughter.
Maru Sanniya:	Patient--I will cook and eat one of your fingers (he blows into the patient's ear).
Drummer:	Speak up. (This is said to Maru Sanniya who seemed to be whispering to the patient).
Maru Sanniya:	Buddha's mother! This is like trying to get an audience with the D.R.O. (The District Revenue Office is one of the most important locally based Government officials. Individuals must be registered at his office for such matters as entering their children in school and receiving their rice rations.) I have sent something like twenty petitions to this woman and I still haven't got a reply. I'm off to send her a telegram!
Drummer:	Lead her on a little. Talk to her as if you know what has caused her illness.
Maru Sanniya:	(to patient) If you have suffered from a sickness . . . say so, ha, ha, ha, ha . . . (patient shakes her head).
Drummer:	Use your mouth, don't shake your head. Say out loud whether you had an illness or not, we can't hear you.
Maru Sanniya:	Seven Deaths! (to patient) If you had an illness, can't you say so? What were the symptoms of your illness?

Further exhortations to the patient from Maru Sanniya and the drummer followed, as yet to little avail. Maru Sanniya then lept away and somersaulted through the audience. Maru Sanniya's appearance ended in a similar way to others in the Dahata sanniya with his passing of an offering basket three times over the patient's head.

Analysis

Dialogue and dramatic action is clearly organized to evoke comedy and laughter not just from an audience but also from a patient. Laughter, in the view of exorcists, is in itself cleansing and purifying and assists the re-equilibration of the bodily humours.[21] When a patient laughs it also indicated to exorcists and audience that a cure is being successfully effected, that the patient is able to look upon the reality presented before him in a manner apparently similar to those non-afflicted assembled in the audience.

Of more immediate concern at present is the contrast, both in the medium of presentation and in the organization of symbolic object and action, between these later dramatic sequences and the earlier parts of the ritual. It is of note that dramatic dialogue and action proceeds, unlike the verbal and non-verbal drummers, and without the stylized symbolic gesture of dance. The language is the rough urban patois of working class Sinhalese, spoken with everyday gusto. It is neither the esoteric language of the earlier ritual episodes nor is it sung or intoned in that conventional ritual mode which most men use to commune with the supernatural. The dramatic presentations assume a secular form within an overall ritual frame which was initially established according to principles relating to the construction of a supernatural reality.

I suggest that it is the hallmark of much religious ritual that language and stylized non-verbal media for the carriage of meaning, such as dance, music and/or special forms of verbal intonation, are combined in the same action setting. The importance of this is that it has the effect of controlling or restricting the range of meaningful symbolic reference. It results from this that the conditions are created for the redundant accumulation of symbols and for the condensation of multiple meanings into symbols (V. Turner 1967: 28-30) which is a feature of so much religious ritual. Susanne Langer (1960: 75-76) has written of the "transparency" of language and that words or vocables are in themselves worthless. "Our conceptual activity seems to flow *through* them, rather than merely to accompany them, as it accompanies other experiences that we endow with significance... But the greatest virtue of verbal symbols is, probably, their tremendous readiness to enter into *combinations*." According to Langer, language is essentially *discursive* and is composed of permanent units of meaning which are combinable into larger units which have wider ranges of meaning and connotation. This wider connotation indeed requires non-verbal acts such as finger pointing to enable the denotation of specific meanings. The combinative property of word and language leads Langer to label language as a discursive symbol system in contrast to non-verbal symbolism or *presentational* symbolism where the meaning is "understood only through the meaning of the whole, through their relations within the total structure. Their very functioning as symbols depends on the fact that they are involved in a simultaneous, internal presentation" (op. cit. 97).

111

This is not to deny the multivocal character of presentational symbols. Individually they are capable of a vast range of meaning perhaps, as Langer suggests (1960: 86-87), more so than individual discursive symbols which are more easily amenable to dictionary definition. What I emphasize is a presentational symbolic mould whereby in the medium of ritual performance a number of presentational symbols are simultaneously linked. By this certain facets of their meaning become fixed, each mutually reinforcing the other in this. Given that, as V. Turner has stressed, ritual is transformative this probably explains the marked presence of presentational/iconic symbols in rituals. Their great connotative range gives them a central position in effecting and expressing ritual transformations. But the principle I stress is that the range of their connotative potential becomes realized and their ability to express and effect transformations in meaning is produced by their being set in a discursive symbolic medium. But if the presentational symbolic mould is broken down, individual presentational symbols are taken out and in a sense treated as discursive symbols.[22]

I consider that where the presentational symbolism, like music, dance and mode of intonation is of a closed and highly integrated kind, as in the ritual exorcisms I have described, then this will override and suppress any broad connotative potential of language or at least restrict it to an overlapping meaning set. Moreover, the audience and participants in ritual are likely to respond more to the non-verbal activity as a vehicle for meaning that to a language as a carrier of meaning. Because presentational symbols cannot easily be broken down into smaller constituent units of meaning and because of the particular form they take in religious ritual they are the natural medium by which mystical and supernatural realities can be created and represented by men to other men. To refer back to an earlier point, religious ritual as a system of presentational symbols rather than a system of discursive symbols is better able to guard against threats of subversion to the reality it supports emanating from other realities in the wider context of ritual performance. This is so because the meaning of presentational symbols is emergent from their interrelation within a total structure so that each symbol mutually supports and reinforces the other. Symbolic meaning and behaviour which intrude from the world outside that created by ritual often do so as bits of meaning, independent of structures which complete and strengthen them. Such occurrences are easily overcome by the integrated presentational symbolic form of religious ritual action. Indeed it is possible that behaviour if based on discursive symbols is more open to subversion because smaller units of meaning can be more easily separated out and exposed to individual attack.

The above discussion is important for gaining an understanding of the significance of drama in ritual. I have already argued that the processional creates and further confirms a reality the effects of which it seeks to avoid. Dramatic action and dialogue in Sinhalese exorcism is such that discursive symbolism is liberated from a restaining presentational symbolic mould and verbal symbols freed to combine and produce a wide range of meaning. Alternatively, the selecting out of individual presentational symbols and their discursive treatment allows them to be linked to a reality as others define it and enables transformation in their meaning. A condition is established for meaning to spiral out of the confines of earlier ritual symbolic reference systems exemplified by the selections from dramatic dialogue reproduced above. Thus an umbrella representative of the one which is held above the sacred tooth relic when carried in procession from the Dalada Maligawa is likened to that carried by a school mistress and to a bat.

The language of dramatic dialogue permits elements of a secular reality to flood into the ritual, while the drama organizes the symbolic reference of secular reality into a form which at once parallels the world developed in the earlier ritual episodes and renders it more capable of potentially overthrowing that reality. Presentational symbolism, dramatic gesture and other body movements, is of course apparent, but unlike previous ritual sequences it is the servant, rather than the master of the discursive symbolism of language. This is facilitated in that the dramatic gesture and other bodily movement is a non-verbal communicative mode, though exaggerated, recognized and used in everyday social intercourse. Although these gestures and other bodily movements comprise a communicative code specific to Sinhalese culture they are not as tightly integrated, as highly interconnected, as the gestural form of ritual dance and magical action. While the non-verbal activity in the dramatic episodes is essential in narrowing the connotative range of verbal symbolism it does not imprison it within a tightly focused reference system of its own.

As the dramatic episodes progress, a reality, alternative to that already erected about the patient and drawing heavily upon the secular world for its content, it constructed and begins to override and subvert that which already surrounds the patient. The audience is actively drawn into the proceedings and occasionally joke at the actor's expense and engage him in verbal interchange. Dramatic dialogue and action combined with the response of spectators effects and expresses an important re-organization in ritual roles. In the earlier ritual sequences the patient, the patient's close kin and other spectators have relatively distinct at well-defined roles. Close kin seated nearby assist the patient with placing offerings in the baskets and comfort the patient during terrifying (for the patient) episodes. But with the start of the dramatic interludes the patient is expected to take conscious note of the proceedings and to be active in giving offerings on his own behalf. With the onset of the drama, too, some of the behaviour distinguishing the patient's kin from the audience disappears and they join together in sharing a common enjoyment of the antics before them. Kin who formerly comforted a patient exhort him to laugh and show amusement rather than to express terror or fright.

Both exorcists and the lay members of an audience state that a non-afflicted person, participating normally in a secular world should not explain or see all facets of his everyday experience unidimensionally. To the healthy, the objects and actions which crowd mundane experience are capable of a variety of interpretations and meanings. It is the expression of this which is one thematic aspect of the dramatic dialogue. Symbolic objects, characters from myth and legend, apparitions and demons are presented in the verbal exchanges as having supernatural and mundane reference, as being terrifying supernatural monsters and also cranky old men, flighty young girls, and so on.

Patient and audience distinguish the way they define and understand the dramatic performance by their response. For the audience the drama is indeed a play in which ordinary human beings act roles as demons or malign apparitions. A patient by refusing to laugh or otherwise show amusement shows, in the view of an audience, that he perceives as real what is, in fact, unreal.

It is only such a resistance by a patient which sustains the reality developed in previous ritual episodes against the subversive threat of the dramatic performance. Often exorcists, as well as kin and others in the audience, become extremely agitated by this. In these instances, exorcists as actors will take advantage of the discursive symbolism of the drama and the relative consciousness of the patient to cajole and bully him into expressing amusement and publicly stating that he is cured and no longer has any fear.[23] Once a patient expresses enjoyment in a publicly received and understood manner then he is regarded as having crossed the threshood from a frightening malign world into a mundane reality as the healthy and non-afflicted should perceive it. The patient is no more a patient but now one with the audience. Like the others gathered around, he is outside, apart from those elements of a malign, supernatural world performed before him. As the magical incantations and acts of the previous episodes effectively cut the relationship between patient and demon, so through a discursive symbolic drama the patient is psychologically separated from an involvement in a demonic world. Until he laughs, there is no distance between him and elements of the malign supernatural world around him. With the expression of amusement a patient signifies his rejoining the secular, earthly world of the normal and unafflicted, who recognize that the secular world is a reality separate and distant from supernatural realities. The world conjured in the earlier ritual sequences is without the focus of a patient and is finally subverted and dissipated.

The main offering and magical acts of ritual exorcisms develop through a presentational symbolism in which meaning is condensed and fused, but locked within the reference system of a world dominated by the supernatural. In contrast, the discursive symbolism of the dramatic episodes permits of the combination of verbal units so that the sense and meaning of symbol is extended. In some way there is a similarity here with V. Turner's (1968: 44-45) distinction between the analytical form of divinatory symbols and the synthetic form of ritual symbols. Thus, in the dramatic episodes of exorcisms, and in divinations, a series of meanings is teased out in the course of dialogue (for example, see the foregoing excerpts from the *Mangara pela paliya*).

Two other consequences of this process might be noted. First, through the extension of symbolic meaning out of the ritual world of the supernatural into an everyday world, symbols and symbolic representations are denuded of some of their mystically dangerous attributes. They are, in a sense, defused and so rendered that members of a ritual audience can adopt and express attitudes towards them consistent with the way the normally healthy should interact with them in a secular world. In ordinary daily secular activity, at least for Sinhalese urban working class, demons and deities should not dominate and occupy every waking thought. Demons and malign ancestor spirits *(pretaya)* can be the subject of jocular comment and form the basis of abusive language. Secondly, the dismantling of symbolic meaning through the manipulation of discursive verbal units permits in turn their re-assembly in accordance with the way patient and audience should see reality relating to their world.

This last point requires further elaboration for I have, so far, concentrated the analysis mainly on processes which lead to the subversion of a supernatural reality constructed around a patient, and not its reassembly in accordance with the way healthy people should see it.

Something like the Durkheimian distinction between "sacred" and "profane" is applicable to the Sinhalese situation and is useful in illuminating aspects of my argument. As described earlier, the type of offering given to a supernatural being signifies the position of the supernatural recipient in the cosmic order. I stress that in my usage the terms "sacred" and "profane" refer to elements of a supernatural reality and its manifestations or representations in a mundane world. For this reason, these terms should be used distinctively from the term "secular" which I have used throughout this paper to refer to the ordinary everyday reality of human beings. The torm "profane", therefore, should not be used synonymously with "secular." The tendency of some anthropologists to use these terms interchangeably (e.g., Leach 1961: 134) in my opinion provokes confusion and misunderstanding.[24]

No exorcism of the type I have described ends without a re-affirmation of a supernatural order as healthy people should see it; with deities placed in a position of clear superiority to demons, with what is sacred clearly distinguished from the profane, and with the supernatural world, particularly its malign aspect, distanced and set apart from the world of the secular. For this, certain transpositions and reversals of symbolic statement made in earlier ritual sequences, and not only subversions, must be effected. It is here that the importance of comedy in the dramatic episodes, so much their dominant motif, is evident.

The discursive symbolism in dramatic dialogue permits what is sacred, profane and secular to be recognized and separated. In the previous episodes sacred and profane meanings are so fused in the manipulation of symbolic object and in symbolic action that they become confused and difficult to distinguish. For instance, a tree resin (*dummala*), used throughout the ritual, has sacred properties, it is produced from the same type of tree under which Buddha was born and when burnt repels demons, but it also has profane aspects, for when smoked over a brazier it produces an aroma which attracts demons. The demons themselves although given profane and impure and polluting offerings are addressed as deities and otherwise shown a respect in word and action normally reserved for gods. It is by passing elements symbolic of the supernatural reality through the secular reality created by drama that their sacred and profane aspects are distinguished.

It is in the nature of the drama, in that opposes and interweaves different realities (Bateson 1973: 193), that the potential for the realization of comedy and humour is established.[25] But it is with the recognition by an audience that the utterances and actions before them are comic and funny that sacred, profane and secular aspects are ordered in some relation to one another and not just separated. The points throughout the drama when the audience suddenly recognizes, expressed by explosive laughter, the incongruities and absurdities of the bahaviour portrayed before them – for example, a demon travelling "first class" in a bus, impersonating a monk, defecating and urinating on temple grounds – is when the true lowly profane station of particular supernatural beings is realized and their position in a supernatural order transposed. It is a property of comedy that events are juxtaposed in such a way that they "call forth a transformation of the original understanding" (McHugh 1968: 41). Bateson is making a similar observation when he states, "The explosive moment in humour is the moment when the labelling of the mode undergoes a dissolution and resynthesis. Commonly, the punch line compels a re-evaluation of earlier signals which ascribed to certain messages a particular mode (e.g., literalness or fantasy)" (Bateson 1973: 175).

Such humour, of course, enables the reduction of the status of demons to a position lower and inferior to human beings. It also distances their malign reality from the secular world for they are represented by the exorcist actors as being incapable of bahaving adequately in it. Demons are portrayed as being unable to speak adequate Sinhalese. When they do speak in Sinhalese they stutter and continually commit improprieties and mouth obscenities (see Kapferer 1976).

Ritual: Its sacred and secular form

I have described some of the key elements of major Sinhalese healing rites in terms of how they effect transformations in patient and audience understandings and in ritual structure. But my central concern in the paper was to examine the shift in symbolic medium as the ritual progressed from its more supernatural, mystical and occult phases to the later dramatic sequences which were dominantly secular in content. In the early phases, the symbolic mode is such that meaning is rendered highly redundant or else limited in reference to a mystical or supernatural reality. In the later dramatic sequences, the symbolic mode allows for the expression of a much wider range of meaning and its transformation: symbolic action does not have its meaning potential restrained by its form. The first symbolic mode, following Langer, is characteristic of presentational symbolism; the second is a discursive symbolic mode. Thus the early ritual episodes are dominated by a presentational symbolic mode: dance and music interweave with stylized bodily movement and verbal intonation "sealing off" the ritual action and removing it from the world of everyday behaviour. The later dramatic sequences are cast in a discursive symbolic mould, stylized music and dance cease, the interpretative potential of symbolic object and action is broadened and the secular world begins to override that of the supernatural. In Sinhalese exorcisms a supernatural reality, both its sacred and profane aspects, the world of religious thought and action, is created through a presentational mode and couched in it. The mundane world introduced into and constructed in the course of ritual employs a discursive symbolic medium in which sacred and profane symbolic meanings intermingle and jostle with interpretations not necessarily derivative from and referenced to a supernatural reality. The sacred and the secular aspects of Sinhalese exorcism are clearly distinguished and recognized as such by the participants. There is in exorcisms a succession from "ritual" through to "drama" whereby participants, and especially the patient, become progressively separated from the reality in which they have been involved and come to see it as "play."

I have stressed the medium in which meaning is communicated, realized and understood as a factor in distinguishing religious ritual from secular ritual, especially where the organization of symbolic object and action seeks to make exclusive reference to a supernatural reality separated from everyday life. The approach taken is one which emphasized the performance elements of ritual behaviour. This is in addition to the nature of the propositions expressed in ritual and the particular meaning and reference attributes held by specific symbolic abjects and symbolic concepts independent of ritual performance. Rappaport, for example, states that religious ritual is distinguishable from secular ritual in that the former proceeds in accordance with sacred propositions which are ineffable or non-discursive. In religious ritual, "Ultimate sacred propositions are taken to be unquestionably true because their enunciation in ritual or in symbols kept in holy places elicits from the faithful a non-discursive, and therefore, unfalsifiable, affirmation" (1920: 70). Again, Ortner (1973) argues a distinction between summarizing and elaborating symbols. She does not develop this on the basis of any religious secular opposition but the distinction she makes is nonetheless pertinent to it. The meaning-content of summarizing, or in the broadest sense sacred, symbols is "by definition clustered, condensed, relatively undifferentiated, 'thick' while the meaning-content of elaborating symbols is by definition relatively clear, orderly, differentiated, articulate" (*op. cit,* 1342).

All this is probably true. But the point which I emphasize is that sacred propositions are, to a degree, rendered unfalsifiable and incontestable, and symbols further confirmed in their summarizing nature by the medium of display and the organizational form of performance. Thus, the early sequences of the exorcism involve treating demons in a sacred manner suppressing their profaneness. Through the presentational medium of the sequences, a reality dominated by capricious, malign demons, a reality contrary to the view of the non-afflicted in the audience, is constructed. Symbolic objects and materials which have their meaning-content fused in the opening exorcism episodes have, in the course of their operation in a later discursive dramatic medium, their meaning elaborated, defined and differentiated.

The presentational symbolic mode of the ritual performance in the early exorcism episodes is such that its broader combinative potential is reduced and, therefore, cannot easily generate meaningful connections outside an inter-related system of meanings, simultaneously presented, referring to a supernatural reality. The rhythm of drums and gesture of dance, although no doubt aesthetically appreciated by an audience, only acquires meaning in the context of the supernatural reality, and its attendant assumptions, conjured by the exorcists. The verbal content of magical verse and songs, through being set in such a presentational symbolic mode, has any combinative properties it might possess restricted by and subordinated to the medium within which it is carried. In the move to a discursive symbolic medium, the combinative and elaborative potential of verbal symbols is facilitated through the cessation of musical and gestural modes which lock them into a closed reference system of a supernatural world. Full play is given to the eleborative properties of verbal symbol by it being shifted from the monological context of its usage in the early ritual sequences to the dialogical context of drama. It is probably a feature of much religious ritual which seeks to enclose participants in, or orient them towards, a supernatural reality (or at least which aims to exclude significant reference to everyday secular life) that its verbal content is monological in form and not dialogical.[26]

In more general terms the form of Sinhalese ritual exorcism whereby there is a transition from a presentational symbolic mode to a discursive symbolic mode is suggestive of a possible distinction between some religious and secular rituals. Thus my analysis has indicated that where ritual action is addressed to a supernatural reality or is directed towards constructing a supernatural world independent and removed from the secular, then it is likely to do so in terms of a dominantly presentational symbolic mode. Alternatively, where ritual is directed towards either making religious statements relevant to mundane social conduct or is simply stressing values and ideas central to everyday behaviour, then a discursive symbolic mode will be used.

There are broader implications of this argument. It is commonplace for anthropologists to discover in religious and secular ritual alike, similar wider sociological significance. For example, religious ritual can define socio-economic and political units, it can be expressive of central guiding principles organizing social behaviour, it can re-affirm basic social values and redress rifts and conflicts in the social order and so on. These consequences of ritual might, however, lie outside the awareness and understanding of participants. Such ritual functions might only be clear to the anthropologist once he has ingeniously joined and tied up, through his distinctive analysis, the disparate elements of the social systems he studies. Consideration of the symbolic mode of ritual, however, would not just provide some index of the likelihood of ritual participants also receiving and understanding the wider social and political import of their activities, but also might indicate where ritual, in the context of performance, is consciously making statements which are applicable to secular life.

119

One final point needs to be made. If some religious and secular rituals can be distinguished by their symbolic medium, then care should be taken against indiscriminately transferring concepts and ideas developed in the study of the one and applying them to the other and *vice versa*. It is fashionable in anthropology to analyse and describe all kinds of social behaviour in an idiom particularly derived from the study of religious behaviour. While this is legitimate in many cases, it runs the danger of failing to see that the organization of symbolic object and action in one kind of ritual context can be very different from its operation in another.

NOTES

[1] The field work on which this paper is based was carried out between August 1971 and September 1972 in the area of Galle Town in the Southern Province of Sri Lanka. I am grateful to the S.S.R.C. for a grant which covered this research and also to the Department of Social Anthropology, University of Manchester, which also supported aspects of the research. Marvyn Meggitt, Adrian Peace and Tom Ernst commented on earlier drafts of this paper and I am grateful to them. A longer version of the paper was delivered at a conference on "Secular Ritual" at Burg-Wartenstein and much is owed in subsequent revision to the participants and particularly erence Turner, Victor Turner and Barbara Myerhoff.

[2] Descriptions of exorcism ritual which serve as a useful background for the ideas in this paper are Wirz 1954, Raghavan 1967, Sarachandra 1966, Ames 1964, Obeyesekere 1963, 1969, Yalman 1964, 1973 and Kapferer 1976. The reader should note that there is a variation in the structure and content of exorcism rituals from one area to another along the western and southern coast of the island. Nevertheless, my evidence suggests that the overall structure of the rituals is essentially the same.

[3] Exorcists in Galle normally come from low caste communities such as Oli and Bereva.

[4] Exorcists are frequently appealed to for assistance, especially in urban areas, after other individuals and specialists have been consulted. Ayurvedic and western medical treatment, if the symptoms are primarily physiological and not clearly mental, are usually sought first and it is later, should the treatment in the view of the patients and his family not be completely successful, that an exorcist is called in. Often the patient, with the advice of kin and neighbours and perhaps an astrologer (*sastra karaya*), has arrived at a diagnosis of his condition and its cause. I have encountered a number of instances where the patient, together with his kin, has overridden an exorcist's diagnosis and has emphasised he should receive treatment contrary to that suggested by the exorcist. In those instances where an exorcist is not faced with such a situation, he strives to obtain the patient's agreement that his diagnosis is accurate.

Finally, it should be noted that exorcism is certainly not opposed to ayurvedic methods of cure and is not necessarily in conflict with western treatment. It is not unusual to find patients following three different courses of treatment at the same time.

[5] V. Turner (1967 has made an extensive ethnographic survey of the symbolic meaning underlying the three colours, black, red and white, and his conclusions accord very much with their usage in the Sinhalese context.

6 A sudden unsettling state experienced while alone is usually the first indication which patients report as suggesting to them that they have attracted the gaze of a demon.

7 Known in Sanskrit as Vaisravana who in the Buddhist texts is the guardian of the Northern Quarter (Obeyesekere 1969: 176).

8 Ames (1964: 34) states that the word, *dola,* although denoting "offering," "giving," also has the meaning of "craving" and "desire" which is against Buddhist virtue.

9 There are variations in the type and number of offerings made to demons and this often both signifies the status of the demon and the number of forms he can assume.

10 Obeyesekere states that "All the minor rites have a *sima,* i.e., they are effective for a limited period like three days, seven days, one month. If the disease is not cured within the specified period, one of the major rituals, like the *Sanni Yakuma,* may have to be performed ... these minor rituals are viewed as *apa,* or "bail," i.e., a promise made to the demon that a longer ritual in his honour will be held within a certain period if the disease is not cured" (1969: 178). If the disease is cured, Obeyesekere goes on, then a longer ritual will not be held. This last point is not supported by my observations in the Galle area. A patient or his household might decide not to have a larger ritual but they do so at their own risk for the tying of a thread only alleviates a condition, it does not remove its cause. It should be added that the smaller rituals I have referred to in the text need not be of specifically the thread-tying variety, which are usually very simple. There are many small offerings *(pideni)* made to ancestor, spirits and specific demons, for instance, which might be tried as cures before performing a larger exorcism.

11 The *Rata Yakuma* is performed for women or for small children who are suffering from ailments as a result of their mothers attracting the malign eyesight of a demon. The name of the exorcism implies that it is for the foreign country demon (i.e., *Kalu Kumaraya*) who lived in India. But some exorcists have told me that *Rata* also contains a reference to the fact that the unborn child or newborn child can be conceptualized as coming from another world into this.

12 The offering baskets are made from coconut-palm leaves, and, dependent on the demon concerned, have internal partitions *(gabe).* Within these partitions are placed offerings either for the various forms the demon takes or the female demons *(yakkini)* associated with him. The design formed by the partitioning of an offering basket is the same as the magical geometrical design *(yantra)* drawn on thin metal strips and worn as protective amulets.

13 Tambiah (1968: 176-177) is correct when he notes that the verses uttered and sung are not only mantra but also employ other verbal forms such as *Kannalavva* and *Kaviya* which are in Sinhalese. The point which I develop is that even though some of the verses are intelligible, the medium and mode by which they are presented restricts and limits the range of participants at the ritual occasion who can understand and follow them. I do not agree with Tambiah, however, that the redundancy in them and the "lengthy recital and staging are contrived to achieve that crucial understanding by the patient of his illness which is a necessary prelude to and a condition of the cure" *(op. cit.* 177). This is more the case later in the ritual but not in the early stages. In the early period the patient is relatively "unconscious" of the ritual proceedings.

14 I am grateful to both Terence Turner and Barbara Myerhoff for urging me to deepen my analysis of the second dance phase of Sinhalese exorcisms and impressing upon me their transformational significance.

[15] This is the correct and respectful term of address towards an exorcist. Dialogue usually begins with disrespectful modes of address being used such as *Bera karayo* (drummer). As the dialogue progresses, disrespectful terms normally give way to respectful terms.

[16] The *Mangara pela paliya* is also performed in large rituals devoted to the deities such as the *Gam Maduva* and the *Devol Maduva*.

[17] There are many myths and legends relating to Mangara. One which is related most frequently by exorcists is that he was a magician living in the vicinity of Kataragama (a sacred pilgrimmage site in the Eastern Dry Zone of the island where every July festivities are held celebrating God Kataragama's visit to his mistress, *Valli-amma* – Wirz 1966). He was transformed into a deity after being killed by a wild buffalo. Another myth (see Wirz 1954: 51 fn.) states that God Mangara was the father of God Kataragama who killed a bull, on which he had ridden, and made a whistle (the *vas danda* used in the ritual exorcism) out of its windpipe. The important point about the myths relating to Mangara is that they link the Mangara pela paliya episode very clearly with Kataragama. Most exorcists will state that the Mahasona ritual originated in the Kataragama area.

[18] An excellent description of this exorcism appears in Obeyesekere (1969).

[19] Usually only eight or so masked demons are presented in this episode. The gestural behaviour of each masked demon is linked closely to the type of illness he represents (see Obeyesekere 1969).

[20] Obeyesekere states that none of his informants could give a satisfactory explanation of the *Kapala Kuduva*. He goes on to suggest that kapala in Sanskrit means "skull" (which has all kinds of polluting associations because of its linkage with death) and that the *Kapala Kuduva* is erected on a rice pounder which is conceptualized by exorcists as the axis of the world. It is also seen as the walking stick of *Maha Brahkma,* and which this deity uses to punish demons. I have been told by one exorcist that the spinning of the *Kapala Kuduva* by the masked actor when he enters the arena is symbolic of the threat by demons to the equilibrium of the world.

[21] This view shows some affinity with Indian dramatic tradition to which the dramatic episodes in Sinhalese exorcism are related. Bharata's second century B. C. treatise on dramatic convention, the *Nataya Sastra,* states that a dramatist's purpose should be to "balance the onlooker's emotions (not purge them, as in accordance with the theory of *Katharsis*) and harmonize his being from within, resulting in his experiencing an unalloyed joy" (Alphonso-Karkala 1971:384).

It must be stressed, however, that elements of catharsis are by no means absent from exorcism rituals. Some masked presentations of demons, e.g., the masked appearance of Mahasona, are designed to so frighten a patient that the afflicting demon will be caused to loosen his grip. But not all apparently frightening masked demons are considered by exorcists to have this effect. Rather the use of their terrifying aspect, as often performed in the *Maru Sanniya* episode, is to test the patient to see whether fear, and therefore a cause of the illness, persists. On occasion laughter and fear are combined by exorcists as therapeutic aids. Thus the mind, soothed and lulled by fun and laughter, is left unprepared for the fright attendant upon the sudden appearance of the masked actor causing the afflicting demon to let go of the patient.

[22] I am grateful to Terence Turner who impressed upon me the importance of this point in a way which I had hitherto not fully grasped.

[23] It should also be apparent that the shift in the medium of the ritual to discursive symbolic mode permits exorcists to use the word, not as a magical aid as in the

earlier ritual sequences, but as a means to directly convince the patient and bring about a cure. The use of verbal forms in a presentational and in a discursive mode is a clear feature of ancient Greek therapy, which in many other respects resembles, both in treatment and in ideas relating to the causation of illness, Sinhalese exorcism (see Entralgo 1970).

[24] Stanner (1967) is highly critical of Durkheim's distinction between "sacred" and "profane" and emphasises the importance of using a third category "mundane" which is more or less equivalent with my use of the term "secular." Stanner is still unhappy with this trichotomy, and, in the light of his criticisms, I am wary of using them. But I consider that I have applied them in the more acceptable dynamic way he recommends, "at the level of human interaction or ... operations and transactions about things of value" (*op. cit.* 234).

[25] Of course, it is not just the discursive medium which allows for the realization of comedy but the general expectation of an audience, most of whom have attended exorcisms before, that ludicrous and humourous action will be performed in the dramatic sequences. One additional point should be mentioned. While the combinative property of a discursive symbolic mode is ideal for the development of humour, humour itself serves a critical function in using the full potential of verbal manipulation and symbolism in constructing alternative realities. The combining and re-combining of verbal units and utterances in varying and unexpected ways is an important devise used by actors in evoking the recognition of the comic from an audience whom the actors strive to please.

[26] It is worth noting that spirit mediums, for example, who relate the supernatural to secular problems and difficulties adopt a dialogical style.

Chapter VII
CEREMONIES OF CONFRONTATION AND SUBMISSION:
THE SYMBOLIC DIMENSION
OF INDIAN-MEXICAN POLITICAL INTERACTION

Eva Hunt

"Social cohesion demands a creed, or a code of behavior, or prevailing sentiment, or, best, some combination of all three."

Bertrand Russell, 1938

1. Introduction[1]

The purpose of this paper is to discuss two political ceremonials which involve the interaction of Indians and Mestizos in Mexico. These two ceremonials are considered an oppositional pair, one emphasizing confrontation, the other submission, as part of the formal manifest message. At the deeper level, however, both are said to emphasize submission. The analysis is also an attempt at delimiting the causal mechanisms which favor the occurrence of formalized behaviors, as well as an attempt at enumeration of the functions of ceremonial behaviors. The relation between secular and sacred aspects of behavior are also discussed. The empirical data comes from the Cuicatec Village of San Andres Teotilalpan, in the state of Oaxaca.[2]

2. Brief Ethnographic Background

Mexico is a nation state made up of the intricate blending of two distinct cultural traditions which met in the sixteenth century. This nation state is a new breed of man and society, the Mestizo (Wolf, E., 1959). Neither Native nor Spaniard, Mexico is genetically, socially and culturally a strong hybrid specimen.

Mexico is too young an industrial state to have reached its own hinterlands. The country continues to have a basic agrarian economy (Solis, L., 1970; for the Cuicateh see Attolini, J., 1949-1950). In the rural areas of low ecologic potential and geographic isolation, older, distinct cultural traditions and structural forms have persisted for nearly 500 years. These areas have been called refuge regions (Aguirre Beltrán, 1967). Their inhabitants survive in village communities which preserve anachronic institutional elements. About 1/10th of Mexico belongs to this different sociocultural tradition called "Indian" or "Indigenous." However, *Indio* does not mean autochthonous, untouched or pristine, as compared with Mestizo.[3] Indian society and culture are also evolved forms like Mestizos, historically, a product of the colonial process. Indians are bearers of structures which are peculiarly different from Mestizo, and which have been described in type by Wolf (1955, 1957) under the name of the Closed Corporate Community.

The 1/10th of Mexico which is Indian speaks nearly seventy languages other than Spanish. Isolation, language differentiation, and other complex factors have kept Indian communities from forming an organized minority as a political block of the nation state. All Indians, however, share a roster of common cultural characteristics and diagnostic institutional features inherited from the prehispanic past and the colonial experience as well as preserved at present by their common inferior status in the social structure of the nation (Caso, A. *et al.*, 1954). One of them are the Cuicatec, who illustrate this paper. Because of their lack of socio-political integration in the nation state, Indians are a neo-colonial rural enclave; that is, Indian communities are basically dependencies of a modern system of internal colonialism (Gonzales Casanova, P. 1963, 1965). The Indian is wedged in the modern class structure of the society, at the bottom level of the hierarchies of power, economic evolution, prestige or degree of national identification (Stavenhagen, R., 1969; Gonzales Casanova, P., *op. cit.*).

There is no racial barrier for mobility, no real apartheid. But although there is no official ideology of domination, profound differences of institutional frame, of *Weltanschauung,* have created a nation with several antagonistic, symbiotically tied ethnic groups, a plural society. One group is economically dominant, politically powerful, and identified with nationwide institutions. The others are subordinate in number and power, cantonalized, heterogenous poor and inward oriented (Nash, M., 1957).

Nowhere is this situation more obvious than in political institutions and processes. Mexico as a whole is governed by an official, single party system, the PRI (Partido Revolucionario Institucional) which directs the nation's political destinies through a complex system of balances and coalitions of interest groups (c.f., Scott, R., 1964; Padgett, V., 1966). There are three major branches: Agrarian, Labor and Popular. Each of these has a three layered territorial organization. The first two are Federal and State, the last a District Committee. This three-layered structure corresponds with the government territorial levels, the bottom one being Municipal local governments. The government is the tool used by the party to shape the nation's future. But there is an exception to this picture.

The Indian Municipalities do not participate in any effective way in this involved political process. Their autonomy is internally maintained (and their political participation preempted) by the survival of a different, traditional local system of government. This has been called in the

125

literature the Civil-Religious Hierarchy or the Cargo System (Hunt, E. and Nash, Jr., 1967; Cancian, F., 1967).[4]

The hierarchy rules Indian communities internally. The political and ritual roles are filled by villagers. The ladder has four role levels, men taking rests between serving in a role for a year. Men enter the system at the bottom, in the post of policemen (*Policia* also called *Alguacil, Topil* and other local names). After they are married and become household heads with their own nuclear families they serve by taking higher posts in a double ascending ladder of responsibility, power and prestige. The levels above contain the posts of Mayordomos (Church Stewards) in the ritual side, and the civil posts of *Regidor* (junior positions), *Sindico* and *Alcalde* (senior positions). One alcalde acts as village Judge. The top post is Municipal President, also sometimes called Alcalde. The civil positions involve administrative, judicial and executive functions, as well as some ritual functions. The Mexican government, however, only recognizes the civil functions, and the post of Mayordomo is outside of the national legal system, which constitutionally separates state and church (c.f., Gobierno de Oazaca, 1963). Two roles outside the hierarchy, *Secretario* and *Sacristán,* serve as administrative links between village and outside. The first is a civil, the second a church post.

In small traditional communities most men serve the full roster of ranked posts for which they are eligible. In other, larger villages, only some reach the top. This top is the position of *pasado* (one who has passed) and makes a man eligible to be a village elder (*principal*). A principal is a member of a sometimes corporate, sometimes informal advisory board or council of village political experts. When Principales form a corporation it has a fixed number of members and posts are for life.

There are two major variants of this institution. In one the civil and religious branches of the hierarchy operate in conjunction as a single ladder. In the other they are dual, similar but separate ladders, and service in each is more or less independent of the other. The more traditional communities exhibit the first form (Camara, F., 1952).

In the village of San Andres discussed in this paper the civil and religious branches of the hierarchy function separately. Not all men reach the top posts. The mayordomias are financed by levying a household tax rather than being the single responsibility of the Mayordomo, and the elder's council is not a corporate body, with a fixed number of elders. In other words, San Andres exhibits the least traditional form of the civil-religious hierarchy.[5] Obtaining a position in the elder's council is an Indian's major achievement in the political sphere. The civil hierarchy does not push Indian men into the national political arena. To the contrary, it does much the opposite, by containing political careers in a set of institutions whose major function beyond that of internal rule os to defend the autonomy of the Indian community vis-a-vis the Mestizo who rules the nation-state.[6]

In brief, the civil hierarchy functions to (a) maintain a system of Indian common law quite distinct from the laws of Mexico (c.f., Hunt, E. and Hunt, R., 1969; Nader, L., 1964, 1965, 1966, 1969); (b) conserve a system of religious rituals and beliefs which are tied to civil government, and ultimately are, from the Mexican point of view, unconstitutional; (c) reallocate or redistribute income within households in a community, as well as to disperse political power and responsibility according to age grades and wealth levels; (d) preserve and defend the Indian style of life from encroachment by Mestizos; and (e) serve as an interface institution, a brokerage agency between the Indian and Mestizo sectors of the nation.

The requirements of a democratic nation for universal political participation and the needs of the state to impose control over all its territories, makes the Indian Municipality autonomous only in a relative sense. While it preserves *internal* autonomy, it also links the community with the state in a dependent position. Legally this is possible because the Municipio is the lowest level form of government in a Federal system of three levels: federation, province and municipality. The Mexican political system can exert authority, force, influence and control over the Indian social process, legally, because the Indian Municipio is a government territorial unit.

Particularly since the 1930s[7] the Mexican government has been dedicated ideologically and to some extent in action to the task of "incorporating and integrating" the Indian sector into the nation. However, the Mestizo rural elites have consistently opposed in their policies (if not in words) such integration. Rural Mestizos live, to a large extent, from the exploitation of the neo-colonial Indian situation.

A long history of ravages by the Mestizo has taught the Indians, also, that little may be gained from integration but further loss of autonomy. But the fact remains that relations between Indians and Mestizos are characterized by strain, structural ignorance, and above all by economic, political and social symbiosis and interdependence. Even the most isolated Indian village has learned that to survive, it must obey and adjust to the presence of Mestizos in their world. The symbiosis is not comfortable, but is not avoidable. Since the 1910 Revolution (in the Cuicatec since the Colonial period) there have not been any major Indian uprisings. Interaction is strained but peaceful.

It could be argued that the major factors operating to maintain peace are (a) the positive action of the federal political elites in passing protective laws and measures in favor of Indians (e.g., the land reform laws, the creation of the Indian Institute and special school programs, community development agencies, etc.); (b) the trickle down effects of economic progress, industrialization and so on, which has had slow but visible effects in creating new forms of ethnic entente. It could also be argued that Mestizos have systematically manged to co-opt, dispose of or repress Indian political innovators before they acquired more than local prominence (Padgett, L. V., 1966: 229-230).

But another major factor in operation is the ability of Indians themselves to cope with Mestizo pressures through the creative use of their own institutional frames. Above all, Indians delimit the areas in which their submissive participation is normal, and areas in which confrontation, avoidance or opposition are possible. In these two arenas Indian traditional ceremonials of political action are quite different. When integration with the nation is inevitable or non-threatening, Indians utilize what I call ceremonials of submission. When participation threatens the integrity of the Indian way of life (particularly when it implies the abandonment of their religious or communal traditions or danger to the physical survival of their village communities) Indians utilize what I call ceremonials of confrontation. The first includes such activities as celebrating the Day of Independence or other national holiday, voting in nathional elections, and so on. The second involves Mestizo actions about the internal life processes of the Indian community.

3. Ceremonies of Confrontation: The Town Meeting in San Andres

Public meetings in San Andres are ceremonial performances. They have a patterned format, a prescribed choreography which delimits the use of space, time and speech by distinctly named roles, and a symbolic structure which condenses cultural meaning.

The stereotypic, "rigid" quality of the form serves to delimit the normative arrangements of social hierarchy, provides a frame for predictable structured interaction, minimizes interpersonal risk for the participants and, ultimately, reduces potential entropy in terms of the community's definition of peaceful social exchange and consensus formation. Like ritual in a sacred context, the predictability of behavioral formulas insures the community's well being, because it both reduces personal anxiety and group tension as well as provides an outlet for the handling of potential conflict. Ultimately the form of a meeting is a public reaffirmation of the ideal social structure.

Town meetings are called, like sacred ritual, to avert potential crisis, when social dramas are likely to unfold, when the normal routines of everyday life do not provide ready solutions for decision making or action. Public meetings occur when there is a possibility of conflict either from internal or external sources, which involve all village members: e.g., a struggle between San Andres and a neighbor hamlet over the boundary of a new government land grant.

The format follows what Rosaldo (1968) has called *metaphors of hierarchy* in the context of religious ritual. These metaphors are embedded in each other, balanced, and displayed by the participants in several complementary juxtaposed codes: spatial, temporal, behavioral, kinesic, etc.

Public meetings take place in the *Cabildo* (government building). There is a main room, approximately 20x40 with the length in the East-West line. The south wall has two double doors, in the extreme quarters. There are no windows.

Starting the day before at sunset, the village policemen walk through the town blowing a conch which can be heard everywhere, crying the news of the approaching meeting. The day itself the announcement is made before men leave for their fields. Meetings are held after the men have had their evening meal, at sunset. All formalized social encounters start or are held at "charged" liminal times: sunrise or sunset. When the meeting opens the Church bells toll as for the opening of religious rituals.

In the Cabildo, participants are initially arranged in a standardized, predictable fashion. The village authorities sit at the eastern end, the hot ritual side of the new-born sun. The officers arrange themselves in a row, preordained by rank. Seniors sit to the south side (left) and juniors to the north side (right). The area in front is left open (the hearth of the meeting) to be used later by those who stand to make speeches. The western half of the room is filled with several rows of benches facing the officers. Here sit the household heads of the village, again, according to ceremonial rank etiquette. Older men who in the past held high office, heads of extended families, sit in the front near the east. Junior men, with little political experience, sit to the back, nearer the west wall or cold ritual side.

When the benches are filled they represent a hierarchical spatial map of the village households: the powerful in front, the junior in back. As men enter, the hierarchy is also expressed in bowing and releasing salutations which are also formal expressions of dominance behavior.

The bench rows signify categories of offership when the men have "passed through" in public service, but unlike the officers who are individually ranked, householders are category ranked. This, I believe, serves in its ambiguity to minimize possible conflicts of relative individual ranking between bench sharers.

There are variations in this arrangement. If men and women are both present, they segregate to the left and right of benches. If incipient politi-

129

cal factions rally beforehand about an issue, they may also segregate spatially. Factions are issue aroused an not permanent village features.

At the door of the Cabildo stand the policemen on duty, to prevent men too drunk to participate from entering the room, and ready to intervene in any visible growing disturbance. The town meetings often include "outsiders," who do not sit with the villagers, but in a "marked" space, on seats between the two south doors. Outsiders include a varied category of roles and persons: government inspectors, the local school teachers, Mexican merchants with some business requiring town approval, curious anthropologists, and so on. It may also include Cuicatec Indians from other towns. Outsiders are thus defined as anyone who is not an Indian and/or a permanent resident of the town. Outsiders, also, do not sit haphazardly but are guided by the policemen to sit in what the authorities (after consultation among themselves) consider a place of appropriate ranking. Hence, the outsiders also form a ladder of rank, superiors to the eastern end, inferiors, graded, towards the western end. Thus the seating orders three categories of roles, into equivalent metaphors of hierarchy as follows:

Category	Senior Rank +	Junior Rank —	Section of Room
officer	south, left (+)	north, right (—)	east (+)
householder	front, head (+)	back, feet (—)	west (—)
outsider	east (+), right (—)	west (—), left (+)	South wall (+ —)

These isomorphic metaphors of hierarchy are not identical in form, perhaps symbolizing the different role categories played by participants. However, there is a single opposition (difference) which separates insiders and outsiders. Insiders (officers and householders) arrange with seniors towards the east (+), the hot powerful ritual direction, and juniors to the west, cold, weak ritual direction. Outsiders appear to follow the same ordering. But there is a secret ceremonial "joke" involved; by seating outsiders against the south wall, facing the room, seniors are right while juniors are left, reversed from insiders. Since left is the hot side, the spatial symbols left (+) with west (—), right (—) with east (+) cancels the power of outsiders in the village communal context, neutralizes them as part of the hierarchy. Symbolically, outsiders are equated to $+ — = 0$! However, outsiders are recognized as potentially powerful. This locates them in the south (hot) rather than north (cold) wall.

After a meeting starts people may move about. They may come forward to the center section to speak. Here seniors stand in the center while juniors stand nearer the north wall. Outsiders also may manipulate and be manipulated by their seating and moving strategies. These changes are permissible manoeuvers, never meaningless, and some movements (like in chess), are absolutely not permitted except for errant dogs and naughty children. (For comparison, see Goffman, E., 1963, 1967). Moving, in fact, may be a form of voting in a non-verbal code.

Figure I: Seating Arrangement at the Cabildo

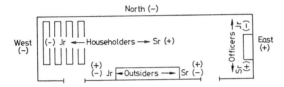

Similar spatial use follows for every Cabildo meeting involving officers and householders, although not all Cabildo affairs involve all household heads.

Hence, public performances created by situations of structural drama, create a symbolic normative spatial frame based on the overall hierarchy of village roles. The frame is predetermined by the rank of parties involved, as defined by the ideal Indian social structure. The metaphorical frame is highlighted in town meetings involving Mestizos, because the Indian view of the hierarchy of the total society is, as it were, undressed in public in explicit and implicit symbolic form.

Space is not the only code in which the social structure is displayed. Order and style of speaking is also preordained. Meetings are opened by the senior officer present, with a highly stereotypic discourse in a specialized verbal style. The discourse is an exhortation to those present to "think slowly and speak good words," i.e., keep a level head, maintain order, control feelings and contribute to a satisfactory resolution of the problem at hand. This style is similar to the speech patterns used by ritual specialists in opening prayers of ritual. The officer speaking, like the ritual specialist, adopts a position of humbleness, requesting that his simple words be "heard with kindness and received with good hearts." (For an illuminating discussion of Indian speech style, see Gossen, G., 1973).

The speech also states that officers would not decide on their own without consulting "the heart of the community." This text both ratifies the legitimacy of officers who are not "acting for their own benefit but

131

that of all," as well as establishes the need for creating community consensus.

After the opening formulae the actual topic of the meeting is publicly brought to the audience's attention. Then, other officers are allowed to speak to ask clarifications, offer helpful comments, etc., until it is clear that all participants have understood why they have been called to the Cabildo. The next speakers are persons occupying roles which are immediately involved in the topic of discussion. If Mestizo outsiders are present, these may speak first, because they are *visitas de categoria* (guests of honor). Finally, the villagers, up to this time a passive audience, are allowed to participate. Again, seniors speak first. The audience may use official speech style, but they can also use normal everyday style. Their choice is determined by their skill in handling formal speech. But in either case the speech usually opens with an apology for their "poor words" (lack of eloquence). This formula prevents those lacking in eloquence from being criticized and highlights the skill of those who "know how to speak."

The format is carried throughout the meeting. Even when issues are best handled by junior men, elders speak first if they wish. Upcoming young men with political aspirations may be in fact major protagonists in encounters and may be the ones whose opinions carry the day. But they could not succeed if they were unable to wait their turn, or use proper speech style. The ceremonial format is, in fact, a school of political style and successful strategy.

The pace of the discussion is also coded, and it occurs in "rounds" like a boxing match. The discussion of rounds is not presented in this summary because of space constraints. Let us just say that the round cycle includes (a) speech, (b) silence, (c) hushed discussion of audience, (d) murmers and comments from benches, (e) silence, (f) officer asks for new speaker (optional), (g) previous speaker sits, new speaker starts again at (a). A meeting may contain many rounds, lasting four or five hours. The tone varies with issues, but there is an overall development from formal to less formal back to formal in the end.

The closing is also a stereotypic discourse. The officer in charge says words to the effect that everyone should accept the decision because it is best and most popular, no one should maintain grudges or wish sickness on their opponents (an euphemism for witchcraft threats which may issue between "heated" opponents at the closing of the meeting), and that everyone should carry joy because the village has been served from the goodness of people's hearts. The closing words are so standardized that little boys playing Cabildo can imitate them quite accurately. After this, the meeting adjourns.

The actual flow and content of discussions, given this "ritualized" frame, is free. Beyond these requirements of common acceptance of community-wide conventions of respect, order, hierarchy and precedence, every man is unobstructed to express his opinion, present a point or argue a case. Just in the same fashion, a shaman's performance is stereotypic, but the content of prayers is adjusted to the needs of the patient being treated. There are variations in formality of public encounters, related to several factors: e.g., age of participants, nature of problem, etc. Meetings may last from a couple of rounds to more than thirty.

It is in meetings involving outsiders where the most formal frames occur. The greater the common threat, the more formalized the frame, the longer the preparatory speeches, the larger the number of rounds, the more obvious the hierarchization of interaction. However, although the opinions expressed may indicate great opposition to Mestizo demands and the meeting a major political confrontation, the form is polite, appeasing and deferential on the part of Indians.

The functions of the civil hierarchy as a defensive mechanism, which Wolf notices (1955, 1957) is never more obvious than when the village as a whole faces a common external danger. It is clear that these contrasts that patterned solemnity, ordered arrangement, restrictive prescriptions, in a word, ritualism, serves in a primary sense, both at the manifest and latent levels as a mechanism to neutralize and avert entropy as well as a school for normative action.

Ritualization may not, ultimately, cancel out individual idiosyncratic unpredictability, or group anarchy, nor in the final view can it control the effects which the Mexican state has on the internal affairs of its subordinate Indian populations. But in its immediacy as an ordering device, it makes the behaviors of others more predictable, and it functions to sustain the order which metaphorically it expresses. Rosaldo presents the view that in the village of Zinacantan "the main subject of ritual performed by members of the religious hierarchy is hierarchy itself expressed in the conventional code . . ." (1968:526). In San Andres, the subject of political ceremony varies with the occasion. Hierarchy is the form, not the content of interaction. This suggests to me that in Indian society in general, like in San Andres, religious rituals are models of shaped interaction, teaching the positioning of actors in a fixed hierarchy frame with a variant content. This frame to some extent determines behavior, and it seems that it is in ritual that the model of political interaction is learned. Like other rituals, it has an "exemplary, model displaying character" (Turner, V., 1969:117), or in Geertz' apt phrase, ritual is a "model of" and "model for" normative behavior (Geertz, C., 1966).

It seems that I am also arguing for a Freudian view of ceremonialism as a form of collective compulsion utilized to cope with social anxiety. This is not untrue. I believe that for Cuicatec Indians ceremonialism is a major coping device within a society which constantly suffers from uncertainty for survival, physical and social. Overpopulation, poor land, lack of health facilities, low technology and unpredictable weather, which cause unstable harvest yields and famine, everpresent interpresional conflict create sources of anxiety from within the system. Exploitation by Mexicans, political, economic and cultural demands which appear arbitrary, unjust and repressive from the Cuicatec point of view create sources of anxiety coming from without the Indian village. In this world of unpredictable danger, Cuicatecs agree with Malinowski, men need ceremonialism. It does provide as one of its latent functions a psychological shield.

However, there is more to ritualization than being an anxiety reducing device or a teaching technique. Because by creating predictable frames for social intercourse in situations of potential stress, ritual actually defuses the situations in which it enters. Hence, it is not simply a symbolic psychic device, but a social instrument, not just an expressive mechanism but a useful, goal-oriented instrumental frame; it is not simply a grammar but a message acted out in a complex action code.

4. *An Example of Confrontation: The Mestizo Teacher's Proposals*

Although there may be strong feelings swinging village opinion in one direction, the outcome of ceremonies of confrontation is not known until they have actually taken place. That is, the outcome is not certain.

On one occasion, the Mestizo town secretary brought to a town meeting the risky proposition that the village householders plant a communal corn field for five years, and utilize its profits to rebuild the church roof and towers which had fallen during an earthquake many years before. The project required interrupting the traditional *majordomía celebrations*, levying household taxes instead, and utilizing most profits towards the purchase of materials and labor rather than in the traditional consumption pattern of *fiestas*. In the beginning there was much opposition, but since this was a community task, which would bring pride in their village Church, the Indians, after much discussion, agreed. They made the Mestizo into Municipal President for the next period, so that he should be responsible for the management of funds and scheduling of labor, and this more than revolutionary change from traditional *Cargo Mayordomía* to collective public enterprise was made without major conflict.

Another time, however, the local Mestizo School Director proposed that twenty householders build cement floors in their houses, for a project of "community development." This project, innocuous as it sounds, was totally defeated, because "no one in the village is to work for the benefit of a few," that is, this project dealt with household rather than community affairs, and it was seen as irrelevant for a town meeting, threatening to village harmony and financially irresponsible. This was true even though the amount of money was minimal (the state supplied the cement at wholesale price) compared with the previous church project, which the Mestizo teacher had seen as the model for his proposal. He had confused, from the Indian point of view, communal and family or individualistic oriented tasks.

In the next type of ceremonies, however, the outcome is always known beforehand.

5. *Ceremonies of submission: The National Presidential Election*[8]

Village internal elections follow the format of political confrontations. Selections are made after elders and officers prepare a slate of candidates. A town meeting makes the final choices, considering (a) previous service of candidates, (b) skills for a particular job, (c) willingness te serve, (d) ability to serve in terms of health, income and so on.

Cuicatecs know that they have no voice in the selection of Mexican presidential candidates unlike the situation in internal municipal elections.[9] Here, as in other areas of Mexican-Indian relations, the neo-colonial position of Indians emerges clearly. National elections in San Andres are ceremonials of submission, in which Indians declare, symbolically and in general terms, their acceptance of Mestizos as superordinate political figures, and ultimately, the village's limited autonomy.

San Andreseños know that they have no national voice but that they are obligated to vote in national elections under the threat of incarceration if they do not do so (Comision Fed. Electoral, Chap. XII). Village officials may fine or actually jail a man who refuses to register, pay dues or vote. Actually, registration and voting are required by law, but dues are for optional party membership (*op. cit.* Chap. IV, Art. 52). But San Andreseños believe that they are also required to register and play dues to the PRI. They receive voter registration cards and party membership simultaneously. Both are seen as obligations like "paying municipal tax." This is encouraged by the local Mestizos who believe that by delivering the vote for the official party, some benefits may accrue to the community (e.g., building an all-weather road).

In fact, this may not be the case unless a special patron-client relation exists between a state or federal candidate and a village. The PRI tends to increase investments in areas where voters' support has been low, because voting percentages are seen as general indications of mass attitudes towards party policies. But investment policies are designed in broad terms to improve the gross national product. "The most developed, best capitalized states are the ones which receive larger amounts (of the federal budget) both in relative and absolute numbers" (Gonzales Casanova, 1965:39, translation mine). These are *not* states with high percentages of Indians. Oaxaca, in fact, has one of the lowest state budgets in the nation.

San Andreseños are also convinced that voting against the PRI may bring reprisals against the village, because "the PRI is the only party which gets elected." I was told of a village where "Federal troops were sent for punishment because they did not vote right." Whatever the truth, San Andreseños believe this is possible.

The formal frame of elections, according to Mexican law, is, however, disregarded. Many electoral law articles and constitutional regulations are broken, unknowingly. Most San Andreseños were not aware that their ceremonies of election are illegal.[10]

First, a special committee is selected, which is required by law (*op. cit.*, Chap. VI and VII). Its members must be able to read and write since they are in charge of preparing voters' registration cards, electoral lists, final voting ballots and all documents sent to the District Committees for counting. These men cannot be those in office. The law is designed with the intent of protecting citizens from undue pressure by local officials in their voting choices. San Andresños believe that not only Cabildo officers cannot serve, but that they cannot be physically present during elections. Village officers, it was consistently interpreted, " are the village." If they are absent, the town cannot be blamed, officially, for its voting record or for errors in the election procedure. If officers are "absent" the potential confrontation between village and state is avoided. Inrites of passage, often parents are replaced by ritual parents, and they abstain from being present. Gluckman (1956:130) has suggested that this device rechannels potential confrontation between adjacent generations. Thus it could be interpreted that the electoral committee stands in loco parentis for the village officers, that they are "the election's Godparents." It could also be interpreted that the officers themselves are in a liminal period of seculsion, since elections signify a period of separation leading to a change of status of political actors. Officers thus represent "government" in the abstract, in a separation phase. San Andreseños go much further than national legal requirements, because during elections the authorities close themselves up in the Cabildo, in darkness, like initiants in an isolation hut, and do not come out until elections are over. The only time we observed this event not only the Cabildo officers were hidden but also the officers of the Women's Church Sodality, which is the female branch of the ritual hierarchy. The Electoral Committee, to the contrary, places it-self outside, in full view, in the corridor of the village school, facing the town's plaza. As in other rituals of submission, sacred or secular, action occurs outdoors.

According to law voting polls open at eight and close at five. No one can vote without a registration card or vote for another person. In San Andres 10% of voters did not have cards, which had been lost or never received because there were not enough when they were issued. However, every one "voted" unanimously for the PRI. Second, officers appeared at 9:30 to arrange their papers and the booths did not open until eleven. Then, many persons left their credentials with a kinsman, in charge of all votes of his household. This was particularly true of women who, after appearing for roll call, left their ballots with their husbands and went home to cook the midday meal. The Indian norm that a kinsman can act for another occurs in other legal contexts (c.f. Hunt, E. and R. Hunt, 1969).

The election was marked like other rituals by the call of the village conch. Otherwise, much which takes place is unusual, as far as ceremonials go.

The mood is light, with villagers dressed in new clothing, bathed and combed, smiling to each other, standing in clusters in the village plaza waiting for their names to be called. This only visible structure of personnel is that men and women stand in separate clusters. When the whole village is congregated, the Municipal President appears briefly, and delivers with formality the ceremonial election paraphernalia: a rubber seal with the word "voted," a list of villagers of voting age, an ink well, several pencils, a bundle of ballots, an ink pad and an eraser to "correct improperly marked votes." These objects are treated like sacred paraphernalia, handled with respect, head bowing, with touching and releasing gestures. The most significant object required by law, the ballot box (*ánfora*), is totally missing. In Mexico the vote is legally secret, and there is a complicated procedure to insure that the ballot box is sealed before votes are deposited, opened to determine that it is empty, sealed again while voting takes place, and reopened with formality, by the committee, to count the votes deposited. Elections in San Andres, however, take place in full view of everyone, there is no ánfora, ballots are not secret, and there is no attempt to insure either voter's privacy or secrecy.

After delivering the paraphernalia, the President withdraws to the inside of the Cabildo to join the other officers. Until elections are over they stay inside, in the dark, sitting quietly.

The ceremony opens with a roll call to determine how many villagers are present. The whole event is highly informal as if an effort is made to

137

eradicate hierarchy distinctions. No one bows to elders, people move rapidly around, making casual remarks, joking, pushing each other around, crowding to see the voting table. As one informant put it: "this day we are all equals."

The next step is to mark and register votes and give them to a Committee member who folds it and checks it in the master list. Pencils are passed around. Everyone is supposed to mark his vote with an X "over the Mexican flag," i.e., to vote a straight party ticket. The Mexican parties are recognized by colored seals, so that illiterate persons can vote by "color." The PRI has the colors of the flag, inverted, up and down. This inversion is necessary since no party can use the flag itself. But one is tempted to interpret this inversion as part of a larger set of symbolic distortions and inversions. While usually gatherings are arranged by hierarchy of age and office, here committee officers tend to be young and unimportant, are not ranked by age, and the audience acts en masse. National elections are an expression of village *communitas*, of the erasing of the normative social structure. Electoral law requirements are either ignored or exaggerated. Moreover, they are elaborated in symbolism beyond the Mexican law but according to Indian rationales.

In usual spatial symbolism men and women stand left and right of each other, and officers (or other ritual mediators) in the east from south to north in rank. On election day the committee stood facing south, outside instead of inside, and women rather than men stood on the left side. I was not able to determine if this symbolic inversion of sex positions was conscious or accidental. Given San Andreseños' usual concern with symbolic expression of behavior, I suspect it was not accidental.

Again, unlike the situation in the traditional ordering, voters were called alphabetically rather than by age rank. This procedure does not reoccur except in school attendance calling. Moreover, while in rituals there is always a mediating figure or figures of authority present (shaman, mayordomo, civil officers) they were absent here. Finally, Mestizo and Indians act in this occasion in an unusually friendly casual manner towards each other. One of the officers of the committee was a young Mestizo. The school director who in section (4) of this paper is the villain of the piece, was happily going around helping people mark votes, and the anthropologist was offered the opportunity to vote "as a guest of the town" even though she is a foreigner. Villagers were in fact somewhat offended that I considered it improper to vote, while they would have been quite angry if I would have intervened in village internal affairs.

There are several ways of interpreting the shape of national elections in San Andres. First, there is the very secular threat of being jailed if they do not vote. This insures participation even though the procedure could be considered a meaningless legal act. Second, the ceremony has been elaborated in such a way that it serves to make a distinction between internal affairs ceremonials and those external or Mestizo originated and controlled. What makes presidential elections meaningless using national criteria, makes them meaningful at the level of the Indian corporate action. Third, some of the ritual aspects suggests that elections are perceived as liminal times of collective danger, and that the ceremonial is designed to act out submission and thus avert danger.

The very liminal position of officers, who embody the notion of hierarchy and normative structuring of the political level, their being absent, enclosed, in darkness, suggests the position of certain roles in passage rituals and other liminal times. Fourth, the disappearance of structural cleavages suggests that villagers are not acting out in the roles of persons, but in unison, as undifferentiated members of the corporation. The encounter is between the community as a whole, all distinctions momentarily erased, and the state, represented by the Mestizo government machine. Unlike ceremonies of confrontation, when hierarchy is acted out in full detail, here hierarchization is avoided or inverted. Finally, choice, bargaining, and balancing of power is not worked out in a dramatic frame. Instead, there is a preordained, predictable outcome. Villagers vote unanimously accepting the political order which dominates the country, in an inevitable, submissive manner. This itself is formalized: the Indian village yields automatically to the superior power of the Mestizo state.

Some contrasts between the town meeting and the election appear in the chart below. Many of these attributes also apply to other rituals of confrontation and submission.

Variable	Confrontation Ceremony	Submission Ceremony
Location	Inside	Outside
Time	Sunset	Midday
Mediators	Officers, senior men always present	Committee, juniormen officers sequested
Bargaining and choice	Yes	No
Conflict expressed	Yes	No
Participants' behavior	Hierarchic	Non-hierarchic
Alchohol consumed as part of ritual	Yes	Forbidden
Sacred symbolism (hot-cold, right-left, etc.)	Same as standard ritual performance	Absent or reversed

6. *The sacred Dimension of Mestizo-Indian Interaction*

"Ideas about the relations between supernatural agencies and human beings or about the potency of particular ritual behaviors are modelled on first-hand experience of real life relationships between human beings. But conversely, every act by which one individual asserts his authority to curb or alter the behavior of another individual is an invocation of metaphysical force. The submissive response is an ideological reaction . . ." (Leach, E., 1969:526).

One of the dramatic contrasts between ceremonials of confrontation and submission is the presence of hierarchy in one and its absence in the other. However, in both types of encounters there is an underlying acceptance of the dominant role of Mestizos. Although the content of some interactions shows that Indians may be willing to oppose Mestizos in internal political issues, the form is always one of subordination, always maintaining extreme positions of respect, deference, politeness vis-a-vis them. In fact, Indian-Mestizo face-to-face interactions are marked by submissive symbolic behavior from Indians, even in private domains. When Indians enter a Mestizo home or store they always hold their hat in hand, bow their head down, speak softly and deferentially look at the floor. Mestizos of any age are spoken to in submissive tones and vocabulary. They are often addressed as *patrón*, and always with the honorific Don or Doña, even if much younger than the Indian speaker. Mestizos instead speak at best with a paternalistic style, as if addressing a child, or in high voice as if addressing a feeble-minded or deaf person, and at worst act purposefully rude and with threatening voice and gesture. Sitting, standing, moving in public spaces (e.g., market) or private domains (e.g., inside a house patio), using objects of material culture are also ridden with symbols of Indian deference. One could argue that such deference is simply the outcome of a healthy understanding of the ultimate ability of Mestizos to utilize the power of their side in any issue. This is obviously true. But beside this secular explanation lies a set of sacred ones.

As already indicated, Cuicatec political ceremonials have a sacred symbolic ideology behind them. The use of time and space, for example, corresponds with basic Cuicatec notions of the sacred space-time continuum. Association of heat, direction, and power follow from sacred orderings. The links of left with south and east, hot and political power correspond also to the ones in ritual and supernatural domains. The village Church is on the south side of the plaza, the Cabildo on the north, fitting the total symbolic arrangement of village sacred features (water holes, crosses, magic roads, etc.). The Church altar is on the Eastern side. When icons used in ritual are manipulated to reenact myths, positive figures are placed left and east/south, negative figures north/west, right. In the Nativity rituals, the "insider," white baby Jesus is placed in the East altar, the "outsider" black baby anti-Jesus is buried under a tree, outside, in a straight line west of the patio of the Church. Inside the Church, women stand right of the nave, men left. North and west represent the dry, dark season, south and east the region and time of light, the wet season. Of the year's ritual moieties the wet is male, the dry female. The placing of persons in Cabildo rituals follows this arrangement consistently, so that Senior : junior :: male : female :: east/south : north/west :: left : right:: summer : winter :: divine : secular :: powerful(hot) : west(cold) :: Church : Cabildo :: Officers : householders.

In the supernatural world, a world of the powerful, the Gods, ancestors and spirits, the "streets are on the left." But the real order of Cuicatec society includes Mestizos as well as Indians, occupying a higher economic, political and social position. This is also built into the Cuicatec pantheon, that is, into the divine given order of society.

The pantheon is a complex transformational system. There are many Gods, of four types: Fire, Water, Earth and Air. The first three types represent the ideal social order. The last, air, represents anti-structure-social disorder, communitas (Air are Gods representing social and sexual licence, inversion, witchcraft and so on). The first three types are arranged in a civil hierarchy, a Government of the Cosmos, in imitation of human society. The top God is *Cheve*, Buyer, Creator and Destroyer of souls. He is a rancher, a rich elder Mestizo. He is also a merchant, and other occupations only exercised by Mestizos. Unlike the other Gods who are rural, "peasant like" (*tocho*: uncouth, of the earth, rustic), he lives and rules an underworld supernatural city, in the center of the divine cosmos. This city is modeled on the experiential knowledge of Mestizo urban centers. Like Mestizos, who are powerful, arbitrary, unpredictable, amoral and the opposite of the common Indian man, so is Cheve. But like Mestizos he also created and rules the social order at the divine level.

The next sets of Gods, Water, and Earth, represent married Indian adults. One pair, water, are rich Indians, a senior officer couple who rules over shamanism. The next pair, earth, is a junior officer couple, poorer, plain peasants and shepherd. Below these are a large group of deities of water and earth, divided into those of adolescent age and unmarried, and those who are child age. Their occupations are delegated by parental deities. But the deities are not only arranged by sex, age, kin ties and division of labor. They are also assigned positions in a territorial government hierarchy. Cheve is a President who rules Mexico. Water and Earth God couples are officers who rule the Cuicatec District; adolescent Gods are policemen and children deities, like real children, do not have posts, but locate themselves in the domestic realm, in small places. Moreover, of the Air Gods, one occupies the post of *Secretario*, which belongs in the non-hierarchic set of Gods because in real Cuicatec villages Secretarios are posts outside the civil religious hierarchy.

Figure II: Abbreviated Chart of the Divine Social Hierarchy

Male Deity's Name	(Creator) Čeve	(Lightning) Dabe	(Earth Lord) Sa?iku	(Charmer) Enkanto	(Goblin) Čaneke
Element	Fire	Water	Earth	Water|Earth	Water|Earth
Ethnic Group	Mestizo	← Rich → ← Poor → ← Indian			→
Occupation	Store Owner -Rancher	Shaman, Rain maker	Farmers and other Indian occupations (weaver, shepherd)		
Age	Eldest	Sr. adult	Jr. adult	adolescent	child
Marital Status		married		unmarried	
Position in "government hierarchy"	"President"	Sr. Officers	Jr. Officers	Policemen	none
Territory They Supervise	Mexico, The World Centre,	The Cuicatec District		Villages	Domestic Realm
Direction	up/down axis of Universe	The four directions of earth surface		Specific Village Locations	Any small location

Hence, as Mestizos rule over Indians, Cheve, the Mestizo God, rules over the other Gods, from his Capital city. He is the idealized Mestizo, they the abstracted Indian categories of political persons. This imagery not only pictures the real social order in simple Durkheimian terms, but it also declares it normative, eternal, divine. As in political rituals, Indians ultimately define themselves at the supernatural level as uniformly inferior, subordinate and obedient to Mestizos. The pantheon provides the eternal measure of social order, and Indians have opted for a sacred idealization of their own subordinate human condition.

Cuicatecs not only believe the social order to be God given, they also believe that if they break the normative regulations of appropriate interaction with superiors they will be supernaturally punished with illness. Persons deviating become ill, villages deviating suffer epidemics. As Mestizos may retaliate in real life, Cheve and his assistants retaliate at the supernatural level. Mestizos do not need even to act. The Cuicatec Gods take care their interests are protected!

The Cuicatec would have made a good case for Marx's view of religion as the opium of the masses (Marx, K., 1956 edition:27). It is possible to argue that changes in the social order must come from exogenous secular forces outside the ideology. But in terms of the topic of this paper we are left with a major question: Are truly secular rituals possible? Is there such a thing as a-theistic symbolism?

My position is that discovered by Durkheim long ago. Societies tend to imagine themselves as projected into the divine cosmic landscape. Or said in less mystical language, the men in a society imagine their collective condition as natural, immanent condition of the universe, of divine origin.

Insofar as societies tend to deify, sacralize and idealize their own social condition as the condition of the cosmic order, secular rituals would always be tinged with sacred aspects, with deeply buried divine symbolism, with norms which originate in the religious experience, as well as the social experience of life. If this is the case, it may not be possible to speak of purely religious ritual or of purely secular ceremonial. (This is one of the reasons why throughout this paper I have at times used the terms synonymously.) It may be the case that the ethnographic roster many show either (a) a continuum of behaviors from most to least secularized, or (b) a separation of secular or ritual action which can be made exclusively in analytic operational terms, but which has little meaning for the members of the society. Secular and sacred may not be different behaviors but different analytic aspects of the same behaviors. It may even be the case, that in all societies, historically, the secular order models and shapes the sacred order, and that, in a contiguous systemic feed-back loop, the sacred order models the secular collective behavior. Only the future historical emergence of a non-theistic, totally secular society, may create a phenomenon we can call, exclusively, secular ritual. Not even industrial society seems to have achieved this type, as every American who pledges simultaneously allegiance to Flag and Country under one God can testify. Whenever the supernatural hides behind the rationalization of behavior, we cannot truly speak of secularity.

7. Conclusion

This paper has been an exploration of political ceremonialism in the relations between Indians and Mestizos in a rural District of Oaxaca, Mexico.

The evidence presented suggests a series of generalizations which may be applicable to other ethnographic cases. Interpretation of the Cuicatec Indians' ritualism is based on an eclectic theory of meaning in behavior. The analysis suggests that:

1. Ritualism tends to appear in situations where there is opposition, structured social antagonism or potential conflict between structurally defined segments of the society, in the case at hand, that between (a) different persons, roles or groups in the hierarchical structure of political roles among Indians, and (b) different potentially antagonistic ethnic segments of a plural or dual society. For the same reasons it operates in Indian society in curing rituals involving conflict in the domestic realm, encounters between potential affines, etc.

2. Ritualism tends to appear where there are no dynamic structural outlets for the open expression of conflict, that is, when social relations cannot be restructured by open battle, and where the possibility of social revolution, rather than balanced rebellion, is not forthcoming. In a sense, behaviors are formalized when potential hostility is accompanied by the impossibility of breaking relations or interactions permanently, or of permanently changing their power balances. Gluckman, M. (1956) as well as our Mexican data support this view.

3. In these situations, ritualism provides a safe outlet for the expression of potential conflict, as well as a restrictive frame in which the potential anomie or entropy is under control.

4. Simultaneously, ceremonialism acts as (a) a defense mechanism in the psychological sense (by reducing the anxiety about outcomes among participants), (b) a neutral behavior frame in which hostilities can be acted out and still remain under social control, and (c) a maintenance mechanism, in Parsons' (1966) sense of the term, of the structural status quo. This latter function is possible because rituals and ceremonies serve as *models for* normative behavior, *codes of* legitimate conduct and examples of guiding strategies of interaction.

5. Formalization of behavior is more likely to occur when uncertain, potentially dangerous outcomes may emerge from social encounters. Ritualism is, in this sense, a mechanism for rechannelling potential crisis situations.

6. The formalization of behavior is framed in complex, multivocal symbol systems characteristic of a culture. These symbol systems determine the use of space, time, language style, the presentation of the self, body movement, and the definition of the relations between actors and actor-situation.

7. The major elements or dominant symbols which occur in ritualized behavior tend to be congruent, within a culture, from one actor-situation

to another, and they form sets of transformations, coherently structured. It is this highly predictable, rigidly stylized pattern of symbols underlying normative behavior which defines the behavior as ritualized rather than informal.

8. The symbols of secular rituals, like those of religious rituals are multivocal, logically structured, transformational and arranged in sets built of dyadic opposition.

9. Ultimately ritualism serves to preserve the social order which, metonymically and metaphorically, it expresses, by becoming an instrument which defuses the dramatic situations in which it enters. Ritual is thus not only an expressive grammar but a vital process, a message acted in a complex, symbolic action code.

10. Among Cuicatec Indians political ceremonials follow patterns dictated by religious rituals and creeds and their structured symbolism is isomorphic with that of Church rituals.

11. Inasmuch as all societies perceive the contemporary social order as given, eternal and unchangeable, and project it into the divine order of the cosmos, secular and sacred are aspects of action rather than different behaviors. The degree to which secular ceremonialism and religious rituals can be separated may be, hence, a function of the emphasis which a particular society places on the belief that there is a divine-given order of its social organization.

NOTES

1 The data for this discussion comes from the field work of myself and my husband in several field work seasons. This field work was done primarily in four Municipalities of the District of Cuicatlan, in the state of Oaxaca. Three of these communities, Santa María Tlalixtac, and Concepción Pálalo are Indian communities of Cuicatec speakers. The last, San Juan Cuicatlan, is a mestizo community with a marginal migrant Indian population (10 percent of the total number of inhabitants). Cuicatlán is also the District Capital. The case studies utilized in the discussion both come from observations made in San Andres in 1964. Much work done outside the Cuicatec, among Maya, Mixtec and other Indians by myself and others also forms the background of this analysis. I am grateful to the University of Chicago Chiapas Project, The National Institute of Anthropology of Mexico and the National Science Foundation (Grants GS-3000 and GS-87) for financial support of field work.

2 San Andres is a village of 1014 inhabitants, all speakers of Cuicatec. Only 49% of the villagers are bilingual in Spanish. Of these only 115 were literate, and 62 of these male. Less than 50 were barely old enough to be elected to office (above 17 years) according to the law, and even a smaller number were eligible according to San Andres home rule that a man must be married with children and head of his household to take positions in the civil hierarchy.

The village is organized into (approximately) 30 localized ambilineal descent groups, residing in 186 occupied houses. There are also two Mestizo extended families (six households) who are quite influential in village affairs, being major sources of credit and employment, serving as Secretarios, running the two village stores, and so on. These two families were instrumental in changing the Mayordomía system, in 1955, into a modified system of public financing by taxes levied on households. The head of one of these Mestizo families functions as a benevolent *cacique* (political boss), serving as major political broker between the village and the state. His position is informal, and has been held since the nineteen-twenties when a village delegation asked him to move into the town to serve as Secretario.

San Andres is the capital of a Municipality containing several hamlets. The municipal population is 3417 persons. All but eight persons are subsistence corn peasants with a marginal cash crop of coffee. The eight persons with other occupations are all Mestizo and include a nurse, three school teachers, two ranch owners and store owners, a mason and a town Secretario. The village is "relatively acculturated," but there is no electricity, potable water or all-weather roads near by. People still use the traditional costumes with women wearing huipiles made in a waist loom. Houses are mud huts with straw or palm roofs, and except for the Cabildo house, a massive colonial Dominican Church and two Mestizo homes, there are no brick or adobe buildings.

³ Neither does it mean race although the word *raza* in Spanish is sometimes used (Wagley, C., 1959; Pitt-Rivers, J., 1965). The vocabulary of ethnicity is extensive. Indians often call Mestizos *gente de razón* (rational men) while they call themselves *naturales* (natives). Mestizos use the words *indio, indigena, natural, indito, or tribu* withe moore or less contemptuous or patronizing effect. But the two groups may be distinguished by calling the Indians *peones* (peons, workers) *montañeros* (people of the mountains), *gente cerrada* (closed up people), *los pobres compecinos* (poor peasants) and so on, while Mestizos are *gente de categoria* (people of high category) *los educados* (educated people), *los mas blancos* (the whiter ones), and so on, mixing terminologies of class, prestige, color, position in the system of production, education, level, etc. In any of these taxonomies, the implication is always that Indians are inferior.

⁴ *Cargo* (Spanish: burden) refers to the ritual and financial burden of the officers who take turns in carrying out public rituals. It should not be confused with the cargo cults of the Pacific. In Indian villages, the religious aspect of officership looms large. San Añndresenos like other Indians cling with tenacity to their traditional religion, a highly syncretic version of prehispanic polytheism and Roman Catholicism (c.f. Madsen, W., 1967; Mendelson, E. M., 1967). The form is to some extent Catholic. The content is mostly Indian. Much adult activity outside of the domestic routines deals with ritual performances. There are two major forms: (a) public rituals (cargo) dealing with cyclic calendric, corporate, universal aspects of community welfare (e.g., asking for rain for crops), and (b) private rituals performed by shamans dealing with sporadic, domestic, family controlled, affairs of the well being of domestic groups (e.g., curing the sick, advice through divination, etc.)

Public and private religious rituals also serve as complex symbolic mechnisms for modeling the social order. They determine agricultural and other schedules on the basis of a calendar adapted to the Roman Catholic calendar but much more ancient in origin. They allocate the households of the village in a complex hierarchy of rank according to service in the ritual officerships. They define mental, physical and moral health. Finally, they serve in Geertz' apt phrase as "models *of* and models *for*" the ideal, normative behavior which San Andreseños adhere to (Geertz,

C. 1966). All other domains of action, from serving a meal or indicating respect or deference, to political behavior in public meetings, are modelled on the symbolic pattern of religious rituals.

[5] Public financing of the Mayordomía has created a separation between the civil and the religious branches of the hierarchy. The Mayordomos continue to have great importance in the carrying on of successful cargo rituals. But the monies are collected by a committe (Junta) especially selected for the *fiesta*. The Junta posts have enlarged the number of positions in the civil administration of the town, but do not count in the hierarchy for advancement to higher posts. Moreover, the religious Mayordomias no longer serve to redistribute income within the village, which was one of its major latent functions.

[6] Although Mexicans are fond of pointing out that Juarez, one of the national hero-presidents was an Indian, in the normal flow of events Indians do not actively move up into the political realms of national life, and those few who did, like Juarez, were "ethnic migrants."

[7] The Revolution of 1910 produced a fundamental reorganization of leftover colonial institutions including economy, politics and the class structure, and, simultaneously the ethnic outlooks of the national elites.

[8] Given the fact that national elections for president are rare occurrences, the following section is based primarily on one single field observation. Numerous conversations with other Mexican anthropologists have led me to believe that this case is not exceptional. It is possible, however, that the ethnographic particulars vary not only with other Mexican Indian communities but even within the Cuicatec district.

[9] The complex process by which national political figures emerge has been extensively explored in the political science literature dealing with Mexican elections. (Padgett, L. V., 1966 is, perhaps, the best account.)

[10] There are so many articles of the electoral law broken during this event, that it would be hard to list them all. Some of the major ones, which would legally invalidate the election, were Chapter V, article 62; Chapter VI, article 77; Chapter VII, Section II, articles 84, 88; Chapter IX, article 121; Chapter XI, article 135, 136; Chapter XII, articles 140, 146.

Humorously enough, the next week one of the major daily papers carried the headlines: "Mexico has accomplished the most brilliant of its journeys: An exemplary election."

PART 3

GROUP ASSEMBLIES

CHAPTER VIII
POLITICAL MEETINGS
AND THE SIMULATION OF UNANIMITY:
KILIMANJARO 1973

Sally Falk Moore

More and more often today, not only religious, but secular collective occasions come within the purview of anthropological observation (see Richards and Kuper, 1971). Are the conventional frameworks used in the
description and analysis of religious ritual helpful in the study of secular
collective occasions? Indeed, are they always adequate to the study of religious ritual itself?

Collective ceremonies are matters to be explained. A staple of every
field diary, they are ways into a complex of information (Turner,
1968:2). A ceremony is ethnographic evidence, but of what? The number
of meanings, explicit and implied is immense, requiring at the very least
what Geertz calls "thick description" to get at the layers of significance
(1973:3). But how far in the direction of a full ethnography does one
have to go to provide a sufficient context for interpretation?

That, obviously depends on one's purpose. This paper presents a selective account of a citizens' political meeting in Tanzania in 1973,[1] emphasizing the ways in which the meeting embodied and elicited apparent consensus. Some allusion to the ethnographic background is essential to understanding the inexplicit local significance of the occasion, but for reasons of space these will be brief. The focus of the present account is on
the ritual-like elements in the meeting itself. The meeting is taken as a
type, as this kind of gathering was a regular occurrence at the time in
many Tanzanian communities. No attention will be given to the ways in
which the particular occasion was used for the strategic purposes of individuals.

Why call such a meeting a "secular ritual?" Because the analogy to a
religious rite draws attention to the general symbolic and doctrinal representations made in the course of business. It keeps the analytic focus from
being entirely on the practical purposes listed on the agenda. Traditional
religious symbols have the weight of time, repetition and ideological legitimacy behind them. The ideas, forms and formalisms of a new socialist
government are by definition straight off the planners' typewriters. But
these socialist ideas, symbols and forms of organization have been pro-

mulgated with the expectation that they will become permanent. A "tradition" is being initiated, a doctrine represented. The ward meeting on Kilimanjaro can be analysed partly as a celebration and propagation of these new doctrines, partly as a means of attending to certain local public business. It lies on the boundary between mundane-practical-technical activities and special occasion-ceremonial-representational activities and mixes the two modes throughout.

Connected with both ceremonial and practical aspects is the appearance of unanimous support for the leadership which the form of the ward meeting elicited. The way in which consensus was achieved made the citizenry in to what I call "ratifying body public." In many parts of the world in societies of varied political type (including our own) there exist corporate organizations in which it is ideologically anathema for the leadership openly to dictate to the followership, and in which the leadership has no right to act independently on behalf of the organization. In these settings a popular mandate of some sort must be obtained, however *pro forma* the manner of its realization. The analytic interest of *ratifying bodies public* is that they constitute a common, garden variety of group political behavior, *not* that they are in any way special to Tanzania. In fact, it is often asserted that unanimous decisions by consensus were once characteristic of pre-industrial societies. Yet it is less often acknowledged that apparent unanimity can be a matter of style and form, rather than substance. Public unanimity regularly achieved may mean either that disagreements have been worked out and bargains struck behind the scenes, or that for some other reason the public occasion is understood not to be the proper forum for the expression of serious stubborn conflict (Bailey 1965:1-20; 1969:148). There is no doubt that many of Tanzania's high level ideologues genuinely wish to provide a format for public discussion and popular participation in self-government. But the permissible parameters of political action on the lowest levels of organization are fairly specific, and on the ground, other men are in charge.

The uses of citizens' meetings as a vehicle for the celebration of new political doctrines and its symbols has been noted. But the repetitious elements in the rhetoric and the procedure may serve other purposes as well. Political meetings fall within a type of secular collective occasion common in modern societies: proceedings which are set up specifically to effect situational transformations. Some of these are: judicial procedures, negotiations, elections, as well as the meetings of decision-making bodies. All of these have explicit practical purposes. But all frequently are elaborated with what seem to be digressions, formulae and formalisms. These appear ancillary to the declared purpose, conventions or diversions which "surround" it, having no direct cause and effect relation to the stated ends, seeming arbitrarily or indirectly attached to them. Why is the "business at hand," the practical part of the activity, so often interwoven with seemingly gratuitous rhetorical ceremonial and formulaic elaboration?

One can only guess at the meanings imbedded in this. Formal, collective, choice-making institutions publicly acknowledge the control of men over social affairs, and the control of some men over others. These are, in many settings, perilous things to acknowledge. Formalities and formulae are effective ways to organize, mark and order these events, and in their symbolic content may serve as reminders of the constraints of the larger social/cultural milieu. This being so, much public formality and ceremonial invites interpretation as a dramatization of order.

It makes sociological sense that symbols of social order should be presented and particularly stressed on those very occasions when situational changes actually are being consciously enacted. The elaborate formalities and formulae of some courtrooms and meetings could be described as the magical aspect of a rational activity. Formality in such contexts can convey the message that certain things are socially *unquestionable* (the secular equivalent of the sacred) and by so declaring in such a form, formality helps to make them unquestionable. The public making of choices implies a certain situational uncertainty, a degree of indeterminacy and openness in the social reality (Moore, 1975). Institutionalizing the settings in which choices are made, and formalizing them decreases the amount of openness. It "domesticates" the indeterminate elements in the occasion by surrounding them with fixed forms. Some of the orderliness is undoubtedly a practical necessity, a consequence of the fact that if it plans to get anything done, a large group of people getting together needs to be organized in some orderly way. But the formality may go far beyond any organizational requirement. Formality and repetition can help to define and confine an immediate situation, to keep it within bounds. They can limit the range of improvisation within a particular staged event.

If that event is a political meeting of citizens that is supposed to propose development projects, in a country ideologically committed to popular participation in government, the ways in which the limits of choice are communicated are as interesting and important as the exhortations to action. A new government, like that of Tanzania, which undertakes to radically remake its society into a socialist state, not only introduces many specific organizational and economic reforms, it also produces synthesizing symbols and explanations of them which it tries to put quickly into circulation. Public meetings are among the principal vehicles that carry the new political faith far into the countryside. On Kilimanjaro, for the Chagga people, these innovations are introduced into an ongoing scene, an established way of life. For the Chagga, in 1973, their own history, customs and recent experience dominated their particular version of the new socialism. TANU (Tanzania's one political party, the Tanzanian African National Union) and local government meetings are intended to present to the citizens the ideals of socialism, the plans of the leadership, and to provide an opportunity for democratic participation in government. The Party/Government is supposed to be the universal forum in which peasants and workers *learn about* and also *take part in* the building and management of the new society.

Significant for those local people who participate in it, a ward meeting thus is also a part of large scale events. An important element in the background meaning of any particular convocation is the regular holding of similar self-government meetings in all the wards of the nation. The ward meeting exists, among other things, to connect separate domains. Just as religious sacrifice connects the discrete worlds of men and gods, and is an attempt to establish contiguity through the act of sacrifice (Lévi-Strauss, 1966:227) so the Party or ward meeting similarly is an act that establishes contiguity. It puts the village in touch with that unseen and unseeable entity, the state. It does so partly through the presence of leaders who have contact with the next steps up in the Party hierarchy. It also makes connections through the standardized statements that are made, through ideologically prescribed words and categories and concepts used and through the uniform organizational apparatus shared with other political units throughout the country. The local political meeting is in its way (and due in part to its form) more than a local event, and more than a momentary incident. It is one of a long series of parallel occurrences that constitute the base of the national political edifice.

Tanzania, independent since 1961, is a tiny country (population roughly 12,000,00) and is largerly rural – agricultural. Her people belong to many dozens of different tribes. The ethnic heterogeneity of the country is compounded by urban-rural differences, and economic, educational and religious differences. In such a setting 'nation-building' is a formidable problem.

There is another difficulty that afflicts Tanzanian politics. There is an inherent contradiction between the idea of a country run from the grass roots by a party of peasants and workers, and a country which has a small educated élite which in fact makes the most important policy decisions (Cliffe: 1971-72:275). In a way the political meeting of farmers in a rural area embodies this contradiction. It sustains the legitimizing appearance of participation. Meanwhile it also serves as a platform for publicizing the latest campaigns and directives emanating from central agencies.

On Kilimanjaro, the Chagga population is at least 350,000. In 1973 the Chagga lived, as they had since precolonial times, on permanently cultivated plots of land, normally given to them individually by their fathers. Many Chagga still live in localized patrilineal clusters with strong internal ties. A localized network of lineage-kin and neighbors exchanges labor internally, gives other forms of mutual aid, and celebrates together all the major moments of the life cycle. Nowadays some land rights are bought and sold, and sometimes land has been distributed by the government, but ordinarily land is still acquired through patrilineal kinship. The Chagga long have been half-way into a cash economy, as they grow coffee as well as subsistence foods. Many are literate. Most are Christian. Every sizeable lineage has one or another educated member who has a salaried job, some working nearby, some in the cities.

The Chagga like it very much that Africans are now ruled by Africans. But as might be expected, not all government measures are equally well received. The government has taken the view that as the Chagga are in a better economic and educational position than many of the other people of Tanzania, they must make way for the development of the more backward peoples, and contribute toward it, rather than continuing to leap further and further ahead themselves. Some Chagga perceive this as a form of discrimination against them, particularly with respect to student places in the secondary school system.

In 1973 independence had touched all rural Chagga, but had reorganized their local social relations very little. To be sure, some individuals such as Chiefs, who were prominent in the pre-independence period were ousted from office and new offices had come into being. There was a general administrative reorganization. 'Chiefdoms' became 'villages' and later each village was divided into two 'wards'. Ten-house cells were organized.[2] But except for the consequence to the office holders themselves, these were not deep changes. Private property in land had been abolished, but traditional individual rights to *use* land continued, so the same people occupied the same coffee gardens as did before independence. The patrilineal clusters and neighborhood ties persisted.

The meeting to be described here was to take place out-of-doors on a large open grassy space in front of a coffee-weighing and storage warehouse that belonged to the coffee cooperative. It was to start at nine and about a thousand people ought to have attended, but nothing began until eleven by which time about 55 men had assembled. The warehouse had a veranda on which the paid local party leaders sat on chairs. Everyone else sat on the ground wherever there was a spot of shade, or a wall to lean on. It was a sunny day, and hot.

In theory, at least, all the adults who reside and work in this part of the ward were obligated to come to the meeting, all who were neither ill, nor looking after small children, nor in some indispensable form of work,[3]

155

such as the manning of the dispensary. It was a meeting for all citizens of the ward which contains at least 1000 households. There are thus at least 2500 adults and at least 100 ten-house leaders in the area. The meeting had been well publicized and it seems probable that everyone was well aware that it was taking place. It was called on a Monday, the day on which everyone is supposed to contribute his full time (unpaid) for public works. On this particular Monday, all labor obligations had been called off to free people to attend the mass meeting. I had first heard the announcement the previous day at a church service attended by about seven hundred people. A 'town crier' also went up and down the paths among the farms of the subvillages blowing a *kudu* horn on the day itself announcing the ward meeting. There was no question but that most everyone knew about it.

Not surprisingly, the first men to have turned up were the paid party officials. Later others arrived, and eventually after a two hour wait, some of the leaders began to grumble and urged the Chairman to begin. All local meetings of any kind start late, except for church services, and the nine o'clock time stated as the time of convening the ward meeting was taken as a figure of speech, meaning, 'in the late morning.' Eventually, some time after the meeting of the original 55 men was in session, about 30 more straggled in, one at a time, bringing the total attendance to about 85. The context of such overwhelming absence from the meeting is as important to interpreting its meaning as what took place.

Looking around at the Chagga farmers sitting on the grass at the meeting it is evident that they are poor by any urban standards, but well off compared with many other tribes. Many of their clothes are the castoffs and stolen clothes of city men that find their way into the country markets. There are also tailors on the mountain who make clothes, and the more dapper, salaried young men are seen in their tailor-made suits on Sundays. Work clothes are worn and patched and muddy and of a marvellous variety of sizes and shapes and colors and styles. One old man wore a huge ancient khaki army overcoat, stained and torn, over his dun-colored ragged cotton shirt and trousers. He carried a cane like any Edwardian British gentleman, and bore himself with the immense dignity of the respected elder he was, his bare feet no incongruity. A prosperous butcher wore a black tail coat with satin lapels, a maroon T-shirt and dark work trousers, a red fez on his head. In fact, the numbers of kinds of hats one sees at such a gathering is a surprise and a delight. Some, like the butcher, wear the tarboosh, others wear knitted hats with pompoms in wild stripes and patterns. Some old men wear felt hats with brims, oily with age. Leather, plastic or wool caps with visors are seen on other heads. Still other men wear the embroidered pill-box hats of the Moslems of the Coast, though they are not Moslems, but Christians, most of them. Here and there one sees hats that are relics of discarded uniforms; a stiff-visored officer's cap, darkened with vintage sweat; a battered campaign hat with leather binding, brim up on one side; a navy blue sailor's hat, grosgrain ribbon and all. From what navy, one wonders, did this inland sailor's headgear come? Some of the hats are new and store-bought, some are old and cherished. No one is exactly like any other.

It is not my purpose to ask how these hats came to be on the heads they graced, but to stress the cheery individuality which they represent. Each man has a personal style, in dress, in bearing, in talk, in laughing, in everything. Looking at this colorful variety of personages one reflects on the party message echoed at this meeting and often stated in the press,

"In order to accomplish your sacred mission, your deeds, behavior and belief must be in line with those of the Party . . ."

Daily News, East Africa, Feb. 21, 1974. Article Headed, "Youth Told: Eradicate Colonial Mentality," quoting Mbeya TANU Regional Secretary.

In Party ideology the political restructuring of the country is not treated solely as a material matter of reorganizing government, reallocating the means of production, and equalizing distribution. It is pictured as a task involving the making of a new kind of man.

"Tanu . . . realises that the building of socialism means the building of a completely new society and a new Man. This new socialist Man must be forged through a new dynamic socialist culture rooted in socialist activity and consciousness."

Daily News, Tanzania, Feb. 14, 1974. Column headed, "Comment."

In such an ideology, too much individuality may be a sign of 'individualism' which is a 'bad tendency' and is assumed to be inimical to the goals of cooperation and collective well-being. Chagga farmers have no wish to give up their plots of land to pool them with their neighbors. Yet they cannot conveniently be classified as capitalist exploiters since most of them work their plots themselves. But they nevertheless are suspected by the ideologues of being enemies of socialism. Most Chagga are deeply attached to their land, and fear it may be taken from them. They know that in the capital city they are considered political wrong-minded. They perceive this as a misunderstanding.

Nyerere has described socialism as "an attitude of mind" to which the actual wealth or poverty of the individual involved has no relevance. It is possible to be a poor capitalist (he would exploit his fellow man if he could) or a rich socialist (he does not believe in exploitation), (Mohiddin, 1971-72: Vol. I, 165). Without speculating on what the range of visible signs of a socialist or capitalist attitude of mind might be, it is worth noting the abstract quality of the definition. Socialism in these terms is a form of faith in certain moral principles, a matter of mental attitudes. As a very well-to-do government official on Kilimanjaro once said to me, just before he drove away in his car, "Socialism is not a matter of how much money you have. It is a matter of what is in your heart."

Such abstractness and ambiguity make it possible for local Chagga party leaders on the mountain, the farmers who are simultaneously salaried party men, to reassure themselves and their constituents that they are all good socialists. As one Ward Chairman said to me when I asked him what he thought about a Tanu directive that implied that all Tanzanians should be in *ujamaa* villages by 1976,

> "The Chagga," he replied, "have no problem with this. *Hakuna shida*. We have always done things in an *ujamaa* (socialist) manner. We share everything with our brothers. We do everything together with our neighbors. You can ask anyone. We already have *ujamaa*."

The men sitting on the grass waiting for the ward meeting to begin often had heard exhortations to become new men, to end all exploitation, to cooperate, to be socialists, to develop their country by working hard, to condemn the colonialists and support the freedom fighters, and the like. These are delivered in an official terminology coined for the purpose in Swahili. The mention of any of the new words evokes the whole set, so often have they been repeated. But most local political meetings, and this one was no exception, while giving voice to these terms, do not dwell on such abstract or distant matters at any length without tying them to the legitimization of specific local projects. The moralizing rhetorical style is generally used to glorify extremely mundane practical matters of local public work and organization.

While the political leaders say, *"Serikali ni sisi,"* "The government is ourselves", the farmers at the meeting know that in fact the Ward Development Committee mediates between them and higher levels of government in Moshi. Ideologically "the people" are the government. But on the ground, there is a clear hierarchy of administrative bodies which runs things. The more centralized administrative levels are closer to the source of government money. In theory, ward plans for local development and requests for funds feed into district offices, and then are forwarded to the regional level and thence to the office of the Prime Minister. National and regional funds and plans flow back in the other direction. Only the level of the ward and those below are of immediate concern in this paper.

In each of the 31 wards on Kilimanjaro, once a month a small, core group, the Tanu Development Committee, met to plan the next Ward meeting, to generate plans to be ratified, and te set up the agenda in general. Then, each month, as planned, there followed a Ward Development Committee meeting. The W.D.C. includes a much larger group of citizen representatives and local officials than the steering committee. On occasion, the whole citizenry of a locality may be summoned to a Ward Development Committee meeting. Such was the case at this meeting.

The Chairman started by welcoming me, then read the agenda, and said that anyone who wanted to comment on the items he and the others would be discussing were welcome to do so. They could ask for the floor by raising their hands. BUT THEY WERE NOT TO INTERRUPT. The invitation for popular participation was thus hedged with warnings about orderly procedure. Since speech-making on these occasions is rather like filibustering, the order not to interrupt is a significant restriction. The agenda included as major items, the obtaining of materials and labor for building additions to a local school, and the locating of a suitable site for a new clinic. The Chairman started reading the minutes of the last meeting when the Tanu Party Secretary interrupted him and said, "Shouldn't we have a short prayer?" Virtually all meetings on Kilimanjaro open with a Christian prayer. Everyone rose, recited a prayer in unison, and then the meeting began in earnest. It continued for more than three and a half hours, so that it must be understood that the description which follows is radically abbreviated.

The minutes of the previous meeting included a denunciation of the sale of beer by unlicensed persons and at illegal hours, both very common practices which had been going on for many years and which had been denounced regularly for just as many. It is not unusual to see politicians drinking along with everyone else at these establishments, or at prohibited hours, which rather undermines the force of their eloquent public condemnation of these illegalities. Another item that had been discussed at the previous meeting was the illegal resale of coffee insecticide that had been distributed free by the government. It was in short supply and a small-scale black market had sprung up. The meeting had been instructed to arrest people selling the insecticide and bring them before the Magistrate. (A check of the records of the courts of several villages for several months thereafter revealed no arrests or accusations on this ground). These two items of illegal behavior were balanced in the Minutes by discussions about the establishment of a nursery school, the extension of piped water, the repair of a bridge, the state of the local Party treasury, some remarks about the coffee cooperative, a report on the cost of doors and windows for the school, and a discussion regarding school funds.

The general pattern of the previous meeting, the inclusion of a set of items regarding local projects, and a set of items regarding local sinners virtually are standard. The three themes: public works, public funds, and violations of law were the major substantive topics at all the local meetings of various levels that I witnessed, and were threaded through the Minute books I consulted. These dominant themes embody three faces of government: *the state as giver* (of funds and sponsor of public works); *the state as taker* (of funds and local labor); and last, *the state as rule-maker and enforcer.*

Once the minutes had been read and mechanically accepted, the floor was open for the proposal of new business to be added to the agenda. A man in the crowd rose to his feet. The Chairman recognized him and he started to speak about the problem of transportation to the distant *shambas* at the foot of the mountain. It was the time of the year for hoeing the fields on the plain to prepare them for the hoped-for rain. Most people living high on the mountain in the banana belt also have the use of auxiliary fields in the lowland. It is a long walk to the *shambas*. One must get up early in the morning before the sun has come up, to arrive before the worst heat of day. The land must be worked, and then the slow climb back up the mountain is made in the afternoon heat. Sometimes lorries on the roads pick up the cultivators and carry them down or up for a fee, though they are restricted by their licenses to the carrying of goods, not people. The police interfere, chase people out, threaten the arrest of the drivers, and otherwise disrupt this thriving illegal business. The speaker wanted to know what was to be done. Why couldn't the police be told not to interfere. The Chairman said authoritatively that cars and trucks and buses had their own law. There was nothing to do but obey.

He then gave the floor to the next citizen-speaker. This man asked why certain accessible schools had been closed so that people in his area now had to send their children to a school much further away than formerly. One of the Party men answered that there were now fewer children than formerly, hence two schools had been consolidated. In fact, the population is burgeoning, and it is hard to believe that there are fewer children anywhere than formerly, but the statement was made with an authority that suggested that the issue was closed.

Both of these matters, like most of the issues raised by individuals at these meetings are matters decided "higher up" and are things the local, small-time politicians consider it useless to pursue. But they do not admit that they are powerless to do anything about these questions, nor that they choose not to do anything. Rather they suggest that all is for the best. They take the role of *explaining* the state of things, giving rational reasons. This involves no admission of impotence on their part, nor of any failure to represent the needs of their constituents. Instead it associates them with "the powers" and the tone taken, that the farmers are ignorant and need things explained to them, is a statement of the authority of the leadership, and their access to higher councils.

Meanwhile on the road, two women passed, each carrying on her head a few sticks of sugar-cane. They ambled by at a leisurely pace, theire full, flowered-cotton skirts swaying left and right as they walked. They were listening to what was going on, but not attentively enough to stop and join. Then a young girl appeared on the road with a basket of coffee on her head. She came to the veranda where the Party leaders sat and went into the coffee weighing room behind them to have her beans weighed. The meeting went on without a ripple.

There were further comments on the question of transportation to the *shambas*. If the government didn't want lorries to do it, couldn't the government arrange to transport people some other way? What about the publicly run bus company, KIDECO, which was operating some routes on the mountain? Couldn't it do this transport work? The Chairman said KIDECO could be asked to run a bus where the private services were inadequate, but it was no use asking them to take people to the *shambas*. Besides, the passengers paid on KIDECO buses just as they paid on any other, at fixed rates by the mile, said the Chairman. The implication was that any bus would be too expensive.

After the airing of these citizen complaints about the closed school and the bus service, the Party leaders had their own complaints to offer. It is a regular pattern of these meetings that the leaders respond to complaints about the government by complaining about the citizenry. What about the repair and maintenance of the roads? Why did people not turn up for the weekly contributed labor? How were the roads to be kept in order if the citizens did not report for work when they were supposed to? Without roads nothing could be done. There could be no development. Ten people could fix a stretch of road, but where are they? The leaders cannot do the work by themselves. People said they did not hear of the work parties, or that notice never reached them. "The roads belong to all of us," said the Chairman, "and we must all take care of them. People must report the names of those who do not come to the public work."

A young man in the audience stood up and said, responding to these exhortations, "Yes, we should make a labor plan for each day until the work is finished". The Chairman agreed and asked the audience, "Did you understand?" There was a weak murmur of assent. I have not seen any counted voting at any of these meetings nor do I know of any Chagga tradition of voting in earlier times. Meetings proceed as if palavering and consensus were the only possible outcome.

Then the Chairman changed the subject and interjected an admonitory tale. Perhaps the connection with the previous discussion was that more effort should be made to catch wrongdoers. A thief had stolen a goat in M - - subvillage, and cut its feet (a sacrificial counter-measure against witchcraft). The people in the neighborhood had made a hullabaloo, caught the thief and eventually he was taken to the police. "I ask you if you see a thief, make an outcry and catch him, so that he may be taken to the police, even if the Ward Leader is not around."

The road work then was discussed again. This time there were many speakers from the platform all reiterating the same general substance. The imagery used in these supporting speeches, and which is conventionally used on Party occasions is that of a great battle, or a great struggle. The fight ahead is always linked to the ones past. The struggle against colonialism and the success in winning independence are cited as if they were precisely parallel to the struggle against everything from bad roads, to inequality, poverty, ignorance, low productivity and the like. There is a rhetorical matching of the past (bad) to the future (good) as a pair of opposites. The present is represented by allusions to the Party and its activities and organization, and by the occasion of the meeting itself. The present is described as transitional, the past and future as fixed conditions.

Unlike many religious presentations of time which reach back to the beginning of all things and look forward to some sort of ultimate end of time, these secular allusions to time evoke a very shallow past and imply a fairly proximate future. Moreover, their imagery usually is drawn from the social-cultural world of men, not from nature and the cosmos.

The reversability of the social universe is declared. The poor are to become well-off, the bound to become free, the exploited to be made whole. The weak countries are to become strong, the ignorant to become lettered, the dependent to become independent, and modern things will be everywhere. All this in the future. In one mode of argument, all deplorable conditions are blamed on colonialism, imperialism, exploitation, on the bad outsiders who dominated the past and who plot to undermine the future. The theme of this message is, "Now that we are masters of our own destiny, we can make our world as we want it." It is almost invariably followed by another mode of argument, "All this is possible only if we work for it, only if we give up capitalistic ideas, if we develop a new spirit." It all becomes possible if the directives of the Party are followed and everyone cooperates. Not nearly enough of the people who should come to public work or to mass meetings, or even to official committee meetings actually come. Meetings do not "make." Work parties do not turn up. The double message is almost always there: that what is bad is the fault of others, that what is bad is our own fault.

The Chairman said the ten house leaders were responsible for getting their people out, but that surely no one would come if the ten-house leaders themselves did not come out to work. "We must build the nation," said the Chairman. "We are messengers, we leaders. We must not fail to deliver these orders." He spoke of the delinquency of the whole ward. By thus time two hours had passed.

The Chairman then called on a school master who was on the local education committee (and was seated on the veranda with him) to speak. He stood and said, "It is our great fortune to have obtained the help of the government . . ." What he was reporting was the fact that a plan had been approved to add a class to the existing school. A building had to be built. The government would supply some of the money, for the cement, bricks, plaster, nails, etc. He read a long list including many figures, how many bricks, nails etc. and their prices. But the people of the area would have to supply the labor, and some cash as well. To increase the fund to 5000 shillings every local citizen would have to give five shillings. The necessary supplies would have to be moved by truck and some of the money would go for that. Some of the rest would be used to hire a *fundi*, an expert, in this case a builder, to direct the work and lay out the measurements, etc., and another *fundi* to do the plastering, and other such specialized tasks.

Following the schoolmaster's speech, the Chairman made a speech in favor of raising the money, and after him a series of men made similar supporting speeches. After this barrage of eloquence, and each was quite lengthy and full of exhortational rhetoric, an old man, bare-foot and in rags, leaning on a staff made his way to the platform and laid five shilling on the table in front of the Chairman. The Chairman thanked him and there was a small round of applause. Then other people came up one by one to contribute. Each person on the platform contributing a speech as well as his five shillings. Suddenly it occurred to the secretary that he should be making a record of the contributions, and he started to write down the names of those who had paid and that of each new contributor. While this was going on, the Chairman embarked on a new tack: individuals would have to be appointed from each *mtaa*, each sub-village, to be responsible for the collections there. He named someone, to collect in *mtaa* K - -. The nominee stood up glumly and accepted the assignment. The crowd laughed. Everyone knows that no one wants such a job. The next man named tried to refuse. The Chairman insisted. A kinsman of the reluctant nominee, a prominent Party man sitting on the platform, made a speech in his defense, saying he was ill sometimes and should be excused. The whole incident provoked much laughter in the crowd. The Chairman backed down, and named someone else.

Then there was a long discussion about who should keep the money and what the accounting procedures should be. Money is a big responsibility. A man who handles it can always say that thieves came in the night and stole some of it while he slept. There are many problems about cash disappearing Discussions about what to do about money take a long time and involve many intricacies of allocating responsibility. Needless to say, the farmers are not too happy to contribute unless they feel their money will in fact go to the cause specified, and they have some skepticism about it, as there have been some spectacularly bad experiences. Finally after much talk the procedures were settled on. It was clear that the danger of pilfering was on everyone's mind. The ten-house leaders would deliver the money and lists to the Ward Leader.

At last the second item on the agenda was reached: the clinic. The first step to be taken was to choose a suitable site, accessible to two of the sub-villages. A labored discussion ensued about who should choose the site. Again there were many speeches. Eventually the Chairman simply named a committee with two representatives from every *mtaa*. That seemed to satisfy, since the *mtaa* are the traditional political units, and are still very much alive, though they are not part of the official organization.

Three hours had passed. One of the men on the veranda said some of the Committee members were tired. "No matter," said the Chairman, "We must talk about the campaign against short dresses." Such a Party campaign had just been started, nation-wide. The rule was that skirts should reach several inches below the knee, and men's shorts to the knee, though current fashions were much shorter for both sexes. The specifics of this very interesting campaign aside, it is a recognizable part of a general ideological style which identifies the enemies of socialism with sexual depravity. The new-Swahili term used for explotation, *unyonyaji*, derives from the term for sucking at the breast. It thus evokes not only vague echoes of jealousy of younger siblings, but also the taboo against an adult male sucking at the breast. Imperialism is *ubeberu*, derived from the term for he-goat, a creature whose sexual rapacity is reflected in our own term "an old goat." There is a consistency in the imagery that associates sexual license with capitalism (economic licentiousness) and associates sexual orderliness with socialism (economic morality).

"Short dresses and short shorts dishonor the nation. It is a law of the government and a law of the country," said the Chairman, "We must obey it and see that others obey it." The order was, in fact, a Party rule, but legal niceties of that kind are not given much attention in the countryside. A citizen stood up and was recognized. He was a tailor and dress-maker. He asked exactly how short or how long clothing was supposed to be. "Two inches below the knee for dresses, and . . ." A man got up to show that his shorts were the right length and did it in a clowning way that made everyone laugh. "And pants must be as long as those of brother X . . . here." More speeches were made about decency in dress. No one should be allowed to walk on the road in improper clothing. Nor into a church. Nor into a market. Nor should any tailor be allowed to stay in business. "We will close his business if he dares to make a short dress," the Chairman said. "A committtee for enforcing this law must be chosen, to watch for the young girls who break the law." A committee was named to make lists of violators. Each man named stood, and was applauded. Several men who were named to committees were not at the meeting. The basis of the distribution of committee members was again by *mtaa.*

A small boy drove three cows by on the path while this was going on. At last the nominations were finished and the Chairman began to take cognizance of the lateness of the hour. We had by then been in session for three and a half hours. The next items on the agenda were hurried through by comparison with the earlier ones, but each still merited a speech. The first of these items was a call to pay up all membership dues in Tanu and obtain up-to-date memberships cards. The Chairman said, "Not only all men, but all women should belong." But there was some indication that none of this was being taken too seriously as no one could remember who was the head of the UWW, the women's organization of the Ward. This discussion was interrupted by some more clowning about the proper length for men's shorts. A man got up to show his shorts were long enough. He clicked his heels and saluted in an exaggerated military manner. Everyone laughed and applauded, drowning out some of the discussion about membership cards.

When that subsided, the Chairman said that butchers should be on their guard as some clever rogues were travelling the countryside saying that they were veterinary inspectors and collecting samples of meat. They were really thieves. He went on to emphasize that the presence of any stranger in the *mitaa* should be reported at once. Then, like a homing pigeon, he returned to his earlier topic: the collective work. "Some people say to stay at home and not to come out to work. That is wrong. We must all work together." Then he thanked me for attending the meeting, thanked everyone for their contributions to the school fund, and ended by saying "Thanks be to God that we may all build the nation together.

Sally Falk Moore

The meeting is over." Nearly four hours after it began, everyone got up to leave, presumably eventually to make their way toward the beer shops where a great many worthy Chagga citizens spend their late afternoons.

Conclusions

An obvious feature of the meeting described here was its double message. For all the explicit verbal commitment to popular initiative, participation, and self-government, to welcoming suggestions from the citizenry, the autocratic and peremptory behavior of the Party officials running the meeting made the opposite quite clear. Only certain very limited proposals made by the rank and file would be welcomed. Also, despite occasional statements to the contrary, the general indifference of the Kilimanjaro citizenry to local Party/Government activities was well-known to all present and evident in the poor attendance. Hence the apparent unanimity achieved by the meeting cannot be taken at face value. What was said in the speeches could be "seen through" and behind it lay unofficial messages and meanings.

This visible underlayer gave the occasion a high degree of what might be called "transparency". The contrived and manufactured quality of the event showed through. The Party rhetoric did not have the "rightness" of long tradition, the legitimacy of custom and habit behind it, nor was behavior consistent with statement. The Ward meeting could be seen as something newly "set up" and arranged, an obligatory and *pro forma show* of support, a required ratification. It is hard to judge how many participants may have experienced that sense of transparency, when all one has to go on are the comments of a few of the men who were there. Some certainly did since they said so. But even if most perceived the contradictions, that does not mean that such meetings lack effect or importance. Among other things Ward meetings serve to support a leadership (both at the local and at higher levels) which depends for its legitimacy on an *apparent* popular mandate, repeatedly given. Meetings make it possible for the citizenry to constitute a "ratifying body public." Thereby, the leadership, from the bottom ranks to the top, can collect universal symbolic tokens of support. The meeting manufactures legitimacy.[4]

In order to make social life operable people must behave as if much that is socially constructed is as non-negotiable, as real as something in the natural world. The dramatic format of ceremony is a powerful way to show the existence of a social construct. Collective social rituals can dramatize political postulates. Dramatic styles seem particularly penetrating and "unquestionable" ways to convey social messages (Rappaport,

166

1971). They are, in part, addressed to psychological levels that are not completely conscious. Seeing is believing. Kilimanjaro political meetings served to give life to new offices, new organizations, and to the new ideological language, by presenting them in action as visible, audible, unquestionable entities.

Durkheim said of religious ritual, "the essential thing is that men are assembled, that sentiments are felt in common and are expressed in common acts" (1961:431). In this tradition some have described ritual as essentially an occasion when believers *express* their beliefs (Wilson, 1957:7; Beattie, 1966:60). The tautological implications of taking such a stance become evident when, in interpreting field material, anthropologists examine rituals to discover the beliefs of the participants. This postulation of a correspondence between acts and thoughts obviously is misleading in many contexts secular as well as religious. Far from "expressing" what was already believed, the TANU Ward meeting was designed to instruct and convert.

But display and communication of what Apter has called "political religion" were by no means the only things that were going on (1965). Borrowing a term from Tambiah and Austin, such political meetings could be described as performatives (Austin, 1962; Tambiah, 1972:222). Like performative speech acts, political meetings and rituals do not just communicate information, they *do* something. The performative quality of a ritual is the efficacy attributed to it. A marriage ceremony is not the same as a rehearsal for it, nor is it the same as a marriage depicted in a play. The "real" thing has social/legal effectiveness. In that sense, the performative quality of the Kilimanjaro meeting is of major importance. What took place constituted an official public meeting of the citizens of a ward. To say that it was a dramatization of government is merely to make an analogy. It *was* local government, whether those attending "believed" in African socialism or not, and whether they were permitted to make important decisions or not.

In Tambiah's words,
> " . . . ritual acts and magical rites are of the 'illocutionary' or 'performative' sort, which simply by virtue of being enacted (under the appropriate conditions) achieve a change of state, or do something effective (e.g. an installation ceremony undergone by the candidate makes him a 'chief')" (Tambiah, 1972:221).

Tambiah is extending Austin's notion of illocutionary or performative speech acts to cover complexes of ritual (and/or magical) acts. The concept can be just as usefully applied to certain secular words and actions. A signature on a contract or the installation ceremony of a judge are as much performative acts as are any magical words or object-manipulations. The secular formalities affect, not the spirit world, but an equally "made-up" social reality in which they have meaning and efficacy.

Because performatives have a normatively defined relationship to the effects they are supposed to bring about, they can serve as ethnographic clues to those larger social/cultural complexes of meaning and "thought" from which they derive their "efficiency." In the easiest case these are systematic doctrines. A religion may make the saying of certain words the proper way to contact the gods. The law may make a document effective only if signed in the presence of witnesses. Thus a specified set of efficacious symbolic acts may be attached to a worked-out, connected, body of explicit rules and ideas. I have called this "doctrinal efficacy" in the introduction to this volume. A whole cluster of assumptions about causality (social or cosmological) often lies behind the doctrinal norms.

A political doctrine may incorporate just such causal ideas about how freedom or equality may be brought about. It may postulate that undertaken in the right spirit regular open meetings of particular persons (workers or peasants) will necessarily be democratic, egalitarian and constructive. Such an ideological doctrine lies behind the form of the Kilimanjaro meeting, and the occasion gains some of its performative efficacy within that frame of explanation.

But there is more to it than that. Doctrinal efficacy of an ideological sort is not the only source of performative significance. The Kilimanjaro meeting also acquires performative efficacy from its place in an organizational plan. In Tanzania government is organized into local units of a particular kind, having prescribed activities. That is, there is a corporate framework in which the procedural meaning of a political meeting is prescribed. Thus the Kilimanjaro meeting enjoys a combination of an ideological/doctrinal and an organizational/"doctrinal"-procedural base for its performative efficacy. It is performatively legitimated in two systems, ideological and organizational. Within these two frameworks of officially attributed meanings the sheer performance, the regular holding of the meetings in the precribed manner is sufficient to "do something effective" in Tambiah's magical sense (1972:221).

It is true that the ideology holds that a particular state of mind, a socialist attitude, must genuinely underlie the performance for it to enjoy complete success. But should the attitude be absent, it is also assumed that the right ideas will eventually be produced by the political education provided by the meetings themselves. Yet in practise, as there is no way to insure that the inner attitude will always accompany the outer performance, the performance itself becomes the measure of a presumed attitude. The leadership comes to rely on the performance. The appearance of unanimity is not only necessary, it becomes sufficient.

The Kilimanjaro meeting was a form of political co-ceremoniality staged in such a way as to allow the interpretation that it was an outer sign of political agreement. But to allow this inference, all that was required were the common acts. Attendance, an appearance of polite attention, applause when given the sign, some supporting speeches, and an absence of expressions of serious objection were needed. The leadership could interpret these as a sign of success, as legitimation of its role, and as a carrying forward both of immediate practical tasks and long term political education. What was being actively elicited at the meeting was general non-objecting behavior.

Co-ceremonial behavior produces a multiplier effect. It hints that what is hidden in everyone's mind is as conventionally proper and uniform as what everyone is *seen* to be doing in concert. Each person knows only about himself whether this is so. He may be silent and appear attentive yet not be listening at all. However, he does not know about the others for certain. That is why, on some solemn occasions when two people whisper or laugh, they create a disproportionately serious disturbance. They destroy the illusion of unanimity. They reveal that the conventional prescribed thoughts and sentiments are not entertained by everyone.

Certain collective ceremonies probably are designed to evoke as much as possible the feeling that there should be congruence between outer appearance and inner thoughts, and to produce a sense of guilt where this is not so. The Kilimanjaro meeting seemed to stress that every man attending (as well as those absent) should think of himself as a political sinner, as one who has not done enough, who does not believe enough, who is not committed enough. The exhortations of the leaders communicated quite explicitly to the participants what they ought to be feeling and what their behavior ought to mean. But because the society (or some persons in it) imputed a particular belief to those who perform a particular formal action does not say that the ethnographer has to do the same.

A central quality of conventional, formal, collective procedures is that they are not spontaneous expressions of feeling at all, but involve some *conventional form of acting, and the acts have an explicit performative significance given in advance.* As such, the ritual aspects of a collective gathering can as often be a means of masking feelings and thoughts as of expressing them. Amending Durkheim, the "essential thing" may be that "men are assembled" and engage in "common acts" *not* that they necessarily feel "sentiments in common" (Durkheim 1961:431).

The meeting on Kilimanjaro attached fixed conventional meanings to the conventional act of attending such a meeting. In doing so, and in other ways, it communicated the non-negotiability, the unquestionability, the sacredness of certain official interpretations of social life. Such meetings dramatize a political arrangement that is being constructed in part by the drama itself. The repetitive themes in the speeches and format are parts of an attempt to define and teach an official version of social reality while acting it out.

In any social setting, whether traditional or innovative, fixed social forms, rules, symbols and ideas can be considered elements in the effort to construct a common, durable social reality, to hold it firm, to make it knowable and reliable. Elsewhere I have called all the ubiquitous processes that feed into this attempt "processes of regularization" (1975). But it is evident when one looks closely at the unfolding details of any particular social situation, that there are counter-processes continually at work. Individuals (and groups) may reinterpret the constructions others put on social "reality." They may redefine matters or renegotiate them as suits their advantage, or as fits their perception of the circumstances in which they find themselves. They may play openly on such ambiguities, conflicts, inconsistencies, and lacunae in the "system" of rules and symbols and categories as suits their immediate strategic purposes. Or they may do so covertly, even passively, without explicitly seeming to alter anything, simply by not acknowledging the performative efficacy of the acts and interpretations of others.

Because any intentionally engineered social change betrays the degree to which social life is a man-made construct, it intimates an underlying plasticity and indeterminacy in social affairs. The attributes of liminality and states of transition discussed by Victor Turner have echoes here (1969:95-96). Moments of consciously-designed social change afford a fleeting glimpse of non-order. Radical political reorganization demonstrates the great malleability of social forms. Hence, when a new political regime is decreed into existence, the dangerous alternatives it faces are not only from some other kind of programmatic order, but from any kind of non-order, openness and indeterminacy. Perhaps the repetitiveness and the ritualized style of many radical reformist governments is at least partly to be understood in this light? Such polities understandably have a preoccupation with orthodoxy.

In the one-party political meetings of Chagga farmers in Tanzania, the twin messages are prominent: 1) that more changes must come and that they must be instituted by "the people" and their organs of government; and, at the same time, 2) that exhortations to institute change and enlist popular participation must not be mistaken for open social choice and ideological indeterminacy. Voluntary involvement, grass roots control, and an un-doctrinaire style are inherent in the Nyerere approach. Yet in many quarters of Tanzania there are others who assume that a politically educated peasantry will ineluctably choose to organize itself and to act in particular, predictable ways, and that if it does not do so, there is no harm in using some pressure to hurry the peasants along on a path that is historically inevitable anyway. The public ward meeting on Kilimanjaro carried both of these communications and a host of others. Its actions and words *appeared* to elicit unanimous support.

The Party leaders were pleased. The matter of the large number of eligible citizens who did not attend, as well as much that is known of the attitudes of local Chagga farmers could be officially ignored. Nevertheless, that unacknowledged social context silently spilled its significance into the meeting. It introduced a potentially unsettling element of indeterminacy into a well-staged production. No matter, the ratifying body public had played its part. The performative efficacy of the meeting was unimpaired.

NOTES

[1] This paper is based on observations made in Tanzania. The author wishes to acknowledge with gratitude a grant from the Social Science Research Council which made field work possible in 1968-69, and a grant from the National Science Foundation No. GI-34953x which funded work done in 1973-74. None of this work would have been possible without two periods as a Research Associate of the University of Dar es Salaam for which the author is duly grateful.

[2] The administrative pyramid was as follows:

    Tanu Development Committee
    Ward Development Committee
    Representatives of 10-house leaders
    10-house leaders

Or rather, this is the administrative pyramid through which proposals for development were to be generated and implemented. Those generated from below could then be presented to the District Development and Planning Commitee for approval after having passed the tests of the District Development Team, a technical group which receives proposals, draws up budgets, puts them into technical language and presents them to the District Development and Planning Committee.

In short, the Ward organization fed proposals into a local center, the District organization. As of 1973, summer, there were 31 wards on Kilimanjaro. There had been some administrative reorganization in July 1973, and some new procedures laid down, hence there was still some confusion about them during the period of field work. Each ward is a piece of what was formerly a Chiefdom. The pieces, however, are composed of very old political units, the *mitaa,* sometimes called parishes, or sub-villages.

In actual working fact, the old *mitaa,* which were sub-sections of the Chiefdoms, (and in fact long ago, some were themselves tiny chiefdoms) are the underlying political units, though they do not exist officially. These are intricately knitted into the modern structure through manipulations of the representational system. There are a varied number of *mitaa* in each ward. Virtually all local organization of committees and boards involves representation by *mtaa.*

171

Meetings of the whole citizenry of these local units are called from time to time for various purposes, and meetings of the ten-house leaders of these *mitaa* are held regularly. Such meetings are addressed by a variety of Tanu and Ward Development Committee officials, depending on the occasion.

The meeting described in this paper was a meeting of all the citizens (supposed to be) of four contiguous *mitaa* and held by the Ward Development Committee. Readers need not disentangle all of this, which is offered only to emphasize that the official hierarchy and the local structure have accommodated each other, even though officially the local structure does not exist and is hidden behind official descriptions of what is going on.

It should be noted that the Party men and Ward leaders were and are farmers like the others, though not always of the locality which they lead.

[3] All Chagga men on the mountain are farmers. A few have craft specialities in addition: tailoring, shopkeeping, carpentering, house building, and such, but the farmers without auxiliary occupations predominate. Not present at ward meetings, unless they occur on the weekend, are the men who reside on the mountain but work in the nearby (25 miles) town of Moshi in clerical jobs of one sort or another. Nor, of course, do those men attend who work in far-away places, but whose wives and children remain on the land. But these migrants and absentees with skilled jobs are a small percentage of the population.

[4] No doubt some Tanzanians who will read this account will be pained by it and will say, "What can you do when the leaders at the local level do not understand socialism? They need re-education." Be that as it may, it is instructive to consider the actual significance of ratifying bodies public in political systems today, even where that is not the intended design of government.

CHAPTER IX
ON POLITICAL RITUALS IN CONTEMPORARY MEXICO

Evon Z. Vogt and Suzanne Abel

Contemporary Mexico abounds in political rituals.* Some are "rituals of reiteration" that are common to all modern nations. The *grito* on Independence Day, performed with a distinctive Mexican cultural flavor, is a type example. Others are "rituals of consolidation" which weave diverse cultural strands together and weld diverse segments of the population. The rites (and myths) surrounding the Virgin of Guadalupe provide a notable Mexican instance. More complex and perhaps more puzzling to the outside observer are the political rituals that have evolved in the "official" political party – the *Partido Revolucionario Institucional*, the "Institutionalized Revolutionary Party" (hereinafter referred to as the PRI). Here one finds rites involved in the selection and unveiling of "official" candidates, in the political campaigns that follow, and in the balloting process, that together form a symbolic complex that has mystified us for years, for, to an observer brought up on North American democracy the procedures, even including the balloting, are not decision making processes as we normally understand them. The puzzle is this: if the selected "official" candidates always "win", what is the point of the enormously expensive and time-consuming campaigns and the elaborate attention to balloting procedures adopted from Western European and North American models?

In his stimulating paper on "Political Anthropology: the Analysis of the Symbolism of Power Relations", Abner Cohen argues that "the central theoretical interest in the study of symbols is the analysis of their involvement in the relationships of Power" (1969:218). He goes on to argue that we must distinguish between symbolic *forms* and symbolic *functions*: that the same symbolic function can be achieved by a variety of symbolic forms in a particular society; and that different societies often adopt different symbolic forms to achieve the same types of symbolic functions (1969: 218-219).

Cohen also makes some cogent theoretical statements concerning "mystification" which are relevant in this context:

173

Through the "mystification" which it creates, symbolism makes it possible for the social order to survive the disruptive processes created within it by the inevitable areas of conflicting values and principles. It does this by creating communion between potential enemies ... The degree of "mystification" mounts as the social inequalities between people who should identify in communion increase (1969: 221).

Finally, Cohen calls attention to the fact that to date there has been scant analysis of "political ritual" in contemporary politics in spite of many years of research by political scientists (1969: 228).

In this paper, we hope to move in a modest way toward filling in some gaps in our knowledge of "political ritual" in contemporary societies by examining a "ritual of reiteration" and a "ritual of consolidation" in Mexico; by showing how "mystification" in symbolism has developed in the whole process of selecting "official" PRI candidates; and, finally, by suggesting how we might look at the other side of the coin (than that proposed by Cohen) with respect to symbolic forms and functions – that is, how the Mexican PRI has adopted symbolic forms that are similar to West European and North American "democratic" procedures, but utilizes these forms for quite different symbolic functions.

The Grito on Mexican Independence Day

At 11 p.m. on September 15, 1810, the creole priest Miguel Hidalgo led the call for independence from Spain in the little town of Dolores Hidalgo in the state of Guanajuato. The bells of the parish church summoned his small flock of Indian parishioners, and before them he raised the banner of the Virgin of Guadalupe, protector of the Indian poor, and cried: "Long live Our Lady of Guadalupe and death to the gachupines!"[1] Although Hidalgo's rebellion was a disastrous failure and he was himself executed less than a year later, he is today remembered as the father of the independence movement. His was the first episode in a long succession of rebellions which culminated in nationhood for Mexico. Hidalgo was the first of a triumvirate of nineteenth century liberals who are today regarded as heroes in the Revolutionary tradition. Equally honored are Morelos, a mestizo priest with black blood who took over the cause at the death of Hidalgo, and Juarez, an Indian who rose to the Presidency of Mexico.

Precisely at 11 p.m. on September 15th, the President of the Republic of Mexico emerges with the tri-colored flag from the National Palace, located on the eastern side of the large plaza, or *zòcalo*, in the heart of

Mexico City, stands on the presidential balcony overlooking the plaza packed with celebrating citizens, and shouts the ceremonial *grito*.[2] "Viva La Independencia! Viva Hidalgo! Viva Morelos! Viva Juarez! Viva Mexico! Viva Mexico!" the President shouts over the loudspeakers, while the amassed citizens answer "Viva!" to each phrase in an affirming chorus. Each President is expected to add some distinctively phrased "Viva" of his own, but essentially the shouts are for Independence, for Hidalgo and for Mexico. The effect of this simple but powerful ritual of reiteration is stunning; after the *grito* and the shouted responses from the huge crowd the President rings the bell from Dolores and the bells peal out from the tower of the ancient National Cathedral; fireworks, including colored skyrockets, are ignited, and the spectacle culminates with the setting off of a great *castillo* (castle) displaying the face of Father Hidalgo shouting out the original "Viva" of 1810.

While the President is reenacting the *grito* in Mexico City, the Governor of every state in the Republic is emerging from the State Palace and shouting the *grito* to the citizens of his state, and the Presidente Municipal (mayor) of every town in Mexico is emerging from the Municipal Palace and shouting the *grito* to the large or small mass of citizens in the plaza below. And these, too, are always followed by the ringing of church bells and fireworks. In one massive and simultaneous *grito* throughout the Republic, the independence of Mexico from Spain is ceremonially reiterated on this most important national holiday.[3] Political speeches delivered on this day also serve to recall the colonial times and the days of the Porfiriato, before the Revolution: "Today it is easy to shout 'Long live liberty' because we are free. There was a time when those who had shouted this died for having shouted it."[4]

The shouted reiteration of the *"grito de Dolores"* each 15th of September is a major symbol of Mexican nationalism. The celebration of this historical cry is a crucial part of the whole process of mystification which envelopes the party of the Revolution and the nation as an independent state. Throughout Mexico, from the National Palace down to the Municipal Palace, the PRI leaders simultaneously become celebrants of a rite in which each becomes in effect another Hidalgo. The men who lead the *grito* are the heirs of a tradition of heroes of the Independence movement; in turn they enjoy identification with the mystical continuity of the Revolution. A great unbroken sequence is created in *personalities* as well as events, from Hidalgo to Morelos to Juarez to Cardenas to Lopez Mateos to Echeverria.

The timing of the *grito* – on the evening before the official holiday on September 16th – is important ritually. For not only does it occur at the time when Hidalgo supposedly shouted the original *grito* but on the vispera (vespers) of the holiday. The evening before a Mexican saint's day celebration is always the time of the peak emotional experience, when larger crowds gather and there is more music, dancing and fireworks. Following the great cathartic *grito* comes the very solemn ritual of the President viewing the military parade during the day on September 16. The contrast resembles Da Matta's (this volume) distinction between rituals of license (Brazilian Carnival) and rituals of constraint (Brazilian Independence Day). Mexicans, of course, also celebrate Carnival, most exuberantly in lowland coastal areas like Veracruz and Guerrero, but not with the same national vigor found in Brazil. It would appear that some of the kind of social energy going into the communitas-type Brazilian Carnival is, in the Mexican case, expressed in the ritual of the *grito* and then followed the next day by the ritual of constraint, the military parade, which symbolically becomes a representation of hierarchical distinctions, which celebrates *structure* rather than creating *communitas* (Turner 1969).

The implications of the ceremonial *grito* for town and architectural planning in contemporary Mexico are worth a comment or two. The pressures are enormous to construct two-story Municipal Palaces (or town halls) complete with balconies on the second floor where the Presidente Municipal will stand while delivering the *grito* – even in the smallest Mexican pueblos. Further, the ritual requires a relatively spacious plaza to hold the masses of standing citizens who will respond to the *grito* of their President. On this point, Mexican officials often seem shockingly insensitive to ecology-minded North Americans when they proceed to renovate lovely old colonial plazas. An example. Some years ago the Presidente Municipal of San Cristobal Las Casas in the highlands of Chiapas proceeded to "modernize" the *zòcalo*, a process which involved cutting down all the trees, repaving the plaza, and generally making more space for crowds of people. The result was a great uproar from the North American colony in San Cristobal – delegations were organized to call upon the Presidente, petitions were circulated requesting that the old, colonial character of the *zòcalo*, with all its lovely trees and garden plots, be maintained. But it developed that the roots of the trees were literally tearing up the sidewalks. Besides, the Presidente explained, trees grow fast in the highlands of Chiapas with some 60 inches of tropical rain falling each year. Furthermore, if people wanted a country-side park, they could walk a few minutes in any direction and be in the open country. The function of a *zòcalo*, the Presidente explained, is for political meeting; they are places to mass large groups of people, as for the *grito*. Significantly, at about the same time the same process of "modernization" took place in the central *zòcalo* in Mexico City. The trees and gardens were removed, and today the *zòcalo* is bare and paved with large blocks of cement, and can hold thousands of citizens. If the people want a park, they can go to Chapultepec; the *zòcalo* is a place for large political meetings like the celebration of Independence Day.

The Virgin of Guadalupe

The patron saint of Mexico is the Virgin of Guadalupe. The symbolism and rituals which form the cult of this saint now " . . . enshrine the major hopes and aspirations of an entire society" (Wolf 1958: 34). Hidalgo first raised the banner of Guadalupe in 1810 and she continued to lead the insurgents into battle until Independence was won. Emiliano Zapata and his rebellious *campesinos* fought beneath her emblem in the Revolution of 1910. Today her image adorns houses and churches, bull rings and gambling casinos, trucks and buses, restaurants and bars. She is celebrated in popular songs (Wolf 1958: 34). Her shrine at Tepeyac, at the northern edge of Mexico City, is visited by hundreds of thousands of pilgrims from throughout Mexico (Turner 1973). She is a figure of religious symbolism, a continuity from the aboriginal past, and a political symbol because of her strong associations with Mexican nationalism and independence. Her cult may be seen as a kind of "rite of consolidation". The Virgin of Guadalupe has become a "master symbol", as Eric Wolf expresses it, for contemporary Mexico.

The image of Guadalupe and her shrine at Tepeyac are surrounded by an origin myth. According to this myth

> . . . the Virgin Mary appeared to Juan Diego, a Christianized Indian of commoner status, and addressed him in Nahuatl. The encounter took place on the Hill of Tepeyac in the year 1531, ten years after the Spanish Conquest of Tenochtitlan. The Virgin commanded Juan Diego to seek out the archbishop of Mexico and inform him of her desire to see a church built in her honor on Tepeyac Hill. After Juan Diego was twice unsuccessful in his efforts to carry out her order, the Virgin wrought a miracle. She bade Juan Diego pick roses in a sterile spot where normally only desert plants could grow, gathered the roses into the Indian's cloak, and told him to present cloak and roses to the incredulous archbishop. When Juan Diego unfolded his cloak before the bishop, the image of the Virgin was miraculously stamped upon it. The bishop acknowledged the miracle, and ordered a shrine built where Mary had appeared to her humble servant (Wolf 1958: 34-35).

The shrine is today a basilica. Above the altar hangs Juan Diego's cloak with the miraculous image: her head lowered, a young dark-skinned virgin is clothed in a flowing gown; she wears an open crown and stands upon the crescent moon of the Immaculate Conception.

In pre-Conquest times, Tepeyac had housed a temple to the earth and fertility goddess Tonantzin, "Our Lady Mother", who, like Guadalupe, was associated with the moon and was the focus of large-scale pilgrimages. So a crucial syncretism occurred as Spanish friars like F. Bernardino de Sahagun attested:

> Now that the Church of Our Lady of Guadalupe has been built there, they call her Tonantzin too ... The term refers ... to that ancient Tonantzin and this state of affairs should be remedied, because the proper name of the Mother of God is not Tonantzin ... It seems to be a satanic device to mask idolatry ... and they come from far away to visit that Tonantzin, as much as before; a devotion which is also suspect because there are many churches of Our Lady everywhere and they do not go to them; and they come too from faraway lands to this Tonantzin as of old (Sahagun 1938: I, lib. 6).

Wolf points out that the cult of Guadalupe has come to have important symbolic connections both to the play of relationships within families, and to the political aspirations of Mexicans. Within the Indian family, Guadalupe is identified as the mother who provides food and consolation, emotional warmth and protection. Within the more typical Mexican family, which is distinguished from the Indian by the overbearing sexual, authoritarian figure of the father, the image of Guadalupe is the embodiment of hope in a victorious outcome of the struggle between generations. Guadalupe stands in defense of the more submissive women and children; she defies male authority. Thus she comes to represent the successful waging of the Oedipal conflict (Wolf 1958: 36-37).

She is the antithesis of La Chingada, the violated Indian mother who submitted to the rape of the Spanish and betrayed her people. Guadalupe is the respected mother, the woman of inviolate integrity and compassion (Paz 1961: 85).

But more important for our purposes are the symbolic connections of the cult of Guadalupe with political aspirations. To Mexico's Indians, Guadalupe is more than the mother who can offer solace in an arduous existence; she gives them once more hope of salvation:

> The apparition of Guadalupe to an Indian commoner thus represents on one level the return of Tonantzin ... On another level, the myth of the apparition served as a symbolic testimony that the Indian, as much as the Spaniard, was capable of being saved, capable of

178

receiving Christianity . . . The myth of Guadalupe thus validates the Indian's right to legal defense, orderly government, to citizenship; to supernatural salvation, but also to salvation from random oppression (Wolf 1958: 37).

The myth of Guadalupe came to stand for every person's right to a place in heaven, but also to a place in society. The orphans of New Spain – the illegitimate children of Spanish and Indian parentage, the financially ruined, those ostracized from either Spanish or Indian society – all came to embrace Guadalupe as their particular patron in the search for hope in life and afterward. The sons of La Malinche – La Chingada – turned to the Virgin of Guadalupe for love. For did not Guadalupe choose to reveal herself to an Indian, while the highly-placed Spanish cleric refused to believe? Was not the poor man honored by her and the wealthy man shamed by his own skepticism and scorn for Juan Diego?

Guadalupe is the symbol for a heterogeneous society with a divisive history, linking "together family, politics and religion; colonial past and independent present; Indian and Mexican" (Wolf 1958: 38). The symbolism of the cult provides an example *par excellence* of a "rite of consolidation" for a contemporary nation.

The Institutionalized Revolutionary Party

Out of the agonizing altermath of the Great Revolution which began in 1910 came the gradual development of the Partido Revolucionario Institucional (PRI) which today symbolizes that the Great Revolution has become institutionalized, has become a permanent feature of Mexican life.

The PRI is the third in line of the Revolutionary parties which have in turn dominated Mexican political life since the Revolution. The PRN (National Revolutionary Party) was established in 1928 by Plutarco Calles, during the presidency of Emilio Portes Gil. Ten years later Lazaro Cardenas dismantled the PNR to replace it with the new PRM (Mexican Revolutionary Party) in a move which repudiated the figure of Calles and his political hegemony and re-established this primary political symbol of the Revolution in a new mold as "spokesman for popular distress" (Johnson 1971: 31). During Cardenas' term of office, the PAN (National Action Party) was permitted to emerge, as this was seen as constituting no true threat to the Revolutionary majority. From that beginning, the PAN has, contrary to the expectations of the ruling party, grown into a solid, permanent political opposition to which certain concessions have to be made. The PAN traditionally has been the more conservative party, sometimes violently opposing the official development policies which it has interpreted as Marxist and suicidal for Mexico. However, in very recent years, the PAN has become more centrist in its philosophy and other parts of the political spectrum are now represented by parties of less influence or permanency. In 1945, under Avila Comacho, the PRM became the PRI. The party, under its 1965 statutes, is divided into three sectors: the *campesino* or agrarian sector, the workers' sector, and the *"popular"* sector, composed of small business and professional groups. The PRI is the sole custodian of political legitimacy in Mexico; this is the primary reason behind its consistent electoral victories, despite practices at the polls which tend to make these victories appear greater than they truly are. The PRI maintains its image as the party of the "continuing Revolution" and the party of the *"pobres"*, for, to many Mexicans, the party remains the only legitimate political entity – all other parties and candidates are suspect. Much of the political ritual associated with the perpetuation of PRI dominance in government derives from this image and status as *the* party of the Revolution. The men who become President of the Republic are seen to be the next in a long line of charismatic figures of the Revolution, men whose personalities have become obscured by the height of their office and its inherent mystery.

"Tapadismo": Rites of "Mystification" in the Selection of Candidates

Contemporary Mexico has no primary elections and no political conventions (unlike the United States) for the selection of candidates for public office. Instead, in the current pattern, the PRI candidate for President of the nation is selected from among the ministers in the cabinet by the incumbent President in consultation with living ex-Presidents and heir representatives and with the leaders of the various organized sectors of the Mexican political system (what Frank Brandenberg has called the "Revolutionary Family"). The PRI Presidential candidate in turn selects the candidates for Governors of the various states, and the Governors select the candidates for Presidente Municipal (mayors) of all the municipios in their states – again consulting with ex-holders of these offices and their representatives.

In the typical case a candidate for Governor is one who was born in the state, but who has spent time in Mexico City – either in professional or political life establishing connections with the central hierarchy of the PRI – and is then "sent back" to his state to govern the people. The national leaders of PRI thus avoid the difficulty of having a local "cacique" gain control of that office, a man who may be very powerful and very popular but who is neither beholden to the central hierarchy nor has the necessary connections to siphon needed funds into his state for public programs and public works. The same process is evident in most of the municipios where the candidate for Presidente Municipal is expected to have had some experience and connections with the state political machinery.

Once the selections have been made there follows a period of *tapadismo* in which the candidate, called *"el tapado"* is "covered" and everyone attempts to guess who he is and to adjust their "radar" and political responses accordingly. Finally, the "unveiling" of "el tapado" is done with considerable ritual – in the case of the President, often at a meeting of the national organization of *campesinos*, i.e. agrarian workers, but sometimes at a press conference at which the President of PRI opens boxes of telegrams in favor of the chosen one. He then becomes "el verdadero *tapado".*[5]

The process known as *"tapadismo"* lends a religious-like aura of mystery to the whole political process. Cohen points out this quality of a political symbol such as *el tapado* and explains it in this way:

> Symbols also objectify roles and give them a reality which is separate from the individual personalities of their incumbents. Men are trained for their roles, installed in them, and helped to perform their duties in the course of a series of stylised symbolic activities (1969: 220).

The man who is chosen as *el verdadero tapado* is the recipient of all the cumulative charisma which has become the soul of the office of the Presidency since the Revolution. Although the Presidency is limited to a six-year term for each incumbent and re-election is unconstitutional, the office remains part of a long tradition of *caudillismo*. Personalism in Mexican politics has always been perhaps its most necessary element; the person of the President is popularly seen as the magical figure from whom all beneficence flows and in whom all power rests. The President is possessed of almost limitless power, subject only to the constitutional restraint of no re-election. The *tapado* is therefore the man in whom the continuity of Mexico's historical and mystical identity resides. Leal Cortes in his book *La Sucesion Presidencial* describes the President as this omnipotent, syncretistic being:

> The President unites in his person everything from the ancient figure of the Indian cacique whose mandate was considered unequivocal and never discussed, to the vibrant and attractive personality of the caudillo (?1963: 9; trans. is ours).[6]

Joseph Hodara (1972) hypothesizes that "tapadismo satisfies the requirements (personal and collective) of a culural framework which is fundamentallen magical, and constitutes, at the same time, a *rite de passage* between traditional and modern political institutions."[7] With all of this in mind, the reason for the secrecy of the selection of the *tapado* becomes clear. Of the candidate were revealed too soon, allegiance to the incumbent President would be abruptly removed, and as political re-alignments began to take shape, there would occur a crisis of authority in the government. Thus the crucial element of mystification which surrounds the decision and the revelation of the *verdadero tapado* has a pragmatic basis which is itself founded in a powerful, quasi-religious symbolic reality.

Political Campaigning

Now come even more mystifying questions. If the selected PRI candidates always "win", who go through an enormously expensive and time-consuming campaign every six years (*irse a la cargada*)? And campaign they do with great vigor and great Mexican flair. A presidential candidate visits every state in the Republic, often more than once; a candidate for governor campaigns in every municipio in his state; and a candidate for mayor repeatedly visits each small hamlet in his municipio. Banners are everywhere; mountainsides are painted in large white-washed letters reading "Todo Chiapas (Michoacan, Oaxaca, etc.) Con Echeverria" (All of Chiapas with Echeverria).

When a presidential candidate arrives in a town like San Cristobal (the market town of some 30,000 Mexicans and political control point for the whole Indian zone of the Chiapas Highlands, containing some 200,000 Indians), the public plaza is packed with 10,000 Indians hauled into town by truck and bus at the expense of the PRI. When the PAN presidential candidate arrives, he has a crowd of perhaps 200 listeners, and my (Vogt) PRI friends in their stores and banks around the plaza watch the proceedings with sly amusement, commenting that "a little opposition is good, but not too much."

Candidates typically go to great lengths to present an image of being "of the people". For example, Echeverria traveled in a bus, as most people in Mexico travel, rather than in a Mercedes Benz.

What is all this campaigning about? After patient and lengthly explanations from a PRI political friend (whom I (Vogt) have known for sixteen years now and who *loves* to discuss politics endlessly), I think I finally understand the function of campaigns. It is diverse, but perhaps the most important *single* aspect is to set up a process of communication between the President and the various states, and between the governor and the various municipalities in his state, that later facilitates administration. (Perhaps it is more than coincidence that the term *tapado* probably derives from the name given the *"oider"* of early colonial days – he who came disguised or cloaked to the Indian communities to "diagnose" the political situation there (Hodara 1972: 3)).[8] Let us take the example of a candidate for governor. As he travels to every small pueblo, the local leaders have a chance to meet him personally and to present in detail their local needs: a new bridge over the river, a health clinic, a new school, etc.

This campaigning, in a word, is a remarkably sensitive means by which the people of the Republic come to know the man who will be President and by which the President and his staff can sense the political temper of different regions and inventory the most important local needs. This does not mean, of course, that all the local needs will be taken care of. For there is a strong tendency among elected officials for local attachments and ties to weigh heavily in the allocation of funds. A President from Veracruz will be most likely to favor the state of Veracruz in his decisions about allocations of resources. A local wag in San Cristobal once commented to me that the only way to get the streets paved in every *barrio* in San Cristobal would be to select the mayors in rotation from *each* of the *barrios* of San Cristobal! And there is much truth in his comment.

There is also an observed tendency for each recent President of Mexico to reach for immortality by selecting one great public work and pushing it to conclusion. For example, under Aleman the new University of Mexico was constructed with all its beautiful buildings; Lopez Mateos built the magnificent new Museum of Anthropology in Mexico City; under Diaz Ordaz, the new subway system of Mexico City was nearly completed.

But there is more to the campaign than this vital establishing of communications throughout the country with the centralized government.

The campaign helps convince the people that the right man has been chosen for office; as a corollary, it also helps to reaffirm the political system itself (and the process of *tapadismo*) by demonstrating that the correct choice has been made (Tannenbaum 1962:91). In the tradition of the Great Revolution, the campaign gives support to the fundamental *moral* justification of the whole system. Further, the candidate himself must become convinced that he is *presidenciable* – after all, this office is greater than the man himself and after having been in the shadow of the powerful incumbent for six years, he probably needs some self-affirmation. His image must be developed and consolidated through the campaign: he must become transformed into the *new* symbol of national unity and the continuing Revolution (what Hodara called "the sequence made sacred by the Revolution").[9] The candidate's worthiness to inherit the office of the Presidency is therefore established through the ritual of the campaign, which assures contact with the vast network of leadership throughout the country as well as the transferral of that magical and necessary quality of a great leader – political charisma.

The campaign can act in addition as a cathartic for the whole nation: if the opposition parties are never in a position to offer any viable alternative to PRI dominion, then the campaign at least allows discontent to be vented on the part of the people. That's a lot of what all the politicking is about. In this particular sense, the campaign is a major instrument of social control for the ruling elite (Hodara:1972: 52).

The political hierarchy is in itself pretty fluid. During each election year, there are literally thousands of "elected" political posts open, the candidates for which are selected or at least approved by the President and the governors. The campaign permits those in power to evaluate the many claims and requests for offices and to make the necessary decisions which become crucial in the working of the new administration. The posts which are purely appointed are, of course, of even greater political importance.

The repetitive, dramatic, collective, affirmative character of the campaign is a ritual of long tradition. It is also cyclic. It is as if time itself were suspended for this critical period, then abruptly resumed with the arrival of the next *sexenio* (six-year term). The campaign in most practical terms, gives everyone the chance to come out for the candidate, to declare their political positions, and to bargain with the temporarily flexible system before it becomes once more rigidified by the new administration.

Balloting on "Election" Day

So much for political campaigning. But why bother to go through the balloting process? – especially, when I (Vogt) know from first-hand experience that votes are not cast and counted in a decision-making process in local communities in Chiapas, and my PRI friends at the highest level in Mexico City admit in confidence that they are not counted at the national level either. It is always reported that such-and-such a candidate wins by so many votes, but my information indicates that the totals reflect a PRI judgment about the political situation in a particular state or municipio and *not* an actual counting of the ballots. I am told that there are certain areas of Mexico, especially in the northern states (which are much more North Americanized) and in some areas of Mexico City where local officials are beginning to actually count the votes. But this certainly does not yet happen in Chiapas.

And, by way of example, we will describe election day in July 1970 in the municipio of Zinacantan, an election in which I (Vogt) and two of my field workers personally participated.

First, a word or two about Zinacantan, the Indian municipio I have been studying for the last eighteen years.[10] Zinancantan is a Highland Tzotzil-speaking municipio of some 11,000 Indians, located just to the west of San Cristobal, along both sides of the Pan American highway. Tzotzil is one of the Mayan languages and the Zinacantecos are descendants of the ancient Maya who lived in the Highlands of Guatemala and the Lowlands of the Yucatan Peninsula. Today they occupy a ceremonial center, where the political and religious officials serve in the town hall and perform ceremonies for the saints and for the ancestral gods who live in the mountains around the center. Some 800 people live in the ceremonial center, but the bulk of the population lives in fifteen scattered hamlets in the mountains. They live by cultivating maize, beans, and squash; they are organized into extended families and patrilineages. Their religion is superficially Catholic and they consider themselves "good Catholics", but the ancient Maya concepts and practices show quite clearly through the veneer. Their ceremonies include offerings to the ancestral gods in the mountains and to the earth god who lives beneath the surface of the earth. Their 200 shamans are constantly busy with curing ceremonies, rain-making, corn-growing, and new house dedication rituals. They have an Indian presidente municipal (and other officials) who are officially members of PRI, but who also have many ritual duties. For example the presidente must attend the Year Renewal Ceremonies of the shamans at the beginning, at the middle, and at the end of the year. He also serves as a godfather for the re-enactment of the birth of the Christ children on Christmas Eve . . for there is not just one Christ Child, but *two*, older and younger brother Christ!

On election day that summer we arrived in the ceremonial center at 9 a.m. to find the town hall crowded with some 300 Indian men. There were only a handful of Indian women, and they sat in the background and watched. These men were representatives from the ceremonial center and each of the hamlets. They had come to do the voting for the whole municipio, the emphasis being upon those men who could read and write and help keep things straight. Six polling booths has been set up, representing six regions of the municipio. The political leaders from each hamlet supervised the process: (1) a group of literate Indians counted carefully all the ballots to see that the number exactly equalled the number of adult residents (men and women) in the official count of registered voters of each hamlet list. Then a second man would take a turn at the voting, marking about ten ballots with an "X" for PRI, as one of the literate Indians checked off names on the hamlet list. Then a second man would take a turn, marking another ten or so ballots and have ten more names checked off. (Nobody voted for other than PRI . . one man explained:

185

PRI is the party for the *pobres* (poor), PAN is the party for the *ricos* (rich), we are *pobres* and that was that!). Finally, after all the representatives from each hamlet had a turn – needless to say, no women voted, even though they were on the list – there were still hundreds of ballots left over. So work parties were formed to efficiently divide the labor. Two or three literate young men would mark "X's" on the ballots, another group would fold the ballots, a third group were carriers that took the ballots to the ballot box, where another man put them in the slot. The process continued until about noon when finally all the ballots were filled out and all the names checked off!

Meanwhile, the Ladino secretary (Ladinos are non-Indians) was in a flap because of all the official papers he had to fill out in fifteen copies each. They had to be typed and he could never finish the job by the time the government officials were due to arrive at noon to pick up the ballot boxes. None of the Indians present could type, so my two students were pressed into service, typing the official papers in fifteen copies. One paper said, in essence, that the polls opened at 8 a.m., another that they closed at 5 p.m., another that there were no irregularities in the balloting! Then the poor Indian presidente had to sit down and laboriously sign all the copies of those papers, again before noon. About noon the officials arrived from San Cristobal and collected the ballot boxes and that was the end of the voting on what one Indian cacique significantly called, in Spanish, "el dia de las selecciones", "selection day", not "election day".

On our return to field headquarters in San Cristobal my students and I puzzled and puzzled about this balloting process. What, in God's name, did it all mean, either practically or symbolically? A testimonial, yes, like an election in the Soviet Union. (The view of the Mexican PRI officials about the balloting in the local Indian villages is that it sanctions decisions that have already been reached within the Indian communities.) But wasn't there something more to it, at least in terms of political symbolism?

I finally came up with this hypothesis: that one could think of the ballots as offerings to the political leaders in Tuztla Guitierrez (the capital of Chiapas) and in Mexico City, much like the offerings that the Zinacantecos regularly make to their ancestral gods in the mountains. In the case of the rituals, the offerings consist of white candles (that are symbolically conceived of as tortillas for the gods), copal incense (cigarettes for the gods) and prayers which plead for services from the gods: prayers to restore the lost soul of one's wife or husband, to cure the illness of a child, to bring the rain for the corn crop. I believe that one way of looking at these ballots – with the ritual-like emphasis upon counting them all, just as they count candles they offer to the gods – is that they are offerings in a kind of ritual transaction with the high political leaders. The Zinacantecos are saying "here is our political support, our offerings to you, now in exchange we want a new bridge built across the river and the roof of the schoolhouse repaired and some more *ejido* land".

The idea that a few representatives from each hamlet can cast the ballots for everyone also fits perfectly with the Zinacanteco pattern that a shaman represents his patient in praying to the gods in the mountains, or that a priest can say Mass in the local church and as long as he does his ritual business, the others do not have to be present, or if they are, there is no sense that people have to keep quiet and participate in the ritual. In a word, the Zinacantecos have no sense of congregation – no sense that a larger religious group inside a church is participating in the ritual, or that a larger political group exists and that each man and woman have to cast their own ballots. I have attended Catholic Masses when the priest was obviously very perturbed with the amount of talking and coming and going in the church. I have frequently observed a shaman praying at a mountain shrine when ten feet away groups of Zinacantecos would be talking, drinking, smoking – as long as the ritual practitioner does his ritual work, he represents everyone else and they can ignore him. This is precisely what the handful of men from each hamlet are doing in this balloting process – doing their ritual business on behalf of the whole hamlet. A related point is that the Zinacantecos also show a strong tendency to defer to those who are, for a variety of reasons, better qualified to "speak" on their behalf. This is a pattern which manifests itself in the existence of several classes of "spokesmen": shamans, "lawyers", caciques, cargoholders, articulate Spanish-speakers.

What the balloting means in Mexican villages, as opposed to these Indian villages, we can only surmise. But there may also be a parallel here between offerings to the saints, in exchange for services and favors, and the offerings in terms of political support provided by filling out all the ballots properly.

These hypotheses need further testing next field season, but this makes, we think, at least a beginning in the unraveling of the political process in the relationship between municipios like Zinacantan and the state and national government.

Among others, Gluckman (see especially his 1962 paper) has called attention to the importance of the ritualization of social relationships in society and to the fact that there appears to be more ritualization in tribal than in modern societies. However, that this ritualization continues as an aspect of social relationships, especially political relationships, in contemporary Mexico seems clear.

NOTES

* The field research on which this paper was based was part of the Harvard Chiapas Project which has been supported by the National Institute of Mental Health (Grant No. 02100). The senior author is Professor of Anthropology at Harvard and Director of the Harvard Chiapas Project; the junior author is a Research Assistant of the Harvard Chiapas Project. We are indebted to Felisa M. Kazen, Jan Rus III, and Mara Turok for their comments on the first draft.

[1] "Spanish-born"

[2] In 1972 *Hispano Americano* estimated there were more than 200,000 citizens packed in the *zòcalo*.

[3] In 1972, the *grito* was also celebrated in major U.S. cities, with members of the cabinet fanning out to New York, Chicago, San Antonio, Houston, and Los Angeles to address members of the Mexican communities in those cities and their invited guests.

[4] "Ahora es facil gritar *Viva La Libertad* porque somos libres. Hubo una vez en que quienes asi gritaron murieron por gritar." – Lic. Jose Lopez Portillo, Director de la Comision Federal de Electridrad, 16 September, Mexico City.

[5] "the true candidate"

[6] "El Presidente resume en su persona, desde la antigua figura del cacique indigena cuyo mandato era considerado inenquivoco y jamas discutido, hasta la brillante y attractiva personalidad del caudillo" (1963:9).

[7] "...el tapadismo satisface requiermientos (personales y colectivos) de una estructura cultural fundamentalmente magica y constituye, al mismo tiempo, un *rite de passage* entre instituciones tradicionales y modernas" (1972: 49).

[8] It is possible that the *oidor* was historically prefigured by the Aztec *pochteca,* the merchants who travelled in disguise throughout Tenochititlan's sphere of influence to "diagnose" the economic situation of various other Indian communities.

[9] "la secuencia sacralizada por la Revolucion" (Hodara 1972:51).

[10] Further ethnographic details on Zinacantan may be found in Vogt 1969 and other books sponsored by the Harvard Chiapas Project.

CHAPTER X
THE LEAST COMMON DENOMINATOR

Elizabeth Colson

The inspiration for this paper was the chance attendance at a birthday party celebration at a Senior Citizen Center in the San Francisco Bay area in 1974, at a time when I was puzzling over the utility of applying the term "ritual" to secular occasions. The birthday party was clearly a secular occasion in that it contained no explicit reference to the cosmic order, made no use of religious symbols, and did not pretend to sacralize its participants in any fashion. Yet in the course of the proceedings, a clientele was being transformed into a community honoring the common characteristic which linked them all and stressing the value of their shared experience. Durkheim would have recognized the celebration as a manifestation of community and characterized it as a intensification and social holiday.

The community was one composed of elders. It was defined by age since it is age alone that makes one eligible to join a senior citizen center. In the events of the Birthday Party, participants celebrated their distinctive status and reassured themselves, and told outsiders, that it is good to be old. In this they reversed the value placed on youth and age in so much of American experience and became reconciled for the moment with the fact of age and their own withdrawal from the settings, activities and interests of the wider community associated with the actively employed.

Age-Grading, Elders, and Senior Citizen Centers

Elders or senior citizens are becoming a distinct element in the American population. The creation of retirement homes and communities and of specialized associations with membership restricted to those over the age of sixty two, along with legislation relating to elders, are all clear indications that elders are now seen as belonging to a distinct category with special needs and attributes. Membership in that category is attained on the birthday of the year in which one reaches that crucial age, although many delay assuming the status associated with the category for some years longer.

Rose (1968) argues that elders are forming a new American subculture. If so, this is occurring within a system increasingly dominated by the play of ethnic politics and by claims to recognition based upon a demonstration of cultural differences. Streib (1968) believes that elders cannot yet be regarded as a minority group since they are linked to other Americans by kinship and other cross-cutting ties and share with them in a common culture. For the anthropologist it is tempting to examine what is happening in terms of the age-grade paradigm and to make comparisons with societies which classify members into age-grades with unique rights and obligations.

Full-blown age grading is probably associated with two kinds of rituals; (1) rites of passage which make entry and exit from a grade and (2) rites of solidarity. Rites of passage take their primary symbolism from transition and from inversions that underline the differences between what has been and what is to be. Rites of passage associated with entry into a new age grade therefore presumably include within themselves some reference to the characteristics of all the age-grades in the set making up the system and play upon explicit contrasts among them. Periodic rites of solidarity on the other hand emphasize some common feature or features which all members of the grade share and give occasion for members to be recognized as participants in the social unit. But what is *not* said within the context of a ritual may be more interesting than what *is* said, for the silence betrays implicit assumptions about the participants' relationship to the larger society and to the political and economic framework that provides the order within which all the age grades operate.

American society may not yet have a full-blown age-grade system, though one appears to be rapidly emerging. At least, as yet, it has not developed a full set of appropriate transition rituals to mark entry and exit from the various stages now generally recognized as marking the life trajectory of its members: infancy, childhood, youth, adulthood, and senior citizen or elder. Exit from the stage of full adulthood may be marked by a transition rite associated with retirement, since full adulthood is linked to regular employment of some kind. Entry into the new age grade of elder appears to be without supportive ritual. Rituals associated with Senior Citizen Centers, if they exist, appear to be rites of solidarity rather than rites of passage.

In this paper I shall be concerned with the implications of the symbolism of one such ritual for the way the role of elder is perceived by elders themselves and by their fellow citizens.

Many who join a Center have been through the ritual of retirement. Although men and women become eligible to join a Center by virtue of reaching a given age, probably few do so until retirement or some equivalent event removes them from the earlier stage of full adulthood. Those who can postpone retirement postpone elderhood. Women who have been employed only as housewives join a center with their husbands when the latter retire. Or if widowed or divorced, and with no children dependent upon them and so in a sense retired from housewife status, they are likely to join with other friends at some point after they reach entry age. Because of differential rates of mortality, more women than men are to be found at most centers. Some centers have a diversified membership: others cater to a particular religious or ethnic clientele.

Centers vary in organization, in the amount of support they receive from public funds, and in the kinds of activities they sponsor. But however much they involve their members in a flow of events, the events cluster within the range associated with leisure, vacation time, and a non-working life. They also emphasize that elders should associate with other elders and share common interests. The typical center involves members only with each other or at most with other elders who are seen as needing their help. It does not attempt to bring them into closer association with kin or with members of other age groups: it does not remind them that they are citizens of political units; it does not attempt to find ways for them to serve within their churches or various other associations with which they may have been affiliated. A center rather attempts to provide an alternative for job, family, neighborhood, and community. Sally Falk Moore suggests that this may be consequence of receiving support from public funds, since this typically places restrictions upon the support of political or religious activities by the receiving agency. Centers supported by an ethnic or a religious community, such as the one described by Barbara Myerhoff, are able to define their role more broadly and so to involve their members in the support of common objectives not defined in terms of elderhood.

For publicly supported centers, my limited investigation suggests that the majority of events sponsored are seen as ends in themselves: or, if they look to the future, it is to a very short-range future. Centers sponsor classes in public affairs, as an academic subject; crafts as hobbies; bridge and other games; and the learning of languages. Language classes are taken primarily to pass the time or to acquire a little fluency in a language to be used in a forthcoming trip. Languages are not professional tools at this stage in life nor regarded as a long-term investment. Centers also organize tours to scenic, recreational, or historic spots. They hold dances, bridge tournaments, and craft shows. They celebrate such festive holidays as Thanksgiving, Chanuka, and Christmas. They have small libraries. Some provide an inexpensive lunch. They are a place to drop in to see if something is going on and to find people with whom to talk.

Members may sign up for as many events as they can fit into a schedule now dominated by a desire to find occupation rather than by the demands of a work schedule. Some members become involved in service to the center and find their new purpose in the many small tasks associated with its running: serving on its council, writing and duplicating notices and newsletters, arranging flowers, setting up chairs and tables for special meetings, working in the library, helping serve at an entertainment.

Active elders who become involved in other kinds of service organizations, including some that cater for elders, are drawn away from the centers, perhaps to give time to transporting elders to clinics or shopping, visiting those in hospitals or care units, or paying home visits. Those who associate themselves with a center find that attendance at classes or other meetings or working about the building can become almost a full-time occupation. Eventually it absorbs much of their day and most of their thoughts. If they have contact with other friends and kin, much of their time is spent with fellow elders at their center.

But this is true principally of the daytime hours. Centers frequently are located in the central city area since this is most easily accessible by public transportation and many elders must use public transport if they wish to move around. They are reluctant to expose themselves to the dangers of the city after the main body of workers have left. The special low fare for elders applies only during the hours when the system is not needed to transport workers and school children, and so they arrive late in the morning and leave in mid-afternoon. This fact in itself underlines the fact that while the centers may be an alternative to the office or other place of employment, they are not alternatives which are given high priority by society at large. Nevertheless as the job was once the most important determinant of status and provided the rhythm for the day, week, and year, so now the centers have this responsibility and become the focus of their members' lives. Their separation from the rest of society is associated with an allocation of a separate time and space to their activities.

The Birthday Ritual

Retirement has its rituals. Ritual associated with entry into a center is minimal or non-existent, though joining a center is almost certainly a statement of intention to associate oneself with other elders. Fred Walden, who was present on several occasions when people came to a center for the first time, assures me that neither then nor at any subsequent point is there a formal acknowledgement of the new status which could be interpreted as a ritual. This is confirmed by a number of people who have joined different centers. The new member signs the forms and provides essential information, including date of birth. Then the entrant is likely to be greeted by one or more of those sitting in the lounge area near the door. They may invite the entrant to join in the lunch provided by the Center. In conversation, the entrant learns about the relative advantages of various events on the Center's schedule. An elder brought by a friend may begin by following the same routine as the friend.

All this indicates that entry is treated as tentative and involving no commitment to a new community or to standards of behavior associated with a community. It should also be noted that while the entrant pays a fee for using the center, the fee can be paid a month at a time and so commitment is minimal. At this stage the entrant is purely a client expecting a service.

The majority of a center's activities must be seen as mundane in nature. The stress is upon the diversity of interests among members and upon their patent desire to fill time left vacant by the falling away of other claims. Members need not commit themselves to any internal order within the Center any more than they commit themselves to the Center itself, since they sign up for a particular trip or event or a limited series of classes. To many entertainments they may come to on the spur of the moment without prior notification.

Nevertheless various centers appear to be feeling their way, under the guidance of their separate staffs, towards the creation of a ritual that will acknowledge the existence of a Center as a social unit larger than its separate interest groups and at the same time make a statement, at least by implication, about the meaning of elderhood and the importance of a community of elders. The monthly birthday party is the vehicle commonly adopted. The one observed at the San Francisco Bay Center is more elaborate than birthday parties observed by Walden in the center in a small California city, but other information suggests that it is not atypical.

At the San Francisco Bay Center, the Birthday Party is an occasion for all members of the Center, though the Birthday People honored are those who have a birthday falling during that month. Only they receive a special invitation from the Center to attend the party. The Birthday Party is also one of the rare occasions when members can bring to the Center friends and kin who have not reached the entrance age. Those who invite guests are not necessarily Birthday People. Even though only a few guests are present at any one time, it appears to be important that some outsiders be present to underline the common identification of Center members. The total number of members present is some indication of the significance they attach to the Birthday Party. On the occasion described, on a beautiful day which had brought crowds of people into the city area near the Center to enjoy the many attractions the area offers to the passerby, some 200 people chose to go to the Party. Some thirty of these were Birthday People. At a guess, Center members who were present represented a thirty year age span, since several pointed out to me were said to have reached ninety.

The Birthday People were seated at tables arranged in a horseshoe, while behind them on folding chairs arranged in long rows sat other elders and the guests. The Center's recreational director was master of ceremonies, first for a short musical program and then for the ceremony which recognized each birthday celebrant. The ceremony was simple and composed of very few elements. What it left out was as striking as what it included.

Beginning at the right end of the horseshoe, and proceeding in a clockwise direction, the Director stopped behind each Birthday Person and asked each one to give two pieces of information; name and the place where his or her first birthday had been spent. He joked about this person or that, playing upon the common knowledge members have of each other. Some of the Birthday People expanded upon the value of age or pride in place of origin, but only the Director, who represents the Center, held the limelight for long. As each person finished, he or she was applauded. When the last one had spoken, there was general applause for the Birthday People and a reminder that another Birthday Party would be held in the coming month. With this the ritual was completed and those who wanted to leave did so. Although ice cream, cookies and coffee or punch were handed around, first to the Birthday People and then to others, this was not treated as a communion meal. Nor did people feel obliged to take part in the dancing that began when the tables were cleared.

The elements stressed overtly in the ritual include the following: membership in the Center, the Center's appreciation of each member, the values of elderhood and so of age, the enduring values of masculinity and femininity, and the existence of individuality signalled by recognition of birthday, name, and early residence. These provide the common denominator that merge participants as a category and at the same time recognize their continued existence as individuals. All else that goes to make up personality and status was ignored. Indeed, it was not only ignored but was positively tabooed within the context of the ritual. Several speakers who began to give their year of birth or their age in years were quickly hushed by the Director who allowed participants no chance to compare relative ages and so deemphasize their common seniority. On the other hand several who found a way to stress pride in age won approval from both Director and their fellows. One who managed to announce her age placed it within a message that youth is not to be envied.

She said, "If someone tries to tell me that I am seventy years young, I tell them, 'I am seventy years old and proud to have lived' " This was loudly applauded. So was the short poem composed by another elder in honor of the value of age.

Age then is a good in itself and a common attribute of all, but it should not be associated with the counting of years. This may avoid the implications of continued aging and the fear of a transition either into helpless old age or death, but it also eliminated the possibility of creating new statuses within the Center community based on relative age.

The Birthday People had celebrated their first birthdays in all parts of the United States and in Australia, England, Middle Europe, Russia, Scandinavia, France, Italy and Canada. Each place won applause, though the loudest applause came for localities in California and especially for San Francisco. Inclusion of the locale of first birthday in the message of the ritual was a neutral way of emphasizing that the Center is a common home to which all are drawn by their elderhood despite their diversity in backgrounds. It also linked beginnings with the present moment and so gave continuity to each life. But this is my interpretation: the symbolism was not made explicit by any additional comment either by Director or by Birthday People.

In moving around the horseshoe, the Director represented the Center in direct relationship to each participant. He also used the occasion to give recognition to what he must perceive as enduring values of masculinity and femininity. A man might be clapped on the back or given a poke on the ribs to show him as a fellow male. This was usually accompanied by a word of praise for the man's help in some way that required a show of strength, as in moving chairs and tables. Women were enveloped with a supporting arm and called "a sweetheart" or some other term that suggested they were endearing creatures.

Now let us look at the important attributes of status ignored completely in the ritual. Each Birthday Person gave his or her name but without any title. The Director did mention the marital status of several couples where husband and wife were both Birthday People, but for no others. Marital status therefore was largely ignored. The existence of children or grandchildren was never mentioned. Even more strikingly, no one was ever identified in terms of any job or position which they had held or currently held outside the Center. American society has long been described as dominated by status linked to occupation. In elderhood this had vanished: doctor, lawyer, beggarman, thief were no longer significant aspects of personality. Identification with neighborhood had also vanished. The locality stressed was that at first birthday, at least sixty years back. Current addresses or association with particular parts of the city which might signal clues to status were suppressed. In praising Birthday People, the Director never referred to any special honors in the larger society nor suggested that people had memberships or interests outside the immediate group. Only once did he drop his guard when he commented that one woman continued to be an opera buff. His other jokes and comments stayed with experiences and incidents from the Center world, but even then did not relate to different interest groups or various offices associated with the center government that could provide a basis for internal status differentiation. All were reduced to a single role – that of elder.

The birthday ritual therefore displayed that collapse of the status system into its broadest, most inclusive categories, which Victor Turner has pointed to as a characteristic feature of rituals. There is both a rejection of the former roles of active adult life and a refusal to recognize new status differences among Center members based on age differences, the pursuit of different activities, length of association with the Center, or the holding of Center offices. The collapse is even more striking when the Birthday Party is compared with the graduation ritual held at the Jewish Senior Citizen Center described by Barbara Myerhoff. Those who created the graduation ritual after all shared much common experience upon which to draw in creating a symbolic statement about the common meaning of their lives. At the San Francisco Bay Center, members had in common only the attributes of being over sixty, the quality of vigor which allowed them to attend, and their present residence in the same city. Given that they might vary in age by as much as thirty years, that they came from different countries of origin and differed in religion, and that they had grown up and spent their youths in very different worlds, no common denominator could be sought in childhood or youthful experiences. They could draw, however, on exposure to certain aspects of American culture associated with other attempts to create an atmosphere of community and with the media. Office forces, church groups, and other collectivities very commonly sponsor an official monthly birthday party. Most participants would find the roles of master of ceremony and celebrity of the day familiar from radio and television programs. These familiar roles helped to define appropriate behavior on an occasion already defined as an appropriate symbol of community.

The Birthday Party then assured participants of their membership in a community of equals and of their importance in the here and now of the Center. The Center's ability to absorb all who came to it as elders despite any differences in previous experience was dramatized. Participants were told that elderhood was an achievement and their status one in which to take pride. Here they were honored members of a community rather than exiles from the working world of adult life and a society that values and clings to youth. They could take pride in the continued vigor which permitted them to be present and which distinguished them from the dependent very old. Max Gluckman suggests that they were recognizing the joy of being alive on an occasion that emphasized the continuity of life itself through the symbol of the recurrent cycling of the months and years.

The simplicity of the ritual may have masked its wider meanings until one contemplated the pleasure with which the Birthday People rose to participate within it and the attention with which the others watched and listened. Something of significance to them, either as individuals or as a group, must have drawn the 200 people who gathered in the hall, abandoning the gaiety and color of the street life just outside its door.

The effectiveness of this Birthday Party as a vehicle of community and continued self identity becomes more marked when contrasted with birthday parties held in a Middlewest retirement home for elderly men and women confined to its care center. Here too those in charge of the Center had seen in the birthday party a common denominator in which various persons could share, but those for whom the parties were held were anything but moved by the ritual to a sense of acceptance of a common identity. Perhaps some enjoyed a birthday party, but those whom I visited took no joy in an institutionalized birthday. The contrast between their dislike of the occasion and the pleasure taken by members of the Bay Area Center needs to be explained.

The patients in the Care Center thought a birthday ought to be an occasion on which they ought to be joined by friends and family. In the past for them a birthday had been a time of ingathering, with messages from old friends, visits from those nearby, and general recognition of their continued importance as valued members of the community they had known. They had come to the Care Center as old people no longer able to live independent lives. They had had to accept hospitalization because of various disabilities which they found humiliating. They had no choice in their new associates. They found it difficult to make friends or even to find common interests across the various barriers of their physical disabilities. For them the monthly Birthday Party became an added insult because it associated them with others whom they would have repudiated if they could and placed them in a common category which they neither respected nor easily tolerated. The official monthly birthday party, with its contrast with former occasions, also served as a reminder that they were no longer part of a common life with family and friends but instead had been sent to live out their days among strangers. They had no option of withdrawal from the situation, as had members of the Senior Citizen Center, and even their recognition of the comforts provided by good nursing care only underlined their helplessness in their own eyes. As long as they could, they tried to maintain their independent personalities, but these were derived not from activity in the care center but from their former lives and were based upon the multitude of experiences they had known as professionals, hired workers or housewives, as spouses, parents, neighbors and active workers in their old communities.

They were interested neither in their own nor in other people's birthday celebrations which marked them as members of the Care Center. A birthday for them should be a unique occasion and not a common denominator. They resented less the celebration of Thanksgiving and Christmas, for these had always been general festivals as well as family occasions.

The elders of the San Francisco Bay Senior Citizen Center saw a common birthday party in a very different light. They were free to come and go. Most of them were still vigorous and able to live independent lives. They could and did celebrate their individual birthdays with friends and kin. They had apartments, houses, or at least rooms of their own, and maintained some kind of status in the wider society from which they were not completely withdrawn even though they may have lost many of the statuses they had once occupied. In coming to the Center they were searching for a new basis that would join them to their fellows and for new experiences that would compensate them for the responsibilities they had lost on retirement. Those who found nothing at the Center to interest them dropped their membership and sought elsewhere. Those who remained found in the Birthday Party a ritual that served to dramatize their common membership in an age grade of elders and a chance to state that as elders they had experience, intelligence, and vigor to offer each other and to the world.

This paper is based on a single observation of a birthday party at a Senior Citizen Center in the San Francisco Bay area, California; numerous observations in the care center of a retirement home in the Middle West; discussions with residents of the care center, several members of the San Francisco Bay center, and members of other centers in various parts of the United States. Victoria Durant and Fred Walden, who had carried out research in senior citizen centers in a small California city, discussed their observations with me while I was formulating this paper and I have drawn on this information. Dr. Ruth Sawtell Wallis commented on the original draft and provided information on the ceremonial birthday in other contexts. I am also grateful to members of the Conference on Social Rituals and to students in Anthropology 141, Berkely, Fall 1974, who commented on this paper.

CHAPTER XI
WE DON'T WRAP HERRING IN A PRINTED PAGE:
FUSION, FICTIONS AND
CONTINUITY IN SECULAR RITUAL

Barbara G. Myerhoff

A Working Definition of Ritual[1]

Ritual is full of contradictions and paradox. Most paradoxical of all, by selecting and shaping a fragment of social life, it defines a portion of reality. The very act of consciously defining reality calls to our attention that, indeed, reality is merely a social construct, a collusive drama, intrinsically conventional, an act of collective imagination.

Rituals are not only paradoxical intrinsically, they are built out of the paradoxes suggested by their symbols. They cope with paradox by mounting the mood of conviction and persuasion which fuses opposing elements referred to by their symbols, creating the belief that things are as they have been portrayed – proper, true, inevitable, natural. How this is accomplished is one of the most challenging of the analyst's tasks.[2]

A working definition of ritual may be suggested, each element of which points to its capacity to achieve one of its special tasks – persuasion. Ritual is an act or actions intentionally conducted by a group of people employing one or more symbols in a repetitive, formal, precise, highly stylized fashion. Action is indicated because rituals persuade the body first; behaviors precede emotions in the participants. Rituals are conspicuously physiological; witness their behavioral basis, the use of repetition and the involvement of the entire human sensorium through dramatic presentations employing costumes, masks, colors, textures, odors, foods, beverages, songs, dances, props, settings, and so forth. Critical, analytic thought, the attitude which would pierce the illusion of reality, is anathema to ritual. The fiction underlying ritual is twofold: first, that rituals are not made-up productions, and second, that the contradictions embraced by their symbols have been erased. The enemy of ritual is one who is incapable of or unwilling to voluntarily suspend disbelief – the spoilsport.

Because of its repetitiveness, formality, and rigid precision, rituals can take on dangerous matters. V. Turner has made the felicitous comment that rituals are to symbols as is a metal container to a radioactive isotope, containing without snuffing out its content (1974). Rituals are stylized because they must be convincing. People must recognize what rituals are saying, and find their claims authentic, their styles familiar and aesthetically satisfying. Rituals can be distinguished from custom and mere habit by their utilization of symbols. They have significance far beyond the information transmitted. They may accomplish tasks, accompany routine and instrumental procedures, but they always go beyond them, endowing some larger meaning to activities they are associated with.

The most salient characteristic of ritual is its function as a frame. It is a deliberate and artificial demarcation. In ritual, a bit of behavior or interaction, an aspect of social life, a moment in time is selected, stopped, remarked upon. But this framing is a fiction. Artificial, its very artifice is denied and the claim is made that its meanings are discovered rather than made-up. It claims that things "are as they seem," as presented. This applies to rituals large and small: the encounters and separations in ordinary human transactions are punctuated by ritual gestures or statements, announcing our agreement on what has occurred – we have met, been amiably disposed to one another, parted with regrets, and so forth. Something of note has occurred. Ritual gestures announce instrumental activities very often. As such they call the subject's attention to his undertaking. He is acting with awareness. He has taken the activity out of the ordinary flow of habit and routine, and performed the gesture to arouse in himself a particular attitude, demonstrating that his actions mean more than they seem.

It is this very feature of framing which coincides with Durkheim's (1915) conception of the sacred as the set-apart. But being set-apart is a matter not of kind but degree. Rituals are not either sacred or secular, rather in high rituals they are closer to the sacred end of the continuum, entirely extraordinary, communicating the *mysterium tremendum* and are often associated with supernatural or spiritual beings. Or, they are closer to the mundane end of the continuum, perfunctory genuflections to form, "good form," meaning good manners that acknowledge and punctuate social interactions, smoothing them, eliminating potential disruption, unpredictability and accident. Whether more or less set-apart, rituals are always rhetorical and didactic, inducing certain attitudes and convictions, blending wish and actuality until history and accident assume the shape of human intention.

The Nonce Ritual: Sequencing and Guiding Metaphor

The case at hand is an illustration of what might be called a nonce ritual, a common form in Western, urban, mobile societies. It is a complex ceremony parts of which are sacred and parts secular, parts unique improvisations (openings) and parts stable, recurrent and fixed (closed). This arrangement is very characteristic of rituals among strangers and acquaintances gathered together on an *ad hoc* basis for the nonce, once only bringing with them diverse experience and personal histories.

Non-repeating or nonce rituals whose participants have only secondary ties to each other must overcome special handicaps in achieving their ceremonial goals. Blatantly made-up and designed for specific occasions by one or more "masters-of-ceremony," nonce rituals must nevertheless convey a sense of rightness and inevitability. Nonce rituals are those awkward, self-conscious "first annual" events, laboring under their obvious contrivance, and the often touchingly transparent hopes and intentions of then participants. Such rituals do not have at hand those powerful, consensual, "self-evident" basic symbols that convey the rightness which endows authenticity and conviction to any circumstance where they occur. Lacking reservoirs of shared beliefs, deities, and histories, having none of the ready sources of emotional dynamism available to intimates, people in traditional societies, or stable circumstances, the masters-of-ceremonies in nonce rituals must use symbols which refer to the most basic common denominators of belief and experience – usually general, shallow and abstract, and little able to arouse deep emotion or profound conviction.

This presents a serious problem in a ritual. Without the emotional response provided by basic, deep symbols how are rituals to move and persuade participants and witnesses? A common solution found in many rituals in secular situations involves sequencing – of two kinds, sacred/secular, and open/closed. The first is an alternation of secular and sacred themes or symbols. Here, the secular elements – usually quite particular and unique – are juxtaposed with those regarded as unquestionable and permanent. By this juxtaposition, particulars are painted with the colors of the sacred, so to speak, borrowing the latter's sense of specialness and significance. Such sequencing is found everywhere – in political meetings which may be begun, closed and intermittently punctuated with references to deities. All the business in between, it is suggested, has the tacit approval of the gods. And rhetorical speeches often follow this pattern, weaving together National Destiny and the raising of funds for a particular candidate until the candidate somehow becomes a manifestation of that Destiny. Local affairs are considerably aggrandized by the process, and, conversely, remote abstract ideas are vitalized and specified. A fusion of sacred and secular can substitute in ritual for the work done in other circumstances by strong, collective symbols.

In addition, open/closed sequencing occurs in complex secular rituals. Rigidly fixed, recurrent, highly specific ritual acts, gestures – set forms such as toasts, poems, salutes, dances, songs, pledges and oaths – alternate with open spaces, which are used for improvisation and particularization; in secular rituals these are often given over to speeches. These openings provide opportunities for participants to establish their individual emotions, identities, motives and needs, and allow the ritual masters-of-ceremony to convey the specific, idiosyncratic messages which are unique to the occasion at hand. The fixed segments are highly predictable, allegedly unchanging, and are the traditionalizing ingredients in a complex ritual. The open segments are the particularizing opportunities, available for the purpose of the day, preceded and followed by closed sections.

The open or improvised sections may be short or protracted, may involve several people or one, may be rather conventional or truly new, but withal they must convey a sense of accuracy and authenticity. They must communicate to the participants and audience what is being done at any given moment. Clearly such communications are redundant in the established, familiar sections of rituals. But within the improvised sections, co-ordination between participants must occur in order for those involved to be certain that they are in the same play, so to speak. In cases of nonce rituals, it is especially important that communication and coordination be done well, lest emotional momentum flag, self-consciousness develop and the made-up quality of the occasion become conspicuous.

One way in which the improvisations are guided and coordinated in secular rituals is through the use of a mnemonic device in the form of a metaphor. The guiding metaphor in ritual serves to remind all concerned who they are, where they are, and what they are doing there. It is essential that the metaphor have ample and emotionally vital referents, sufficiently specific to be used as the basis of enactments. Metaphor cross-references domains of meaning to supply information from one well-known realm in understanding another, lesser known realm. It operates by analogy, and ultimately by blending the domains, to some extent. Reference to a guiding metaphor obviates the questions, "what do I do next?" for participants, and "what are they doing now?" for the audience. By naming the event, with a familiar name, (i.e., "graduation") audience and actors are quickly oriented within the less familiar sections of a nonce ritual. Ritual drama is a complex form requiring precision, flow and details. Ritual dramas must be fully staged, abounding in vocabulary and props to flesh them out, conceptually and sensually. The guiding metaphor provides these details as well as basic orientation.

The ritual event presented here, a nonce ritual, is characterized by the sequencing of sacred/secular, and open/closed elements, and by a clear and fruitful guiding metaphor, "Graduation-Siyum."[3] The ritual was a totally unique event, blending the sacred and secular, and successfully linking two entirely distinct realms of meaning and experience into a strong, convincing ritual drama. It was an occasion which transcended many contradictions, fused disparate elements, glossed conflicts, and provided a sense of individual and collective continuity in the course of mounting a bold and original fiction.

The Graduation-Siyum, Participants and their History

A graduation is a common secular ritual in which a class of students marks a termination of a course of study, prescribed by and occurring within an educational institution. A *siyum*, (Hebrew, "completion") refers to the ceremonial recognition of the completion of a course of self-assigned study of a Jewish sacred text. In the context of this case, siyum refers to the ceremony held in 19th and early 20th century small Jewish villages and settlements of Eastern Europe called *shtetls*. There, the siyum was a simple affair which took place in the synagogue after the Saturday morning service; the individual who had completed his studies provided refreshments, received congratulations and announced his plans for another round of study, since "the Torah has no beginning and no end," and "a Jew studies all his life." As will be seen, graduation and siyum were drawn from utterly distinct domains of meaning and experience – cultural, religious and historical. Nevertheless, the graduation-siyum achieved a fusion among many conflicting ingredients; it was used once and once only, but for that occasion it was more than adequate as a guiding metaphor.

The Graduation-Siyum took place on a November Sunday afternoon in a small dilapidated hall which housed the Jewish Senior Citizens' Center on the Boardwalk at the beach in a California city. Assembled there were the graduates, thirty-one members of the Yiddish History Class which had just completed a year of study, and an audience of about a hundred and fifty. The graduating students, all women save eight men, were in their eighties and nineties. All were Eastern European Jewish immigrants, all had grown up in shtetls. The Senior Citizen's Center, sponsored and supported by a large city-wide organization, was made up of a very stable membership with a common history and culture. It was a highly visible and well-bounded community with a distinctive life style, some thirty years in the making. Three decades before, it was founded by retiring Jews from East Coast urban centers of America, who were drawn to the climate and the *Yiddishkeit* which flourished there.[4] As recently as the late 1950's there were an estimated 10,000 such people in the area.

Losses due to death and urban renewal had shrunk the present population to approximately 4,000.

A collective portrait can summarize the history of the people participating in the Graduation-Siyum, and with varying goodness of fit, the same outlines characterize the majority of the 300 Center members. Shtetl life has been well-documented, and here I shall limit my comments to those features most pertinent to the ritual at hand.[5] Shtetls were tiny ethnic enclaves surrounded by hostile peasants; anti-semitism was legal and traditional. Life was precarious and relentlessly poor. But the culture within was strong, rich and stable. The shtetls from which these people came were profoundly religious, conservative, ethnocentric and provincial, separated from Jewish and non-Jewish centers. They were late in receiving the full impact of the secular and religious movements which swept the rest of the Jewish world in the late nineteenth and early twentieth centuries, and ultimately drew shtetl youth away from their parents' traditional way.

Shtetl folk were tradesmen, peddlers, petty artisans, craftsmen, and the like, legally forbidden to own land or grow crops. In this highly stratified community even the powerful and relatively affluent were impotent outside their limited world. A pogrom might wipe out a family or a whole village at any moment. In education, all shtetl people were literate, in contrast to the surrounding peasantry whom they disdained accordingly. Though legally forbidden to attend public secular schools or institutions of advanced learning, nevertheless, religious education was pursued with passion in the shetl. Yiddish, the everyday language, was read and written by all; Hebrew, the sacred language, was read and written by all men and some women, though proficiency varied considerably.

These communities were self-regulating, jointly administered by the Rabbi and a social elite based on a wealth and religious scholarship. There was little sustained interaction with the surrounding world of non-Jews except for peripheral exchanges in the market place or occasional intimate relationships with trusted servants. Cultural and social separatism were very thorough. A dual but conflicting social structure existed, one – internal, indigenous, sacred and politically impotent; the other – external, coercive, powerful and hostile. In these circumstances one would expect family and community ties to be exceedingly strong, and so they were.

Age and sex, as always in such groups, were major determiners of role allocations, with women's participation in religious and educational realms sharply limited. Family stability and harmony were highly valued and occasionally attained. Life was hard but folkways were treasured – in Redfield's sense (1956) it was a sacred society, in its peoples' feeling of the complete rightness of its way of life, their unquestioned fusion of place, tradition and primary group, and their total indentity with community.

In many ways the shtetl was similar to one of the small, traditional, well-integrated, stable pre-literate groups that anthropologists usually study, with two major exceptions: their link to a religious Great Tradition through literacy, and a sense of unity as a people through time and space with a common destiny and sacred history.

This way of life was ended definitively by Hitler's physical destruction of the shtetl, but before the Holocaust many thousands of young people had left their homes in a search for a new life. Soon everyone had a relative in America who could help him or her come over and get started. They came in masses, fleeing poverty, anti-Semitism and often the restrictive orthodoxy of their parents and community.

Most of the people involved in this study came to America in their late or middle teens, and soon became petty merchants, retailers, wage workers, artisans and peddlers. None had more than a year or two of secular or religious education behind them. They struggled with poverty and loneliness in America. All who could manage to de so went to night school to learn English. They married people like themselves and with determination dedicated themselves to their childrens' future. So successful were they in assuring an education for their children that they constituted what has been called a one-generation proletariat. Their children were lawyers, doctors, professors, scientists, artists, businessmen and entrepreneurs. And they were "real Americans." They disdained Yiddish, abandoned religious orthodoxy, firmly turned away from the cultural baggage of their parents. Herberg (1955) points out that theirs was an age of militant secularism "since a clean break with religion seemed the best and surest way of becoming an American."

In many ways the immigrants were highly successful. Their children were secure, respected, accomplished people. The parents had, by middle age, acquired the possibility of a respectable and secure retirement, and they had flocked to the beaches of California.

For the past decade the beach neighborhood in which they now live has been becoming increasingly marginal. Housing costs are rising, and muggings and violent crimes keep the elderly off the streets after dark. Other retired Jews like themselves are not moving into the neighborhood. There are almost no other younger Jews in the immediate area; the nearest large Temple is several miles away. Their little community is distinctive and set apart – a closed enclave.

Thus the people described here constitute a highly stable, cohesive, relatively small group, whose members share a common cultural and religious historical background. They are alike in education, work history, income, age, language, and family status. Despite their long and intense relationships with each other and despite their well-developed community life, they are lonely, quite cut off from their families and from other and younger Jews. Most live in tiny rundown rented rooms and economically are well below the national poverty level. They are unwilling to accept any assistance in the form of "charity" and maintain a dignified, genteel facade of independence, while in actuality they are under more stress every day, due to the growing losses of physical and sometimes mental powers, exacerbated by the torments of living on a small, fixed income in times of soaring inflation.

Ritual Elements of the Graduation-Siyum

The Yiddish History Class is the elite of the Center membership, those most involved in all its activities and most committed to the highest goal of the entire membership, the study of Jewish life in general and Yiddishkeit in particular. The program for the Graduation-Siyum was designed by the Center director, several of the graduating students, and the teacher of the class, Kominsky, a dynamic younger man of 68 possessed of great energy and charisma. For the ceremony he had two clear purposes in mind: to bring the students back to the religion they had abandoned as teenagers in America, and to bring them to the attention of those who were neglecting them – their children and wealthier Jewish organizations in the city.

The little hall was filled with folding chairs for the Graduation-Siyum; the students sat together facing the audience. At one end of the room, a platform served as a stage, flanked by flags of Israel and America and decked with flowers. The walls were adorned with the seniors' art work, and photographs and drawings of important Jews, especially Zionists and Yiddishists.

The audience consisted of other members of the Center, friends, representatives of the Jewish Alliance, the philanthropic organization which funds and sponsors the Center, and officials from Temple Beth Shalom, a well-to-do synagogue a few miles away which had "adopted" the Center the previous year in an effort to assume some responsibility for it unmet needs. Also attending were the director of the city senior citizen programs, and approximately fifteen individuals who were kin and progeny of the graduating members, twelve from the family of the Center's President. As important to the ceremony were those who did not attend: members (as opposed to officials) of any of the organizations mentioned above, and any significant numbers of the family of the seniors.

Gathered on the platform were the representatives from the formal organizations, the Center Director, and the teacher, Kominsky. Though those to whom the event was ostensibly addressed were absent, the hall was packed with well-wishers in a festive mood. Flowers of blue and white – the national colors of Israel and the Jewish flag – adorned tables and the graduating elders, who wore finest clothes beneath blue and white satin banners crossed from shoulder to waist. For the next three hours, the program proceeded as follows:[6]

1 The Pledge of Allegiance to the American flag was recited. (secular/ closed)
2 Kominsky introduced the students and officials to the audience, and made some general remarks concerning the significance of the occasion. He then explained,
   "First we are Americans, then we are Jews. According to the Talmud, the law of the country precedes the law of the Jews. That is why we are beginning with the National Anthem." (open/secular)
3 The 92-year-old, greatly esteemed Center President read a Yiddish poem he had written about his childhood in the shtetl. (closed/ sacred)
4 Class valedictorian delivered a short speech in English, the major theme of which was a eulogy to America, the land of freedom and democracy. (open/secular)
5 A 20-year-old Hebrew student of Kominsky's read a poem by the poet laureate of Israel. (closed/sacred)
6 Greetings and congratulations were read by the Alliance president from "Jewish civic and community leaders" throughout the city. There were some messages from national Jewish organizations commending the class members for their accomplishments and citing them as exemplary Jews and senior citizens. (open/secular)
7 The "Commencement Address" was delivered by the Rabbi of Temple Beth Shalom lauding the students, stressing the connection between Judaism and scholarship, and the good fortune presented to retired Jews by the opportunity to finish their lives in study and learning. (open/ secular and sacred)
8 Diplomas were distributed by the Rabbi. These were in Hebrew, printed forms actually intended for children graduating from Hebrew schools and temple confirmations. As such, they carried messages referring to "Hope for the future," "Passing on the religious heritage to the young who will improve the world," and "Creating a brighter tomorrow." The diplomas bore the date 5733, following the

ancient Jewish calendar. Inscribed on them were the names of the senior citizens in Yiddish, ending in the diminutive. Leahle, Rechele, Schloymele, and so forth. These were shtetl names for children known to each other, but not generally used in everyday affairs. (open/secular and sacred)

9 The Rabbi's young daughter and her friend entertained the group with Israeli folksongs. (closed/sacred)

10 The president of the Temple's Men's Club read messages from organizations and individuals all over the world, congratulating the senior citizens. These had resulted from class members pooling their contacts in Israel and elsewhere, requesting their friends to find "dignitaries" to send telegrams and cards to the graduates. The project was facilitated by the Center's reputation as a reliable and generous supporter of Israel. One message came in the form of a tape recording made of young orthodox Jews praying and reciting their lessons in a religious school immediately adjacent to the Western Wall in Jerusalem; this wall is a remnant of the Temple of the Jews in Biblical times. (open/secular and sacred)

11 Kominsky read "The Charge to the Class." Here he discussed his students' exemplary conduct, told the audience how despite their poor health and bad weather, they came eagerly and prepared to each class session. Limited means notwithstanding, they had their own libraries. Despite their lack of formal religious training in childhood and rejection of religiosity in youth, despite an adulthood devoted to becoming Americans and earning a living which left no time for study, now, as older people they were learning the Hebrew alphabet and beginning to be able to read the sacred texts. He closed his remarks by explaining the importance of the Law and Learning to the Jews in general and in his family in particular, closing by saying,

> "In my family, when Papa opened his book we were all quiet. Sha! Papa studies. Papa looks in a book. All the house respects it. When a book is dropped, it is kissed. A worn-out book is buried. We don't wrap herring in a printed page, not even if it's a newspaper" (open/sacred)

12 Kominsky led the students in the "Class Song," a shtetl folksong in Yiddish describing the warm room in which the hearth glows as the Rabbi teaches his little children the Hebrew alphabet. (closed/sacred)

13 The Center Director made his address which included the following comments:

> You are our parents and we honor you today. You are the people

the world, by your efforts, the finest doctors, scientists, professors, philosophers, artists and musicians that have ever been seen. Your children have given you "nakhes" (pride and pleasure), and now it is the time for you, the parents, to give your children "nakhes."

Then, addressing the audience,

How proud you must be of your parents and grandparents today. You can rejoice over them; it is your turn. All their lives, without recognition, they worked for others, raising children, sending money to Israel, and now it is time for you to express your appreciation.

Their lives have meaning and they are a model to us. Look at Mr. Abraham. He has written a book, and produced four devoted, successful sons. He writes poetry every day. From him we learn what life can be. He is always learning. He is a "filosophe." Learning is lifelong. We Jews are the People of the Book. Study is the highest activity for any phase of life. Old and young, every Jew is supposed to study a little bit each day. Learning is what makes us stay young forever, so a real Jew is ageless. (open/secular and sacred)

14 Hatikvah, the national anthem of Israel, was sung. (closed/sacred)

15 A group of teenagers, the class of the Temple Beth Shalom, served cookies and punch to the graduates and the audience. (open/secular)

16 An important but unplanned event occurred next – the provision and service by several class members of brandy, herring, and honey cakes. This was done rather furtively, so that no one could be sure who was responsible, for Kominsky had been adamant that on this one occasion the senior citizens should be the receivers of applause, praise, food and service; today, at least, they should not provide for or serve those younger than themselves. (open/sacred) A blessing was said in Hebrew before eating. (closed/sacred)

17 Another unexpected event took place; one of the class members took to the stage to present "Reb Kominsky," "Our chaver" (Hebrew: companion) a "filosofe" (philosopher) with a certificate indicating that the class had gathered contributions from among its members to enter their teacher's name in "The Golden Book," where a record is kept of donors of $ 100 or more in funds for Israel. (open/sacred)

18 The ceremony was officially closed with the singing of the American National Anthem. (closed/secular)

Barbara G. Myerhoff

Axiomatic Symbols in the Ritual: Being-a-Jew and Learning

Rituals when they succeed do so in large part through the power of their axiomatic symbols. In this case, two such symbols operate, unifying and condensing a vast array of referents; these symbols are Being-a-Jew, and Learning.[7] Being-a-Jew is a particularly complex, dense symbol, referring to four distinct forms of Jewish experience: the Great Tradition of scholarship, the Little Tradition of Yiddishkeit, The Jews as One People (Klal Isroel), and American Temple Judaism.

Loosely following Redfield (1956), the "Great Tradition" is used to refer to the abstract, eternal, impersonal verities in which a culture participates. Local institutions expressive of the Great Tradition may exist but are controlled by literatti remote from the community. And indeed, the great centers of learning, the great scholars, and the great historical events were spatially and temporally removed from the experience of the shtetl. The Great Tradition of Judaism is learned, exalted, specialized, pure and perpetual. Awesome and somewhat forbidding to these ordinary people, it is quite distinguishable from the meaning of Judaism as folk religion, the Little Tradition, in this case Yiddishkeit. This form of Judaism for them was a matter of everyday life and mundane concerns, but no less authentically Jewish because more homely. This is the Judaism which guided everyday decisions, the interpretation of events, the folkways, local histories, styles, and customs. It is Judaism in the form of the Little Tradition which makes a Jew from Berditchev nearly unrecognizable to one from Morocco or Berlin; the folk traditions separate Jews from different locales, and the Great Tradition provides the overarching connections between them. The Great Tradition, manifested especially in the use of Hebrew, prayer, study, and an awareness of sacred history allows Jews to experience most powerfully a sense of peoplehood; though they are spatially dispersed and culturally heterogeneous, nevertheless they are a unified group, "One People," Klal Isroel.

Among these people the Great Tradition was and is incompletely woven into everyday life. It might be said that it covers their local forms of Judaism like a fine bedspread on a straw pallet. In fact, a very few of those participating in the Graduation-Siyum were deeply learned people. The Great Tradition of Jewish scholarship was venerated by them but not part of their direct experience. A reading knowledge of Hebrew among the men, enough to get through the Psalms, knowledge of some prayers and a little Jewish history, was all that time had allowed them. None of the women knew Hebrew and only two had had a year or two devoted to Jewish study.

Local traditions are matters of daily life, occurring first and foremost in the familial setting, in association with the child's earliest experiences in the safety of the home, in the routines of ordinary affairs. They have a kind of sacrality, despite their mundane nature, which comes from being so completely embedded in every feature of a culture. Judaism as Little Tradition was learned pre-verbally, intertwined with nurturance and survival, occurring in the form of the small, prysical and sensory events and experiences which correspond to V. Turner's (1969) orectic or physiological pole of dominant symbols, "relating to desire, appetite and feeling." Local tradition is largely unconscious and unconsidered, a profoundly familiar mix of household odors and habits, gestures, sounds, tastes, and sentiments which set down the deepest roots in the individual.

In the Graduation-Siyum, the Great Tradition of Judaism was brought in by means of a mediating symbol, representing another expression of Judaism-Israel. Israel was always and a still a very personal matter to these people, regarded by them almost as a child, precious and precarious, needing their help, making mistakes but deserving complete faith and devotion, forgiveness and indulgence. For them, Israel contains and refers to the Great Tradition theme, for it is a historical place of sacred origins and the place where the sacred language and history flourishes and is preserved. At the same time it elicits profound responses which are more immediate and less lofty. Their identification with the Holy Land goes back to their childhood and has constituted one of the most continuing, passionate concerns throughout their lives. Israel is for them the Millennium, representing spiritual salvation, but in addition, it is a worldly, historical salvation, the ingathering of the Jews as a people, the real and symbolic homeland for their depleted families. Here is the site of the total Jewish community, Klal Isroel. Through Israel, identification with the broadest reaches of group membership is achieved. It links these people to a larger destiny, beyond Yiddishkeit; as such it is part of the Great Tradition, but less awesome and unattainable than its scholarly expression. For though they hold scholarship in the highest regard, the elders know full well that they are not and will never be deeply educated people. But for the maintenance and support of Israel, even the most ignorant and humble are needed and welcome. As a mediating symbol, Israel coalesces the highest and most fundamental forms of Being-a-Jew for the senior citizens.

American Temple Judaism offered its own special meanings and conflicts which had to be incorporated into the ritual. For most of the graduates, since adolescence, Being-a-Jew had become associated with being old-fashioned and un-American. In this country for the first time Jewish identity became optional to some extent. It was a somewhat bewildering condition, sometimes a little embarrassing – a social impediment. Being-a-

Jew in America as young adults was never satisfactorily resolved by most of these people. Judaism in this country lacked the firm roots and social supports of the shtetl, and the Great Tradition part of Judaism had never really constituted a compelling, immediate way of life for them. What, then, did it mean Being-a-Jew in America during their middle years? On this there was more variation among them than the other meanings of Being-a-Jew. Some individuals had expressed their Judaism by joining Yiddish political or cultural groups. A few joined small orthodox temples. Most had no time for these activities, and Being-a-Jew became blurred and uneasy. The distinctly American institutions referred to in the Graduation-Siyum were the modern, less orthodox temples and schools. In these institutions the elders had never participated directly. The features in the ritual ceremony associated with the temple were viewed with some indifference by the graduates. They constituted a kind of ritual cargo that the seniors had to include so as not to be overtly rude. Men's Clubs, Confirmation Classes, Sisterhoods, English prayers led by beardless, bareheaded rabbis were not part of Judaism as they had known it. These were forms without emotional resonance.

A symbol of a different kind is also active in this ritual, Learning. Like Being-a-Jew, it is an axiomatic good, an end in itself, but it is also a means, a strategy for appropriate social and spiritual action.[8] As a symbol and strategy it has been relevant throughout the many phases and changes in these elders' lives. It is one of the strong, unifying concerns of their personal histories. In the shtetl, Learning determined a family's social as well as religious standing. Learning benefited community and the individual, and was a certain source of upward social mobility.

Later in America, in their middle years it was Learning, as symbol and strategy, which served these people and their children so well. Now, Learning was for secular, instrumental and more individualistic purposes but it retained its aura of sacrality. The seniors could not achieve it for themselves but they could and did provide higher education for their children.

Now, in old age, Learning assumed a somewhat different form while remaining a major concern. At this point, it had become the means of expressing the successful culmination of a life. Jews, they say, need never stop Learning, and old age provides the leisure they never had before for its pursuit. "We are the People of the Book," they often said, and as such more fortunate than other retired people. Pursuit of Learning is regarded as a blessing, defiant of time. In this stage of life, Learning included secular and sacred meanings, an activity intrinsically and extrinsically valuable. The content of the Graduation-Siyum repeatedly employed the symbol, Learning, in the speeches, songs, and poems, lauding a man by referring to him as a "filosophe," reverence demonstrated for the teacher of the Yiddish history class, signified in many ways, including the use of the respectful term "Reb," and honoring him by entering his name in the Golden Book. And of course the very form of the ceremony, commemorating completion of studies, is based on this axiomatic symbol.

Both axiomatic symbols, it must be said, are touched with irony and ambivalence. One of the major postulates of "Being-a-Jew" is that "We are one People, Klal Isroel." It is generally agreed, certainly by these people, that the ultimate expression of Being-a-Jew is not praying but taking responsibility for other Jews. "Among Jews one is never lost," goes the proverb. But it is no secret that these senior citizens are being neglected by the wider Jewish community as well as their own progeny. This realization is close to the surface and a very delicate matter. No less painful is the uneasy recognition that the solidarity among the members of the Center is strained and fragile, for many reasons. The people help one of their members in distress but are reluctant to share each other's joys. In the end, they are fellow Jews but not family. Internal discord breaks out with great intensity and frequency and on ritual events such as this one, the harmonious atmosphere is understood to be temporary. Being-a-Jew makes them One People but the sense of Peoplehood is strongest when external threats are grave, and correspondingly weak in times of relative external peace.

Ambivalence toward Learning is also distinct, but subtler. Though Learning was the key to the success of the peoples' children, it was also the path by means of which their progeny escaped from them and their traditions. All children leave their parents behind, but the speed and completeness of the break between the generations here is extreme. Their American-born children were exceptionally well-equipped to make their way up and out of the ghetto, and their parents were genuinely proud of their accomplishments. But at the same time, there is sadness and bitterness as well as pride in the elders' talk about their children. Hannah's daughter told her, "Mamale, you are sweet but so stupid." "And," Hannah agreed, "I know it's true. After all this time in America, I still can't spell." Learning was the strategy for assimilation and success in America, but as it became an escape route for the children it was also an irony, and a source of great hurt for the old people.

Functions of the Ritual: Fusions, Fictions and Continuity

The Graduation-Siyum served several functions: it was an occasion in which the axiomatic symbols, Being-a-Jew and Learning, were activated and used to fuse disparate domains of experience, to dramatize a fictive version of themselves made in the form of assertions and denials, and to provide a sense of individual and collective continuity. It was an elaborate staging of a great fiction, an official, if momentary, collective interpretation of the participants' past and present lives. Being-a-Jew, and Learning, as symbols, provided form and substance which were used to build the ritual, the symbolic sources sustaining the metaphor which guided the ceremony – the Graduation-Siyum.

The Fusion of Domains: Graduation and Siyum

The Graduation-Siyum was a fusion of two disparate domains, and in this, it was a fiction. Some of the features of both domains were selected and used, and others overlooked, in order to present a definition of self, by participants, for themselves and the world. The coherence and conviction of the ritual were achieved despite its fictive nature. On close look it becomes evident that the guiding metaphor is connecting and fusing extremely different domains of meaning. Indeed, graduation and siyum stand in an analogous, not homologous relation to each other, as is seen in Table One.

Outside of the context of a ritual drama, persuasively mounted, it is hard to imagine that such a connection between domains would be credible, but in fact the differences between them were not in the least troublesome the afternoon of the ceremony. Both were essential sources of form and emotion. The guiding metaphor, it can be seen, is very useful in coordinating assorted cultural materials, resulting in a ritual which addresses diverse populations with differing perspectives, beliefs and experiences. The audience, in this case, comprehended and had directly experienced graduation ceremonies. It may be assumed that this domain constituted the most meaningful dimension of the ritual for them. For the seniors, the greater emotional response was clearly provoked by references to the childhood associations. The graduation domain provided most of the formal ingredients in the ritual (Charge to the Class, Valedictorian, and so forth), while the siyum domain was the source of the deep emotional significance at least for the participants. Altogether, the event was generally accepted as authentic and traditional by audience and participants, though no one had ever witnessed such a unique creation before.[9]

Fictions: Claims and Denials

Rituals not only fuse disparate elements but they also make assertions, claims that are at the same time denials of unacceptable realities. In part

214

Table One: Graduation and Siyum Contrasts Domains Connected by the Guiding Metaphor

Traditional graduation ("commencement")	Traditional siyum ("completion")
1 secular content	sacred content
2 associated with adulthood	associated with childhood
3 English language	Hebrew language
4 occured in America	occurred in Eastern Europe
5 public school setting	synagogue setting
6 rite of passage marking lineal progress and clear transitions through fixed stages	repeating rite marking cyclical movement, without transitions or stages
7 benefits the individual	benefits the community, all Jews, and mankind
8 direct means of achieving worldly success	may lead to worldly success indirectly; primarily leads to understanding for its own sake
9 materials selected by and learning paced by the institution	materials selected by and learning paced by the individual
10 learning occurs in a group with secondary relations between members; group usually disperses after ceremony	learning occurs in a group with primary relations; group endures after ceremony
11 group is age homogeneous; sexually hetereogeneous	group is age heterogeneous; sexually homogeneous—only men undertake the course of study and participate in a traditional siyum
12 ceremony marks beginning of adulthood; growing social and biological capacities and prospects; associated with hopes for the future	ceremony is ostensibly age-free, actually here associated with waning social and biological capacities and prospects; associated with a restricted future
13 ceremony is not part of the direct experience of the seniors; it is their children's experience, and the experience of the audience	ceremony is part of the direct experience of the senior men; it is not a direct experience for the senior women; not for their children or the audience

the ritual dramatized an interpretation of the consequences of coming to America. In this drastic move, the elders had exchanged many cherished features of life in the Old World for a new life. As always, a trade-off was involved, and America had brought them gains and losses. They had gained religious freedom but lost their sacred traditions; they had gained physical safety and security for themselves and their children but had lost their natal families and communities; they had gained the educational and economic accomplishments of their children but ultimately this led to the isolation and loneliness of their old age. Sonya summarized matters this way:

> Well, of course, life in America isn't what it was in the old country. There, we loved our parents, we took care of them. Now, look at us ... On the other hand, this is a wonderful country. Look at my children. My daughter is a teacher, my son is a doctor. In Glowno my mother couldn't keep shoes on our feet. You know what that means to a parent? So, if I'm a nobody here, who cares? Who needs an old lady like me anyway? I'm happy. I did all I could and I didn't do so bad.

The ceremony, while making claims and denials, also stressed gains over losses. Here is a summary of principal assertions.

Table Two: Claims and Denials

---

1 *One People*
   Claim being dramatized and asserted:
   We Jews are One People through time and space, sharing a single identity and destiny.
   Denial of the reality that:
   Jews are diverse in nearly every way, from belief to life style, sometimes more different than alike.

2 *Common Fate*
   Claim
   As One People, we Jews share each others' destiny—all are part of each other, a community.
   Denial
   The seniors are neglected by family and neighboring well-to-do Jews; they are needy and isolated.

3 *Judaism is Forever*
   Claim
   Judaism is timeless; it will endure. Though America is a secular state, Jews here will not be assimilated and disappear.
   Denial
   Judaism practiced by young Americans is so different and so diffuse as to be nearly unrecognizable to the seniors. The most important aspect of Judaism for them, Yiddishkeit, will die out with their generation, almost certainly.

4 *Lifelong Study*
   Claim
   We Jews practice lifelong study. This is appropriate for old people as well as young; though old age means many losses, we are fortunate since we can always pursue our studies and thus always live a meaningful life.

Denial
Study is extremely difficult for these older people. They have severe handicaps in the form of short concentration spans, poor eyesight, poor hearing, memory lapses, difficulties in sitting for long or holding a pen, impatience with each other in discussions.

5 *Meaning and Use of Learning*
Claim
We have always loved learning. We have been trained to study and understand. We need never cease growing. We are becoming educated even now.

Denial
They study what is, in actuality, very thin fare. Lacking formal preparation, their attitude is one of awe and respect before almost all printed matter. The act and attitude of studying is more important than the substance.

6 *Successful Lives*
Claim
We have realized our dearest goals in life; it has all been worthwhile. Our children are educated, wealthy, and they respect us. We know they are too important to have time for us, but we don't expect that. Who could ask for more than we have? We know children must live their own lives. After all, we left our parents when we needed to.
Denial
Family ties are the only connections that are counted as completely trustworthy and valuable. It is terribly painful for them to be so cut off from children and family. They feel isolated and useless, and wonder, "Is this what our parents felt like when we left them? Did they deserve such treatment? Do we deserve such treatment?"

In addition to the fusion of separate domains of experience and the demonstration of a set of fictions, there is also a more mundane function being achieved in this ritual drama – an accusation is being made against those who neglect them. To address to their children and their better off fellow Jews the overt statement "You are treating us badly" would embarrass and alienate them. By making their self-definition and protest indirect and ceremonial, the old people arouse guilt without having to state openly the humiliating facts of their condition. Their self-esteem is built upon their conception of themselves as independent, even supporters of others. The statement of need in any form, especially to those they need most, is unthinkable. And the very point of the ritual is that it need not be thought. Fortunately, in ritual, fictions can be presented which disguise truths, save face, and convince all concerned that matters are in order. For rituals allow people to maneuver, fight on their own terms, choose the times, places, conditions and shapes of their assertions, as Burke (1957) says of proverbs. Such maneuvering may result in action, encounter and change, or may end in poetry, "... where instead of being moved anywhere we are accommodated in many subtle ways to our condition in all its contrarieties and complexities" (Fernandez, 1971:53). Here, in the Graduation-Siyum the old Jews can present themselves as people

217

of significance and dignity while they are shaming those who deserted them, and at the same time bolster and define their own sense of worth. In this ritual they exercise that basic human prerogative, the right to indicate who they are to the world, to interpret themselves to themselves instead of allowing the world, accident, history and reality, if you will, to provide an interpretation for them. Here eloquently demonstrated is mankind's undying insistence on stating not only that life has meaning but also specifying precisely what that meaning is.

Continuity – Individual and Collective

Rituals provide continuity of two distinct but related kinds, the individual's sense of unity as a person (individual-biographical continuity), and the sense of being "One People" on the part of the whole group (collective-historical continuity). Despite great changes and disruptions, the individual must be convinced of his/her continuity; thus, must be able to re-experience parts of the past in the present, and of course, the most charged and essential segments of this retrieval come from the remote past, the events of childhood. Continuity is, in this case, especially critical, due to a combination of factors: the extreme age of the ritual participants, their proximity to death, and the drastic rupture with the past caused by emigration. Reviewing one's life and reminiscing, much practiced by the very old, are expressions of the concern for integration, efforts to experience oneself as the same individual through time. As elderly and as Jews, their striving for a sense of integration and continuity, unity and oneness, were parallel, powerful concerns, addressed in this ritual.

The sense of being One People is especially important to Jews, a collectivity dispersed all over the world for centuries.[10] The group, to think of itself as One People, must connect with those of their kind who have gone before and those who are yet to come. The difference between "us then" and "us now" is enormous. This sense of unity, of identity, with one's past and future, "We have been here and we will continue, despite so many changes", is a very important function frequently managed by ritual. It has long been characteristic for Jews to achieve a sense of oneness by means of ritual. The question "What makes us a people?" is never far from the lips of the thoughtful Jew, ancient or modern. Not race, geography, mother tongue or way of life unite them. Above all, it is the commitment to the study of the sacred books. Several times weekly, Jews come together to read synchronized portions of the Law all over the world. The ceremony described here signified the unity and perpetuity of Jews as a People at several important points: in its inclusions of messages from widely dispersed Jews, in the presence of representatives from nearby Jewish organizations, and by the participation of the young people who signified the survival of Judaism in the future. The most numinous symbol of the history of the Jews was the tape of students praying beside the Western Wall in Jerusalem. The Wall is the *axis mundi* of the Jewish world, the physical remainder of the Second Temple of Biblical times. Its inclusion in the program did much to sanctify the entire ceremony.

The Graduation-Siyum established individual and collective continuity by using at least three distinct cultural-historical layers as the sources of symbols and specific ritual details. First, it drew heavily upon the participants' childhood experiences in the East European shtetl; the emotions, meanings and particulars associated with this cultural level were drawn upon for the siyum domain in the guiding metaphor. A second cultural level was provided by the graduation domain of the guiding metaphor, referring to the experiences of America, adulthood and, to some extent, old age. Yet a third layer was incorporated, referring to Judaism in all its forms, a consistent theme running through all the historical phases of the lives of the people.

All these layers supplied cultural materials, employed in the ritual in a highly eclectic fashion. The Graduation-Siyum usually drew on peoples' associations rather than their direct and historical experiences. Most had not been to Israel, had not belonged to an American temple or attended an American school (though many went to night school for a time, none graduated ceremonially), most had not participated in a siyum. Nevertheless, they assembled bits and pieces from their common past and present lives, memories and fantasies, gathering thus sufficient ritual and symbolic element to make their own statements about the meaning of these occasions. Secular rituals, like myths, thus appear to be susceptible of construction with whatever diverse and heterogeneous materials are at hand. Lévi-Strauss (1966) used the word *bricolage* to describe this process in myth and mythic thought. Though their ritual was made of fragments, assembled willy-nilly, they were adequate, allowing the people to write their own history, fight on their own terms, frame and interpret events that never actually happened to them but were no less vital and real because of that. By calling upon all these layers, sources of their axiomatic symbols, personal and collective continuity, the sense of oneness, as Jews and as individuals, were dramatized and experienced. One of the means by which continuity is experienced is through the use of axiomatic symbols, those storehouses of meaning and emotions that carry over shades of all their referents to each particular situation in which they appear.

The three cultural layers drawn upon to develop the Graduation-Siyum bear an interesting relation to each other. On one hand they constitute a series of sharp shifts over the life span, discontinuities which must be knitted together for the people to experience a sense of coherence and integration when reflecting upon their histories. On the other hand, there are some strong continuities, especially between the worlds of childhood and old age. The total picture is complex, but in general it can be said that the ritual event emphasized, subtly and often unintentionally, the continuities in social and cultural phases of their lives and glossed the discontinuities. The existence of the continuities made the work of the axiomatic symbols much easier, since they had references which obtained throughout the life cycle. Table Three summarizes and compares these continuities and discontinuities across the seniors' lives. The summary was compounded of individual life histories and represents a kind of collective profile, emphasizing features most mentioned by the senior citizens themselves.

The table clearly reveals the materials out of which the present subculture was built, freely, unsystematically, using materials at hand to meet present needs. No doubt it would not have come into being, at least in this elaborate form, if the seniors had remained embedded in a context of family and community. Their very isolation gave them much of their freedom and originality; they improvised and invented, unhampered by restraints of tradition and social disapproval, with only themselves to please. For the first time since coming to America, they were able to fully indulge their old love of Yiddish and Yiddishkeit, without fear of ridicule from their sophisticated children. The beloved *mamaloschen*, the language which their children rejected in order to be modern, which the old people gave up as a marker of their status as greenhorn immigrants, could come into its own once more.

Living again in a small, integrated community, which emphasizes Learning, where Yiddishkeit flourishes, where individual freedom and autonomy are exercised in isolation from mainstream society, all of these are familiar – replications of earlier phases of life, revitalized and useful now in old age. Poverty, impotence, physical insecurity and social marginality reiterate shtetl existence. Such continuity is adaptive despite its painful contents. People who have always known that life was hard, and fate unreliable if not downright treacherous, are not surprised to encounter these hazards again. They know how to cope with them and they are not discouraged.

Most continuities are between childhood and old age; between childhood and adulthood, discontinuities are more evident. Above all, the dissolution of the family as they knew it stands out. The centrality of a stable family group was essential to a *Weltanschauung* which held that *le Three: Continuities and Discontinuities in Life Circumstances*

Locale	Eastern Europe	America	America
Community	*Gemeinschaft of small settlements and villages	Gesellschaft: urban centers and suburbs	*Gemeinschaft of an urban ghetto
Family	extended, patriarchal, stable, cohesive	nuclear, more egalitarian, less stable and cohesive	shallow and narrow; infrequent contacts with family members
Generational continuity	*rejection of their parental traditions; geographical and social separation between generations due to immigration	strained relations with children as assimilation occurs; social separation grows, geographical proximity	*virtually severed relations between generations; strong geographical and social separation between generations
Religion and Ideology	*Zionism; growing agnosticism; Yiddishkeit; "Learning" a major form of religious expression: pronounced identity as Jews	*Zionism; agnosticism; Yiddishkeit; "Learning" as a religious expression is superceded by "learning" for assimilation and social success; less pronounced identity as Jews	*Zionism; less pronounced agnosticism, more preference for traditional religious forms; "Learning" a major form of religious expression; pronounced identity as Jews
Language	*Yiddish; some Hebrew for men; Slavic languages for some	English gradually acquired and replaces Yiddish to some extent	*Yiddish assumes more importance; some study of Hebrew; all fluent in English
Age, sex distinctions	sharp division between sexes; males dominant economically and ritually; seniority valued	age and sex roles blurred; women become important economically; seniors largely absent; juniors dominant socially	age and sex roles no longer relevant; females dominant; males largely absent; younger generations absent
Autonomy and nurturance	nurtured by family and community; dependent on others	nurturant of own children, independent	some nurturance by others (health and economic matters); some nurturing of others (Israel); partially dependent on others
Economic circumstances	*poverty; little or no social mobility; insecurity	relative affluence; security and much social mobility	*poverty; no social mobility; pronounced insecurity
Relation to outside, dominant society	*physical danger; religious oppression; social and cultural separation, enforced externally and self-imposed	no physical danger; very little religious oppression; moderate and diminishing social and cultural separation, more enforced than self-imposed	*physical danger; no religious oppression; moderate social separation; pronounced cultural separation, some external enforcement but primarily self-imposed

ndicates distinct continuity

though all Jews were one, non-family Jews were only to be trusted more than the gentiles. The breakdown of the natal community, the segmented social relations in the American urban centers, the rapid social change, and social and geographical mobility constituted a profound contrast with the stable rhythms of the past. Not less important as a discontinuity was their sense of hope and potency, characteristic of the American middle period when new, undreamed of possibilities seemed to open at every turn. These senior citizens went from a small, stable folkworld, familiar and predictable, guided by a tight consensus of family, rabbi and community, in one sudden movement to an entirely different world. This shift coincided with changes in the life cycle which lent the latter additional force, no doubt. Their biological dependence gave way to biological maturity, and this was paralleled by social autonomy which occured within the expanding circumstances provided by immigration.

But in the end, it was the continuities between the world of childhood and the world of old age which provided the basis for their creation of an authentic and distinctive subculture, fragmented, contrived, often thin, constructed out of desperate need, nevertheless, to be counted as a major gain over and against losses in the history of their lives.

Conclusion: Success in Ritual

Did this ritual succeed in its purposes? This requires that we consider what constitutes success for ritual in general. I suggested earlier that above all rituals are dramas of persuasion. They are didactic, enacted pronouncements concerning the meaning of an occasion, and the nature and worth of the people involved in the occasion. In many ways rituals may be judged like any drama – they must be convincing. Not all the parties involved need to be equally convinced or equally moved. But the whole of it must be good enough to play. No one can stand up and boo. Not too many people can shift about in embarrassment, sigh or grimace. The appearance of attention is essential, and everyone is in it together – stage hands, master-of-ceremony, audience, players - all must collude so as not to spoil the show, or damage the illusion that the dramatic reality coincides with the "other, out-there reality."

Why should people collude as much as they do? As Goffman (1956) has demonstrated so well, most individuals sharing a social scene wish to preserve the surface appearances, to reassure themselves and others that "things are going well," "are as they appear to be." Courtesy is a norm always, and ritual is an instance of high courtesy. Unless it is downright bad, wanting all knowledge, art, and care, rituals are likely to be received with courtesy. The ritual participants and designers owe themselves and the audience sufficient competence to aid the pre-existing wish to support it. All involved are offended if the suspicion develops that most of those present are bored, confused or self-conscious. Craft may replace genuine emotional involvement without damaging the ritual; the reverse is not true. Ritual, in general, may be judged a success when it is not a conspicuous failure.

Was the Graduation-Siyum ritual convincing? It was. Not only was its success unhampered by the fact that those to whom it was ostensibly addressed were absent (the graduates' children and families), but it was more successful because they were absent. As a group, the proper audience was represented by a few individuals who were disposed to agree with the justice of the claims being made in the ritual. It is likely that the mood of self-confidence, even self-pride on the part of the graduates would have been impaired if the older people had to face their own children as they made their claims. Instead, the senior citizens were able to make their interpretations of themselves with subtlety and even without completely conscious intent, while they shamed those delinquent in their obligations to them, stated their own importance as people, and the basis of that importance. In their ritual, they emphasized their accomplishments while minimizing their losses.

Did the old people themselves believe in what they were doing? It must be assumed that they did. In ritual, not only is seeing believing, doing is believing. A fine example of this is provided by a Hasidic tale called "The Sabbath Feeling." Two rabbis decide to make a test, to see if their Sabbath feelings are "genuine" by conducting a Sabbath meal on a weekday. After their services, they find they have the Sabbath feeling and are alarmed because it is a weekday. They bring this problem to a third, more learned rabbi. He tells them,

> If you put on sabbath clothes and sabbath caps, it is quite right that you had a feeling of sabbath holiness. Because sabbath clothes and sabbath caps have the power of drawing the light of sabbath holiness down to earth. So you need have no fears. (Buber 1947:241)

In the case of the Graduation-Siyum, the people involved were certainly better off having undertaken this venture than had not they bothered. The very actions, the mounting of a major, complex event of consequence – public, sustained, original – gave them intense pleasure and satisfaction. For the time, they were what they said they were, despite the most pressing contrary realities. They were a community, a people agreeing on their past and present lives, individuals learning and growing, ageless and indominable.

Barbara G. Myerhoff

NOTES

1 Some of the research on which this paper is based took place between 1972 and 1973, funded by a National Science Foundation grant GI-34953X administered through the Andrus Gerontology Center of the University of Southern California, Social and Cultural Contexts of Aging Project, Los Angeles, California. All proper names of individuals and organizations are fictitious.

2 See especially V. Turner (1967, 1968, 1974) for a description of the processes by means of which contrary and paradoxical referents of ritual symbols are fused and reconciled.

3 In addition to the sequences mentioned in this ceremony, a series of alternations between sensory/presentational and discursive symbols occurs (cf. Langer, 1942). Usually the discursive symbols appear in the open segments, but not always. This set of sequences is probably general to all kinds of rituals, whereas the other two are especially germane in secular rituals, for reasons mentioned.

4 Yiddishkeit is a difficult term to translate or explicate briefly. It refers to the culture which centered in the home and communities where Yiddish was the mother tongue. It flowered in the shtetls of Eastern Europe in the late 19th and early 20th centuries, continuing for awhile in other parts of the world, particularly America. In general, the term signifies a local, folk version of Judaism, which I refer to later as the Little Tradition.

5 Zborowski and Herzog (1952), Heschel (1950), Dawidowicz (1967), Levitats (1943), Dubnow (1916-1920), Samuel (1943), Roskies and Roskies (1975), Howe (1976) and Shulman (1974). Sholom Aleichem, Mendele Moher Sefarim, I. L. Peretz and I. B. Singer, great writers of Yiddish fiction also provide valuable and ample ethnographic information about shtetl life.

6 Sacred and secular are not always clearly separate. All references to Judaism are somewhat sacred; more clearly sacred are references to Yiddishkeit, life in the shtetl, Jewish Law and scolarship and Jewish historical and collective identity. Bases for these classifications are discussed in more detail later.

7 A third major symbol appeared in the ceremony, patriotism and Americanism, including modernity and freedom in its referents. It is not treated as an axiomatic symbol of the depth of Being-a-Jew and Learning because compared to these it appeared only in the elders' middle years, whereas the other two have been passionate concerns throughout their lives.

8 This corresponds to what Ortner (1973) calls a "key scenario," a method for attaining a valued cultural goal.

  While considerable freedom is available in the use of a guiding metaphor, traditions require the inclusion of certain critical elements. Thus the seniors debated at length as to whether a real graduation could take place without a procession. They did not feel they could manage a slow, stately walk down the aisle. Fortunately, Manya remembered attending a graduation in which students stood in place when their names were called. Thus, they too could do this and it would be proper. And without a formal discussion, several had agreed that traditional shtetl foodherring, honeycakes and brandy – were essential for a genuine siyum.

10 Cf. R.-E. Prell-Foldes, 1973, for discussion of this point.

PART 4

MASS OCCASIONS

CHAPTER XII
ON DRAMA, AND GAMES AND ATHLETIC CONTESTS

Mary Gluckman and Max Gluckman

Drama

Most ceremonies and rituals are spectacles; and among the problems set
for this seminar, is the question whether games, athletic contests, sports,
and dramas are "secular rituals".[1] After wavering towards thinking they
might profitably be so considered, we have decided that they do have similarities with rituals, but have also elements which are so very different,
that it is wiser to keep them distinct. Like rituals and secular ceremonies,
dramas and even contests may involve powerful moral and ethical themes,
but they exhibit these both in different contexts of social relationships
and through different mechanisms of action (contrast Turner 1969:
Chapters 4 and 5, where phases in Ndembu rituals, and aspects of the
Crusades, of modern communes, and the Woodstock music festival are
treated similarly – see below). This statement does not deny that on occasions games or masquerades formed parts of ritual ceremonies; nor does
it deny that ceremonies of one kind or another can be attached to the
playing of games, or the staging of dramas. It does deny that all – perhaps most – games and dramas can be so regarded, without putting them
out of context and distorting the means by which they exhibit moral
values.

Our main argument is well stated in judgments ascribed by Cornelia
Otis Skinner in her book on "La belle epoque", the gay 1890's in Paris –
Elegant wits and grand horizontals (1969: 152)[2] to Tristan Bernard,
the French dramatist and critic: "The audience always wants to be surprised, but surprised by what they are expecting ... Write any sort of play
as long as the subject amuses you ... But if you burn Moscow and upset
thrones, do so because the little blonde no longer loves her husband on
account of the dark young man who lives on the third floor of one of the
houses you intend to burn ... The principal quality of the successful author is a special gift for handling subjects which are not new, without
being stale." In short, the essence of successful drama for Bernard was
that the playwright take some well-known theme, possibly a conflict of

socially defined moral imperatives, or a conflict between personal drives and moral imperatives, and works it out through the story of specific individuals, battered within a particular social context. The outcome is uncertain: the audience has to be suprised by what it is expecting, and a subject which is not new is handled, in a way that is not stale.

This characteristic of the successful drama can be observed strikingly in those dramas which have lasted through many centuries, and which, by their presentation of the dilemmas of the principal characters, have moved audiences in centuries and places very distant from the period and place of their composition. One of us recently (Max Gluckman, 1974a) worked through Sophocles's *Antigone* in order to evaluate the sense of Antigone's soliloquizing defence, after she is sentenced by King Creon to be incarcerated in the cave because she symbolically buried her brother Polyneices in defiance of the orders of Creon. This defence begins by stating that she was impelled by the sacred duty, established by the gods, to perform the last rites for dead kin, instanced by her apostrophising her dead parents: "when ye died, with mine own hands I washed and dressed you, and poured drink-offerings at your graves; and now [my brother] Polyneices, 'tis for tending thy corpse that I win such recompense as this" (translation by Jebb, lines 904f). The plea that follows was taken by critics, from Goethe to Jebb, in the nineteenth century, and even Lesky in the twentieth, to be spurious: "And yet I honoured thee, as the wise will deem, rightly. Never, had I been a mother of children, or if a husband had been mouldering in death, would I have taken this task upon me in the city's despite [here she repeats the words in the opening scene of her sister Ismene who refused to aid her]. What law, ye ask, is my warrant for that word? The husband lost, another might have been found, and child from another, to replace the first-born, but, father and mother, hidden in Hades, no brother's life could ever bloom for me again. Such was the law whereby I held thee first in honour; but Creon deemed me guilty of error therein, and of outrage, ah brother mine! And now he leads me thus, a captive in his hands, no bridal bed, no bridal song hath been mine, no joy of marriage, no portion in the nurture of children; but thus forlorn of friends, unhappy one, I go living to the vaults of death."

This passage specifying varying obligations to brother, to husband and to child, is then followed by an appeal again to the gods: "And what law of Heaven have I transgressed? Why, hapless one, should I look to the gods any more – what ally should I invoke, – when by piety I have earned the name of impious? Nay, then, if these things are pleasing to the gods, when I have suffered my doom, I shall come to know my sin; but if the sin is with my judges. I could wish them no fuller measure of evil than they, on their part, mete wrongfully to me."

Nineteenth-century critics, beginning with Goethe in 1827, thought the personal paragraph detracted from the high theme of the conflict between obedience to the gods and disobedience against the king's edict. Goethe, indeed, as quoted by Jebb (1888, 1900 edition: 259), thought the passage, "ganz schlecht", so absurd as almost to border on the comic. Hence the passage was thought to be a spurious interpolation, not worthy of the master Sophocles, and indeed to be a poor copy from the passage in Herodotus's *Histories*, Book III, in which when Darius has condemned all the family of Intaphrenes to death, the lamentations of Intaphrene's wife moved Darius to grant her the life of one of them, and she chose her brother, not her husband or a child.She explained her choice by argument akin to Antigone's. Later critics (but not Lesky 1966: 282) are now inclined to accept the disputed passage as genuine, since Greek dramas by that stage were seen as dramatic confrontations between the central characters, rather than philosophical debates. In his article Max Gluckman considered how the passage would appear to an African audience, involved in a set of kinship relatiinships not very different from those we believe to have characterized the Greece of Sophocles's time: some kind of system of agnatic lineages, with conflicts over claims of siblings, parents, spouses, and children crucial in the system.

Antigone was of course performed on the occasion of the great Dionysian rituals in Athens, so it had a ritual setting. Yet it remains a great drama, a tragedy that moves us with its moral dilemmas in a time when the gods involved are for us "fairy-tale" fantastic creatures. And it can move us time and time again, at each new reading or at each viewing. If it had any ritual significance in Sophocles's time, it has long outlived that significance. Modern critics can debate the themes of the play: the *hubris* with which Creon sets himself above the gods, as the *hubris* of a man who does not recognize that there are limits to kingly power, an ever-present problem in political life; the great courage needed, markedly in Antigone's isolation, to defy that power in defence of the right; and so forth; – analyses partly made in the light of other ancient Greek plays and texts, partly in terms of general social and emotional understanding. An anthropologist can even try to introduce another set of conflicts – the pulls between natal kin and spouses, the pulls between filial obedience (for Haemon, Creon's son and Antigone's betrothed) and love for bride-to-be. The themes are found in most societies, and bear, when dramatically presented, frequent repetition. If the dramatist is great, the dilemmas, whether those set in the writing or in later times, are present each time, and there is a kind of emotional hope that the outcome may be different – though it cannot be. This hope, despite the known outcome, is present at each reading or viewing of *Hamlet* and other great tragedies.

It seems probable that the Greek dramas developed out of ritual masquerades of some kind (Harsh 1944; Lesky 1962 [1957]; Aristotle, *Poetics*). If so, the great tragedies we know had become liberated from the prescribed forms of ritual. The tragic writers took mostly themes from Greek myths and legends, and exploited them in diverse ways: they surprised the audiences with what the latter were expecting, and handled subjects not new, without being stale.[3]

What is most significant for our present problem, is that the new forms, even when they dealt with old stories, varied the course of events and the outcome, leaving this outcome in some sense uncertain, and emphasizing that men and women themselves had choices, even though they still remained subject to the ultimate influence of Fate and the control of the gods. Antigone insisted on defying the king to fulfill her duty to her dead brother and to the gods by burying Polyneices; Ismene, their sister, argued for the path of helpless acquiescence: when Antigone was condemned Ismene took courage to remain faithful to the bond between siblings and wished to die with Antigone, but Antigone rejected her, repeating her own words, because she was first cowardly and rejected that bond as weaker than the king's commands. This is the dramatic working out of the conflicting ties of obedience to king and obedience to sibling loyalty, shown by the adherence of one sister to the latter, and of the failure first of the other sister in that loyalty, and then by the emphatic statement that she can never again be worthy of it (Max Gluckman, 1974a). Dramatic irony, when the audience had foreknowledge from the prologue, often replaced uncertainty of outcome.

Much recent research on the rituals of the tribal peoples has emphasized the extent to which these are marked by the process which one of us (Max Gluckman, 1962) called "ritualization", by which he meant the use of secular relationships and roles in rituals, by acting of them on special occasions, either directly, or by inversion, or in some other symbolical form. That is to say, in such rituals the actors have selected roles in the rituals according to their roles in secular life, and it is believed that by their actions they influence the fertility, fruitfulness, success, prosperity, victoriousness, health, and so forth of the central group, category, or individual of the ritual, through in some way influencing the occult, variously conceived. In that essay, discussing the work of Van Gennep, it was stipulated that the word "ritualization" was thus used specifically to describe the fact that, e.g. father or mother's brother, kind and princes and subjects, men or women, old or young, initiates and novices, and so forth, performed actions or recited prayers or spells for a specific congregation constituted by the specificity of day-to-day secular relationships. The word "ritualization" was thus used to define a particular means of operating on, or influencing, occult powers, for the good of the congregation as a whole or some of its members. This form of ritual was seen to differ markedly from the rituals of "universalistic" religions, in which adherence to the beliefs was sufficient to give membership in congregations. We stress this operational, stipulated use of the term, defined as a form of ritual distinct from, say, the "ritualism" of the Catholic Church as against the lack of "ritualism" of many Protestant sects. And "ritual" as an embracing category was seen to be part of a whole field of behavior which could by stipulation be called "ceremonial", in that such behavior was marked by high formality and conventionality, perhaps organized into larger units appropriately termed "ceremonies". "Ritual" ceremonialism was stipulated to cover actions which had reference in the view of the actors, to occult powers: where such beliefs were not present, it was suggested that the word "ceremonious" be used: so that for our present problems, "secular rituals" is a contradiction in those stipulated terms (not, of course, inherently so), and "secular ceremonial" would be a better title. We repeat, what was attempted was an essay at suggesting a series of stipulated terms, defined in relation to one another, in order to further a particular analysis. We have to repeat that these suggestions, because in discussions with two other members of the seminar, we found that they had worried over these definitions after reading a comment by Leach (1968: vol. 13, 521) that the terminology was not useful, since words were only concepts and could only be defined operationally. Leach had not taken it into account that the series of definitions were in fact advanced with reference to a specific problem, as he insists (correctly) definitions should be advanced. And this series of definitions does seem to be particularly relevant here.

For it seems that while it is clear that the dithyrambic hymns to Dionysus were ritual, the acienyt Greek tragedies that have survived for us were not ritual. It was not believed that with their enactment of major conflicts in the society's social organization, they in themselves influenced the course of events within specific congregations, even if their performance, in the ritual setting, honored the god. We consider that similar conclusions can be drawn about the burlesque satyr-plays, and about the comedies. The tragedies were not prescribed in their course of action or in their outcomes; and in fancy at least, and as perceived the audience, the protagonists had choices which would allow them to alter the course of events. As some classical scholars maintain, when Oedipus, to evade the Fate ordained by the oracle, fled from what he believed to be his parental home at Corinth, he should still have avoided killing, in anger, an older man, and then marrying a woman so much older than himself. In

Sophocles's *Antigone*, Antigone had some choice: she could have harkened to Ismene and obeyed the king, and been spared since she failed in duty to her brother under *force majeure*. But Creon above all could have changed his course of action: once he committed the impiety of refusing burial to the rebel Polyneices, he could have altered his action when warned of that impiety, rather than insisting that the dead man should not be buried even if the eagles of Zeus carried the remnants of the corpse to the throne of the most high.[4] Again, when Ismene reminded him that the condemned Antigone was betrothed to his son, he could have recognized the attachment of betrothed to each other, not said contemptuously, "Nay, there are other fields for him to plough" (Jebb translation, line 569). Finally, he resisted Haemon's own plea that one man cannot lay down unjust law and insist on its being obeyed. This finally provoked Haemon, mourning over Antigone's corpse, to attack his father, come too late to resque her, and then, in horror at his potential "parricide", kill himself.

This play like other ancient Greek tragedies, was cast to show the working out through the lives of individuals of conflicts in relationship inherent in the society (individual king vs. the duties of kingship; the pull of sibling loyalties as against the edicts of the king; the strength of sexual and personal attachment of betrothed against absolute obedience to father; the strength of the tie between spouses and potential spouses in a culture where that tie was not always dominant), conflicts all cast against a religious background in which men and women were warned against the uncertainty of Fate and the danger of *hubris*, of setting oneself up to assume that good fortune would continue and that one was favored of the gods. And the most fruitful form of interpreting ritualization has been to see it as the acting of the conflicts which lie deep in the structure of society itself, in the independent, discrepant, inconsistent, principles on which social relationships are built (dating most clearly from Fortes and Evans-Pritchard 1940: 16f). But though they have this common element, of representing the acting of these deep social conflicts, drama and ritualization are very different in their mechanisms.

Turner has pointed out (1968:135-150) that ritualizations in ceremony involve and organize certain persons, relationships, groups or categories, but leave other persons, relationships, groups and categories unorganized. He argued that those euements that are not organized penetrate, so to speak, into the interstices of the ritual, and may raise trouble there. Thus in his example, initiation rituals organize the categories of men and women, and of initiates und uninitiated, but not villages and their headmen: hence competition between villages and headmen for high status in the rituals may cause difficulties. In this competition the outcome is uncertain and there is choice over strategies; but clearly, he implies, the course and the observable outcome of the ritual is prescribed and predetermined. And we would argue that it is characteristic of ritual as such, that theoretically at least, its main activities are always known in advance, and conformity to rule and tradition is important. The ritual moves to its prescribed ending: the outcome, in the sense whether it will be successful in achieving its "ostensible purpose" (Radcliffe-Brown) of securing fertility, etc., is of course uncertain – occult, hidden, not known by the senses till some future events demonstrate whether or not this success has been achieved.

The point of Max Gluckman's stipulated definitions set out above, is that they give us the term "ceremonial" to cover all highly conventionalized symbolic forms of action or speech which define social status, relationships, roles, etc. but enable us to distinguish two categories. We can describe as "ceremonious" those actions and words which do not involve beliefs in occult power, and as "ritual" those which do involve such beliefs and which frequently also exhibit conflicts deep in the social structure, conflicts that are portrayed in many rituals, above all in "ritualization" of social roles. Leach does not like this, *ab initio*, because in his *The Political Systems of Highland Burma* (1945: 10-11, but cf. 16) he asserted that ritual was no more than a symbolic expression of status. But great ceremonies, in the common sense use of the word, such as May-day parades of Labor, or military marches past like the British "Trooping of the Colours", or parades on the anniversary of the October Revolution in the USSR, or the ceremonial movement of Barotse king between flood-and-dry-season captials, and so forth, exhibit clearly enough status and social and political relationships, in a way very different from, say, the great first-fruits rites of the Swazi nation. In the former there is parade, with signs of strength exhibitions of ruling status, and so forth. In the Swazi ceremony, what are employed are not signs but symbols (for distinction see Turner, 1964). These symbols both ramify their significance in the unconscious psyches of the participants, and refer to underlying conflicts and struggles within the nation – manifested, for example, in the national songs of hatred of subjects against the ruling king, insults to him, and so forth, expressions of disloyalty and resentment which are nevertheless believed to strengthen the king as well as the nation by occult or mystical means (Kuper 1945:Chapter 13; Gluckman 1963 [1954]. It seems sensible to reserve the word "ritual," and its sub-category in this case of "ritualization," to describe these ceremonies as against the "ceremoniousness" of "Trooping of the Colors," etc., because in the instances here defined as "ritual" we are dealing with activity which depends for its social effects on mechanisms which evoke emotion not directly by signs of unity and status, operating patently on emotion and mind, but indirectly in a complex process of "sublimation." Thereby (in Turner's 1964 formulation) psychical energy is evoked by a set of symbolical physiological referents and transposed to strengthen social and moral values which are simultaneously exhibited in the symbols. There is a belief in occult power; and in very fact the process of transfiguration of emotion is occult, operating to a large extent outside the consciousness of the psyche. And it is important to note here that such a restriction on the use of the word "ritual" was adopted by the great ethologist Tinbergen. He stressed that, for example, some of the behavior of herring-gulls could be understood as displacement leading to "compromise" formations. Thus what he calls the complex signalling "rituals" involved when a male and female meet for the first time, and are caught between hostility as strangers and attraction as potential mates, involve a compromise from initial hostility. In the non-human world, it has been thought sensible to see a distinction between signalling a single mood, and symbolizing a compromise from duality of mood, when moods are in conflict: *a fortiori* such a distinction must be made when we deal with the more complex activities of human beings in social relationship. Van Gennep and Durkheim, Simmel and von Wiese, and other of our great predecessors, were struck by the shift in the modes of dealing with the series of conflicts that arise from clashes of particular with general interests (Fortes and Evans-Pritchard 1940:16f.) and with the conflicts of mood and emotion begotten by the human predicament, as we compare ancient and tribal societies with societies based on more advanced technologies. This shift, involves increasingly less of the "ritualization" in our terminology that marks the ceremonies of the former set of societies, with their small-scale view of the universe in which what happens in social relationships is inextricably intertwined with what happens in the physical environment and the relations of occult powers (Max Gluckman 1965:Chapter 5). Increasingly ceremonies involving statements of social status (cf. Leach 1954: 10-11) are made with only (in some modern societies) initial prayer to God, but no "ritualization" of social relationships and roles themselves. In these ceremonies, even if in some humility before God is expressed, social conflicts are not enacted: the emphasis is patently and observably on social strength, unity, etc., which are assumed to exist. There is no suggestion that harmony and unity exist despite the open, indeed the exaggerated, difference of role and relationships with all their conflicts (as summarized in Max Gluckman 1955: Chapter 5: 1962); and this kind of ritualization of roles, it has been argued, can no longer be used when the conflicts involved are such that they threaten revolutionary as against rebellious change (see Max Gluckman 1963 [1954]; and reconsideration in Max Gluckman 1965: 260-3).

We have started with ancient Greek drama which was performed on ritual occasions, in order to emphasize that here were crucial differences between the dithyrambic hymns to Dionysus and the tragedies performed to honor him – until there developed a saying in ancient Greece in 494 B.C. "nothing to do with Dionysus," arising from the paradoxical absence of his story from the forms intended to do him honor (Lucas 1969: 630). In ritual, actions and words were more stereotyped, set in advance; the actors' roles were prescribed; the outcome was predetermined (i.e. the outcome of the ritual, not of its appeal). In the drama, actions and words were increasingly less stereotyped; the actors had choices set for them; and the outcome in theory (even if by the device of dramatic irony) was uncertain. In the greater dramas, the actors were individuals with specific characters, flawed in some way, acting in terms of their fit and lack of fit to their prototypical social roles: in ritualization, actors played their social roles independently of their characters. If this distinction is clear even in ancient Greek drama, and becoming more manifest from the time of Aeschylus through that of Sophocles to Euripides, the distinction must be accepted as even more marked in later drama, even among the classical Romans, and certainly in drama from the Middle Ages on. The medieval mystery and miracle plays were indeed religious; and it is significant that the non-ritual morality plays were a later development.

We point the difference in another way. The medieval mystery and miracle plays, like the recitations, songs and prayers on the Jewish Passover night, exhibit events that were and are performed out of time, even if they were and are believed to have occurred in time. Each re-enactment renews a covenant with God between performers and audience established at a point in history. In an occult sense, the long-past event is symbolically occurring in the performance. This indeed is the essence of tribal rituals, whether these be the Swazi first-fruits rites (Kuper 19945:Chapter 13), or some initiation ritual, or say the fertility rituals of the Australian Aborigines which at the same time re-enact and act the doings of the Wawn-Being (on this general point see Max Gluckman 1965:268-178). When an ancient myth is re-enacted in a drama, there is no idea that the events are in any way occurring then and there, with the actors becoming the heroes and heroines of that distant event, and the audience participating in that event itself. The drama is a presentation, not a representation as ritual is. And this may be true of the present-day passion play at Oberammergau – though some may feel it is a genuine enactment of the story of Christ. Yet since ritualizing ceremonies so often involve the statement – often the exaggerated statement – of standardized conflicts in order to transpose emotional energy from the physiological pole to the ideological pole of social value (see above, and Turner 1964), and dramas also enact, through the events affecting legendary of historical or fictional individuals, the conflicts that are current in social life, both types of action achieve some similar effects: the catharsis which Aristotle described in his analysis of tragedy, a catharsis in which the excitement evoked is purged through pity and terror. But again there is a difference. In ritual, and particularly in ritualization, the ultimate emphasis is that harmony among people can be achieved despite the conflicts, and that social institutions and values are in fact harmonious – ultimate statements that are belied to some extent by the ritualization itself. Ritual can do this since each ritual selects to some extent from the gamut of moods, of cooperative links and of conflicts. Ritual is acted out of time. In what we classify as great drama, the problems are left unsolved, since drama is set in a specific time for a particular set of individuals. The values emphasized are uncertainty not certainty, of human fate; the difficulties of decision; the pulls of irreconcilable duties and obligations. In lesser drama, the situation is simpler: goodies win and baddies lose. What is socially valuable triumphs. This is why George Orwell in his *Inside the Whale* (1940) urged that the radicals should produce penny horribles and comics in which anarchists and revolutionaries and strikers, and not the police, were the heroes and heroines, the good, triumphing over the wicked, so that the "ritualistic" lesson might be conveyed dramatically.

We argue, in short, that though the emotional effects, and the exciting and purging of emotion, in ritual and in drama show and overlap, that the final effect is not the same, and that the means by which that effect is achieved is not the same. Hence while some overlap has to be handled in analysis, we consider it would be wiser not to bring drama under the rubric of "secular rituals".

We have thus far written of tragedies. Comedies and clowning take a somewhat different course. It does seem that where clowning is allowed in ritual settings among tribal peoples, it gives more rein to innovation: the clowns are allowed to invent new jokes and pranks, even if their general form be stereotyped. We noted this when watching the masquerades of *makishi* masked dancers (all men) of Mbunda, Cokwe, and Lubale immigrants to Barotseland (see Max Gluckman 1949 and 1974b). Each of the masked dancers is in a complicated way, into which we need not enter here, an "ancestral-spirit", with some of the varying characters linked with spirits. Some of the *makishi* are connected with circumcision lodges: they are what Baumann and others haye called "ritual" (see Max Gluckman 1974b). Their performances in the dances staged are very stereotyped. Other *makishi*, without specific roles in the circumcision ritual, also perform stereotyped dances with the women as chorus. And they are all silent, they do not speak. But there are a number of the *makishi* which put on highly inventive performances. One represents a young woman, and "she" may do acrobatics on a pole held on the shoulders of two men; very skilled dancers playing "her" do tricks on ropes tied between two poles stuck in the ground, up to (in our experience) thrity feet high. The best of the performers in this character do clown, making up jokes, indulging in antics, bringing members of the audience into the dance. We have seen three other *makishi* characters behave thus, all comics: an old man, an old woman, and a young man with an enormous straw penis which he kicks off his thighs toward the women while making sexual jokes. Obscene and other jokes and actions are also in the repertory of the oldsters. In these roles dancing is reduced, clowning and joking are the mode. We have been told that there is a similar difference between the clowns and the serious characters in Hopi dances. There was a similar difference in the comedies of ancient Greece, with great license allowed the comic writers, who as we all know developed different themes from the tragedians. Attic comedy developed, according to Aristotle, later than tragedy, into satirical and abusive themes, out of the spoken or shouted improvisations of the leaders, with phallic songs, still heard in his time. But where contemporary historical plays were never popular (only two are know from the fifth century B.C. – Harsh 1944:6), comedy dealt with contemporary themes. But the effect of comedy, like that of drama (even where comedy appears in ritual contexts) is quite different from the effect of ritual. Ritual is performed for the benefit of the community, a benefit achieved through its postulated effect on unseen forces, not through its direct effect on the audience.

Games and athletic contests

The argument that drama has to be distinguished from ritual because the actors have a series of choices open to them and the outcome is uncertain, applies *a fortiori* to games and athletic contests. In some contexts, games have been connected with ritual occasions, as notably with the original Olympic Games in classical Greece. But though they were held to honor the gods, and during their course each four years the Greek city-states involved were supposed to observe a truce in their hostilities, the contests were not of themselves ritual. Contestants sought the blessing of their own gods on their endeavors – which might set the gods themselves in competition. And a winner might in thanks make offerings to a god or a goddess, and even raise a statue to god or goddess; delighted fellow citizens were more likely to raise a statue to their triumphant winner. Cheating, it was believed, might be followed by divine punishment. But the ritual took place in the inauguration and ending of the Games, it was not inherent in the contests themselves. Similarly, in the modern Games, which we have witnessed in 1972 and have seen on other occasions on television, there is great ceremoniousness at each inauguration including the taking of the oath by selected competitors on behalf of all their fellows; there is a ceremonious presentation of medals to winners, seconds and thirds; here is a somewhat uncontrolled ceremonious closure. But breach of the oath is not believed to bring occult punishment; and the highly militaristic ceremoniousness with which the Nazis surrounded the 1936 Games in Berlin, as against the deliberately civilian and peaceable ceremoniousness which the Germans stressed at Munich in 1972, show how variable the ceremonial may be. Nor was there any feeling that the massacre by Arabs of Israeli athletes was a blasphemy, as a similar breach of truce at the Ancient Greek Games would have been regarded. At al modern Games, the American contingent even refuses to dip their flag to the presiding Head of State as other contingents do, because of an alleged offence to their flag at the Games in London in 1908. Nor is there any belief that bias on the part of the judges is a "ritual" offence.

We consider that the same observations apply to other situations where games were said to be "ritual" or "religious". In this light, we came to the conclusion, after reading some general accounts in this form of the ancient Mayan ball-court game, that it could not be in itself religious, as was assumed because stelae show sacrifices of players, but must be at best a form of divination.While we are writing this paper, in a lecture at Yale, Professor Richard E. Adams of the University of Texas stated that the ballgame was a form of divination: a question was asked of the Gods, and one side represented the answer "yes", the other the answer "no": and the outcome was settled by whichever side won. (We have not had time to check the source of this conclusion, which was not known to at least two distinguished Meso-American archaeologists we consulted). But the form of divination described by Adams is in clear parallel with the way Azande put questions to their oracles (Evans-Pritchard 1937). Adams did not suggest that the sacrifice of the losers influenced in occult manner events to change their course; and presumably if the losers were sacrificed, this may only have occurred when they represented the desired, auspicious answer.

Again, it has been said that some North American Indian games were ritual; but this does not emerge from the following account taken from Culin's book, or elsewhere there. The contestants may use magic to seek success, and the presiding elders ask for a peaceable game, with none hurt and fair play observed, but there is no suggestion that unfair play or assault or attempts to damage an opponent bring occult retribution, or that the course of the game or its outcome influence in occult manner the course of outside events (see Culin 1907). For example, Culin (at pp. 564f.) cites account from Long in 1791 and Carver in 1796 of games of racket or *le jeu de crosse* among the Chippewa. At that time, the games even took place between different bands, and though they were played with "so much vehemence" that players were wounded and bones broken, good humor prevailed and there were no disputes between the parties. The "rules of the game" apparently provided an ethos which kept the games within bounds.

By 1890, according to the accounts cited by Culin from Hoffman and Mooney, stakes in the game had risen among Indians living on reservations: Hoffman said of the Chippewa in Minnesota "severe injuries occurred only when playing for high stakes or when ill-feeling existed between some of the players." This change in ethos may have resulted from penning the Indians on reservations, or from the increase of stakes made possible by a relative wealth in new types of goods. Certainly Mooney's account of a game, also in 1890, between two groups of East Cherokee in North Carolina stresses the roughness of the game, with everything short of murder allowable: men now sometimes went into the game with the purpose of disabling each other, and even rolled fighting on the ground. These fracas occurred despite an address by an old man who told them that the Sun was looking down upon them, urged them to acquit themselves in the games as their fathers had done before them, but above all to keep their tempers, so that none might say they became angry or quarrelled, and that after it was over each one might return "in peace along the white trail to rest in his white house." (Mooney notes that "white in these formulas is symbolic of peace and happiness and all good things", much as Turner, 1964 and 1966 spoke of "whiteness" among the Ndembu: I would incline to agree with Kuper (1971) that our "bright" is the better English translation.)

This breaking out of violence, despite the ethos of the game and the initial supplication, as well as the fact that players can make choices and the outcome is uncertain, also distinguish most games from ritual. Except when prescribed and limited license, within bounds, is allowed, violence at a ritual may destroy its efficacy. We have cited Turner as reporting the entry of competition and struggle of categories, groups and persons not controlled by ritual prescription, into the interstices of rituals he observed among the Ndembu. But it is also inappropriate, but not blasphemous, for competition and struggle to break the rules of games. It is unfair and unsporting – not "fairplay" in an English phrase seemingly not found indigenously in, e.g. French and German – for Olympic athletes to use drugs, even those not proscribed by rules. But they do. It is not destructive of efficacy of the rules.

It is always possible that deep divisions within the social field from which participants enter into competitive contest may break out into violence that is rooted in relationships outside the contest itself. There are many instances of this, some of which Max Gluckman discussed in a lecture on "Sport to conflict" delivered to a plenary session of the Congress for the Scientific Study of Sport held in connection with the Olympic Games of 1972 (in press). These instances range from the soccer game between San Salvador and Nicaragua in the World Cup which led to actual war, to battles on the field between teams and supporters of each team in the "hick leagues" of Cheshire and Mid-Wales in the United Kingdom. Even out of such amorphous groups as the supporters of rival Manchester soccer teams, City and United, there emerge gangs to battle thus. The battle is exacerbated when allegiance to the teams is associated with religious differences as were allegiances to Glascow Celtics and Glasgow Rangers, or with racial differences, as when the Blacks in Minnesota University's Basketball Team attecked the Whites in Ohio State's team (see *Sports Illustrated,* Chicago, February 7, 1972:18f., and Max Gluckman, in press). Here we are dealing with processes involving deep social conflicts in a quite different context from the expression of social conflicts in ritualization. Games can only be kept going where there is a strong controlling organization, with secular authority, able to expel players and even teams from competition and thus to enforce the rules administered by neutral umpires it appoints.

Yet the rules, and the ethos of games, may contain moral rules as ritual does; and these, together with admiration of a rival's dexterity, may influence participants and spectators as a ritual does. We have space to cite only one example: the admiration which the Black Jesse Owens' powerful jumping and running evoked in a German crowd, many of whom must have been Nazis, despite the Nazi press's contempt for Blacks and its description of him and his fellow-Blacks as "American auxiliaries"; and above all, the assistance given by his German opponent, Lutz Lang, in the long jump, to Owens in measuring his run to enable him to win. From this sprang a friendship by correspondence which continued until the War in which Lutz was killed, a friendship which Owens continued with Lang's widow and son. C.L.R. James's autobiography, *Beyond a Boundary* (1970), shows brilliantly how in Jamaica the ethos of fair play and play for the team was one of the inconsistent moralities developed in West Indians. Though games and rituals may both *express* moral rules, only ritual affects the fate of the participants through its further effects on mystical powers.

As a final illustration of the difference between rituals and games, we refer to an analysis made by Max Gluckman, which has been published in *The Listener* (February 1958). In a memorial broadcast for the Manchester United football team destroyed in an aircrash in 1957, he examined how a team that was easily winning the English Championship became unable to win at home, where winning is "statistically" much easier. Precisely the same thing happened in this last season, 1973-74, to Leeds United who at one time were leading by eleven points; and it has happened in previous seasons to other teams which were far ahead. In the phrasing of sports journalists, they lost confidence. What does this mean? Gluckman had observed that his team's play had become outstandingly good, indeed brilliant, but eventually the team's supporters began to treat it as ordinary. (As a Scottish Heart of Midlothian player, when that team was in a similar position, said: "Man, we were superhuman, and the crowd thought it was ordinary.") Therefore instead of applauding the good play, the crowd began to concentrate on inevitable mistakes, or apparent mistakes, and to jeer at and boo the players for these. This shook the confidence of some: they became more careful, could no longer "do it simple, do it quick" (which a Scots International gave as the formula for success), hesitated against fast and skillful opponents – and were lost. The cycle became vicious. Only the dropping of international players and their replacement by reserves, who were cheered for what they did right, forgiven for what they did wrong, broke the vicious circle and enabled the team to win. This tremulous loss of confidence caused partly by the very supporters of the team, the immediate and only immediate importance of what went on, is a far cry from the emotional excitement and sublimation, and confidence in ultimate mystical effect, that so often marks ritual.

Conclusion

We have here argued that despite the importance of rules which control actions into what might be called formal and conventional patterns, and despite the fact that games embody moral pinciples, it would be missing essential differences to bring them under the rubric of "ritual." This emerges even more strongly than the same conclusion has emerged from our analysis of the differences between drama and ritual: but there the same cautionary note is necessary. We came to this conclusion on reading Turner's *The Ritual Process: Structure and Anti-Structure* (1969). This book has made such a widespread impression and its ideas have been taken up by so many young anthropologists, that we feel justified in pointing out our doubts, however briefly. Most of the first part of the analysis, that which deals with Ndembu ritual, we admire greatly, as our references to his seminal ideas show. But the second part seems to us to be full of inappropriate categorization. The liminal period, and the rites associated with it, are, as Van Gennep stressed, a most important element in all movements in space, in time, and in social status. But the extent to which during this period ordinary rules of enjoined behavior are suspended sometimes for all, but most commonly for some, of the actors, to give a fellow-feeling which he describes as *communitas*, can only be significant, as his analysis shows, within an established structure which is asserted again afterwards, and which indeed is asserted during the liminal period itself, by inversion. Ordinary activities of producing, preparing, eating food; of herding stock where there is stock; of restraining breaches from the allowable license – these and more continue outside the ritual arena. This kind of ritual liminal period, and therefore of any temporary casting off of roles, must be analyzed as different from such large-scale social and political movements as the Crusades, which various people joined for various motives, often with only some standard expressed adherence to the religious aims of the wars. And that in turn is very different from the temporary agglomeration of young people at a festival like the one at Woodstock, an agglomeration in which all temporarily, as they knew, came to feel a sense of unity with one another – a sense of unity very different from what the British called "the spirit of Dunkirk." And these are again different from the sense of unity – often fictitious if hard-desired – of small communes in modern America, communes supported, like Woodstock, often by the affluence of a highly developed economy and political system. Similarity of emotion, or even a few beliefs, does not make for similarity of social action and structure – or anti-structure. Turner himself (1957) has emphasized the importance of differences in social context and of social mechanism in discussing the situations in which Ndembu resort to judicial investigation and to divination, with ritual or accusations of witchcraft, in his study of what he called "social dramas" (see also Marwick 1963; Gluckman 1965: Chapters 4 and 5). If the social contexts, processes and mechanisms involved are different, then we surely need a more differentiated vocabulary to handle those differences. If there are also similarities despite those differences, then the differentiation of vocabulary should be within a hierarchical series of connected terms (see Max Gluckman 1965:198f., for discussion of similar problem in analyzing "law"). To call all formality and ceremonial "ritual" is to blur the distinction between formal activities that address and move the spirit world (which I call "ritual") and formal activities that do not. To lump together what has been analytically segregated is justified only if reclassification illuminates. I neither see that much is gained from aggregating all occasions when men have a sense of brother-hood under one rubric, nor that analytic refinement is achieved by enlarging the heretofore limited category "ritual" to include everything that could be considered collective formality.

NOTES

[1] Professor Gluckman died before this paper could be revised for publication, hence the editors have made a few minor changes which he did not see. The final version is essentially his, and such changes as have been made were added for clarification only.

[2] Thanks to Elizabeth Colson who gave us this book to read. This essay was written at the Yale Law School, where we had suggestive discussions with Professor Stanton Wheeler and Mr. Craig Calhoun.

[3] Since we have cited Sophocles's *Antigone,* it is relevant to state that in Euripides's lost version of *Antigone,* Haemon was married to Antigone, not betrothed to her. So with each playwright the stories of Oedipus, and other traditional myths, were varied in their emphasis to alter the dramatic development and sometimes even the outcome. In Harsh's words, variations in the legends and playwright's liberties encouraged vagueness and uncertainty, and therefore suspense (1944:31). There was a steady and even consistent development away from stereotyped masquerades in ritual dances, though these continued in a sense in the dithyrambic hymns to Dionysus, sung and danced by competing choruses of fifty drawn from the ten tribes of the Athenian citizenry. Social change, as we know well, may proceed by multiplication rather than by elimination and substitution. These hymns survived in the setting of the ritual occasion, with tragedies and comedies, and satyr-plays, the latter written by the tragic writers. In these last some heroic legend was treated in burlesqued manner, the chorus consisting of satyrs, being represented in human form with animal attributes, often a horse's tail. The hand of the past was also stamped upon the tragedies: the actors remained masked, as in the ritual sets of the past. Aeschylus brought a second actor to vary the former dialogue between one actor and the chorus. He presented human actions in relation to the purposes of the gods, rather than giving dramatic structure through portrayal of character. The drama came from an accumulation of tension because of the emotional force of the long lyric passages and the exciting richness of metaphor. Sophocles reduced the importance of the chorus and introduced a third actor: and where Aeschylus tried to make intelligible the workings of the gods to man, Sophocles more readily accepted the gods as there, and aimed to exhibit the values of life as lived within a traditional moral framework. Some human suffering was due to wickedness of human beings themselves, but not all. Euripides, though only ten years younger than Sophocles, wrote in a vastly different time, when traditional beliefs and the very gods were being questioned. He strained and twisted the mythic materials on which he had still to draw to incorporate in his dramas contemporary problems (Harsh 1944; Lucas 1967).

In the course of this development, the gods themselves appeared less and less frequently, though they continued often to speak through the mounts of seers, as with Tiresias in Sophocles's *Antigone* told.

CHAPTER XIII
CONSTRAINT AND LICENSE:
A PRELIMINARY STUDY OF TWO BRAZILIAN
NATIONAL RITUALS

Roberto Da Matta

The purpose of this paper* is to present a discussion of two Brazilian national rituals: Independence Day (Dia da Patria), and Carnival. Both are
rituals which have an effect on all parts of Brazilian society, being celebrated throughout the whole country, and involving the participation of
all classes, categories, and social groups which make up Brazilian national society.

In what follows, I shall try to explain how far Carnival does express
the extreme limit of *informality*, and, conversely, how far the Independence Day ceremony expresses the extreme limit of *formality*. In doing
so, I hope not only to find a wider field of context for these rituals, but
also to discuss the role and the significance of the rituals in the context of
a complex society. Furthermore, I want to place in the same ritual context such social events as are distinguished by divine motivation and carried out under the aegis of the Church, those assuming, in Brazil, a mediating character between extreme formality and extreme informality.
From this point of view I hope not only to look at the role of each group
or category which attends such events, but also to discuss the significance
of the classic distinctions, sacred/profane, religious/secular, formal/infor-
mal, and so on.

Carnival and Independence Day: A Comparison

1. Historic Time and Cosmic Time:

Both Carnival and Independence Day are national rituals which, while
involving the entire population of the cities where they take place, de-
mand a special kind of "time" – what we might call "vacant time," that
is, a holiday. Carnival takes place over three days (the Sunday, Monday,
and Tuesday immediately before Lent),[1] while Independence Day (commemorated on September 7) is officially part of a week known as "a Se-
mana Da Patria" (National Week). Carnival and Independence Day are
the two longest rituals in Brazil, being comparable only with Holy Week,

244

which is devoted to the rites which recreate the Passion and Resurrection of Christ. These three dates suggest, in the case of Brazil, an obvious balance between rituals explicitly concerned with civil society, rituals devoted to religion (Holy Week), and rituals concerning licentiousness and sin, "the other face" of religion.

It is of fundamental importance to appreciate that Independence Day is a ceremony related to a specific historical event – it is a *historical rite*, to borrow an expression from Levi-Strauss (1962b, chap. VIII), – while Carnival is part of the Roman Catholic calendar, marking the period which precedes Christ's teaching among men. Thus the temporality which relates to the commemoration ceremonies of Independence Day is an empirical temporality, a recorded time, which has a starting point and which, moreover, is part of a series of crucial events in Brazilian life which are seen to be interconnected. One cannot therefore understand "Independence" without referring to the colonial period and the Republican period which followed. These being specific events in the history of several peoples of the world, one can see how such temporality is marked by the sense of "progress," of "evolution," and above all, of "non-repetition," like the growth cycle of the individual – in this case, of the Brazilian people. In this sense the time of Independence Day is a unique moment, emphasizing the final break with the Colonial period and the beginning of a political "coming-of-age". It is then a *historical rite of passage* since its performance is not only intended to recreate also a glorious event in the past, but also to emphasize, in a quite explicit way, the shift from the colonial world to the world of freedom and self-determination. Thus these events, which are historical, and empirically recorded, are taken as paradigmatic, and the individuals who caused them to come about are seen as national heroes.

In contrast with that kind of temporality, Carnival is located in a cyclical time scale which is independent of fixed dates. The period of Carnival, in fact, is a time which emphasizes the relationship between men and God and for this reason has a universal and transcendent meaning. Thus, the beginning of Carnival loses itself in time, since it becomes associated with the whole of humanity in that thinking of Carnival-time is thinking in terms of categories of wide extension such as sin, death, salvation, the mortification of the flesh, sexual excess, and continence.[2] Precisely because it is defined as a time of licence and excess, Carnival clearly leads towards an emphasis on values which are not Brazilian, but Christian. The chronology of Carnival is therefore a *cosmic chronology*, being related directly to the Divinity and to actions which lead to conjunction or disjunction with the gods.

It can be seen, then, that each one of these ceremonies creates a contrasting "time". That of Independence Day is historical time – it places the participants of the ritual within the specificity of Brazilian history – while that of Carnival is a cosmic and cyclical time, taking the participants of the ritual outside the Brazilian context and placing them in direct contact with the world of the sacred, the divine, or the supernatural. In terms of temporality, then, both rituals are rites of passage (or "calendrical rites") but which refer to calendars which are distinct and which many see as being mutually exclusive, especially, as I have tried to show, when such calendars are in force in a complex, industrial society.

But the change in time from one ritual to the other is not only conceptual. Time changes also in terms of the practice of the ceremonies. Independence Day is a ritual carried out in the clear light of day and takes place in well-defined space. Since the focal point of the ritual is a military parade, one of the main streets is made ready, marking out the places where the participants in the ritual (the soldiers) are to be, where the public is permitted, and where the authorities are to be. This last consists of a high platform erected near the monument to the patron of the army, the Duke of Caxias, situated opposite the Ministry of Army. By contrast, during Carnival, the ritual takes place by night, there being here a complete inversion of night and day including the division of night into distinct periods. This can be seen in the typical ritual forms of Carnival which are the balls (where a fancy dress parade is always put on) and the processions of the "samba Schools," private organizations whose display consists of the dramatization of a theme, usually relating to the colonial period or to the aristocratic world. Since the processions and the balls take place at night, this part of the celebrations stands out very clearly, creating a dynamism which is an inversion of the normal.

Similarly, in each of these rituals, space is arranged in a different way. As we have seen, during Independence Day the ceremony takes place at a spot consecrated by history and in front of those who represent the political and jural order of the country. But during Carnival, although there does exist a special place for the processions of the "Samba Schools," "the street," taking the word in its most generic and categorical sense, is in opposition to "the home" (which represents the private and personal world), and thereby is the appropriate locale for the ritual. Thus the appropriate spatial universe for Carnival consists of the squares, the avenues, and above all the city-centre, which, during the ritual period, ceases to be the dehumanized locale of impersonal decisions and becomes the meeting place of the people.

2. *The Authorities and the People:*

A basic point of contrast between these rituals lies in the consideration of the groups which are responsible for carrying them out. During Independence Day the organization of the ritual is the responsibility of the established authorities, those officials whose power is legitimized by law and decree. The rites are organized by those groups which control the means of communication and repression – the Armed Forces – so having the support, not of a social group, a club, or a voluntary organization, but of a permanent body representing the national authority. Their internal organization is the responsibility of the Army, the Navy, and the Air Force and, since these institutions are arranged according to a hierarchical scheme, the ritual explicitly takes on the same organizing principle. Thus, there is a clear separation between the public, the authorities (who attend the procession, but for whom the procession ultimately takes place), and the soldiers who march past. Basically, the focal point of the procession of Independence Day consists of the march past the consecrated place where the highest officials of the land are saluted (*continencia* in Portuguese). The participation of the public consist in their role as spectators, which, along with the soldiers, adds importance and a dimension of relevance to the act of solidarity and respect offered to the authorities and the national symbols (the flag and the coat-of-arms of the Republic) by means of the paradigmatic sign of salute.[3] The gesture is carried out in the form of a military parade, the term "parada" (parade) in Portuguese being related to the verb "parar" (to stop) and having a rich symbolic content. Indeed the military procession (the Portuguese word being "desfile," from the verb "desfilar," to pass in a line) appears as nothing short of a freezing or "stopping" (parada) of the social structure. Thus the units march past according to a rigorous internal order (with the officers in front accompanying the flags of the unit and the national flag), and a rigorous order of procession. At all levels the ceremony becomes an actual representation of hierarchical distinctions, being organized in a chain of command going from the civilian and military authorities separated on the platform (the authorities who are saluted along with the flag), through the troops which march past (organized according to their internal hierarchy), to the public who participate in the ceremony by their attendance. The military parade creates a sense of unity, its crucial aspect being to reinforce the idea of corporateness through the gestures, verbal expressions, and uniforms, which are always identical.

The Carnival procession is very different, since here the processions are organized and carried out by private organizations, the Samba Schools, which bring together into a permanent group individuals from the lowest classes of Brazilian society. The Carnival organizations are voluntary associations and can center around a neighborhood, a group of friends, or personal ties formed through a club or some such group. They possess the character of fraternities[4] and their ideology is that of "communitas" in the sense that Turner (1969) uses the term. The procession is organized as a public lottery since the Samba Schools, in marked opposition to the military organizations, are in competition with one another and do not process in any sort of hierarchical order.

It is perhaps even more important to point out that the processions take place with the active participation of celebrities from local high society. This is especially true in Rio de Janeiro. Thus, the Schools recruit millionaires, football stars, film stars, and actors, and the entire population of Rio is divided according to their preferences for this or that School. A striking aspect of the processions is the inversion which takes place between the participant (one of the poor, generally a black or a mulatto) and the figure he represents in the procession (a nobleman, a king, a mythical hero, etc. . . .) and furthermore the active participation of all social classes (including the established authorities who attend the procession) in the role of judges and supporters. Thus, while in ordinary life, the members of a Samba School participate vicariously in the world of the rich, in the Carnival processions it is the rich who participate in that world recreated by the Samba Schools and by the poor.

A further important point is that the Samba Schools go past dancing, so that the onlooker is captured by a constant vision of movement, each participant improvising his own dance out of a set of conventional steps. As a result every opportunity is given within the conventionalized pattern for creative innovation and interpretation while, in contrast, the characteristic march of the military parade produces a total uniformity of appearance. The parade literally takes the form of a dance. In the first case, the march is marked by gestural restraint (continencia), in the second by gestural licence (incontencia).*

The Carnival procession brings together a little of everything: diversity within uniformity, homogeneity within difference, sin within the cosmic and religious time cycle, the aristocratic lavishness of dress alongside the real poverty of the actors. It thus refers to various symbolic sub-universes of Brazilian society and can therefore be called a "polysemic" procession. This is the opposite of what takes place in the military parade of Independence Day where, although the public and the authorities obviously meet in the same place, the separation between them is patent. Here the focus of the symbols, of the ritual behavior and speech, is univocal.

* Trans. note. In Portuguese, the opposition here is expressed as "contencia/ incontinencia." "Contencia" is also the word for a military salute. See page 178 above.

One of the most fundamental points in the comparative study of these rituals is a consideration of the clothing appropriate to each, this being grammatically coherent with the gestures and other general aspects of behavior. In the Independence Day parades, the clothing is military uniform, which makes all men of the same rank equal. In the Carnival parade the appropriate dress is the "fantasia" (fancy-dress), the term in Brazilian Portuguese having a double sense referring both to the dreams and fantasies of everyday life as well as to the costumes used in Carnical. Thus, while the military uniform gives a sense of equality and corporateness (all members of the same corps being dressed identically, the difference being in degree and not in kind), the fancy-dresses make distinctions and bring out individuality since each is free to choose whatever costume he wants. Thus, the military uniform, the formal suit, and other modes of dress typical of certain social positions have the function, among others, of concealing the wearer, protecting the role carried out from he who carries it out, and further, separating the role which defines his position in the ritual from the other roles he may take in everyday life. And consistent with this is the crucial fact that military uniforms (and other forms of formal dress) are exclusively related to certain positions. The contrary takes place with regard to the Carnival costume which reveals much more than it hides since a fancy dress, representing a hidden desire, creates a synthesis between the person who wears it and the roles which are represented and which the person would like to fulfill. In short, formal dress, such as a uniform, operates analytically, creating a separation by segregating firmly and clearly one role from all others which a person might carry out,[5] while on the other hand the fancy dress operates synthetically, by unification, putting together an imaginary role (made explicit in the costume) with the real roles which the individual in fact fulfills in everyday life.

It is still necessary to consider a further fundamental point. Uniforms refer back to central positions in the social structure, being signs of positions in the social order. They are therefore a mode of dress used both in the rituals and in everyday life, there being only a change of degree and not of kind between one kind and the other. The general distinction, in fact, is between "dress uniform" (uniforme de gala) and "common uniform". (In Brazil uniforms are numered from "first uniform" to "fifth uniform" in decreasing order of formal importance.) Such a use of uniforms is consistent with the order of everyday life and its formalization is the result of an acute awareness of such order. Uniforms symbolize real, concrete social realities which operate at all levels of social life. A uniformed colonel does not cease to be a colonel when he is out of uniform – he can only lose the awareness of his position, or try to see that such awareness is lost.

249

The opposite is the case with the Canival fancy dresses. The figures which are brought to life are peripheral to the Brazilian social world: kings, dukes, princes, and other nobles; ghosts, death's heads, devils, and other apparitions from the spirit world; ancient Greeks, Romans, Hawaiians, Scotsmen, and Chinese, from the edges of the known world; thieves, murderers, whores, down-and-outs, vagabonds, convicts, outlaws, and other such liminal figures who appear in everyday life only in unfortunate circumstances. The world of the Carnival characters is, then, the world of the periphery, of the past, and of the frontiers of Brazilian society. Its focal point is the forbidden, the illicit, the impossible, that which is outside the system or which lies in the interstices of it (see DaMatta, 1973).

It is clear, then, that there is little homogeneity in the set of characters created by the Carnival fancy dresses. This means that the social field created by Carnival (especially that created by the costumes used) is not one of the social uniformity, based on univocal organizing principles as is the case with the uniforms of Independence Day. On the contrary, the field is heterogeneous and, frequently, the fancy dresses bring together elements of Brazilian culture which are totally "ungrammatical," as is the case with those costumes worn in the processions of the Samba Schools, or those which emphasize homosexuality. It is a common sight during Carnival to see a "bandit" dancing with a "sherif," or a "death's head" with a young girl. And it is precisely this conjunction of contraries, this combination of symbolic (or real) representations of opposite fields, which constitutes the very essence of Carnival as a national rite.

The Carnival costumes help to create a world of mediation and of meeting. They therefore produce a social field which is cosmopolitan and universal,[6] polysemic "par excellence." There is a place for all individuals, types, personalities, categories, and groups. There is a place for all values. There emerges what can be called an open social field and perhaps, a limiting case of the Brazilian social structure, concerned as it is with its entrances and exits (cf. Douglas, 1970). In this sense the world of Carnival is the world of conjunction, of licence, and of joking; that is to say, the world of metaphor, of the temporary conjunction of two elements representing domains which are normally discrete and whose union is always a sign of abnormality, a sign that something extraordinary is happening.

Some Theoretical Problems:

The foregoing analysis establishes Independence Day and Carnival as two contrasting social events, or to be more precise, two symmetrical but inverted rituals which are part of the fabric of Brazilian social life. At first sight it could be said that Independence Day is a *sacred, formal* rite which celebrates *structure,* in opposition to Carnival which is a *profane, informal* rite creating *communitas.* In that way we would be taking the obvious, visible elements of the central of these social events as the basic features of their definition and further, establishing a dichotomy in just the way our discipline likes to do. On the other hand, one could go on to say that Independence Day closely follows Gluckman's model of rites of passage since, as we have seen, the central point of this ceremony is the clear separation of social roles, in accordance with the formula presented in "Les Rites de Passage" (1962).

But if we consider the context of Brazilian rituals as a whole, such classifications present difficulties since (a) such divisions and components, as Leach has shown (1961:135), are not mutually exclusive, but are part of a set or configuration; and (b) there is another complete set of rites in Brazilian social life which seem to bring together the fundamental components of Carnival and Independence Day. From this perspective it must be explained that Carnival ends on Ash Wednesday with the deep silence of a mass, and the Independence Day parade ends in an informal dispersion where soldiers, officials, the public, and the authorities return to their places in the everyday world. The dispersal of the participants, still formally dressed, but on their way home and accompanied by family and friends in ordinary clothes, seems to create an atmosphere similar to Carnival, based on a conjunction of the formal representations of social positions (expressed most clearly in the uniforms) with the set of other social roles which were segregated and inhibited during the performance of the ritual.

Thus, an analysis of these rituals would have to take into account not simply one particular instance of their occurrence but the entire structural process which leads to their being carried out, from the moment of their preparation to their conclusion.

The point illustrates clearly that although the central moment of Independence Day (the procession) gives emphasis to structure, such a clear priority of structure does not rule out the possible creation of a moment of *communitas.* This clearly, is what takes place at the end of the rite and perhaps even when it is going on, as I tried to show above. Carnival, on the other hand, is an event of *communitas,* which at the same time – given the conditions of Brazilian social organization and its division into classes – serves to maintain the hierarchy and position of those classes. In short, the *communitas* of Carnival is a function of the rigid social position held in everyday life by those groups involved. Its universality and homogeneity act as a reinforcement of the particularity and heterogeneity of everyday life.

251

The other problem concerns the so-called "Church festivals" or "Saints Days" in Brazil, where the focal point consists of a special kind of procession. These rites begin with a mass, are centered on the procession (where the image of the Saint is carried from one sanctuary to another) and end with a fair which takes place in the churchyard to which the image has been taken. There, confectionary and drinks are sold. There is an auction, the proceeds going to the bortherhood of the saint. There are games and dances; an atmosphere of meeting and conviviality is created which is very similar to Carnival. Furthermore, the procession itself has conciliatory characteristics. Its center is formed by those who carry the image of the saint, and it so happens that these persons form a rigid hierarchy, consisting of the ecclesiastical, civil, and military authorities. However, the central nucleus is surrounded and followed by an unorganized crowd of all social types: penitents who are carrying out vows, cripples in search of relief from their afflictions, ordinary people who are there simply to show their devotion to the saint. As a result the procession unites the hierarchical components of the military parade at its center, with the undifferentiated polysemic gathering which surrounds it. Like the Carnival procession, it unites happiness and sadness, the healthy and the sick, the good man and the sinner, and, most significantly, the authorities and the people. Also, while the Saint being honored is carried on a platform and is thereby separated from the people (on account of its status) and through the mediation of the authorities which surround it, he at the same time can be said to be walking with the people, receiving from them in the street (and not in the church) their prayers, their hymns, and their devotions. This seems to be an important point since in the military parade the authorities remain in a set position (as do the people who attend). The only part of that ritual which is in motion is the march past of the soldiers (symbols of the power of authority). Thus, in that case, the mediation between the people and the authorities is realized through the symbols of power, while, in the religious processions, the mediation between the people and the Saint takes place through the authorities (who bear the Saint on the platform and are nearest to him). In the Carnival procession, on the other hand, the people and the authorities attend a procession of the people themselves, disguised, the ritual event being an incarnation of their symbolic power since the people are taking part in an order which is routine (and for this very reason implicit and internalized). It is an event totally orientated *towards the inside* of Brazilian society, where what is emphasized is that which is specifically Brazilian: the national flag, the national colors, the national anthem, the highest authorities of the country, the national language, and the national power. It is, then, a ritual led by the Armed Forces, the search for what is specifically national being a basic component of the ideology of these bodies. This does not mean, however, that in this type of discourse a liminal event is not being created, and/or sentiments of strong fraternity between the participants in the rite. In Brazil the word "vibracao vibrations, thrill) denotes such aspects of high emotional content, indicating perhaps a sentiment of *communitas* when one can virtually "see" this basic aspect of the system through its representation in the military parade and at the moment when the national anthem is sung. Now, "the other side" of the particular and the national is the universal and the international, that is, the other countries of the world which have a close relationship with Brazil. One can therefore put forward the hypothesis that *communitas* also appears when one exaggeratedly reinforced *structure*, especially when a so-called 'breach of protocol" by authority takes place, a phenomenon which demands a detailed study and which, because of its frequent occurrence, can be viewed as a technique to create a "short-circuit" of solidarity at those times when the separation of roles and social positions is dominant.

The second possible discourse is that which focuses on, or brings out, the ambiguous aspects of the social order. This is what takes place during Carnival when the focus of the rite seems to be the set of sentiments, actions, values, groups, and categories which are inhibited in everyday life, because they are problematic. Here the center of attention is on that which lies on the edges, at the limits, and in the interstices of society. Carnival is, then a "popular festival," marked by an orientation which is universalist, and which gives special emphasis to categories such as, life in opposition to death, happiness in opposition to sadness, the rich in opposition to the poor, and so on. But here again it is not possible to say that procession of regal magnificence.

Within the scheme of anthropological dichotomies it would be difficult, if not impossible, to conceive of processions which would be neither *sacred* nor *profane*, neither *formal* or *informal*, and which would neither be creating a *communitas* nor emphasizing a *structure,* but which would be displaying all these aspects at the same time.

How, then, are we to deal with the problems arising from the study of these rituals?

One way of trying to resolve the difficulty is to take the view that each ritual expresses in turn a different way of seeing, a diffferent way of interpreting and representing Brazilian social reality. These rites would therefore be a way of "saying something" about the social structure, as Leach has suggested (Leach, 1954). In other words, Independence Day, Carnival, and the Brazilian religious festivals consist of distinct *discourses* with respect to the same reality, each one bringing out certain critical, essential aspects of that reality. In fact, such discourses constitute the means by which the anthropologist can perceive the social reality, since they are themselves an integral part of the selfsame social structure.

Considering such ceremonies as *discourses* (and/or ways of revealing a social structure) implies studying them from a disjunctive point of view. By this I mean that the ritual life of a given society does not necessarily have to be coherent or functional and can contain elements which are competitive or concurrent, which express different ways of seeing, interpreting, and realizing the social structure. On the other hand, this perspective allows us to verify the fundamental importance of the way such ritual life brings things into conjunction.

Indeed, Brazilian national rituals constitute a good example of three possible modes of *emphasizing* and *making manifest,* by means of a specific symbolic discourse, those aspects considered important in the structure of Brazilian social life. Thus, the first discourse – Independence Day- calls attention to those aspects of the social structure which does not make its presence felt. Carnival is, in fact, a period defined as "preparatory" to a cycle of penitence and remorse, that is, Lent – a period when behavior must be marked by abstinence from meat and when all excess must be controlled. On the other hand Carnival also has its own structure and formalities, there being prescribed ways of participating in the celebration with regard to dancing, singing, and dress. Furthermore, although the focus of the rite is on universal categories and on the edges of social life, the way of representing them is specifically Brazilian.

The discourses of Independence Day and Carnival are, then, related to one another by an apparently simple logic. During Independence Day a *reinforcement* of hierarchy takes place. This is done openly and obviously from the beginning of the event through to its climax, disappearing only at the end when the social roles which are operative in daily life are again reassumed. During Carnival, the festival creates a dissolution of the system of social roles and positions, since these are *inverted* during the ritual, there being, nevertheless, a return to the system of roles and positions at the end of the rite when everything sinks once more into the daily world. Furthermore, everything indicates that Independence Day is marked by an emphasis, in its central moment, towards what is national and specifically Brazilian, but ends by revealing a universality underlying this inward looking orientation, since there cannot be a nation without the existence of "other" nations against which "our nation" can be opposed. And, *mutatis mutandis,* during Carnival, the focus is on the cosmic and the universal, yet it is a cosmos and a universality which are distinctly Brazilian.

The discourse of the religious festivals, in turn, allows the discovery of a perspective of the social structure where the focus is simultaneously on local and universal values. Everything leads to the supposition that there is an attempt in these festivals to reconcile the people and the authorities by means of the cult of God (or of the Saint), allowing diverse, discontinuous elements of the social structure to meet and mingle under the aegis of the Church, a body which holds the monopoly on spiritual matters. Religious festivals, therefore, by putting side by side, at one time, the people and the authorities, the saints and the sinners, the healthy and the sick, thereby express in their discourse a systematic *neutralization* of positions, groups, and social categories, establishing a sort of *pax Catholica*. There are aspects of these ceremonies which are rigidly structured, when, for example, it centers on the two hierarchical levels which are being represented (the divine hierarchy which unites men and God through the priest; and the hierarchy which unites men amongst themselves under the aegis of the priest), and there are also moments similar in form and content to Carnival, since a legitimate encounter is established between categories and social groups both during the procession and at the end of the festival. But nevertheless the religious festivals are neither a Carnival nor a military parade. Its logic, however, seeems to be a logic where relationships are accentuated in one moment only to be inhibited in the next.

To summarize what has been said: it is very difficult to equate these discourses with any substantive elements which have been defined *a priori*, such as sacred and profane, formal and informal, secular or religious, and so on, since each of the ceremonies considered contains, in one aspect or another, components which correspond to these dichotomies. On the other hand, I also tried to show that if these rituals are in any way directed, they are directed by the kind of association of elements which they create and not because they are capable of modifying the everyday in any essential way. There should therefore be a grammar or a system of combination which would give us a way of entering the "ritual world" and the central point of such a study should be this grammar, not the substantive categories which have been traditionally used to describe and interpret these events. From this point of view, ritual is something completely compatible with the world of ordinary events, the elements of everyday life being the same as those of the ritual. A further point in my interpretation was that concerning the crucial relationships which each of the respective ceremonies allows us to isolate. Here I tried to show that the basic mechanisms of Carnival, of Independence Day, and of Brazilian religious festivals were, respectively *inversion, reinforcement,* and *neutralization.* Finally I suggested a definition of each of these events as *discourses* about the social structure. It should therefore be clear that such discourses are symbolic and expressive of positions in the social struc-

255

ture, and hence do not necessarily have to be coherent or functional.

Having made these points, I would like to go on further to suggest a possible approach to the study of what we call "rite" or "ritual." In doing so I would like to consider again, in greater depth, some of the points already made.

One of the most obvious problems in the study of rituals is the notion that they constitute a special kind of action and/or a special kind of event. Thus, rites "do something," "say something," "reveal something," "hide something," "incite something," "store something." Expressions such as these, appearing innumerable times in the literature, are indicative of all sorts of theoretical positions, but they all point towards one and the same problem: rites are to be taken as special events constructed by society. They are situations which are created under the aegis and under the control of the social system. They are programmed by it.

But besides this, what is equally striking is that of all subjects in the anthropological literature, the area of ritual is the most heavily qualified by adjectives. We find rituals described as "sacred," "popular," "economic," "political," "of kinship," "secular," "formal and informal"; the rituals of "games," of "academics"; "civil" and "military" rituals; "masculine and feminine" rituals; rites of "passage," of "interaction," of "segregation and aggregation"; "financial," "magical and mystical," "scientific"; rituals of "expiation," of "affliction" . . . the list could go on indefinitely.

What is the significance of this?

It seems clear that there exist as many "rituals" as there are events or domains in the social world which can be perceived, distinguished, and classified. Thus, for each established domain, the word "ritual" can be applied, and a corresponding "rite" emerge from it. That is to say, all aspects of the social world can be seen as capable of generating a "rite." Obviously this depends on the way "ritual" is defined, but I believe this is a superficial response to the problem. Even in those areas where problems of definition are prevalent, the possibilities of definition do not allow such a plethora of adjectival qualification. We can see, for example, that the field of "kinship" is one of those areas, but the possibilities of attaching qualifying labels to kinship are not so vast.

It is most probable that these immense possibilities of defining rites are the result of something which can be related to a deeper and more difficult problem, which is the simple fact that all social life is, indeed, a "rite" or is "ritualized." Since the social world is based on conventions and symbols, all social actions are really ritual acts or acts arising from a ritualization.

I am therefore taking up a radical position in not trying to draw distinctions between the *materia prima* of the everyday world and that which constitutes the world of ritual. Both these dimensions are built up from more or less arbitrary conventions, and there is no essential or qualitative shift between the categories and relations of the everyday world and those used in the universe of rites. I do not see how we can distinguish types of behavior which are "rational," "communicative," and "magical," as Leach and Turner do (cf. Leach, 1966; Turner, 1968). Even the act of "cutting down a tree" is a problematic action and cannot be so easily classified, as Leach does (1966), into the category of "types of rational behavior." I do accept that on a certain analytical level such an action is rational in the sense that there is a relationship between means and ends, but is this really important? We can see that two individuals from two societies cut down trees in different ways, although both use the same tool. And leaving aside the question that the tools used can be of different kinds, we know that an individual might swing an axe to the right, and never to the left, that he could begin the task by spitting on his hands, that in cutting down the tree he might invoke the gods, and so on, while another, from another culture, would do none of this.

This is the sociological question which reveals that even the most conceivably rational actions are not immune from so-called "communicative" or "magical" behavior. To try to resolve the problem of ritual by means of these classifications, even when one tries to put them together, as Leach does in his second theory of rituals, is no more than a disguised return to butterfly collecting.[7] And in this context one could further add that mystical or magical thought – as Levi-Strauss has shown (1962b) – is a way of "saying something" about reality which does not exclude rationality.

As it happens, I believe that the present study clearly reveals how each festival is related to, or directed towards, a specific sector of Brazilian society. Thus, Independence Day concerns the Armed Forces and the authorities, the religious festivals the Church, and Carnival is seen as a "popular festival." These discourses are reflections of groups which monopolize the rites so that, in a certain sense, those rites well represent the model of organic solidarity proposed by Durkheim and developed by Gluckman (Cf. Durkheim, 1933, and Gluckman, 1962). But the problem is that in a complex society these organically whole and functional domains are constantly disputing for power. In other words, although Durkheim's model is probably correct in pointing out that in a complex society multiple codes are possible (since each group will have a different perspective of the social totality), there exists, on the other hand, the problem of the *contamination of codes*. By the contamination of codes, I want to bring out and call attention to the problem that, in a complex society, oscillations take place between specialized groups moving from dominant to dominated and visaversa. Thus, the Church was dominant during the Medieval period and the discourse of European society of that time was a Catholic discourse. Similarly, the National Socialist Party was dominant in Nazi Germany so that the discourse of German society at that time was the discourse of that political party.

Alongside the multiple codes which divide up "the Stage" into the social roles, as Gluckman describes, there is also struggle caused by the contamination of the whole system by one social group and its ideology. The dynamic of these systems is, as a result, a dynamic of total contamination or of equilibrium: that is, certain periods are dominated by certain social groups and the entire system is organized according to their perspective, categories, and values, other periods being dominated by other groups. In the context of the study of rituals it would seem that the history of Western society is one where various social systems have systematically explored, through the years, the possibilities of having multiple codes which exist together in equilibrium, or to have only one code of one group which is dominant, and which contaminates the entire system.

I believe therefore that complex social systems also suffer from a necessity of over-determination and from a necessity of coherent relation between their domains. This is revealed most clearly on the political and ritual level. Rituals which reinforce the existing rules and social roles, such as, for example, Independence Day, are rituals which proliferate in systems where authoritarianism is dominant. And authoritarianism here means the decrease of multiplex visions of the same social structure, hence the description of these systems as *totalitarian* since they embody contaminated (or total) views of the social order; that is, they represent exclusive perspectives of the order.

It can be seen, then, that it is problematic to define "ritual" as a type of social action specific to a certain type of system of social relations since it is equally difficult to isolate those systems clearly one from the other.

How, then, are we to deal with the problem?

Note that up to this point I have not said that "rituals do not exist." Quite to the contrary, I have throughout affirmed their existence and agreed that rites are special events of social familiarity. My argument is that rituals must not be taken as events which are essentially different (in form, quality, and substance) from those which constitute and inform the so-called routine of daily life. In fact, the present essay established that the three Brazilian rituals analyzed make use of everyday social mechanisms. *Reinforcement, inversion,* and *neutralization* are made use of at all times in social life.

From this approach, the study of rituals will not be a search for the essential qualities of a peculiar and qualitatively different event, but a way of examining how trivial elements of the social world can be elevated and transformed into symbols, categories, and mechanisms which, in certain contexts, allow the generation of a special or extraordinary event.

As with all symbolic discourses, ritual abstracts certain aspects of reality. One of its basic mechanisms is, therefore, to make certain aspects of social life more obvious than others. In fact, it can be said that without these abstractions, which produce discontinuities and contrasts, the entire meaning of the social world would be lost. The ritual world is, therefore, a world of oppositions and conjunctions, of abstractions and integrations, of the emphasis and inhibition of elements. It is through this process that "wordly things" take on a different meaning and can express more than what is expressed in their normal context. In short, the world of ritual consists of what is effectively arbitrary. It is in this world that men can dress and behave as women, adults as children, and man as animals, and, by so doing, reveal how men differ amongst themselves and are similar to animals and/or how men are similar amongst themselves and different from animals. The possibilities are infinitely variable. Thus, as was stated at the beginning of this section, rituals hide and reveal; they can both delude or clarify. This varies from culture to culture and from situation to situation. What is important, it seems to me, is to suggest, if only in a preliminary way, the mechanisms which are made use of in the creation of these events where the meaning is either hidden or clearly revealed, where it is analysed or entirely obscured, where it is for or against that which is least debated in the human or natural world.

I am arguing that rite, as myth, manages to place aspects of the social world in "close up". A finger is only a finger joined to a hand, and the hand to an arm, and the arm to a body. But at the moment when a ring is placed on the finger, marking the matrimonial status of the person, the finger changes its significance. As Ramos and Peirano (1973) have emphasized, a transposition of elements has taken place between one domain and another. The finger normally seen as an element which is an integral part of a biological and individual universe, becomes a symbol of a set of social relations.

It can be seen that the basic mechanism of the above example is the separation and insertion of an element into a new context. As Ramos and Peirano (1973) suggest, a *bricolage* has taken place. Nothing new appears. What happens is that an element is transposed into a context from which it is normally excluded.

The mechanism of separation seems to be fundamental in the process of bricolage and ritualization. Gluckman illustrated this when he tries to equate rites of passage with a certain type of social system where social roles are carried out on multiple levels by the same person in simultaneous contexts. However, separation seems to be a very general mechanism since what is separated on the one hand is integrated on the other. Thus the role of chief is separated from those of father, maternal uncle, and brother, in order to integrate that individual, *qua* member of that role, into a system of authority. In terms of the mechanisms mentioned in this analysis, it can be said that the separation of roles, as explained by Gluckman (1962), is an important instance of ritualization, but with two differences. In the first place the separation does not exclusively (or even with greater frequency) concern tribal societies, since such a way of establishing social identities is a universal mechanism, being part of the world of conventions. Secondly, I consider "separation" to be a special case of what I am calling *reinforcement*, in the sense I used the term in the study of the Independence Day ceremony.

In these cases where social relationships and categories are revealed and emphasized by means of *separation* or *reinforcement*, the elements are not shifted from their normal context in any radical way. These mechanisms simply call attention to the rules, positions, or categories which in fact exist, without altering their position very much. What seems to take place is an exaggeration of what already exists. Therefore, rituals which are based on reinforcement (or on separation) are rituals which maintain a direct relationship with the routine of everyday life. Thus, for example a general is always a general; all that happens is that in a given context, and at a time determined by the group, he uses the dress, decorations, and arms which correspond to his position and identity. The existing position is accordingly reinforced, a position which could be otherwise submerged under all the rest of the routines and social roles. The so-called ritual of separation is precisely this moment when the role of general is singled and given emphasis while all the others are inhibited. Furthermore, we can suggest that mechanisms of reinforcement are employed when routines create conflicting equivalences between systems of social roles, or when situations become ambiguous and it becomes necessary to redefine them in terms of the established system. By this I am suggesting that mechanisms of reinforcement probably become necessary and are brought into action in systems where there is little tolerance for ambiguity.

But even in trivial or spontaneous situations mechanisms of reinforcement are constantly brought into play. Thus, for example, it is common for the situation to arise where a man says: "Let's get it straight – who's house in this anyway?", or: "Who do you think you are? Just remember that *I* am head of this department." Notice that here the emphasis is both on the separation of the roles and on the reinforcement of a system of roles, the attenpt being to resolve an ambiguous situation.

Reinforcement, then, seems to be a mechanism which concentrates on that which is submerged (or that which is being submerged), and therefore not being as clearly recognized as it should be. When the mechanism is applied, and the ambiguous situation resolved, a context of the formality or respect is created. I think this is the implication of Radcliffe-Brown's argument when he wrote his first article on joking relationships (1940, [1952]). He saw very clearly that a theory of joking relationships is impossible without, at the same time, developing a theory to cover those relationships which are symmetrical and inverse: relationships of formality and respect. Nevertheless, these relationships are not special cases. They are specific ways of resolving normal situations which arise in social life, my point being that when social roles are separated or reinforced, a context of respect is created. Separation or reinforcement are therefore the *materia prima* of those rituals frequently called "formal", those rites of respect, where the basic objective is the separation of elements, categories, or rules which have been, at some point or another, confused. To mention a specific case, I believe that this is the mechanism which is characteristic of the social world of the Ndembu and their rituals of affliction (Cf. Turner, 1967: chap. 1, and 1968).

The other basic mechanism referred to in this article is *inversion*. In this case it appears that the process is radical in the sense that it really produces a complete shift of elements from one domain into another from which they are normally excluded. In other words it is case of uniting what is normally separate, creating continuities between the various systems of classification which operate discretely in the social system. It is precisely this which takes place in events like the Brazilian Carnival, where the use of costumes allows a vast array of personalities, social roles and categories, which would in the normal course of events be hidden and marginal, to be brought into relationship with the nucleus (or centre) of the social system. Thus, when inversion takes place, categories and social roles which in everyday life are rigidly separated, come to be joined. The context which we call "ritual" is therefore created when the thief and the policeman, the prostitute and the housewife, the convict and the diplomat, the transvestite and the *macho*, are placed side by side.

The social field thereby created is one based on its own peculiar grammatically: that of familiarity and joking, where what is being searched after are those aspects which are beyond the systems which each of these social roles represent in the normal world. This is the very idea underlying joking, since in this situation (or relation) there is a tendency to ignore systematically those roles most rigidly defined by age, sex, or position in a clearly articulated system of social positions (like the kinship system), in order to reveal what is marginal in this system. Thus, as Radcliffe-Brown pointed out, the grandson pretends that he can marry the grandfather's wife; or attempts to treat her as if she already was his wife (1952:97). That is, tho important aspect of joking is not the division established by age or social position in the kinship system, but the fact that the grandfather and grandson are both, before all else, men, and can have sexual desire for the same woman. This is the essence of the joking relationship, since here, what is sought after is what is marginal (the fact that both are men), the difference in age and social position being eliminated by inversion).

The same thing occurs in academic cocktail parties where pupils and teachers tend to bring out their human side (as husband, father, son, Don Juan, pop-music fan, reactionary or leftist, and so on), allowing them to take on social roles normally excluded in the context of academic routine. In such situations the emphasis always falls on those aspects of social relations which are most universal, such as sex or age (or on more diffuse tastes such as a liking for music, painting, or women), these being aspects which the routines of daily life tend to inhibit in favour of other structural and organizational factors. In other words, the out-come of inversion (and of joking) is the conjunction of position, as Radcliffe-Brown pointed out (1952).

Inversion creates the conditions which make possible a shift between domains and between elements' situation in discontinuous positions. Thus, during Carnival, the social classes of Brazil, "from top to toe", can enter into association. Here, the mediating element between them is no longer power and wealth, but singing, dancing, the costumes, and the festivities, in a word, the opportunity to "play" at Carnival. What is being said at this time is that differences do indeed exist, but at the same time everyone is fundamentally the same in that they are all human beings. Thus, the discontinuities of Carnival are those which separate men as members of humanity, not as members of districts, factions, political parties, classes, and so on.

With regard to the third mechanism, *neutralization*, it becomes more difficult to imagine situations which will demonstrate its, operation, apart from those of ceremony itself. But one could suggest as a working hypothesis that neutralizations correspond to those situations referred to in the literature as "avoidance". Thus avoidance results neither in disjunction (which comes about through reinforcement and/or separation) nor in conjunction (which results from inversion). Here the result simply takes the form of a relationship based on distance and on extreme respect, as Radcliffe-Brown pointed out (1952), and equally, on an extreme inversion of behaviour, since, as an avoidance relationship, there is no visible social relationship: there is only, as the term itself declares, avoidance! This is an inversion of social behaviour since it does not permit social communication through normal channels between the parties in the relationship.

Conclusions:

In this essay I have called attention to the combinatorial aspect of those events which we call "ritual". My intention was to show that rites do not appear to be events which are substantially different from those of the everyday world, but are syntheses of these events. The atmosphere of ritual is created not by means of *essential transformations* of the world of social relations, but by a manipulation of the elements and relationships of this world. Rituals are then to be seen as ways of bringing out aspects of the everyday world, and I looked at three basic ways of bringing this about: reinforcement, inversion, and neutralization. Here, the argument closely follows Leach's suggestion (1954 and especially 1961), where he indicates that ritual is an *aspect* of social relations, and, furthermore, that rite is a technique "for changing the status of the moral person from profane to sacred, or from sacred to profane" (1961: 134). The difference is that the three mechanisms which I have described are different from Leach's. Furthermore my attempt was to produce a fuller articulation of the relationship between these three mechanisms and three other aspects of social relations (respect, joking, and avoidance) which are, all three, quite ordinary aspects of life.

In other words, by developing the argument, I tried to show that the *materia prima* of the world of ritual is the same as that of the world of ordinary life, and that the differences between these are of degree and not of kind. Ritual consists of placing in focus, in close up, elements and relations. From this perspective, it is hardly worthwhile to begin classifying rites, before we have a better understanding of the basis relations which constitute them. And, in fact, understanding the basic relations of the social world is automatically and simultaneously to understand the world of ritual. Rituals say something with respect to all social relations, whether they be sacred or profane, local or national, formal or informal. Everything points to the problem that, in the ritual world, what is said is said more vehemently, more coherently, and with greater consistency. Rituals are, therefore, instruments which give greater clarity to social messages.

If rites help to construct and create time, as Leach suggested (1961: 135), they also create gaps in the social routine. Thus, there is no situation, defined by a group as extraordinary or special, which is not permeated by a certain kind of awareness of an event, of a category, or a relationship, in a word, of ritualization. And there is no ritualization which does not make use of a mechanism which has as its end to neutralize, to reaffirm, or to place everything together "from top to toe."

Finally, I suggest that we pay more attention to social relations and to the systems of those relations than to the effects produced by their syntheses, as appears to be the case with rituals. As happened in the case of totemism (Cf. Lévi-Strauss, 1962a), we should be careful not to take the message for the code, not to mistake the phenomenon for its constitutive elements. To find the proper approach to totemism it was necessary to point out that behind a set of apparently dissimilar types, there lay a few basic mechanisms, without which neither the phenomenon perceived as totemism nor even social life itself would be possible. To rethink rites, therefore, we must first de-ritualize.

NOTES

* In preparing this essay I was grateful for the help given by Lucia Blundi Guinle who collected basic material on Independence Day. Gilberto Alves Velho, Moacir Palmeira, Otavio Alves Velho and Luiz de Castro Faria discussed certain important aspects of the interpretation. Alan Campbell, from Oxford, translated the article and, in doing so, helped me clarify some basic points.

[1] The festivities, however, begin on the Friday.

[2] There is an abundance of such themes in the songs written specially for Carnival which would in themselves constitute a separate subject of inquiry.

[3] That seems to be a form of greeting, where, on meeting, persons emphasize their differences. Thus, instead of the hand and arm being extended towards the "alter", they are turned back towards the "ego". The Nazi salute, on the other hand, indicates one's position with regard to the Führer.

[4] Carnival, especially in Rio, has now become part of the tourist market, and accordingly, the Samba Schools are today organized like permanent commercial enterprises. A study of these organizations, which is being carried out by Maria Julia Goldwasser, has discovered a series of internal difficulties due to the attempt to come to terms with the reality of a commercial business while maintaining the external aspect of "communitas" (Cf. Turner, 1969).

[5] It will be clear that this agrees with Gluckman's formulation which will be discussed at the end of this paper (Cf. Gluckman, 1962).

[6] This certainly explains the obligatory arrival of Hollywood stars to take part in the Carnival of Rio de Janeiro.

[7] It is, of course, curious that this should be so since my own argument developed above is, basically, a repetition of Leach's (1954:12).

CHAPTER XIV
CUP MATCH AND CARNIVAL: SECULAR RITES OF
REVITALIZATION IN
DECOLONIZING, TOURIST-ORIENTED SOCIETIES

Frank E. Manning

Few subjects addressed by anthropologists of religion have received more attention than the revitalization movements which swept large parts of the world in the wake of white imperial expansion. Three general patterns seem to characterize many of these movements, especially those of the "cargo cult" variety. First, there is a foreign incursion which precipitates abrupt changes in native society. Second, there is a native response which works to preserve and enhance selected aspects of the indigenous culture, partly by relating them to symbols drawn from the alien presence. Third, there is an intense manifestation of religious phenomena; prophets arise, millenia are visualized, and rites are dominated by states of ecstasy and dissociation.

It strikes me that this process has a secular counterpart that is a significant force today throughout the Antilles and possibly many other developing regions. The foreign incursion is mass tourism, originating chiefly from metropolitan countries. The native response is a reformulated cultural orientation which synthesizes indigenous development processes and alien images while remaining formally consistent with traditional meanings. Heroes representing the normative antithesis of religion emerge as central figures of the new cultural orientation, offering interpretations and strategies applicable to the changing conditions of native society.

I would like here to consider two commemorative rituals which are part of secular revitalization processes: Cup Match in Bermuda and Carnival in Antigua. The major annual festivals of these countries, Cup Match and Carnival are similar enough to reveal recurrent features of the revitalization pattern and different enough to yield insight into their respective ethnographic settings.[1]

The "Creole Baccanal"

Emancipation from slavery on August 1, 1834 had special significance in Bermuda and Antigua. In other parts of the British Antilles manumitted slaves were required to serve a four-year indenture euphemistically known as "apprenticeship" under their previous owners. But in Bermuda and Antigua emancipation was immediate and unconditional.

The practical social consequences of full freedom were minimal, as the smallness of the two islands left blacks no realistic alternative but to stay in their former psotions. Thus Bermudians remained an artisan class in a maritime and mercantile economy controlled by a resident white oligarchy, while Antiguans remained an agricultural proletariat on sugar estates owned by local and metropolitan whites. Such restrictions, however, did not erase the symbolic impact of emancipation. In both Bermuda and Antigua ex-slaves commemorated the historic event by initiating a mid-summer day of celebration on which they held picnics, beach outings, sports events, and family gatherings.

In the twentieth century the emancipation celebration took on the character of a major festival. This happened first in Bermuda when a cricket game between two lodges became too big for the lodges to promote. Sports clubs were built to sponsor the game, which in 1902 became known as Cup Match. The popularity of Cup Match increased steadily as the game evolved from an interclub rivalry to an all-star match between the island's eastern and western parishes. For several decades the two consecutive days on which Cup Match is played have been legal holidays.

But Cup Match is more than a spectacular sports event. Attended by some ten thousand persons – a third of the black population – it is the occasion, in the words of one informant, "when we eat everything in Bermuda, and spend everything in Bermuda." The excessive consumption of food is highlighted by such traditional Bermudian dishes as mussel pie and conch stew, sold at concession stands, and cassava pie, a homemade recipe of chicken and pork baked in a cassava crust. Along with picnic items most persons carry a quantity of liquor. Drinking in the bleachers begins before the first ball is bowled at 10 a.m., and continues all day. At the club bar there is also heavy traffic.

The custom of "wearing everything in Bermuda" is known as the "fashion show." Women come to the game in chic, sexually arousing clothing. Popular styles in recent years have included sheer blouses that cling to the contours of the bosom, low-cut necklines which amply expose the cleavage, two-piece ensembles which daringly bare the midriff, and hot pants outfits which accentuate the pubes, hips, and buttocks. Also in vogue are Afro-American and Afro-Caribbean styles, especially "natural" and "corn-row" coiffures, leather collars, large round earrings, "slave" bracelets worn on the upper arm, African print dresses and head wrappings, and jewelry made of beads and carved wood chips.

Men, dressed in such counterparts of these fashions as wide-brimmed hats with gold and silver bands, fringed leather vests, shirts slit open to expose the chest, and tight-fitting, "mod"-styled trousers, respond outwardly to the invitation conveyed by the women's clothing. In the bleachers, at the concession stands, and inside the club at the bar, the interactional encouter between the sexes illustrates Wax's (1957:593) observation that clothing and grooming transmute natural attraction into a cultural game. The outstanding game is that of "rapping," the agonistic exchange of licentious double-entendres and flirtaceous gestures that Kochman has described as a "colorful way of asking for some pussy" (1970: 146).

For extravagant spending at Cup Match is most dramatically evidenced in the "stock market", a revival-size gambling tent on the edge of the cricket field. Barkers lure customers with shouts of "Come in here on a bike, go home in a sports car", "Get some money for your honey", "Take your hands out of your pocket and put your money on the table", and "Play the stock market, ladies and gentlemen, play the stock market." The dice game of crown and anchor is played at forty or more tables, while at other tables there are cards and crap rolling. Bets range from one to a hundred dollars and higher. Croupiers keep a supply of cold beer which they share with good customers.

Another attraction of the Cup Match festival is entertainment. Steel bands play on the periphery of the grounds for the listening and dancing pleasure of the crowd. At night there are parties and shows featuring soul-styled musicians. Performances are given by Gombey troupes, masked mimes who dance to an Afro-Caribbean rhythm played on drums, fifes, snares, flutes, and whistles, costume-like caricatured Amerindians by wearing feather headdresses and carrying tomahawks, but whose overall rendition is uniquelly Bermudian and a familiar part of the island folk tradition, having evolved in the context of Christmas mumming on the streets.

Since 1970, however, the main entertainment productions at Cup Match have been a *mas'* (masquerade pageant) and a performance revue choreographed along the lines of the Trinidadian Carnival. While these events were originally organized by immigrants from Trinidad, Bermudians now participate enthusiastically and compete successfully for such exalted titles as Calypso King and Carnival Queen. Members of the public join the celebrations by "jumping up" (dancing and parading) along with costumed *mas'* players.

The recent popularity of Carnival motifs in Bermuda bears witness to the diffusion of the Carnival festival from Trinidad to other parts of the Antilles. The outstanding recipient of this diffusion is Antigua, a Northeast Caribbean island of seventy thousand persons. Antigua held its first

Carnival in 1957, coincident with the mid-summer emancipation remembrance. The festival has grown in size and popularity and is now – like Cup Match in Bermuda – a two-day legal holiday.

The Antigua Carnival follows the general format of the Trinidad prototype. The festivities begin with nightly performance competitions in various categories of entertainment; calypsonians, beauty queens, steel bands, brass bands, and *mas'* leaders compete for titles that convey both coveted status designations and lucrative monetary prizes. These contests are held in "Carnival City", a public park in which there is erected a huge, elegantly decorated stage surrounded by seating for several thousand persons. The actual production of revues is informal, even chaotic at times, although emcees and stage managers strive to project a professional image consistent with the modern notion of Carnival as "show business". There are admission charges to all events, a reflection of the view that Carnival is consumer as well as participatory entertainment.

The round of performance competitions is followed by the Carnival itself, or what Hill calls the "theatre of the streets" (1972:85-99) – the two days when the streets are literally taken over by masquerade troupes accompanied by steel and brass bands playing the repetitive, hypnotic rhythms of the "road march", the locally-composed calypso that emerges as the popular favorite. Revelling spectators line the sides of every parade route. Some are moved to join the troupes or to help push the rolling platforms which transport the steel drums; others tag along behind the bands, having their own "jump up".

Yet Antigua's Carnival attempts to conserve insular identity rather than to copy slavishly the Trinidadian model. It is held on the occasion of the emancipation commemoration, not before Lent as in Trinidad. It has incorporated into its masquerade band repertoire both clowns and mummering troupes (similar to the Bermuda Gombeys) who previously performed on the streets during the Christmas season. Behind the Carnival City stage is a vast panorama of a distinctive Antiguan scene such as Nelson's Dockyard or an idyllic beach with abandoned windmills in the background. The inscriptions "Antigua me come from" and "Antigua where land and sea make beauty" are seen on tee shirts, parade vehicles, and concession stands.

Balancing these expressions of insular identity are various symbols of Caribbean regionalism. The regional theme is clearly depicted in the contests for Calypso King and Carnival Queen. In each category a preliminary competition selects winners from Antigua, who then compete against representatives from other islands in two shows which climax the entertainment revues. In recent years these events have drawn contestants from not only the British Commonwealth islands but from territories under the French, Dutch, and American flags.

Regional awareness is stressed in a number of other ways as well. Emcees, editorial writers, political dignitaries, and others who have access to a microphone or medium make it a point to welcome the many visitors from different parts of the Caribbean. Disc jockeys remind their audiences that special Caribbean programs are broadcast to neighboring islands. Calypsonians lament insular divisiveness, call for regional cooperation, and boast about regional accomplishments in the fields of politics and sports. Masquerade troupes depict folkloric, historic, and aesthetic motifs relevant to the region as a whole. At food stands there is an abundance of items regarded as Afro-Caribbean staples: plantain, breadfruit, black pudding, souse, black eye peas and rice, coconuts, and the various "ground provisions" (tannias, eddoes, dasheen, yams, sweet potatoes). In short, the cultural nationalism that permeates the Trinidad Carnival is replaced in Antigua by a conscious pan-Caribbeanism.

Expressions of racial solidarity, many of which have political implications, have been closely associated with regional awareness. A recent Calypso King, Lord Short Shirt, urged his audience to "pull together, with your black brother." His successor, Mighty Swallow, won the title with the song "Freedom". Each verse recited the oppression suffered by black people in a different world area – Angola, Rhodesia, Antigua; the chorus, which the audience lustily joined, was the chant "freedom". In performance, the song was a striking example of the powerfull call-an-response formula inherited from the rhythmic structure of West African poetry and music (Keil 1966:97).

This sense of an aggressive racial consciousness has helped to popularize the black American aesthetic and attitude. Performance styles and repertoires have become increasingly oriented toward the soul and funky genres; indeed, one group of Antiguan panmen have named themselves the "Superfly Steel Band". Dress, jewelry, and coiffure fashions borrow heavily from Afro-American patterns. Themes of black militancy are expressed through the wearing of emblems depicting the red, green, and black tricolor and through the raising of clenched fists as a gesture of applause at entertainment events. Similarly, crowds of youths following the procession of steel and brass bands raise their fists in rhythmic unison – a response which helps to explain the success of the song "Black Power March" for which eighteen-year-old Mighty Deceiver recently won the junior calypso contest.

In its underlying tone Carnival is essentially comparable to Cup Match, although the considerably greater prosperity of Bermuda allows for a more extravagant display of wealth and spending. The spirit of Carnival, however, is qualitatively if not quantitatively the same as its Bermudian festival counterpart. Liquor is profusely consumed, gambling is openly conducted, and sexual liaisons are freely initiated. In short, the "license in ritual" described by Gluckman (1959:109-136) is readily apparent. As the calypsonisan perennially boast, Carnival is, after all, the "creole bacchanal".

Politics and Tourists

No less than religious ritual, secular ritual must be examined in relation to its total social context. In both Bermuda and Antigua the transition of emancipation commemorations from quiet folk celebrations to centralized, baroque festivals has been accompanied by two major social processes. The first is the struggle of democratic reform movements against archaic sociopolitical traditians. The second is the development of tour ism as the foundation of the economy. Let us look briefly at these processes in each island.

Although the actual decolonization movement began a generation later in Bermuda than in the British West Indies, the black challenge to the white merchant oligarchy known as the "Forty Thieves" can be dated to the political associations which emerged in the early 1900's, a period when Cup Match was begun. Working within a constitutional system which restricted the franchise to property owners, the great majority of whom were white, the associations sought to elect one black from each parish to Parliament. The use of the "plumping" strategy whereby association supporters voted for the black candidate and withheld their other three votes achieved a fair measure of success, culminating in 1953 with the election of nine blacks to the House of Assembly.

The "assault on the oligarchy" accelerated greatly in the 1960's. Popular campaigns for racial integration and universal suffrage were mounted at the outset of the decade, the first political party was formed in 1963 as an organ of the labor movement, the first major industrial strike was called in 1965, and partisan politics brought into effect in 1968 a new constitution which replaced the board system controlled by British civil servants and local white aristocrats with a cabinet of ministers responsible to Parliament. Further democratic reforms limiting the executive power of the Crown-appointed Governor were amended to the constitution in 1972.

These developments, however, have yet to achieve the basic goals toward which they aimed: racial parity in the power structure and national independence. The white oligarchy reacted to the threat of organized black political strength by forming its own party which it has integrated racially on a selective basis. The coalition thus forged continues, after two one man-one vote elections, to hold a sizeable parliamentary majority and to perpetuate colonial status.

Yet while retaining its commanding position the oligarchy has been forced to disavow the values and idioms of the traditional patronage system, which gave to whites the role of paternal benefactors and to blacks that of docile dependents. The power structure is now officially legitimated in terms of partnership rather than patronage; the ruling party proclaims that a "united Bermuda" is the way to a better future for both races.

From the viewpoint of many blacks, "competition" is more readily sought than partnership (cf. Manning 1973:115-145). Yet the end envisaged by both strategies is the same: to benefit materially from the phenomenal boom created by the rapid and sustained growth of year-round tourism since the early 1950's. The effects of this boom, boosted further by the recent expansion of the international business sector, are obvious. A per capita income higher than that of most developed countries has been achieved and the trappings of poverty have been virtually eliminated. Massive over-employment and indirect taxation have combined to encourage Bermudians to work two or more jobs, to become heavily involved in investment and speculation, and to convert sections of their homes into apartments which can be rented at exorbitant rates to the expatriate labor force who comprise a fourth of the island's population. In short, while steady gains have been made toward the achievement of decolonization and racial equality, what has really been democratized in Bermuda is not the sociopolitical system but the economic lifestyle of the Forty Thieves. The role of "adventurer capitalist" (Wilkinson 1958) formerly monopolized by the white elites has become accessible to other segments of society.

The processes of democratic reform and tourist development have evolved rather differently in Antigua. The first trade union, formed during the Caribbean-wide labor unrest of the late 1930's, followed the West Indian pattern of establishing a political party as the means of reaching its long term goals. The union-party achieved a significant breakthrough with the granting of universal suffrage in 1951. Party candidates supported by the black masses were quickly elected to the island legislature, paving the way for the transition from crown colony to representative government. A limited ministerial system was instituted in 1956, the year before the first Carnival. In 1960 a fuller ministerial system was developed, together with the office of Chief Minister. In 1967 Antigua became an associated state, an arrangement granting internal self-government and the right to opt unilaterally for full independence.

271

Impressive socioeconomic gains have been realized during the period of decolonization. In 1950 more than half of the working population were in agriculture, chiefly in the employ of an estate consortium formed by white planters as a defense against the black struggle for unionization and political power. Soon after its election, however, the black government began to take over lands from the plantocracy and to promote the private ownership of small farms. The remarkable success of this program is attested by the fact that in 1961 nearly 95 per cent of all farms were in the hands of small holders (James 1970:105). The planter consortium retained control of the large estates, but their tenant proletariat had been transformed into an independent peasantry.

The rise of a peasant propriety abetted agricultural diversification. While the large plantations continued to produce sugar almost exclusively, the small farmers grew sugar and cotton for export and other crops, notably pineapple, for local consumption. These developments combined to make the agricultural picture brighter in the 1950's than it had been for a century.

The major contribution to economic growth, however, came from tourism. Like Bermuda, Antigua was included in the 1940 Roosevelt-Churchill agreement which gave the United States the right to lease land for military bases on the "outer ring" of British island colonies from Trinidad to Newfoundland. The air field built by the Americans made it possible for Antigua to attract the type of person who emerged as the mainstay of post-World War II tourism – the short-term vacationer. By 1960 tourism had become the dominant sector of the economy and the chief contributor to a standard of living higher than that of neighboring islands of comparable size in the Commonwealth bloc. For the next several years tourism was boosted still further by the granting of liberal tax concessions to hotel builders, the licensing of a gambling casino, and the opening of a deep-water harbor suitable for cruise ships. In 1967, the year when associated statehood was attained, tourism accounted for 89 per cent of the national income (Zinder 1969: 50).

More recently, however, the ebullience generated by prosperity and decolonization has eroded. The government has neglected sugar, a policy climaxed by its refusal to process the 1972 crop, leaving farmers with fields of worthless cane. Food shortages and rising prices have become acute, a situation exacerbated by the growing power of Arabic and Portuguese merchants in the local economy. But the major problem has been the failure of tourism to achieve the optimistic growth rates predicted in the late 1960's (Zinder 1969). Unemployment rose to twenty per cent in 1970, a figure more than twice as high as that of the previous decade

(James 1970: 93). During the 1973 tourist off season the unemployment rate soared to nearly fifty per cent.

Political disaffection has been interwoven with economic decline. A split in the labor movement led to the formation of a rival political party which gained a parliamentary majority in 1971 and has since adopted the style of repression that has become all too familiar in the Caribbean. Newspapers supporting the political opposition have been subjected to exorbitant licensing fees and dissident groups such as the Antigua Freedom Fighters, a black power movement, and the Rastafarians, a religious cult seeking repatriation to Africa and holding the core belief that deposed Ethiopian Emperor Haile Selassie is God, have been suppressed. Counterreactions in the form of strikes and demonstrations have intensified, a trend illustrated by the four-day suspension of water and electricity services preceeding the 1973 Carnival. In the throes of this internal conflict a policy of isolation has been taken, to the extent of remaining outside the Caribbean Common Market for a full year after the organization was brought into being.

Besides their social impact, the processes at work in Bermuda and Antigua have had important symbolic implications. The struggle against a white-dominated, archaic social system has undercut not only British colonial culture but the local-level folk cultures that legitimated the traditional order. The strongest bid to replace these receding cultural orientations has come from the general frame of meaning and purpose within which decolonization has been set. Political rhetoric, media coverage, education, travel abroad, and other sources of stimulation to which Antillean people now have access have made them aware that their own condition and struggle is not unique. Rather, they are part of a global process of change that includes such kindred movements as the achievement of full independence in the larger Caribbean islands, revolutionary nationalism in Africa, and the struggle for "liberation" waged by black Americans. Although abstract ideological and philosophical aspects of these movements have little appeal outside intellectual circles, a general sense of sympathy and solidarity with the awakening of non-white (especially black) peoples has been introduced at every social level.

Introduction, however, is quite different from acceptance. The Antillean brand of sociocultural exclusivism that Lewis calls *isularismo* (1968: 132) has proven stubbornly resistant to modern ideas; the island thus tends to remain the dominant if no longer exclusive symbol of social identification. There are obvious reasons for this type of cultural conservatism both in Bermuda and Antigua. The awareness of Bermudians that their material circumstances far surpass those of black Americans and West Indians is a strong inducement for them to cherish the smugness and security of the traditional identity system in which they are "colored Bermudians", separate and superior to people of their pigmentation in other parts of the world. Similarly, Antiguans know that their government's current isolationism is merely an extreme example of the fragility of Caribbean solidarity. Dissension and distrust have frustrated every attempt at political federation in the West Indies, and continually threaten economic cooperation. Within weeks after the signing of the 1973 Chaguaramas Treaty inaugurating the Caribbean Common Market, the Prime Minister of one of the MDC's (More Developed Countries) took television time to denounce the premiers of the LDC's (Less Developed Countries) as a "bunch of bandits" who had previously wanted God and the British Empire to solve their problems, and now wanted the MDC's to provide the solution.

The symbolic influences stemming from large-scale tourism are generally explained in terms of the North American imitation syndrome, a cultural orientation that is antithetical to that fostered by political decolonization. As far back as 1951 a Bermudian commission of enquiry described the "holiday atmosphere", a social climate reflecting the lifestyle of carefree, spendthrift, pleasure-seeking tourists. The dress and demeanor of the tourists, the commission report concluded, conveyed a notion of relaxed sexual mores that the native population tended to adopt. Hence the decline of "moral values" and the high rate of illegitimacy, amounting to one-third of all births (Report to Commission . . . 1951). Two decades later this view is still given frequent utterance by such diverse personages as media commentators, ministers of cabinet and curch, schoolteachers, social workers, political radicals, and white aristocrats. An editorial in the island's daily newspaper related the imitation syndrome to "keeping up with the Joneses", noting that the Joneses were not the proverbial next door family but the multitude of vacationers seen at the hotels, cabarets, beaches, and boutiques.

The holiday atmosphere interpretation has been taken over by Caribbean commentators as the region's tourist industry has moved toward the proportions of Bermuda's. Conservative opinion sees the imitation of North American lifestyles as a philistine regression from British propriety and folk gentility. Progressive opinion makes an equally perjurative assessment of the tourist influence, conceiving it as a form of cultural imperialism that has eroded the integrity and fibre of native life. From either perspective tourism is viewed as having created a society not only of service personnel but of "mimic men" as well, to borrow a title from the Trinidadian novelist V. S. Naipaul (1967).

The rationale for this negative diagnosis, at least from the progressive side, lies in the perceived threat of psychological recolonization under a white racist system. The tourist industry plants a new metropolitan ethos which serves the same purpose as the old: to gain the allegiance of the population while keeping them in oppression. A pictorial satire on this theme shows a muscular young black man stripped to the waist and holding on his shoulders an obese, fortyish white woman whose bathing suit reveals a substantial part of her drooping bosom. The two are laughing hilariously in an obvious parody of the snapshots that tourists have taken with natives. The caption reads, "Tourism on top – we underneath". *(Journal of Black Poetry* 1973:62).

In sum ,contemporary social processes in Bermuda and Antigua have introduced conflicting symbolic orientations. Decolonization and democratic reform tend to expand the parameters of cultural identity, fostering an awareness of a larger, black-centered social reality. Persistent tradition and insular self-interest tend to stifle this influence, as does the affluent, glamorous, hedonistic "holiday atmosphere" dominated by white vacationers.

Resolution and Revitalization

Within this setting of cultural dissonance, what are the hermeneutics and functions of festival symbolism? The safest line of argument sticks close to the shibboleths of orthodox positivism, conceptualizing the symbolic order as a reflex copy of the social system in which it operates. The diagrams on 276, which schematize the symbolic description of Cup Match and Carnival already given, illustrate this argument.

But the anthropological perspective shaped by the field experience of observation and participation suggests that the epiphenomenal view of festival symbolism is too limited to deal adequately with the depth of its meaning and the range of its impact on social life. It fails to appreciate the role of symbolic *action*. While the symbols that make up Cup Match and Carnival may be presented in analytical form as if they were placed in hrmetically-sealed compartments, no such division of cultural reality exists in the festival situation. Rather, the affectively-charged, euphoric action context of festival works to conjoin, and at least partially reconcile its component symbols.

Two general patterns of symbolic association are discernible in Cup Match and Carnival. The first relates symbols of insular identity stemming from local customs to symbols of pan-black identity drawn from Afro-Caribbean and Afro-American expressive forms. The second relates all of the symbols of identity to symbols of tone embodying stylistic and sensual appeal. These spatial and temporal associations of symbols imply the compatibility of their conceptual and evaluative referents. The associ-

275

Cup Match

I. Symbols of Cultural Identity	II. Symbols of Tone

A Insular (Bermudian) Symbols
  1 The emancipation festival tradition
  2 Gombey dancers
  3 Traditional Bermudian food
  4 The "stock market"

B Afro-Caribbean Symbols
  1 Steel bands
  2 *Mas'* performance
  3 Clothing and grooming styles

C Afro-American Symbols
  1 Performance style/content
  2 Clothing and grooming styles

A Symbols of Sexuality
  1 Dress, adornment
  2 Spirit of license

B Symbols of Affluence/Consumption
  1 Excessive consumption of food, liquor
  2 Extravagant spending, gambling

C Symbols of Sophistication
  1 Elegance of setting and dress
  2 Choreographical professionalism of *mas'* production

Carnival

I. Symbols of Cultural Identity	II. Symbols of Tone

A Insular (Antiguan) Symbols
  1 The emancipation festival tradition

  2 Incorporation of folk mumming troupes into *mas'* repertoire
  3 Island scenes and slogans

  4 Calypso commentary on local issues

B Afro-Caribbean Symbols
  1 Carnival tradition
  2 Regional representation in performance competitions
  3 West Indian visitors
  4 Pan-Caribbean masquerade motifs
  5 Pan-Caribbean food items
  6 Calypso commentary on regional issues

C Afro-American Symbols
  1 Performance style/content
  2 Clothing and grooming styles
  3 Black power motifs

A Symbols of Sexuality
  1 Dress, adornment
  2 Spirit of license

B Symbols of Affluence/Consumption
  1 Emphasis on consumer entertainment
  2 Excessive consumption of food, liquor
  3 Extravagant spending, gambling

C Symbols of Sophistication
  1 Elegance of setting and dress
  2 Professional image of enteritanment revues

276

ation of identity and tonal symbols also illustrates what Turner calls "polarization of meaning" (1964:30) – the principle whereby the action of ritual works to exchange ideological and sensory representations, investing socio-cultural principles with sensate and emotional appeal while at the same time ennobling this appeal with normative legitimacy. In the present case festival symbolism works to endow the three spheres of cultural (ideological) identity with sexuality, glamor, sophistication and such tonal (sensory) allurements, while conversely relating stylistic and sensual appeal to a frame of reference that is Antillean and black.

These meaningful interrelationships are established not only by the festivals as a whole but by the figures who dominate them: cricketers, gamblers, and fashionable spectators at Cup Match; beauty contestants, entertainers, and masqueraders at Carnival. All of these figures are replete with one or more expressions of cultural identity and with the elements of tonal attraction. The Afro-coiffured, sensually dressed, elegantly bejewelled woman at Cup Match is a good example, but some of the personalities at Carnival are even more illustrative. Take, for instance, the calypsonian. The content of his performance – the songs lyrics – is likely to be either a topical commentary on a local issue or an exhortation for regional/racial solidarity. The form of his performance – the calypso genre – is now regarded as pan-Caribbean, although there is continuing emphasis on Trinidad as the source and center of the calypso tradition. Trinidad in turn is seen as the eastern Caribbean capital of glamor, sophistication, and affluence, a reputation derived principally from its strong socio-economic orientation to the "yankee dollar". The calypsonian invariably cultivates an image drawing from all of these clusters of symbolism, as well as the international celebrity image that has been introduced to the calypso world by those of its performers whose recordings have achieved lucrative sales in the North American market.

Another association of identity and tonal symbols is exemplified by the emcee at a recent Carnival Queen show. Visually, he typified the contemporary black American entertainer; he sported a pink shirt with long see-through sleeves, a black vest, a wide, white necktie worn outside the vest, and black velvet pants with white pockets. Verbally, however, he represented insular and regional identity. His speech abounded in Antiguan colloquialisms and references to local events. He stressed the Caribbean-wide participation in the Carnival Queen Contest and the regional character of Carnival as a whole, and assured the many visitors from other islands of Antiguan hospitality. Besides these multiple expressions of cultural identity he was invested with the symbols of tone by the swank sophistication of his dress, the elegance of the stage setting, the presence of photographers from the middle class black American magazines *Ebony*

277

and *Essence,* and the Carnival City audience, who dressed in semi-formal attire and paid twelve dollars per couple for reserved seats.

The attractivenees of personalities who interrelate these symbolic categories helps to explain the significance of the black American tourist, who typically (perhaps stereotypically) combines overt, often aggressive expressions of racial identity with a display of conspicuous consumption and hedonistic behavior that surpasses even his white compatriots. An even fuller embodiment of crucial symbols, however, is the islander who has emigrated to more glamorous surrounding but who comes home for the Carnival. If the returning islander is an entertainer who can be booked for a performance, the image is complete. A faint hint of the importance of such a figure can be gleaned from a new preview about the entertainment card at the 1973 Carnival Queen show: ". . . Barry Harvey, Antigua's mellow voiced young man who has made good abroad (New York), will remind us of what we have been missing through his absence form the island *(Antigua Times* 1973:6).

Moving to another level, the dominant festival figures fit into three types which have overlapping attributes: sportsmen, entertainers, and what Abrahams calls "men of words" (cf. 1970:163-179). Sportsmen (cricketers, gamblers) are gamester-showmen; their popularity depends not only on their success at the game but on their ability to impress their followers with flamboyant displays of personal style. Entertainers (calypsonians, beauty contestants, masqueraders) are performer-competitors; their role is both to render a performance and to compete against others for titles and prizes. Men of words (emcess, "rap" artists) are both sportsmen and entertainers; their conversation is aimed less at conveying informational content than at competing against other talkers in verbal battles of wits and at amusing and persuading an audience.

Throughout the Antilles, as I have argued in a recent paper (1974), the diffuse agonistic and dramatistic tropisms exemplified by sportsmen, entertainers, and men of words are the basis of popular heroism. Hence the personalities who dominate Cup Match and Carnival enjoy continuous heroic status, not merely commanding roles in a single event. The function of festival is to exalt the heroes by providing a meaningful context in which their abilities are on display for an appreciative audience. It might be added that the total form of the Bermudian and Antiguan festivals is based on the agonistic and dramatistic tropisms: Cup Match is a performance-centered celebration of sporting competition; Carnival, conversely, is a competition-centered celebration of entertainment performance.

This approach to symbols, heroes, and tropisms suggests that Cup Match and Carnical achieve what Wallace (1956:468-273) calls "mazeway reformulation" – the synthesis of a new image of society and culture following a period of distortion generally produced by acculturative pressures. In the present cases the distortion stems from a number of conflicts: insular exclusivism versus regional solidarity, black identity versus white material glamor, cultural integrity versus the copying of foreign cultural influences. These conflicts are resolved in the festivals not through the reaggregation and reconciliation of meanings within an aesthetic context that is resonant to the native culture's core tropisms.

The popular heroes who dominate Cup Match and Carnival are the secular counterparts of the prophets who normally lead religious rites of revitalization. Interestingly, the heroes run counter to religion in their own societies, which have been rather thoroughly missionized with the evangelical Protestant taboos against drinking, dancing, wearing jewelry, listening to "devil music," having extra-marital sexual affairs, and many other practices closely associated with Cup Match and Carnival. We have in these festivals, then, a symbol system which is secular not only in the sense of being dichotomized from religion but in the further sense of being regarded as immoral and sinful.

If Cup Match and Carnival can be viewed as secular rites of revitalization, do they give rise to organized movements which subsequently carry on the process? It would seem that this has already happened in Bermuda. The clubs were developed when it became necessary to have permanent institutions to sponsor Cup Match and the dozen other calendrical sports festivals that have originated in this century. As the clubs grew they also became centers of entertainment and sociability. I have argued (Manning 1973) that the clubs' three spheres of ludic action – the game, the show, and the bar – are symbolically ordered in a way that parallels the order of festivals discussed in this paper. Each sphere brings about the meaningful association of tonal symbols heavily influenced by (but not necessarily the same as) those of the tourist environment and identity symbols relevant to the continuous and changing aspects of the native experience. Moreover, each sphere promotes an active response: the game encourages economic competition against the white oligarchy; the show supports modern notion of black cultural consciousness; the bar fosters involvement in progressive political programs. Symbolically and institutionally the club world may thus be seen as the structured implementation of the revitalizing synthesis achieved in such secular rites as Cup Match.

In Antigua a club is a euphemism for a whorehouse, and thus a center for a different type of sport, entertainment, and sociability than that found in the Bermuda clubs. Yet the types of symbolic action observable in Bermuda are also apparent in Antigua, although diffused in a variety of settings – the sports organization, the commercial nightclub, the village

279

rum shop, etc. – rather than centered in a single institutional complex. The symbolic power of Carnival (which is sponsored by a government-appointed committee rather than a voluntary association) is that it has unified these diffuse ludic activities under a single ritual rubric. It remains to be seen whether the cultural reformulation achieved by Carnival symbols will have a structured sequel, as in the Bermuda case.

The absence to date of a Bermudian-type club would in Antigua throw light on hermeneutic differences between the two festivals under discussion. Cup Match reflects of course, both the social buoyancy generated by a democratic struggle in progress and the material prosperity made available by a flourishing tourist economy. Yet it is not a conscious acknowledgment of either of these conditions as much as a toast to the ludic ethos which has developed under them but gained a life of its own in the club world. A celebrant's comment at a sports festival illustrates this understanding

> You Americans, you party on the weekends right? Well, we party every day. But we work at the same time. We'll be out till five or six (in the morning), drinking, maybe pick up a bitch, have a hit, get home and have some shut eye, and then go to work. This is our life. We go to cricket games, drink, work, fuck, play sports, and go to parties

Carnival has a different orientation. The continuous experience of its participants is shaped not in a play world but in a society which in recent years has suffered economic recession and political regression. This experience is given both expression and direction in Carnival performance. The calypso which draws an audience of thousands into chanting "freedom" disposes them to fight for it at home. The emphasis in regional solidarity refutes the government's insular chauvinism. The display of black power emblems is a show of support for the black activist groups that have been suppressed. Even the agricultural policy is parodied; a calypso praisoing Antigua as the "land of cotton and cane" was sung at the very time that the sugar factory reneged on processing the crop.

In a broader framework of consideration differences between Cup Match and Carnival yield to essential similarities. To borrow a Turnerian phrase, the two festivals are liminoid events. They are ritual occasions when egalitarianism prevails over hierarchy, spontaneity over routine, freedom over restriction, communitas over structure. The calypso description of the Carnival J'Ouvert Parade as "back to back and belly to belly" is an apt creolized understanding of what Turner calls the "total confrontation of human identities" (1974: 169). The revitalizing synthesis that is produced on these occasions illustrates the cultural inventiveness that is so often fostered by the *limen*. Temporarily released from the conservative influences of structure, individuals and societies can formulate new understandings of the realities they face.

Turner (1974) has recently applied this Van Gennepian model to pilgrimage systems, showing how travelers to sacred shrines have an essentially liminoid experience on their journeys. Here I have made a diamerically opposite application, dealing with the secular counterpart of pilgrimage, tourism, and focusing not on travelers but on those who live in the profane shrines to which travelers are attracted. The resulting analysis indicates that anthropological concepts of ritual can be a source of insight in examining a range of phenomena that are normally conceived as outside the boundaries of religion. These concepts throw light on the cultural symbolization of a paradox that is found not only in the Antilles but throughout the Third World: the conflict between political decolonization and a growing economic dependency on the metropolis.

NOTES

1 Field research was conducted in Bermuda in 1969-70 and in Antigua in 1972 and 1973. For financial support I am grateful to the National Science Foundation and the Institute of So:ial and Economic Research, Memorial University of New Foundland.

CONTRIBUTORS

Suzanne Abel, Harvard University, Cambridge, Massachusetts.
Elizabeth Colson, University of California, Berkeley, Berkeley, California.
Roberto da Matta, Museu Nacional, Rio de Janeiro, Brazil.
Max Gluckman, Victoria University, Manchester, England.
Mary Gluckman, Manchester, England.
Jack Goody, University of Cambridge, Cambridge, England.
Eva Hunt, Boston University, Boston, Massachusetts.
Bruce Kapferer, University of Adelaide, Adelaide, Australia.
Frank E. Manning, Memorial University of Newfoundland, St. John's, Newfoundland, Canada.
John Middleton, School of Oriental and African Studies University of London, London, England.
Sally F. Moore, University of Southern California, Los Angeles, California.
Barbara Myerhoff, University of Southern California, Los Angeles, California.
Terence Turner, University of Chicago, Chicago, Illinois.
Victor Turner, University of Chicago, Chicago, Illinois.
Evon Z. Vogt, Harvard University, Cambridge, Massachusetts.

REFERENCES

Abrahams, Roger
1970, "Patterns of Performance in the British West Indies." In Norman Whitten, Jr., and John Szwed, (Eds.), *Afro-American Anthropology: Contemporary Perspectives.* New York: The Free Press.
Adams, Richard N. and Arthur Rubel
1967, "Sickness and Social Relations." In M. Nash, (Ed.), *Handbook of Middle American Indians.* 6: 333-356.
Aguirre Beltrán, Gonzalo
1967, *Regiones de Refugio.* México: Instituto Indigenista Interamericano. Ediciones Especiales No. 46.
Alphonso-Karkala, John B.
1971, *An Anthropology of Indian Literature.* Harmondsworth: Penguin Books.
Ames, M.
1964, "Magical Animism and Buddhism: a structural analysis of the Sinhalese religious system." In E. B. Harper, (Ed.), *Religion in South Asia.* Seattle: University of Washington Press.
Ames, M.
1966, "Ritual Presentations and the Structure of the Sinhalese Pantheon." In M. Nash, (Ed.), *Anthropological Studies in Theravada Buddhism.* Yale Uiniversity South East Asia Studies.
Apter, David E.
1963, "Political Religion in the New Nations." In C. Geertz, (Ed.), *Old Societies and New States.* Glencoe: The Free Press, Collier-Macmillan.
1967, *The Politics of Modernization.* Chicago: Chicago University Press. (First published 1965).
Aristotle
The Poetics.
Attolini, José *et al.*
1949-50, *Economia de la Cuenca del Papaloapan.* México: Instituto de Investigaciones Económicas. 2 Vols.
Austin, J. L.
1962, *How to do Things with Words.* J. O. Urmson, (Ed.). New York: Oxford University Press.
Bailey, F. G.
1965, "Decisions by Consensus in Councils and Committees." In *Political Systems and the Distribution of Power.* A.S.A. Monograph 2. London: Tavistock.
1969, *Stratagems and Spoils.* New York: Schocken.
Bateson, G.
1955, "A Theory of Play and Fantasy." In *Psychiatric Research Reports 2.* American Psychiatric Association.

References

1973, *Steps to an Ecology of Mind*. Hertfordshire: Paladin.
Beattie, John
1966, "Ritual and Social Change." In *Man*. 1(1): 60-74.
Berger, Peter and Thomas Luckman
1966, *The Social Construction of Reality*. London: Penguin Books.
Bernstein, B.
1972, "A Sociolinguistic Approach to Socialization; with some reference to educability." In J. J. Gumperz and Dell Hymes, *Directions in Sociolinguistics*. New York: Holt, Rinehart and Winston.
Boas, Franz
1911, *The Mind of Primitive Man*. New York: Macmillan.
Bocock, Robert
1974, *Ritual in Industrial Society*. London: Allen and Unwin.
Brandenburg, Frank
1964, *The Making of Modern Mexico*. Inglewood Cliffs: Prentice-Hall, Inc. Chapters 2 and 6.
Buber, M.
1947, *Tales of the Hasidim: The Early Masters*. New York: Schocken.
Burke, Kenneth
1957, *The Philosophy of Literary Form: Studies in Symbolic Action*. New York: Vintage Books.
Camara, Fernando
1952, "Instituciones Religiosas y Políticas Indígenas." In Basuri *et al. Hechos y Problemas del México Rural*. México: Seminario Mexicano de Sociología.
Cancian, Frank
1967, "Political and Religious Organizations." In M. Nash, (Ed.), *Handbook of Middle American Indians*. 6: 283-298. Austin: University of Texas Press.
Caso, Alfonso *et al.*
1954, *Métodos y Resultados de la Política Indigenista en México*. México: Memorias del Instituto Nacional Indigennista No. 6.
Cassirer, Ernst
1944, *An Essay on Man*. New Haven: Yale University Press.
Cicourel, Aaron V.
1973, *Cognitive Sociology*. London: Penguin Modern Sociology Texts.
Cliffe, Lionel
1972, "Tanzania – Socialist Transformation and Party Development." In Lionel ,Cliffe and John Saul, (Eds.), *Socialism in Tanzania*. Pp. 266-276. Dar es Salaam: East Africa Publishing House.
Cohen, Abner
1969, "Political Anthropology: the analysis of the symbolism of power relations." In *Man*. 4(2): 215-235.
Collins, Fletcher, Jr.
1972, *The Production of Medieval Church Music Drama*. Charlottesville: University Press of Virginia.
Comisión Federal Electoral
1964, *Ley Electoral Federal*. México D. F.: Talleres Gráficos de la Nación.
Culin, S.
1907, "Games of North American Indians." In *24th Annual Report of the Bureau of American Ethnology*. Washington Government Printing Office. Citing: J. Long, *Voyages and Travels of an Indian Interpreter*, 1791; J. Carver, *Travels Through the Interior Parts of North America*, 1796; W. Hoffman, "Remarks

on Ojibwa Ball Play." In *American Anthropologist*. Vol. 3: 1890; J. Mooney, "The Cherokee Ball Play." In *American Anthropologist*. 3: 105f; 1890.

Daily News
1974, Dar es Salaam, Tanzania. Feb. 13th and 21st.

Da Matta, Roberto
1973, "O Carnaval como um Rito de Passagem." In *Ensaios de Antropologia Estrutural*. Petrópolis: Editora Vozes Ltda.

Dawidowicz, L. S.
1967, *The Golden Tradition: Jewish Life and Thought in Eastern Europe*. New York: Holt, Rinehart and Winston.

Douglas, Mary
1970, *Natural Symbols: Explorations in Cosmology*. Barrie and Rockliffe.

Dubow, S. M.
1916-20, *History of the Jews in Russia and Poland . . . Until the Present Day*. 3 Vols. Philadelphia: Jewish Publication Society of America.

Durkheim, Emile
1961, *The Elementary Forms of the Religious Life*. (trans.), J. W. Swain. New York: Collier Books. (1915)
1964, *The Division of Labor in Society*. (trans.), G. Simpson. Glencoe: Collier-Macmillan Ltd. (1893).

Edelstein, Emma J. and Ludwig
1945, *Asclepius: A Collection and Interpretation of the Testimonies*. 2 Vols. Baltimore: John Hopkins.

Entralgo, Pedro Lain
1970, *The Therapy of the Word in Classical Antiquity*. New Haven: Yale.

Evans-Pritchard, E. E.
1937, *Witchcraft, Oracles and Magic among the Azande*. Oxford: Clarendon Press.

Fernandez, J. W.
1971, "Persuasions and Performances: of the beast in everybody . . . and the metaphors of Everyman." In C. Geertz, (Ed.), *Myth, Symbol and Culture*. Pp. 39-60. New York: W. W. Norton.

Fortes, M. and E. E. Evans-Pritchard
1940, "Introduction". To M. Fortes and E. E. Evans-Pritchard, (Eds.), *African Political Systems*. London: Oxford University Press for the International African Institute.

Freud, Sigmund
1907, "Obsessive Acts and Religious Practices." In Sigmund Freud, *Collected Papers*. (trans.), Joan Riviere. 5 Vols. 2:25-50. London; extract reprinted in W. Lessa and E. Vogt, (Eds.), *Reader in Comparative Religion*. 2nd ed.: 197-202. 1965. New York.
1913, *Totem and Taboo*. (trans.), J. Strachy. 150 ed. London: Rontledge and Kegan Paul.

Gargi, B.
1966, *The Folk Theatre of India*. Seattle: University of Washington Press.

Geertz, Clifford
1966, "Religion as a Cultural System." In M. Banton, (Ed.), *Anthropological Approaches to the Study of Religion*. A. S. A. Monograph No. 3. London: Tavistock Publications, 1-46.
1973, *The Interpretation of Cultures*. New York: Basic Books.

Gennep, Arnold Van
1909, *rites de Passage*. Paris.

References

Gluckman, Max
1949, "The Role of the Sexes in the Circumcision Ceremonies of the Wiko of Ba-rotseland." In M. Fortes, (Ed.), *Social Structure: Essays Presented to A.R. Rad-cliffe-Brown.* Oxford: Clarendon Press.
1954, *Rituals of Rebellion in South-East Africa.* (reprinted in 1963 below). Manch-ester: Manchester University Press.
1955, *Custom and Conflict in Africa.* Oxford; Blackwell; New York: Barnes and Noble.
1956, *Custom and Conflict in Africa.* Oxford: Basil Blackwell. (1965 ed.).
1958, "Football Players and the Crowd." In *The Listener.* February.
1958, *Politics, Law and Ritual in Tribal Society, An Analysis of a Social Situation in Modern Zululand.* Manchester: Manchester University Press. (See also 1965 below).
1959, *Custom and Conflict in Africa.* Glencoe: The Free Press.
1962, "Les Rites de Passage." In M. Gluckman, (Ed.), *Essays on the Ritual of Social Relations.* Pp. 1-52. Manchester: Manchester University Press.
1963, "Rituals of Rebellion in South East Africa." In M. Gluckman *Order and Re-bellion in Tribal Africa.*
1964, *Closed Systems and Open Minds.* Edinburgh: Oliver and Boyd.
1965, *Politics, Law and Ritual in Tribal Society.* Oxford: Blackwell.
1972, "Sport and Conflict." In *Proceedings of the Congress for the Scientific Study of Sport.* Munich. (In press).
1974a, "Spouse, child, parent or sibling? – Who should be saved?" (The Disputed Passage in Sophocles' *Antigone).* In B. Chapman and A. Potter, (Eds.), *Essays Presented to W. J. M. Mackenzie.* Manchester: Manchester University Press.
1974b "Makishi Masked Dancers of Barotseland." In *In Memoriam Jorge Dias.*
Gobierno de Oaxaca
1964, *Constitución Política y Otras Leyes.* Leyes del Estado de Oaxaca. Colección de Leyes Mexicanas. Puebla, Mex. Editorial Jose M. Cajica Jr. S. A.
Goffman, E.
1956, *Presentation of Self in Everyday Life.* Edinburgh: University of Edinburgh.
1961, *Encounters.* Indianapolis: Bobbs-Merrill.
1963, *Behavior in Public Places: Notes on the Social Organizations of Gatherings.* New York: The Free Press.
1967, *Interaction Ritual: Essays on Face-to-Face Bahavior.* New York: Doubleday and Co., Inc.
1972, *Interaction Ritual,* London. (1967 ed.).
1974 *Frame Analysis: An Essay on the Organization of Experience.* Cambridge: Harvard University Press.
Gombrich, Richard F.
1971, *Precept and Practice.* Oxford: Clarendon Press.
Gonzales Casanova, Pablo
1963, "Sociedad Plural, Colonialismo Interno y Desarrollo." In *America Latina* 6:3.
1965, *La Democracia en México.* México: Serie Popular Era.
Goody, E.
1973, *Contexts of Kinship,* Cambridge.
Goody, Jack R.
1962, "Religion and Ritual, the Definitional Problem." In *British Journal of Sociol-ogy.* 12: 142-164. (Also published 1961).
Gossen, Gary

References

1971, "Chamula Genres of Verbal Behavior." In *Journal of American Folklore.* 84: 145-167.

Handelman, D. and Kapferer, B.
1972, "Forms of Joking Activity: a comparative approach." In *American Anthropologist.* 74(3).

Handlin, O.
1954, *Adventure in Freedom: Three Hundred Years of Jewish Life in America.* New York: McGraw-Hill.

Harsh, P. W.
1944, *A Handbook of Classical Drama.* Stanford University Press.

Herberg, W.
1955, *Protestant-Catholic-Jew: An Essay in American Religious Sociology.* New York: Anchor.

Heschel, A. J.
1950, *The Earth is the Lord's: The Inner World of the Jew in East Europe.* New York: Harper and Row.

Hill, Errol
1972, *The Trinidad Carnival: Mandate for a Nantional Theatre.* Austin: University of Texas Press.

Hispano Americano
1972, September 25. LXI (1586): 5-9.

Howe, I.
1976, *World of our Fathers.* New York: Harcourt, Brace, Janovich.

Hubert, Henri and Marcel Mauss
1899, "Essai sur la Nature et Fonction Social du Sacrifice." In *Année Sociologique.* II: 29-138.

Hunt, Eva
1969, "The Meaning of Kinship in San Juan: geneological and social models." In *Ethnology.* 8(1): 37-53.
1974, (in press). "Kinship and Territorial Fission in the Cuicatec Highlands." In H. Nutini and P. Carrasco, (Eds.), *Kinship in Mesoamerica.* Pittsburgh: University of Pittsburgh Press.

Hunt, Eva and June Nash
1967, "Local and Territorial Units." In M. Nash, (Ed.), *Handbook of Middle American Indians.* Vol. 6: 253-282. Austin: University of Texas Press.

Hunt, Eva and Robert Hunt
1969, "The Role of the Courts in Rural Mexico." In P. Bock, (Ed.), *Peasants in the modern World.* Albuquerque: University of New Mexico Press.

James, C. L. R.
1870, *Beyond a Boundary.* London: Faber and Faber.

James, D. G.
1937, *Skepticism and Poetry.* London: G. Allen and Unwin.

James, Elijah
1970, *The Economic Development of Antigua: Problems and Prospects.* Unpublished M. A. Thesis. Memorial University of Newfoundland.

Jebb, R.
1880, Sophocles: The Plays and Fragments (with critical notes, commentary, and translation into English prose). Used in 3rd., 1900 edition. Cambridge: Cambridge University Press.

Johnson, Kenneth F.
1971, *Mexican Democracy: A Critical View.* Boston: Allyn and Bacon, Inc.

Journal of Black Poetry

References

1973, Vol. 1, No. 17: Summer

Kapferer, B.
1976, "Entertaining Demons." In *Modern Ceylon Studies*. Vol. 6.

Keil, Charles
1966, *Urban Blues*. Chicago: University of Chicago Press.

Kilson, M.
1972, "Ambivalence and Power: mediums in Ga traditional religion." In *Journal of Religion in Africa*. 4: 171-177.

Kochman, Thomas
1970. "Toward an Ethnography of Black American Speech Behavior." In Norman Whitten, Jr. and John Szwed, (Eds.), *Afro-American Anthropology: Contemporary Perspectives*. New York: The Free Press.

Kuper, Hilda
1944, "A Ritual of Kinship Among the Swazi." In *Africa*. XIV, I: 130-256.
1945, *An African Aristocracy: Rank among the Swazi of The Protectorate*. London: Oxford University for the International African Institute.
1971, "Color, Categories and Colonialism: The Swazi case." In V. W. Turner, (Ed.), *Profiles of Change: The Impact of Colonialism on Africa*. Cambridge: Cambridge University Press.
1972, "A Royal Ritual in a Changing Political Context." In *Cahiers D'Etudes Africaines*. Vol. XII. Ecole Pratique des Hautes Etudes. Sorbonne.

La Fontaine, J. W. (Ed.)
1972, *The Interpretation of Ritual: Essays in Honour of A. I. Richards*. London: Tavistock.

Langer, Susanne K.
1960, *Philosophy in a New Key*. Cambridge: Harvard University Press. (1942).

Leach, E. R.
1954, *The Political Systems of Highland Burma, A Study of Kachin Social Structure*. London: Athlone Press.
1961, *Rethinking Anthropology*. London School of Economics Monographs on Social Anthropology. No. 22. London: The Athlone Press.
1966, "Ritualization in Man." In *Philosophical Transactions of the Royal Society of London*. Series B. 251 (722): 403-408.
1968, "Ritual." In D. Sills, (Ed.), In *International Encyclopedia of the Social Sciences*. Vol. 13. New York: Macmillan and The Free Press.
1969, "Ritual." In *The International Encyclopedia of the Social Sciences*.

Leal Cores, Alfredo
1963, *La Sucesion Presidencial*. Edicion de la Revista de Economia: México.

Lesky, A.
1966, *A History of Greek Literature*. (trans. from the German of 1957-58), J. Wilis and C. de Heer. London: Methuen.

Lévi-Strauss, Claude
1962a, *Totemism*. Boston: Beacon Press.
1962b, *La Pensée Sauvage*. Paris: Plon. (Reprinted 1966 below).
1966, *The Savage Mind*. (trans.), G. Weidenfeld and Nicolson Ltd. Chicago: University of Chicago Press.
1967, "The Story of Asdiwal." In E. Leach, (Ed.). (trans.), N. Mann, *The Structural Study of Myth*. Pp. 1-47. London: Tavistock. (Also published 1958-59).

Lewis, Gordon
1968, *The Growth of the Modern West Indies*. New York and London: Modern Reader Paperbacks.

Lucas, D. W.
1969, "Greek Drama." In *Encyclopedia Britannica*. Vol. 7.
Madsen, William
1967, "Religious Syncretism." In M. Nash, (Ed.), *Handbook of Middle American Indians*. 6: 369-391.
Malinowski, Bronislaw
1955, *Magic, Science and Religion*. New York: Doubleday.
Manning, Frank
1973, *Black Clubs in Bermuda: Ethnography of a Play World*. Ithaca and London: Cornell University Press.
1974, "Nicknames and Number Plates in the British West Indies." In *Journal of American Folklore*. 87 (344).
Marwick, M. G.
1965, *The Social Context of Sorcery*. Manchester: Manchester University Press.
Marx, Karl
1956, *Selected Writings in Sociology and Social Philosophy*. (trans.), T. B. Bottomore. New York: McGraw-Hill Book Co.
McHugh, Peter
1968, *Defining the Situation*. New York: Bobbs-Merrill.
McQuown, Norman A. (Ed.)
1965, *Linguistics: Handbook of Middle American Indians*. Vol. 5. Austin: University of Texas Press.
Mendelson, E. Michael
1967, "Ritual and Mythology." In M. Nash, (Ed.), *Handbook of Middle American Indians*. 6:392-415.
Middleton, J.
1956, "The Roles of Chiefs and Headmen in Lugbara." In *Journal of African Administration*. 8 (1): 32-38.
1958, "The Political System of the Lugbara of the Nile-Congo Divide." In J. Middleton and D. Tait, (Eds.), *Tribes without Rulers*. Pp. 203-229. London: Routledge and Kegan Paul.
1960, *Lugbara Religion: Ritual and Authority among and East African Pepople*. London: Oxford University Press for International African Institute.
1963, "The Yakan of Allah Water Cult among the Lugbara." In *Journal of the Royal Anthropological Institute*. 93: 80-108.
1965, *The Lugbara of Uganda*. New York: Holt, Rinehart and Winston.
1968, "Some Categories of Dual Classification among the Lugbara of Uganda." In *History of Religions*. 7 (3): 187-208.
1971, "Prophets and Rainmakers: the agents of social change among the Lugbara." In T. O. Beidelman, (Ed.), *The Translation of Culture*. Pp. 179-201. London: Tavistock Publication.
1973, "Secrecy in Lugbara Religion." In *History of Religions*. 12 (4): 299-316.
1974, *Les Lugbara de l'Ouganda: Religion et Société*, Paris: Ecole Pratique des Hautes Etudes.
Mittler, P.
1971, *The Study of Twins*. London.
Mohiddin, A.
1972, "Ujamaa na Kujitegemea." In Lionel Cliffe and John Saul, (Eds.), *Socialism in Tanzania*. Pp. 165-177. Dar es Salaam: East Africa Publishing House.
Moore, Sally Falk
1975a, "Selection for Failure in a Small Social Field: ritual concord and fraternal

References

strife on Kilimanjaro, 1968-69". In Sally F. Moore and B. Myerhoff, (Eds), *Symbol anl Politics in Communal Ideology: Cases and Questions.* Ithaca: Cornell University Press.

1975b, "Uncertainty in Situations: indeterminacies in culture." In Sally F. Moore and Barbara Myerhoff, (Eds.), *Symbol and Politics in Communal Ideology: Cases and Questions.* Ithaca: Cornell University Press.

Munn, Nancy
1973, "Symbolism in a Ritual Context." In John J. Honigmann, (Ed.), *Handbook of Social and Cultural Anthropology.* Chicago.

Myerhoff, Barbara G.
1974, *Peyote Hunt: The Sacred Journey of the Huichol Indians.* Ithaca: Cornell University Press.

1976, "Return to Wirikuta: ritual reversal and symbolic continuity among the Huichol Indians." In B. Babcock, (Ed.), *The Reversible World.* Ithaca: Cornell University Press.

Nadel, S. F.
1954, *Nupe Religion.* London: Routledge and Kegan Paul.

Nader, Laura
1964a, *Talea and Juquila: a Comparison of social organization.* University of California, Publications in American Archeology and Ethnology. 48(3).

1964b "An Analysis of Zapotec Law Cases." In *Ethnology.* III (4): 404-419.

1965, "Choice in Legal Procedure: Shia Moslem and Mexican Zapotec. In *American Anthropologist.* 62(2): 394-399.

1966, "Variations in Rincon Zapotec Legal Procedures." In *Homenaje al Ingeniero R. Weitlaner.* pp. 375-383. México: Instituto de Antropología.

1969, "Styles of Court Procedure: to make the balance." In L. Nader, *Law in Culture and Society.* Chicago: Aldine Publishing Co.

Naipaul, V. S.
1967, *The Mimic Men.* New York: Macmillan.

Nash, June
1967, "Death as a Way of Life: the increasing resort to homocide in a Mexican Indian town." In *American Anthropologist.* 69(5): 455-470.

Nash, Manning
1957, "The Multiple Society in Economic Development: Mexico and Guatemala." In *American Anthropologist.* 59: 825-833.

Needham, Rodney
"Percussion and Transition." In *Man.* (N.S.) 2: 606-614.

1972, *Belief, Language and Experience.* Chicago: University of Chicago Press.

Obeyesekere, G.
1963, "The Great Tradition and the Little in the Perspective of the Sinhalese Buddhism." In *Journal of Asian Studies.* Vol. XXII. No. 2.

1966, "The Buddhist Pantheon in Ceylon and its Extensions." In M. Nash, (Ed.), *Anthropological Studies in Theravada Buddhism.* Yale University South East Asia Studies.

1969, "The Ritual of the Sanni Demons: collective representations of disease in Ceylon." In *Comparative Studies in Society and History.* Vol. II. No. 2.

Ortner, S. B.
1973, "On Key Symbols." In *American Anthropologist.* 15(5): 1338-1346. December

Orwell, G.
1940, "Boys' Weeklies." In *Inside the Whale, and other essays.* pp. 89-128. London: Gollancz.

Padgett, Victor
1966, *The Mexican Political System.* Boston: Houghton Mifflin Co.
Parsons, Tlcott
1966, *Societies: Evolutionary and Comparative Perspectives.* New Jersey: Prentice-Hall, Inc.
Paz, Octavio
1961, *The Labyrinth of Solitude.* New York: Grove Press.
Pitt-Rivers, Julian
1965, "Who Are the Indians?" In *Encounter.* 25(3): 41-49.
Prell-Foldes, R. -E.
1973, *The Unity of Oneness: Unity and Opposition in Jewish Ritual.* M. A. Thesis. University of Chicago.
Radcliffe-Brown, A. R.
1952, *Structure and Function in Primitive Society: Essays and Addresses.* London: Cohen & West Ltd.
Raghavan, M. D.
1967, *Sinhala Natum.* Colombo: Gunasena.
Ramos, A. and Peirano, M.
1973, "O Simbolismo da Caça em dois Rituals de Nimonação." Brasilia: Departamento de Ciências Sociais, Série Antropologia 4.
Rappaport, Roy A.
1968, *Pigs for the Ancestors.* New Haven and London: Yale University Press.
1971, "Ritual Sanctity and Cybernetics." In *American Anthropologist.* 73(1): 59-76.
Redfield, R.
1953, *The Primitive World and its Transformations.* Ithaca: Cornell University Press.
Reina, Ruben E.
1967, "Annual Cycle and Fiesta Cycle." In M. Nash, (Ed.), *Handbook of Middle American Indians.* 6: 317-332.
Report of the Commission of Enquiry into the Growth of Population and Illegitimacy. Hamilton: The Bermuda Press.
Richards, Audrey and Adam Kuper (Eds.)
1971, *Councils in Action.* Cambridge.
Rosaldo, Renato I.
1968, "Metaphors of Hierarchy in a Mayan Ritual." In *American Anthropolist.* 70(3): 524-536.
Rose, Arnold M.
1968, "The Subculture of the Aging: a topic for sociological research." In Bernice L. Neugarten, (Ed.), *Middle Age and Aging: A Reader in Social Psychology.* Pp. 29-34. Chicago: University of Chicago Press.
Rosies, D. K. and D. G.
1975, *The Shtetl Book.* N. P. Ktav.
Russell, Bertrand
1938, *Power.* New York: W. W. Norton and Co., Inc.
Sahagún, Bernardino de
1938, *Historia General de las Cosas de Nueva España.* 1, Lib. 6. M éxico.
Samuel, M.
1971, *In Praise of Yiddish.* Chicago: Cowles.
Sarachandra, E. R.
1966, *The Folk Drama of Ceylon.* Ceylon Department of Cultural Affairs.
Scott, Robert E.

References

1964, *Mexican Government in Transition.* Pp. 197-243. Urbana: University of Illinois Press.

Shulman, A.
1974, *The Old Country: The Lost World of East European Jews.* New York: Scribners.

Skinner, C. O.
1962, *Elegant Wits and Grand Horizontals.* Boston: Houghton Mifflin.

Smith, W. Robertson
1894, *Lectures on the Religion of the Semites.* 2nd ed. London.

Solis, Leopoldo
1970, *La Realidad Económica Mexicana: Retrovisión y Perspectivas.* México: Siglo Veintiuno Editores S. A.

Stanner, W. E. H.
1967, "Reflections on Durkheim and Aboriginal Religion." In Maurice Freeman, (Ed.), *Social Organization: Essays Presented to Raymond Firth.* Chicago: Aldine.

Stavinhagen, Rodolfo
1969, *Las Clases en las Sociedades Agracias.* México: Siglo Veintiuno Editores S. A.

Streib, Gordon F.
1968, "Are the Aged a Minority Group?" In Bernice L. Neugarten, (Ed.), *Middle Age and Aging: A Reader in Social Psychology.* Pp. 35-46. Chicago: University of Chicago Press.

Tambiah, S. J.
1968, "The Magical Power of Words." In *Man.* (N.S.) 3(2).
1973, "Form and Meaning of Magical Acts: a point of view." In Robin Horton and Ruth Finnegan, (Eds.), *Modes of Thought.* London: Faber and Faber.

Tannenbaum, Frank
1962, *Mexico - The Struggle for Peace and Bread.* New York: Alfred A. Knopf.

Trachtenberg, J.
1970, *Jewish Magic and Superstition: A Study in Folk Religion.* New York: Atheneum.

Turner, Victor W.
1957, *Schism and Continuity in an African Society.* Manchester: Manchester University Press for the Rhodes-Livingston Institute.
1964a, "Symbols in Ndembu Ritual." In Max Gluckman, (Ed.), *Closed Systems and Open Minds: The Limits of Naivete in Social Anthropology.* Chicago: Aldine.
1964b, "Betwixt and Between: the liminal period in rites of passage." In *Proceedings of the American Ethnological Society.*
1966, "Color Classification in Ndembu Ritual." In M. Banton, (Ed.), *Anthropological Approaches to the Study of Religion.* A.S.A. Monograph No. 3. London: Tavistock Publications.
1967, *The Forest of Symbols: Aspects of Ndembu Ritual.* Ithaca: Cornell University Press.
1968a, *The Drums of Affliction: A Study of Religious Processes among the Ndembu of Zambia.* Oxford: Clarendon Press and the International African Institute.
1968b "Mukanda: the politics of a non-political ritual." In M. Swartz, (Ed.), *Local Level Politics.* Pp. 135-150. Chicago: Aldine.
1969, *The Ritual Process: Structure and Anti-Structure.* Chicago: Aldine. London: Routledge and Kegan Paul.
1973, "The Center Out There: the pilgrim's goal." In *History of Religions.* February.

1974, *Dramas, Fields and Metaphors: Symbolic Action in Human Society.* Ithaca: Cornell University Press.

Twumasi, P. A.
1972, "Ashanti Traditional Medicine." In *Encounter.* 41: 50-63.

Vogt, Evon Z.
1965, "Structural and Conceptual Replications in Zinacantan Culture." In *American Anthropologist.* LXVII: 342-353.

1969, *Zinacantan, A Maya Community in the Highlands of Chiapas.* Cambridge: Belknap Press of the Harvard University Press.

Wagley, Charles
1959, "The Concept of Social Race in the Americas." In *Acts of the 33rd Congress of Americanists.* 1: 403-417.

Wallace, Anthony
1956, "Revitalization Movements." In *American Anthropologist.* Vol. 58.

Wax, Murray
1957, "Themes in Cosmetics and Grooming." In *American Journal of Sociology.* 62(6).

Wilkinson, Henry
1958, *The Adventurers of Bermuda: A History of the Island from Its Discovery until the Dissolution of the Somers Island Company in 1684.* London: Oxford University Press.

Wilson, M.
1954, "Nyakyusa Ritual and Symbolism." In *American Anthropologist.* Vol. 56.

1957, *Rituals of Kinship among the Nyakyusa.* Oxford: Oxford University Press.

Wirz, P.
1954, *Exorcism and the Art of Healing in Ceylon.* Leiden: E. J. Brill.

1966, *Kataragama: The Holiest Place in Ceylon.* Colombo.

Wolf, Eric R.
1955, "Types of Latin American Peasantry." In *American Anthropologist.* 57: 452-471.

1957, "Closed Corporate Communities in Mesoamerica and Central Java." In *South-Western Journal of Anthropology.* 13: 1-18.

1958, "The Virgin of Guadalupe: a Mexican national symbol." In *Journal of American Folklore.* (71279): 34-39.

1959, *Sons of the Shaking Earth.* Chicago: University of Chicago Press.

Yalman, N.
1964, "The Structure of Sinhalese Healing Rituals." In E. B. Harper, (Ed.), *Religion in South Asia.* Seattle: University of Washington Press.

1973, "On the Meaning of Food Offerings in Ceylon." In *Social Compass.* Vol. XX.

Young, K.
1933, *The Drama of the Medieval Church.* Vol. II. Oxford: Clarendon Press.

Zborowski, M. and E. Herzog
1952, *Life is with People: The Culture of the Shtetl.* New York: Shocken.

Zinder, H. *et al.*
1969, *The Future of Tourism in the Eastern Caribbean.* Washington D. C.: Published by the author.